Praise for *De*
by James

"In this vibrant piece of intellectual history, Reston completes the saga of the relationship between East and West he began with *Warriors of God*. Combining a historian's attention to detail and a novelist's narrative flair, Reston focuses on the period when the Ottoman Empire came within a hair's breadth of conquering Europe."   —*Publishers Weekly*

"A readable, enjoyable and professional popular history of a crucial era of Muslim-Christian conflict . . . The obvious relevance of this book is the twenty-first-century challenge to the West of radical Islam. [The book has] fascinating echoes with modern conflicts and strategic dilemmas."
                                    —*The Washington Times*

"[Reston] imposes narrative clarity on a kaleidoscopic array of historical events. . . . Readers wondering why Suleyman did not prevail may depend on Reston's interesting display of fact, description, and narrative to elucidate a pivotal point in history."   —*Booklist*

"Reston helps the lay reader grasp the root causes of religious tensions that exist to this day between Protestant and Catholic, Christian and Muslim, and Sunni and Shiite. Fast-paced and engaging, this is excellent reading."
                                    —*Library Journal*

PENGUIN BOOKS

DEFENDERS OF THE FAITH

James Reston, Jr., is the author of fourteen books, including *Warriors of God, Dogs of God, Galileo: A Life,* and *The Conviction of Richard Nixon.* His 1983 documentary, *Father Cares: The Last of Jonestown,* won the Prix Italia and the Dupont-Columbia Award. His books have been translated into thirteen languages.

Defenders

of the

Faith

✠

Christianity and Islam Battle
for the Soul of Europe,
1520–1536

James Reston, Jr.

PENGUIN BOOKS

PENGUIN BOOKS

Published by the Penguin Group

Penguin Group (USA) Inc., 375 Hudson Street, New York, New York 10014, U.S.A.

Penguin Group (Canada), 90 Eglinton Avenue East, Suite 700, Toronto, Ontario, Canada M4P 2Y3
(a division of Pearson Penguin Canada Inc.)

Penguin Books Ltd, 80 Strand, London WC2R 0RL, England

Penguin Ireland, 25 St Stephen's Green, Dublin 2, Ireland (a division of Penguin Books Ltd)

Penguin Group (Australia), 250 Camberwell Road, Camberwell,
Victoria 3124, Australia
(a division of Pearson Australia Group Pty Ltd)

Penguin Books India Pvt Ltd, 11 Community Centre, Panchsheel Park, New Delhi – 110 017, India

Penguin Group (NZ), 67 Apollo Drive, Rosedale, North Shore 0632,
New Zealand (a division of Pearson New Zealand Ltd)

Penguin Books (South Africa) (Pty) Ltd, 24 Sturdee Avenue,
Rosebank, Johannesburg 2196, South Africa

Penguin Books Ltd, Registered Offices:
80 Strand, London WC2R 0RL, England

First published in the United States of America by The Penguin Press,
a member of Penguin Group (USA) Inc. 2009
Published in Penguin Books 2010

1   3   5   7   9   10   8   6   4   2

THE LIBRARY OF CONGRESS HAS CATALOGED THE HARDCOVER EDITION AS FOLLOWS:
Reston, James, 1941–
Defenders of the faith : Charles V, Suleyman the Magnificent, and
the battle for Europe, 1520–1536 / James Reston, Jr.
p.   cm.
Includes bibliographical references and index.
ISBN 978-1-59420-255-4 (hc.)
ISBN 978-0-14-311759-9 (pbk.)
1. Holy Roman Empire—History—Charles V, 1519–1556.   2. Charles V, Holy Roman Emperor,
1500–1558.   3. Turkey—History—Süleyman I, 1520–1566.   4. Süleyman I, Sultan of the Turks,
1494 or 5–1566.   5. Holy Roman Empire—Foreign relations—Turkey.   6. Turkey—Foreign
relations—Holy Roman Empire.   7. Holy Roman Empire—Religion—16th century.
8. Turkey—Religion—16th century.   9. Religion and civilization—Europe.
10. Vienna (Austria)—History—Siege, 1529—Religious aspects.   I. Title.
D231.R47   2009
940.2′32—dc22   2008054655

Printed in the United States of America
DESIGNED BY NICOLE LAROCHE

for

JOSEPH REGAL

Every era possesses a blessed individual
who is born under the fortunate star of that time.
When a person leaves this world another will take his place.
Truly this world is but a port of call,
he who has departed will not return and he who remains awaits
   his own departure.

—NASUH MATRAKCI SULEYMANNAME

circa A.D. 1534

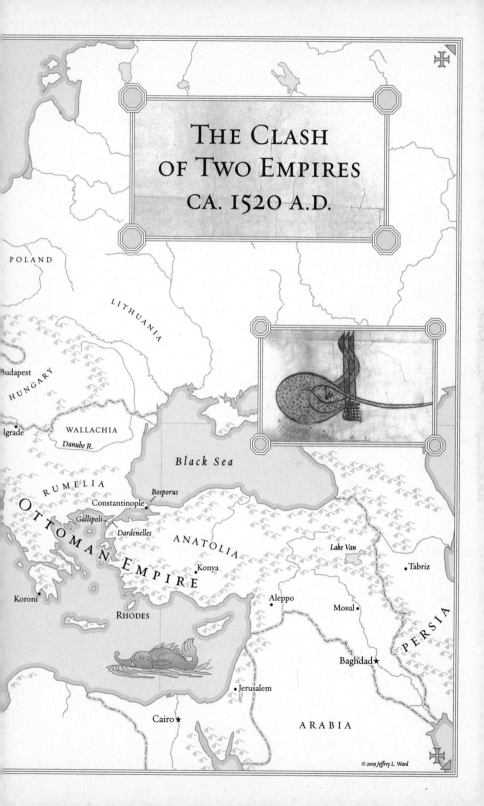

THE CLASH
OF TWO EMPIRES
CA. 1520 A.D.

POLAND

LITHUANIA

Budapest

HUNGARY

lgrade

WALLACHIA

Danube R.

Black Sea

RUMELIA

OTTOMAN EMPIRE

Bosporus

Constantinople

Gallipoli

Dardanelles

ANATOLIA

Lake Van

Konya

Tabriz

Koroni

Aleppo

Mosul

PERSIA

RHODES

Baghdad★

Jerusalem

ARABIA

Cairo ★

© 2009 Jeffrey L. Ward

CONTENTS

FOREWORD

This is a book about an epic clash of civilizations. In the years 1520 to 1536 the fate of Western civilization hung in the balance as two vast and vigorous empires came into conflict along the seam of the Alps. The powerful Ottoman Empire, centered in Constantinople, stood at the pinnacle of its glory and its expansionist ambitions. It was ruled by one of history's most fascinating figures, Suleyman the Magnificent, whose Islamic empire stretched from the Tigris River in the east to the shores of Algiers, up the Balkan Peninsula to the Pannonian plain of Hungary. In central Europe, this juggernaut faced a Christian empire with an equally impressive expanse. The Hapsburg Empire stretched from Denmark and the Netherlands in the north, Austria in the east, to Spain and beyond to the New World. This vast Christian dominion was ruled by a young, dynamic, and deeply devout Holy Roman emperor named Charles V. Both Charles and Suleyman regarded their roles as defender and propagator of their respective faiths against the infidel as an obligation received from the Almighty.

In this pivotal hinge of history, these two daunting empires came into their apocalyptic clash at the gates of Vienna in 1529 and 1532. The consequences of that clash held immense implications for the future of the civilized world. Had Suleyman prevailed at Vienna, as the odds suggest he should have, Europe would have been Islamic to the Rhine River in the early sixteenth century.

Beyond the clash of superpowers, this is a story of the clash of religions and the clash of historical giants, bent on fulfilling the grandiose aspirations of their forefathers and the challenge of their gods. In previous centuries the crusades of Christian leaders in Palestine and Spain had made the Christian side the aggressor against the nonbeliever. In this story, the situation is reversed. Suleyman's ambitions were driven by his aggressive concept of jihad and his desire for world domination as an Islamic Alexander the Great. But his struggle with Charles V was personal, for Suleyman's hostility toward Christian Europe came from his feeling that the sheer magnificence of his superior civilization and religion was not getting from Europe the respect it deserved.

These years encompass other important turning points of history. Both the Christianity of Charles V and the Islam of Suleyman faced "heresies" within their respective established doctrines. In Germany, a simple Augustinian monk named Martin Luther rattled the portals of the Vatican as he lashed out at the corruption of popes and the abuses of the Roman Church. So, simultaneously, Roman Catholicism faced military conquest from without, and rebellion from within. Similarly, the Sunni Islam of Suleyman, who as the official Defender of the Faith now held the mantle of the caliphate in Constantinople, faced the Shi'ite "heresy" in Persia. Suleyman would unsuccessfully attempt to exterminate Shi'ism as his father, Selim I, had before him. As the two emperors sought to engage one another in a final, apocalyptic battle, so they sought to smother the doctrinal dissension within their own respective faiths.

This extraordinary competition would be played out in dramatic ways and in far-flung places: on the island of Rhodes in the Mediterranean, in the desert around Baghdad, in the rathskellers of Swabia, in the swamps of southern Hungary and the fertile fields of Lombardy. The debates over fine points of dogma in such places as Worms and Augsburg would be transformed into battles between Catholics and Protestants and eventually into the Sack of Rome itself, which brought the greatest period of Italian history, the Renaissance, to an abrupt and catastrophic end. A royal divorce would lead to England's breach with Rome and the establishment of the Church of England. Suleyman's desire to purify Islam would take him to Tabriz and to Baghdad.

If the principals were Olympian, the secondary characters are no less interesting. Ibrahim Pasha, Suleyman's childhood favorite and later his grand vizier, will see a dramatic rise and meet a startling end. The woebegone Medici pope Clement VII, powerless and self-pitying, will find himself forever in a vise between Charles V, Francis I, and the Lutheran rabble. Henry VIII of England and Francis I of France, as potentates of the second rank, will forever jockey for power and respect. Side plots include Henry's effort to divorce his queen, Catherine of Aragon (Charles V's aunt), and marry Anne Boleyn, Ibrahim Pasha's longing for supreme power, the capture of Francis I at Pavia, Italy, and the captivity of Clement VII in his own Eternal City and in Orvieto.

I see these sixteen years as a drama in ten acts. I have written it as a work of historical literature, accurate in every respect, but winnowing the number of characters and the number of dates and places to the essentials so that one can see a clear line in the interplay of character and event. I have attempted in previous books on the Third Crusade of Richard the Lionheart and Saladin and on the Spain of Christopher Columbus to integrate the history of the Islamic world with the history of the Christian world. Here as well I have put the two religions, the two cultures, and the two civilizations on an equal footing in an effort to avoid the Eurocentrism or the Islamic centrality or, for American and English audiences, the Anglo-Saxon centrality of past treatments.

JAMES RESTON, JR.
Fiery Run, Virginia

THE DIE IS CAST

✠

I.

An Emperor Arrives
in Europe

In May 1520 a royal flotilla left Spain for the British Isles with precious cargo. He was the twenty-year-old king of Spain, Charles V, the grandson, on his mother's side, of the "Catholic kings of Spain," Ferdinand and Isabella, the grandson, on his father's side, of Maximilian I, Holy Roman emperor. By his maternal lineage, he was also the nephew of Catherine of Aragon, the current wife of Henry VIII. Charles was now on his way to see the English king. The voyage would take seven days, ample time for the sober-sided, determined young monarch to ponder the extraordinary events of the past five years that had taken him from a cloister in the Netherlands to the pinnacle of power in Europe and to his new role as secular leader for all Christianity.

By birth, he was not Spanish but Flemish, born of Austrian parents in Ghent in the Jubilee Year of 1500. His first crown had been that of the Netherlands, which he had acquired at the age of six upon the death of his father, Philip the Handsome. The Low Countries, especially their contiguous provinces of Burgundy, would always lodge deep in the sentimentalities of the youthful monarch. Then at the age of seventeen, the crown of Spain was conferred upon him as well through the line to his Spanish grandparents, Ferdinand and Isabella, though the Spanish nobility was none too pleased to have this dour youth of Austrian and Dutch background as their monarch. Then two years after that, when Charles was nineteen years old, his other grandfather, Maximilian I, the Holy Roman emperor, ruler of Germany, and leader of the Hapsburg line of monarchs, died in Austria. It had been Maximilian's fondest hope to have his grandson officially proclaimed as his successor to the title of Holy Roman emperor. But Maximilian had died with his desires unfulfilled. As a result, a furious competition over this grand and ancient title ensued in 1519. Charles's chief rival was the other most powerful leader of Europe, Francis I, the king of France. Six years older than Charles, Francis stood in marked contrast to his solemn rival. He was robust, impetuous, and fun-loving, and he ruled over the wealthiest real estate in Europe.

In the contest over who would be the next Holy Roman emperor, the pope in Rome held considerable sway, for in theory the holy father was in charge of the spiritual world, while the Holy Roman emperor was Christianity's secular leader. But for three decades, in one invasion after another, Spain and France had feasted upon the fat of Italy. In 1515, just months after Francis I had become king of France, he won a glorious victory over the Swiss at Marignano and took charge of Italy's wealthiest state, Milan. But Charles V, as king of Spain, had Naples and Sicily in his domain. In between lay the hapless papal states and Machiavelli's independent province of Florence. In the face of these powerful countervailing forces, the independence of Florence and the defenseless papal states was always at risk.

Now, ironically, it fell to the pope to adjudicate between ravenous potentates for his secular counterpart. The pope was Leo X, amiable, courteous, and diplomatic, the scion of the great counting house of Florence, House of Medici, and the second son of Lorenzo the Magnificent. Leo had grown up in the company of painters and sculptors and writers. Art, he proclaimed, was "mankind's untouchable wealth." He had been elected seven years before, and upon his accession, as the consummate Florentine he had uttered his most famous remark, "Since God has given the papacy to us, let us enjoy it." And enjoying it he was, staging naughty drama and lavish balls and expensive entertainments in the staterooms of the holy palace. As a result, the Vatican was virtually bankrupt within two years. These indiscretions, financial mismanagements, and indecencies incurred the ire of contemporary critics such as Sigismondo Tizio, who wrote, "It is injurious to the Church that her Head should delight in plays, music, the chase and nonsense, instead of paying serious attention to the needs of his flock and mourning over their misfortunes." But in Rome, this was the minority opinion. In their pleasure-seeking and hubris, Romans loved the ripe atmosphere that Leo created. Unprotected though it might be, Rome had again become the cultural center of the civilized world.

In the campaign for the post of Holy Roman emperor, Leo X liked neither front-runner. For a time, he attempted to maintain strict neutrality, sailing, as one commentator remarked, with "two compasses." Of the two leading candidates (Henry VIII of England was a distant third) he disliked Charles V more, for the pope feared that with Charles's election his increased strength would tip the balance of power in Italy severely, to the disadvantage of the Vatican and of the pope's beloved Florence. So Leo threw his weight behind Francis I, only to find that he had backed the wrong candidate. The election was to be determined primarily by money. In matters of finance, Charles was in the best position to buy off the electors. His managers tapped the coffers of the most important bank of Germany, the House of Fugger, in Augsburg. Its campaign contribution of a half million ducats* proved more than enough to purchase the votes. Only one elector, the fiercely independent Frederick of Saxony, seemed to transcend bribery. At the last moment, Pope Leo X put Frederick forward as a compromise candidate in a last-ditch effort to halt the inevitable, but Frederick declined. On June 28, 1519, at Frankfurt am Main, Charles had been elected unanimously. The election had cost Charles and his investors 850,000 ducats. Before, the Western world had been composed of loose and contentious states under fractious rulers. Now, without really appreciating it, Christian central Europe was girding for the coming battle with Islam under one consolidated rule.

---

* A golden ducat was worth about two dollars. It was the standard coin of medieval Europe, first issued in the twelfth century in Sicily. It bore the image of Christ, and the inscription "O Christ, let this duchy that you rule be dedicated to you," a reference to Matthew 22:21: "Render therefore unto Caesar the things which are Caesar's; and unto God the things that are God's."

Thus the Holy Roman emperor–elect, Charles V, was making his first official state visit to England. This was to be but the first stop in a long swing through the north, a tour that was planned to culminate in October with his investiture as Holy Roman emperor in the great cathedral of Charlemagne at Aachen. Then early in the new year, before he returned to Spain, he would attend his first German parliament, to be called the Diet of Worms. There, among other pressing matters, he was to be formally proclaimed the successor of Maximilian I, the leader of the expansive Hapsburg dynasty.

The reach of this twenty-year-old emperor was now global. His dominion stretched from the Baltic Sea to the Mediterranean, from the Netherlands through Germany and Austria to Spain and Sicily. It stretched beyond the points of the compass in Europe to the New World. As Charles V was making his way north to England, his explorer Magellan was making his way south along the coast of Patagonia in South America. Within a few months, Magellan would find his passage through the Tierra del Fuego to the Pacific Ocean. And in Mexico, his brutal conquistador, Hernán Cortés, was closing in on the island of Tenochtitlán, where the last Aztec emperor, Montezuma II, cowered in the gold-filled rooms of his fabulous palace. Within a month, Montezuma would be dead, and Spain was one important step closer to its conquest of Mexico.

But on his voyage to England, the New World seemed far away. Charles's focus was merely continental in nature. In meeting Henry VIII, and in pondering his relations with his more formidable rival, Francis I, treaties of the recent past were on his mind. After Francis's victory at Marignano five years earlier, when the French took charge of the duchy of Milan, a treaty had been signed at Noyon, which had ushered in a brief period of peace between the natural enemies. Among the treaty's provisions was the promise that Charles would marry Francis's first child, now a babe in a cradle. This was a silly promise, for Charles at age twenty could scarcely be expected to wait for an infant to grow up. A few years earlier than that, however, in another negotiation, Charles had been promised in marriage to Mary Tudor, the daughter of Henry VIII. No doubt on this forthcoming visit Henry

VIII would press for a fulfillment of this treaty "obligation." The Hapsburgs were the masters of such ever-shifting promises, for they had built their empire on marriage ties. Times had changed. Charles's situation was different now, and he was not ready to make a matrimonial commitment. Rather, his attitude toward marriage was to ponder his best arrangement for his dynasty. Moreover, he had been schooled in cynicism about such matters.

"My child," Maximilian I had told his grandson, as the Treaty of Noyon was being solemnly ratified, "you are about to cheat the French, and I the English . . . or at least I shall do my best." It was well understood that the other potentates of Europe were no less cynical. France remained the most threatening power to the Hapsburg empire, and of the French, Charles's advisers remarked, "The French care neither for truth nor for friendship, and it is much to be feared that they will make no exception in their dealings with our master, for they are jealous to see him a greater ruler and a mightier king than their own."

Another treaty was even fresher in the mind of the emperor-elect. It had been signed at a meeting in London in the summer of 1518, convened by the lord chancellor of Henry VIII, Cardinal Wolsey, the archbishop of York. All the powers of Europe great and small had attended. All seemed to be swept up in a brief spasm of international harmony. If in the previous century, the Continent had enjoyed fifty years of peace between the great powers, why not in the sixteenth century as well? Agreement was reached that no state would pursue aggressive war against another. If aggression took place, each signatory was to come to the aid of the victim.

Behind this lofty sentiment lay something darker. If until 1494, when France had invaded Italy, there had been relative peace among the European powers, a new and menacing threat had, at the same time, emerged in the Orient. This was the rise of a powerful Islamic force in Turkey called the Ottoman Empire. Gradually, since the Ottomans had captured Constantinople in 1453, the Turks had spread their dominion north in the Balkan Peninsula, even to the gates of Belgrade in Serbia.

Once again, as so many popes before him had done, Leo X appealed to the major European powers to set aside their differences and unite against the common threat to Christianity. In 1518, before the conclave in London, the portly pontiff had formally preached a crusade. But Leo's crusade found few takers. Opposition was especially fierce in Germany, where a charismatic friar named Martin Luther was causing consternation in the Catholic world. This upstart rejected any call to crusade as a transparent Vatican ploy to extort money from the faithful. Thus, the Treaty of London was a sham, the face of harmony without its substance.

Charles V was traveling to England first. His chief concern, naïve though it was, was to honor the spirit of the London treaty and to foster a rapprochement between Henry VIII and Francis I. A great meeting between the English and the French kings was planned for June at what would become known as the Field of the Cloth of Gold. Charles would remain quietly in the background during the showy spectacle in France. But he was intent to head off any move toward an alliance against his new empire. Europe had only three major powers now, France, the Empire, and England, and of these France and the Empire were the greatest. It seemed inevitable that sooner or later the House of Hapsburg would come into conflict with the House of Valois.

2.

THE SWORD OF OSMAN

In September of that same year of 1520, a continent away, a very different royal flotilla was hastily being organized on the Aegean coastline of Turkey, not far from the ancient biblical cities of Ephesus and Smyrna. It too possessed precious cargo, the only remaining son of the Ottoman sultan known as Selim I or Selim the Grim. His name was Suleyman. The name itself portended great deeds, for it was a derivative of *Solomon,* the figure in the Koran who is thought to be the most perfect monarch, the ruler who perfectly embodies the concept of justice, but who is also a great warrior. According to the legend of holy books, King Solomon held sway over the winds and rode to battle along with his horses, camels, tents, and troops on a magic wooden platform.

Suleyman was born on the banks of the Black Sea in eastern Anatolia in late 1494, and this very date as well gave rise to great expectations. For his birth coincided with the first year of the tenth century in the Muslim calendar (A.H. 900). The number ten was magic and propitious. Mehmet had ten disciples. Allah was said to prefer the ten days of Dhul-Hijjah (the twelfth month in the Islamic calendar) over all other days in the year. The companion of the Messenger had asked, "Not even jihad in the way of Allah?" and the Messenger replied, "Not even jihad, except for the man who puts his life and wealth in danger for Allah's sake and returns with neither of them." If Suleyman became sultan, he would be the tenth sultan of the

House of Osman and therefore destined for glory. In his pronouncements, he could begin by invoking the thirtieth verse of the twenty-seventh sura of the Koran: "Verily, it is the message from Solomon, and verily it reads, in the name of Allah, the most Gracious, the most Merciful."

In 1520, as he prepared for his journey to the throne of power, Suleyman was twenty-six, six years older than Charles V, but the same age as Francis I of France. His experience in government was already extensive, for in the tradition of past sultans, he had been superbly trained for leadership. At the age of fifteen he was made the governor of a small province in northwest Anatolia; then for three years he served as governor of the Crimean port of Caffa, an important emporium for Iranian and Indian trade. Later, he was ordered to Constantinople and Adrianople as those cities' governors. He was now the governor of the province of Manisa in western Anatolia, a strategic province, where for several years he had dealt mainly with the annoying problem of widespread banditry. He was tall and wiry now, with a long neck, a thin face, and a long aquiline nose. It was sometimes said that he derived these fine features from his Circassian mother, the intelligent and beautiful Hafsa Khatun, who was the daughter of the khan of the Crimean Tartars. It was also through her that Suleyman inherited the blood of Genghis Khan (since the khans of the Crimea were descended from Djöchi, the eldest son of the Mongolian conqueror). Suleyman's delicate visage had a pallid complexion and was scored by a thin mustache and small goatee. His demeanor was studious; and his speech was polished, as he had been taught well in the Palace School under the close scrutiny of the chief white eunuch.

Of his father, Suleyman knew little, except that he was formidable, ruthless, and largely absent from the royal estate known as the Sublime Porte. During Suleyman's youth Selim I had spent his eight years as sultan in the east, far from home, fighting the heretics of Shi'ism in Iran and hoping to unite all of Islam under a single creed. Intimidating though he was, Selim I did not command the prestige of his great-grandfather Mehmet II, who had been known as the Conqueror. Mehmet II had crushed the last, woebegone remnants of the Byzantine Empire more than fifty years earlier in

1453. After capturing Constantinople, he had extended the dominion of the Ottoman Empire through the Balkan Peninsula, conquering most of Serbia, Albania, and Bosnia. His navy had overpowered the Venetians and captured Otranto on the tip of Italy. He conquered a number of islands in the Aegean. He had ended Greek rule in the eastern provinces of the Black Sea and annexed Crimea to the Empire. But the great Mehmet II had experienced two major failures and, thereby, had left two points of unfinished business to his successors. He had failed to capture Belgrade: he was repulsed there in 1456, and he had failed to capture the Christian bastion of the Knights of the Hospitallers on the island of Rhodes in 1480. "The great eagle is dead" was the famous remark that had greeted the death of the Conqueror in 1481. The lachrymose inscription on his tomb read:

"I wished to take Rhodes and subdue Italy."

Mehmet II had been succeeded by a much more docile sultan, Bayezid II, Suleyman's grandfather, who preferred the palace to the battlefield, though he extended the empire still farther over Herzegovina in 1496. During Bayezid's reign the Moors of southern Spain were finally defeated by the Catholic kings Ferdinand and Isabella. With that, the center of gravity for Islamic power shifted from Granada east to Constantinople.

Selim I had been the youngest of Bayezid's sons. In Ottoman tradition it was not age but ability or sheer, brute determination that determined succession. When Selim came of age, two of his brothers were dead and the other two, one a poet, the other a popular politician, were less determined. Impetuous and impatient for power, Selim waged a three-year war against his placid father for the throne. In the winter of 1511 he raised a cavalry of three thousand in the Crimea, drove his men mercilessly along the windswept northern banks of the Black Sea, crossed the frozen Dniester and other rivers north of Constantinople on his famous horse, known as Black Cloud, stormed into the city, and forced his father to abdicate. Then to consolidate his hold on power he had his father poisoned on the way to exile and had deaf-mutes strangle his remaining two brothers with a bowstring. Before his poetic brother, Korkud, was strangled, he wrote a poem to Selim complaining of cruelty. Selim was said to shed passionate tears when he read it. For good measure, Korkud's children were garroted as well, as Selim sat quietly in the next room. He burnished his reputation as the Grim One during his reign when he had some seven viziers beheaded, bringing into the Turkish language the wry insult "May you become Selim's vizier!"

Suleyman, therefore, had ample incentive to lead an upright and loyal life, for he knew his father was capable of the most brazen acts. The Grim One could murder and then wax eloquent about it as a poet. "A carpet is large enough to accommodate two Sufis," Selim had once written, "but the world is not large enough for two kings." If his father could tolerate holy men, he would brook no political challenge. As Selim had challenged his own father, so he was suspicious of his own son. Indeed, Selim was rumored to have attempted to murder his son years earlier by sending a poisoned shirt as a gift, but Suleyman's astute mother had a page try it on first.

By 1520 the campaigns of Suleyman's father had doubled the size of the Ottoman Empire. During his rule, Egypt, Palestine, and Syria had come under Ottoman rule. This was a historic achievement, for it meant that the Ottoman sultan now controlled the great cultural centers of Islam: Cairo, Jerusalem, and Damascus. When Selim's campaign in Egypt displaced the Mamluks, the mantle of the caliphate shifted to Ottoman control, along with the three most important holy cities of Islam, Mecca, Medina, and Jerusalem. Holy relics, most notably the cloak and standard of the Prophet Mohammed himself, were transported to Constantinople. In the Islamic world, the Ottoman emperor was now formally the "Guardian of the Faith."

But Selim's effort to unite the faith under Sunnism had met with only partial success. Before his campaign to the east, he massacred thousands of Shi'ites in Anatolia to purify his own land of heresy. For this campaign, he added the title of "the Just" to that of "the Grim." He had sliced into Persia as far as Tabriz. But Shi'ism had survived. It remained a vibrant force in Asia Minor.

In late September of 1520, Selim I was planning his next campaign: to attempt once again to dislodge the Christian unbelievers, the warrior-monks known as the Knights of the Hospital, from their great bastion on the island of Rhodes. The goal was to complete the historical quest of his grandfather, the Conqueror. Selim was on the road from Constantinople to Adrianople when he fell ill and abruptly died, probably from a combination of cancer and an anthrax infection that had developed from his years in the saddle. From this demise, a Turkish proverb arose: "Selim died of an infected boil and thereby Hungary was spared." Hungary was left to his successor. For seven days Selim's death was kept secret, for it was feared that the palace guard, the janissaries, would revolt against Selim's successor. Selim was much beloved by these war-lovers for his persistent campaigns. To quell such a rebellion might prove difficult.

The history of the janissaries stretched back to the founding of the Ottoman dynasty in the thirteenth century. Then, the idea was put forward to seize the flower of Christian youth in the Balkans, bring the boys to Constantinople as slaves, school them in loyalty to the sultan, and groom them for leadership. The practice had the dual purpose of emasculating the opposition to the Turks in the Balkans and of furnishing the army and the civilian establishment with great talent. Gifts and titles were lavished on the best of these slaves. They were trained for high office and became generals and statesmen, governors and royal bodyguards. Their wealth could only come from the spoils of war. Their loyalty was fierce to the sultan who rewarded them, just as the dissension of these warrior-slaves was dangerous to the sultan who left them to languish in idleness. Would Selim's successor be able to satisfy their thirst for conquest?

As the casket of Selim lay in his tent, adorned with seven white horse-tails, the symbols of power, a messenger raced across Thrace and across the Bosporus to Manisa. The message was written by the sultan's grand vizier, the seventy-seven-year-old statesman named Piri Pasha, known to the sultan as "the Bearer of the Burden." The note was cryptic: Come to Constantinople to receive the sword of the House of Osman. Suleyman was suspicious, and his wariness increased with the doubts of his confidant and chief counselor, Ibrahim. Ibrahim was Greek, a slave who had been groomed for leadership with Suleyman in the royal palace. Had not the sultan poisoned his father and strangled his brothers and their children? Why not his only son? Was this some sort of test? Had Selim I not once written the line:

> Those who ride to the hunt, do they ask
> In truth who are the hunters and who is the hunted?

Was Suleyman now sought as the hunter or the hunted? Was the crescent sword of the House of Osman meant for his hand or for his throat?

So Suleyman delayed until he could be sure that his summons hid no sinister purpose. Then, an entourage including his bosom friend, Ibrahim, was organized, and they rode three days to Üsküdar. There, the party boarded three dhows with graceful lateen sails for the short passage across the Sea of Marmara to Constantinople.

In the distance, the outlines of the seven hills of the great imperial city were visible in the mist. As the vessels crossed the boundary between Asia and Europe, the great seawalls of the city came into view on the European side, punctuated by a score of daunting naval gates, then the octagonal towers of the Grand Seraglio itself. His great-grandfather, Mehmet II, the Conqueror, had constructed this massive fortress over twenty-five years on the ruins of Byzantine palaces on a promontory known as Seraglio Point, where three bodies of water came together, the Golden Horn, the Bosporus, and the Sea of Marmara. As Suleyman's galleys drew still closer, the high walls and portals of the immense palace rose before him, and finally, the great sea gate itself, the Cannon Gate or Topkapi, with its twin towers and bristling artillery.

Suleyman knew this inner sanctum well. With his friend Ibrahim he had been prepared for leadership in the Palace School in the Third Court, not far from the Pavilion of the Holy Mantle, the ornate office of the grand vizier, and the throne room of the sultan itself. Here, under the tutelage of the agha and the white eunuchs, Suleyman's education had included the study of the Koran, the history of the forty viziers, the history of Sindbad the philosopher, the Hindu work *Kalila and Dimna,* and naturally *A Thousand*

and One Nights. They had taught him Arabic, the language of the Prophet, and Farsi, the language of the Persian heretic. In the shops he had been instructed in the crafts of silver- and goldsmithing, and then, as a welcome break, he took daily instruction in archery, the martial arts, and horsemanship at the privy stables.

Ibrahim had come into his life as a friend only after Suleyman was twelve. Ibrahim was, at first glance, not much to look at. The son of a Greek fisherman, he was medium in height, with a dark complexion and oval face, with a lower jaw that sported five or six pointed and separated teeth. He had arrived from the west coast of Greece after having been captured by Turkish pirates and sold into slavery. Suleyman was much taken with Ibrahim's charm, his skill at playing the violin, and his intelligence. The two, exactly the same age, had quickly bonded.

Later, as Constantinople's governor, with Ibrahim by his side, Suleyman had conducted his business in the Second Court of the palace, where the divan or Imperial Council deliberated and in whose expansive courtyard the janissaries gathered in formations by the thousands, totally silent and magnificently dressed in their loose-fitting, pink, billowy uniforms. When the janissaries receded, gazelles grazed languidly amid the cypress trees and the graceful fountains, near the gate that led to the harem, which was guarded by the halberdiers-with-tresses. (The false tresses hung down from their tall hats over their eyes so that they could not get a good look at the beautiful women within.) Suleyman guessed that he would be conveyed to the divan now, but for what purpose? The office of the executioner was also in the Second Court. As the city governor, he had witnessed the executioner's work on a number of occasions outside the wall, next to the Executioner's Fountain, where the executioner washed his hands after a decapitation.

Suleyman was coming home, to the playground and schoolyard of his youth and to the precincts of his important business as a governor, to his future destiny. If these spaces were portentous, they could be well loved, for they were exquisitely beautiful. "Never hath a more delightful residence been erected by the art of man," wrote a Turkish scribe. Suleyman's great-grandfather's Greek biographer had said that the Conqueror's creation possesses "vast and very beautiful gardens in which grow every imaginable plant and fruit. Water, fresh, clear and drinkable, flows in abundance on every side. Flocks of birds, both of the edible and singing variety, chatter and warble. Herds of both domestic and wild animals browse here." Above the Imperial Gate, the pride of his ancestor was inscribed in calligraphy: "Sultan Mehmet, Shadow and Spirit of God amongst men, Monarch of this world, Lord of two continents and of two seas, of east and west, and conqueror of the City of Constantinople." The weight of Suleyman's ancestry was considerable.

When the flotilla passed through the Cannon Gate, the grand vizier, Piri Pasha, greeted Suleyman lavishly at the royal dock. Within minutes of his landing, Suleyman's fears that this could be a dangerous paternal trap began to subside. His father was indeed dead. His coffin was en route from Adrianople. Suleyman had been summoned to accede to the throne of the Ottoman Empire.

At sunrise on the following day, Suleyman dressed in an elaborate ceremonial costume: his outer caftan was a brilliant blue, embroidered with a floral design; his inner caftan was gold lined with elaborate red, puffed sleeves. His substantial, bulbous white turban was topped with the traditional red plume. Solemnly, he was conducted to the courtyard of the Second Court, where an impressive dais had been erected in front of the Gate of Felicity, with the gate's massive towers as a backdrop. Slowly, he moved through the throng of dignitaries and learned men to the golden throne. To his right stood the grand vizier, proud and proprietary, dressed in a red floral caftan. Below among his Islamic scholars was their head, the Şeyhülislam, the highest Muslim eminence of the empire, cutting a fine figure with his long, white beard. The chief judges of Anatolia and Rumelia were close by, wearing flat turbans and fur-lined coats, as were the commanders of the janissaries, the captain of the seas, pages of the Inner Service, and the grand mufti himself, the highest official of Islamic law and the issuer of the fatwa. In accordance with the strictest protocol, these dignitaries approached the throne and knelt before their new sultan in deference. When the ceremony was over, Suleyman moved to the steps of the great hall of the divan to greet the throng of his subjects. For all his brutality, Selim I had left a well-organized and much-expanded empire to his successor.

A day later, the wooden coffin of the dead sultan arrived from the west. At the Imperial Gate, the new sultan, dressed now in dark robes and turban, received the body. Thereafter, a solemn procession wound through the streets to the sixth hill of the capital. Imams led the cortege, followed by Suleyman on foot, and a great crowd behind. On a high terrace overlooking the Golden Horn, the body was laid to rest. The traditional belief was that the departed soul would present its case to enter paradise standing on top of its burial place. Suleyman proclaimed that a mosque and a school would be built to honor his father.

At this ceremony, Suleyman, later known as the Magnificent, grasped the sword of Osman and took charge of the vast Ottoman Empire. With that act, he committed his reign, as nine sultans had done before him, to *gaza*, or holy war against the infidels.

3.

Son of Satan

On June 15, 1520, Leo X, the portly, pleasure-loving Florentine pope once called Giovanni di Lorenzo de' Medici, turned his attention from European politics and the election of the Holy Roman emperor to a more direct and immediate challenge to his papal authority. On this day, the pope issued a lengthy papal bull entitled *Exsurge Domine* or "Arise, O Lord." In a declaration replete with lurid images, the vicar of Christ called upon his Lord to punish the wolves, wild beasts, foxes, and one very dangerous wild boar that had invaded the Lord's vineyard and were ravishing the winepress of the true Catholic faith. The bull spoke of heretical errors that were offensive to pious ears, seductive to simple minds, and contrary to Catholic truth. These errors must be condemned at their source lest they spread further. It was regrettable, read the bull, that these errors had sprouted in Germany, whose true and obedient believers had always been held "in the bosom of our affection."

Of these errors, the papal document said, "It is no longer the Gospel of Christ's but of a man's or what is worse, the Devil's."

Who was this wicked man, this vicar of the devil? He was a simple Augustinian hermit, north in the center of Catholic Germany, Saxony, in the town of Wittenberg. The monk's name was Martin Luther. The papal bull brought to a head a three-year struggle of wills. Its language was passionate. Luther "is like the heretics whose last defense, as Jerome says, is to start spewing out the serpent's venom in their tongue and when they see that their causes are condemned, they spring to insults when they see they are vanquished." But at this point, it was unclear whose cause was the most condemned, and who was vanquished. *Exsurge Domine* represented nothing less than struggle to the death. This was Luther's formal excommunication from the Catholic Church. From his writings, books, and sermons, forty-one specific errors from the true doctrine of the Church were defined. Of these several were particularly noteworthy. Error 34 was Luther's remark that "to go to war against the Turks is to resist God who punishes our iniquities through them." Errors 18–21 dealt with Luther's contempt for papal indulgences, especially his assertion that they were worthless, particularly when they were applied to the dead. Error 25 disputed that the Roman pope was even the vicar of Christ at all. The bull ordered all the heretical books, pamphlets, and sermons of Luther to be gathered up and publicly burned.

As for Luther himself, despite the many efforts of the Mother Church to treat him charitably and kindly, to regard him as a prodigal son who would be welcomed back once he saw the error of his ways, his spirit had hardened. Therefore "we can proceed against him to his condemnation and damnation as one whose faith is notoriously suspect and who is in fact a true heretic." Unless he quickly disavowed these erroneous beliefs, he was to be seized and burned at the stake. In the meantime, he was to cease all his preaching. He was given sixty days to recant.

The "reformer," as his admirers now called him, had been expecting this ban for some time. He knew well that his life was in jeopardy. Yet allies gathered around him. Chief among them were the humanists, who were at the forefront of the new age of learning. They prized freedom of thought over ecclesiastical dogma and put their emphasis on human emotions. For years these humanists had railed against the ecclesiastical abuses of the wealthy German church, which had become fat from its indulgences and benefices, which had become the reserve of comfortable sinecures for the sons of the nobility, and whose lavish courts combined luxury with open immorality. The revulsion against these abuses had begun long before Luther.

"The clergy are to be found in taverns and inns, at sports and theaters, more frequently than in the consecrated places," wrote a contemporary. The richest abbeys and monasteries resisted reform most strenuously. Through these humanists Luther's sermons and writings, especially his inflammatory Ninety-five Theses, were widely distributed. They cheered him on.

"They say thou art excommunicated," wrote one humanist. "How great, O Luther, how great art thou, if this is true!"

In the early months of Luther's revolt, the greatest humanist of all, Erasmus of Rotterdam, supported Luther's challenge to the Church. Erasmus had written a letter of support to the powerful elector of Saxony, Frederick, who was now offering Luther his friendship and protection. Another notable admirer was the famous German painter Albrecht Dürer. And the rebel enjoyed the unanimous support of his university.

Luther's rebellion had been a great spur to German nationalism. After his early support, Erasmus's enthusiasm for Luther's cause began to wane for that reason. Luther was, wrote Erasmus, the "tree that bore the poisonous fruit of nationalism." Some allies were unsavory, men who were using Luther for their own political aims. One was the German prince Franz von Sickingen, whose powerful fortresses at Ebernburg and Landstuhl controlled the Rhine Valley. For years he had been warring on various local German princes to expand his dominion and enrich his treasure. He had accepted bribes from Francis I during the competition for the post of Holy Roman emperor, but had then switched to the winning side when Charles V's election became inevitable. In 1520 Sickingen was attempting to undercut the power of the German clergy and advance the power of the secular nobility. Luther's rebellion served that purpose. So Sickingen offered Luther both his castles as a refuge and his soldiers as guards. Another knight, Sylvester von Schaumberg, offered troops as well, invoking Caesar's dictum at the Rubicon that "the die is cast." These offers imparted a sense of safety to the reformer and emboldened him further.

"Sylvester von Schaumberg and Franz von Sickingen have freed me from the fear of men," Luther said gratefully. Perhaps, after all, he could escape the fate of his historical mentor, the Czech reformer Jan Hus, who had been proclaimed a heretic and burned at the stake a hundred years before.

It had been three years since, on October 31, 1517, Luther had tacked his ninety-five theses on the church door in Wittenberg. In that time he had risen from a simple, rustic, violent-tempered monk and obscure professor of theology to an international cause célèbre, hero, and "liberator" to a fast-spreading anti-Roman movement. He had become the archvillain to Catholic traditionalists. It had all begun when the archbishop of Magdeburg was offered the chance to buy another archbishopric, the see of Mainz, on the condition that he raise an additional ten thousand ducats, partly as a contribution to the building fund of St. Peter's Basilica in Rome (whose construction began in 1506). To raise this money, Rome suggested the sale of indulgences that were said to shorten the time of a sinner in purgatory. In Luther's words, Rome sent their "great fleecer of men's pockets" into the population to pay the archbishop's financial obligations. "They went around with indulgences, selling grace for money as dearly or as cheaply as they could, to the best of their ability." The indulgences for the dead were a particular fraud, for the dead man could scarcely express any further contrition for past sin.

"Do souls in purgatory actually want to be redeemed?" Luther wrote wryly in his twenty-ninth thesis. Ran a couplet attributed to an infamous indulgence hawker:

As soon as the gold in the coffin rings
The rescued soul to heaven springs.

Rome's counteroffensive had been fierce. Indulgences had their origin in the First Crusade in the eleventh century when holy warriors were rewarded for their service to the pope and to the Christian God. In recent times they had only been extended as rewards to those who contributed to the building of St. Peter's. The task was referred to the Dominicans, the hounds of God, whose role in the Church was to police and protect the purity of Catholic dogma, including the supreme authority of the pope over Christian ministers and his authority to issue indulgences. A Dominican scholar, Sylvester Prierias, who was the "commissioner of the Sacred Palace" and the Vatican's leading theologian, was put in charge of the theological aspects of the complaint. After studying the ninety-five theses, he drew up a bill of particulars that formally alleged the "suspicion of disseminating heresy." His invective against Luther was lurid: "Just as the devil smells of his pride in all his works, so you smell of your malevolence." When he received Prierias's document, Luther was at first shocked and then contemptuous. In theological discourse, he was in his element, and he responded with force and withering ridicule.

The Curia countered with the demand that Luther come to Rome within sixty days to answer for his words and acts. There could be no doubt now that his summons emanated from the office of the pope himself. In the first two years of his rebellion Luther could rail against the depravity of Rome, but he respected its immense power. In his first year of the rebellion, he had acted like a critic from within, still part of the Catholic family. In one of his first letters to Pope Leo X, he wrote, "It has never been in my mind to attack the authority of the Roman Church. On the contrary, I acknowledge that the authority of the Roman Church surpasses all other and nothing in heaven or on earth, save only Jesus Christ, is to be put above it."

Still, he appreciated that to go to Rome, that place of "hydras and portents," was never to return to Germany. If he was lucky enough to escape the fate of Jan Hus, he was, at least, certain to be silenced forever in perpetual incarceration. He looked for an excuse and found it in the flimsy invocations of poor health and poverty. Besides, he argued, his safety on a trip to Rome could not be guaranteed. The elector Frederick, the most powerful prince in Germany, conspired in this ruse by formally refusing Luther "safe conduct."

Rome had no choice but to compromise. The Holy See dispatched a papal legate to Germany, Cardinal Gaetanus Cajetan, a general of the Dominican order and head of the Inquisition. He was ordered to confront Luther and bring him to heel at a diet of German princes that was being held in Augsburg during the late summer of 1518. Cajetan was a worthy opponent, for he had been among the strongest critics of abuse and extravagance in the Vatican. The cardinal's mission was twofold. He was also charged with persuading the reluctant princes to donate substantial monies to a crusade against the Turks, who were then thought to be threatening Austria. To soften Frederick both in his protection of Luther and his disinterest in the Turkish question, the cardinal held out the prospect that Frederick might receive a much coveted papal decoration, the gilded rose, known as the Golden Rose of Virtue.

Cardinal Cajetan arrived in Augsburg in late July and immediately plunged into the difficult debate over the Turkish question. His plea fell on deaf ears and was answered with a chorus of grievances over ecclesiastical abuses in Germany, including pervasive financial improprieties. The sympathy for Luther in the conclave was clear from the beginning. When the cardinal brought up Turkey, the princes countered with the demand that a general Council of the Church be convened to consider Church abuses, including the indulgences. As the cardinal was suffering this public humiliation, the head of the Augustinian order in Rome was ordering his subordinate in Saxony to seize Luther as an enemy of Christ, manacle him, and turn him over to the papal legate.

Not until mid-October did the long-anticipated confrontation between Luther and the cardinal take place. Upon his departure from Wittenberg, Luther wrote bravely to his university supporters, "Let the will of the Lord be done. In Augsburg, even in the midst of his enemies, Jesus Christ rules. May Christ live even though Martin and every sinner perish."

But Luther arrived in Augsburg sick, exhausted, despondent . . . and terrified that he was staring death in the face. "Now I must die," he moaned. But almost in the next breath, he proclaimed that he would rather die than recant. When the two finally came face-to-face, Luther had regained his vigor. In his simple friar's cowl, with several Augustinian and Carmelite brothers beside him, he faced the elegant and cerebral cardinal, dressed in luminous red and accompanied by several impressive Italian cavaliers. Initially with a tone of deference to the papal surrogate, Luther restated his case forcefully. For his part, the cardinal, initially in the spirit of "fatherly kindness," demanded a recantation. Luther refused. After the first day's argument, Luther wrote that the cardinal as a scholar and Vatican administrator had no more understanding of these issues than "an ass to play the harp."

Over the next two days, the opponents dueled over the fine points of theology. Luther would recant, he said, if his errors could be proved. He could not recant "so long as the passages of the Scripture stand. It would be my greatest joy to see the truth victorious." Soon enough, Cajetan grew exasperated. As he dropped the tone of fatherly kindness, Luther dropped his attitude of deference, and by the third day the two began to shout at one another. The interchange ended badly with Cajetan ordering Luther out of his sight. "Go and do not return unless you are ready to recant!" the cardinal blurted out. That night, Luther wrote, "I will not become a heretic by contradicting the opinions that made me a Christian. I would rather die, be burned, exiled, accursed." A day later, hearing rumors that he was about to be arrested despite Frederick's guarantee of safe conduct, Luther fled the scene in haste.

The following year, 1519, had seen the conflict widen and the positions harden. In March, as if he took Luther's excuse of poverty seriously as a bar to coming to Rome, Leo X offered to pay all the reformer's expenses for the privilege of appearing before a Roman inquisition. Luther scoffed. Rome was nothing short of Babylon, he wrote, a city of evil, the lair of the Antichrist. Romans were out to get him "by Italian subtlety, poison or assassination." At the same time the pope sent an unctuous message to the elector Frederick, accompanied by the coveted gilded rose. "Consider how great an honor we are sending, and how detestable is the overbearing boldness of that only son of Satan, Martin Luther. Consider that he savors of notorious heresy and can blacken the name and fame of the great Elector and his ancestors. Let him crush the rashness of this Luther." Frederick did nothing.

The bombast and ridicule of Luther's antipapist rhetoric grew more violent by the month, and as his rebellion spread across Germany, he grew bolder. His public pronouncements became more and more messianic, suggesting that God was speaking through him to reform His church. A reconciliation became less and less possible. But Luther was still reluctant to debate these fundamental points of theology in public. In February of 1520 he wrote to a friend, "You cannot make a pen out of a sword. The Word of God is a sword. I am unwilling to be forced to come forward in public and the more unwilling I am, the more I am drawn into the contest." Not long after he relented and acquiesced to outside pressure.

In June a public disputation was arranged in Leipzig. He would debate the most famous theologian in Germany, Dr. Johann Eck, the vice-chancellor of the University of Ingolstadt and widely regarded as the reigning genius of the German academy. Like Luther, Eck hailed from humble roots—Luther's father was a miner, Eck's a peasant. He had taken up his pen in defense of the new science and new learning of the Renaissance, but he had pilloried Erasmus and the humanists. A staunch apologist for the Roman establishment, he had no sympathy for the reformers.

Leipzig was an appropriate site for this single combat between intellectual gladiators on the theological campus. Indulgences had sold briskly in the city, including a nasty bit of fraudulence called the *Butterbrief*. For a pretty price to the church, the buyer was permitted to indulge in butter, milk, and other dairy products normally prohibited by the Church on fast days. Leipzig was also situated in the fiefdom of Luther's fiercest detractor, Duke George of Saxony, known as the Bearded One. Duke George was the cousin of the elector Frederick, Luther's most important patron. Wary of Duke George, the reformer arrived in Leipzig guarded by two hundred armed students from the University of Wittenberg.

On the morning of June 27, 1519, an excited throng gathered on Ritterstrasse in a festive spirit and accompanied the combatants and their seconds to St. Thomas Church for a special twelve-part mass that had been composed by the church's cantor for the occasion. Over the next two weeks, the crowd moved to the great hall of Pleissenburg Castle for the main event. There the central question for debate was, is the papacy in Rome of human or divine origin? Christ is the head of the Church, Luther argued. Yes, Eck replied, but Christ's church has a vicar on earth. The church is the kingdom of faith, Luther asserted. Yes, Eck replied, but as it is stated in Matthew 16:18, "Thou art Peter, and upon this rock I will build my church." Skillfully and stubbornly, Eck defended Catholic doctrine against Lutheran "despair" and put on an impressive display of learning against Luther's appeal to Scripture. He trapped Luther into endorsing the heresies of Jan Hus, which did not help the cause of one who was himself accused of heresy. Eck pushed Luther into arguing that belief in the divine supremacy of Rome was not necessary to salvation. They quarreled over the meaning of Christ's statement "Feed my sheep," and over the nature of purgatory and penance. When it was over, Eck was thought to have won on points.

The reformer left the conclave disgruntled. Whatever his reverses in the debate may have been, he left his mark. Students by the hundreds deserted Leipzig University for the University of Wittenberg. After the debate Lutheran sympathizers turned on Eck personally, charging the theologian with vanity, hypocrisy, stupidity, and drunkenness. One slander suggested that in the nine days Eck remained in Leipzig after the debate, he "enjoyed manifold sensual pleasures, for which he had notoriously a great susceptibility." Soon enough Luther himself waded in with ad hominem libels about his opponents at Leipzig. About one he wrote, "The clumsy ass can not yet sing his hee-haw." Of his detractors generally he wrote that they clung to him like mud to a wheel.

"Their armor is so wonderful. They put the helmet on the feet, sword on the head, shield and breastplate on the back. They hold the spear by the point. Leipzig, to produce such giants, must be very rich soil." If he could make sport of his enemies with both sharp and blunt ridicule, so he put himself forward as a victim, and his rebellion forward as noble. "Whoever will, let him freely slander and condemn my person and my life. It is already forgiven him. God has given me a glad and fearless spirit that they shall not embitter for me, I trust, not now or in all eternity."

Early in 1520 Johann Eck traveled to Rome, and the drafting of restrictions against the "Lutherans" and of a specific excommunication order against Luther himself began. Eck joined with Luther's other opponent

Cardinal Cajetan in the initial apostolic commissions. In the spring of 1520 Leo X himself joined the discussions. In May, Eck polished the final wording of the order and presented it to a consistory of cardinals presided over by the pope himself. "It is hoped," remarked an optimistic (and delusional) cardinal, "that as soon as the bull is published in Germany, most men will forsake Luther."

The papal bull of excommunication had three parts. Forty-one errors from Luther's writings and sermons were defined and condemned as dangerous, heretical, scandalous, and offensive to pious ears. His books were to be burned. After sixty days for "reflection," if the culprit did not recant, he was to be ostracized or, better yet, seized and brought to the fire of holy justice. Eck was then appointed as a protonotary apostolic and charged with the privilege of taking the papal order to Germany and seeing that it was enforced.

In the first half of 1520, as the excommunication order was debated and refined in Rome, the fine art of insult was broadly employed in Germany. One Lutheran prince, Ulrich von Hutten, referred to Rome as "a gigantic bloodsucking worm" and its priests as "gluttons who, having first sucked our blood and then consumed our flesh, are now seeking to grind our bones and devour all that is left of us." He argued that if Germany did not have the strength of will to free itself from the Vatican's yoke, then "let the Turks execute judgment on Rome." Meanwhile, the woodblock printing presses of Germany clattered with the production of Luther's books, letters, pamphlets, sermons, and manifestos. Between 1518 and 1520, when the printing process was still in its infancy, the number of his titles in print grew from 150 to 570. In Catholic towns in Germany and the Netherlands, Luther's enemies conducted ceremonial burnings of these works, as if the spectacles were a metaphor for the fate of Luther himself. But the burnings could not keep up with the distribution.

"Farewell, thou unhappy, lost, blaspheming Rome," Luther wrote during the week that the bull of excommunication was actually issued. "The wrath of God has come upon thee, as thou hast deserved. We have cared for

Babylon, but she is not healed. Let us then leave her, that she may be the habitation of dragons, specters, and witches, and true to her name of Babel, an everlasting confusion, a new pantheon of wickedness."

His breach with Rome was now complete, irreconcilable, and permanent.

4.

A FIELD OF FOOL'S GOLD

In the last two weeks of May 1520, Henry VIII posted scouts along the coast of Cornwall to search the horizon for the royal fleet of Charles V. This visit of his nephew was much anticipated in England, as the first official visit of the new Holy Roman emperor–elect. But time was short before the extravaganza across the English Channel with the French king, Francis I, at what was later known as the Field of the Cloth of Gold, which had been two years in the planning. Henry VIII was eager to see Charles V first ahead of his French rival. His queen, Catherine of Aragon, was still more eager, for she was decidedly unenthusiastic about a rapprochement between France and England. But the English king had succeeded in securing only a few weeks postponement for the French visit. The queen of France, Claude of Brittany, was pregnant again. At the age of twenty, she was about to have her fifth child, and the French envoys said emphatically that their fertile queen, with her big belly, could not travel after mid-June (the child was born on August 10). The fecundity of the French queen must have seemed like a quiet rebuke to the vigorous Henry VIII. His queen, Catherine, was now thirty-five years old and had produced only a daughter, the princess Mary Tudor. The future of the Tudor dynasty hung in the balance. Henry was growing impatient and, in the bargain, a bit tired of his stolid and pious queen.

In fact, the offspring of Henry and Francis were at the center of the delicate dance between the three monarchs. In separate solemn treaties, Charles had been promised to Henry's daughter, Mary, now four years old, and also promised to the first child of Francis I. At present, he had no intention of marrying either. The infanta, Mary Tudor, in turn, had also been promised in marriage to a French dauphin, a proposal opposed vehemently by her mother, Catherine. Catherine longed for her nephew Charles to marry her daughter despite consanguinity, for that would link England with Spain, Germany, Austria, and the Low Countries under one dynasty.

Despite the duplicity on all sides, all needed to keep up appearances. Henry needed to be gracious about his defeat in the imperial election, and Charles needed to profess gratitude for Henry's "help" in his election. Charles, though noncommittal about marriage, needed to show deference to his estimable aunt Catherine, and her volatile husband, Henry. Henry, in turn, needed to profess an interest in peace, although the pope, Leo X, was secretly urging an offensive pact of England, Venice, and France against the rising power of Charles. An important commercial pact between England and the Netherlands was on the table. In a few months, Charles's coronation as Holy Roman emperor would take place in Aachen. For that celebratory moment, peace must reign in Europe.

All of these delicacies and subtleties would be moot unless the imperial flotilla arrived promptly. Henry VIII was already eager to sail for Calais and had already moved his entourage from London to Greenwich to Canterbury on the road to Dover in preparation for an imminent departure. But Catherine prevailed upon him to tarry a few days longer. She was determined that the coming lovefest with France be nullified, bracketing it with two visits by Charles V.

On May 27, Whitsunday, the Spanish flotilla sailed into Dover just in time. Fortunate it was for all that Charles had had seven days of clear sailing from Spain. The royal fleet arrived at 10 p.m. Waiting on the dock to greet him was Cardinal Wolsey, full of schemes and proposals. To Shakespeare, Wolsey was a holy fox or wolf, equally as ravenous as he was subtle and "as prone to mischief as able to perform it." In the flickering torchlight, the cardinal and archbishop of York and papal legate cut quite a figure on the quay, draped in luminous red as befit his eminence. At forty-five he was immensely fat, fat as a maggot, the poet John Skelton called him, bold and bragging and prideful as well, for one so "basely borne." (Wolsey was the son of a butcher from Ipswich.) Shakespeare saw him as a "keech" or congealed lump of fat whose "bulk takes up the rays of the beneficial sun and keeps them from the earth." But his brilliance and his cunning were legendary, and he had a driving ambition to be the next pope. A veteran of turbulent European politics, he was by all accounts the king's favorite; Henry deferred to his lord chancellor unfailingly in matters of foreign policy. "Be it black or white," wrote Skelton about Wolsey's influence, "all that he doth is right."

As he came down the stairs to greet the formidable cardinal, Charles, dressed in black, cut a far less imposing figure. At twenty, he was not quite put together, being ungainly and frail-looking, his legs too short for his body. His back was slightly bowed. His head was large and long-faced. His brilliant blue eyes were offset by the famous Hapsburg chin, an overshot jaw that contributed to his lisp and slow speech. What he lacked in physical appearance, he tried to cover up with pomp and decorum. His ship displayed an immense black eagle, the symbol of the Empire. Elegant Spanish cavaliers and Burgundian knights accompanied him. The procession rode off to Dover Castle. Four hours later, Henry VIII came to meet his royal guest.

The following day, they rode to Canterbury with a sword-bearing knight riding between them. Henry was expansive and jolly, Charles dour and deferential. In the shadow of the great Norman cathedral, king and emperor paid a ceremonial visit to the shrine of St. Thomas à Becket; then they sat down to talk. Over the next two days, sometimes under the watchful eye of Queen Catherine, they discussed the state of their world. Henry dispensed a surfeit of avuncular advice, as if Charles were his royal ward: how to deal with the various, far-flung provinces of the vast Hapsburg Empire, how to comport himself as king and emperor. Charles harped upon the need for peace in the spirit of the Treaty of London. He gave lip service to the pope's concern about the Turkish menace and about his call to crusade, expressing wariness about the intentions of Francis I. Later, in a letter, Charles would thank his uncle for "the advice you gave me at Canterbury like a good father." Whether Henry appreciated the steel beneath Charles's unimpressive appearance was not clear. They parted with the agreement to meet again in the Netherlands a month later, after Henry's extravaganza with Francis. On the same day, June 1, they sailed from Dover in different directions.

Preparations for the conference between Henry VIII and Francis I had been under way since February. It had been proposed nearly two years before, in October 1518, as a gesture of "perpetual friendship" between the two traditional enemies, but it had been postponed for a year because of the imperial election. For months English ports along the Channel teemed with armies of carpenters and tentmakers, mules and horses, on their way to the pale of Calais. Rolls and rolls of cloth clogged the docks, especially woven with a weft of gold thread and a warp of silk. Velvet and satin and damask were shipped by the boatload. English carpenters were refurbishing the decaying castle at the village of Guines with spectacular stained-glass work and magnificent tapestries, while English gardeners fashioned a sumptuous square courtyard, appointed with statues of Cupid and Hercules and King Arthur, carved with such mottoes as "A faithful friend is another self" and "A faithful friend is a strong protection." A Bacchus fountain flowed with wine. Among all the nobles who planned to attend were the Knights of the Garter, the master of the posts, the king of arms, and the knights bachelor.

Francis I, meanwhile, would have a royal pavilion 120 feet in height, whose flaps were lined with blue velvet and fringed in gold and whose tent poles were ship masts. For the entrance to the royal pavilion a statue of St. Michael, the patron saint of France, had been carved in walnut. Beyond his great pavilion a tent city arose to accommodate dukes and princes, four cardinals and nine bishops, the chancellor, the admiral, the marshal, and the constable of France, not to mention the king's librarian and the king of Navarre. When all the nobles and their seconds and their ladies were counted up on both sides, the conference brought together about six thousand people.

The ladies accompanying the king of France were the more stunning.

Besides his fertile queen, there was his formidable mother, Louise of Savoy, now forty-three, powerful, refined, experienced in statecraft, and devoted to her son, *"mon roi, mon seigneur, mon Caesar, et mon fils."* The young beauties of the French court were the stuff of poetry and portraiture. Rabelais, the connoisseur of beauty and grace, described them alternately as enchanting, abstract, joyful, charming, ethereal, with glorious feminine bodies and angelic spirits.

Among these belles in the French court was a vivacious and graceful nineteen-year-old English girl named Anne Boleyn. The daughter of an English diplomat of merely high bourgeois lineage, she was in Paris to receive her finishing education and had been drawn into the court of Francis as an interpreter, where she became a favorite lady-in-waiting for Queen Claude. Characteristically, the French took credit for her grace. "She became so graceful that you would never have taken her for an Englishwoman, but for a Frenchwoman born," wrote a contemporary French poet. She had a lovely body, sparkling, welcoming eyes, black hair, and an especially pretty mouth with fine lips. She also had an especially prominent Adam's apple, which she always covered up with high-necked dresses, and which an uncharitable French historian would later describe as a "goiter." The other curiosity about her was a double nail on one of her fingers, which her detractors inevitably called her sixth finger or, worse, the devil's teat.

Queen Catherine, meanwhile, presided over the English ladies. Some naughty snickering about her came from the French side. One French commentator patronized her as a "Spanish saint," whose overweening piety "has rendered her so desolate and dismal that her husband only dares to approach her kneeling on the prayer bench." This was, of course, unfair to both Catherine and Henry. Aloof and exceedingly pious she may have been—she was, after all, the daughter of Queen Isabella of Spain—but she was a much admired woman of substance and refinement, especially as an advocate for the scholars of the New Learning, as a patron of both humanistic education and of humanists themselves, including the great Erasmus of Rotterdam. Though Henry's discontent with her was growing, she was, at this point, very much the queen of England.

Before the festivities began, there was business to conduct. Cardinal Wolsey had been the driving force behind this rapprochement, partially as a matter of self-interest, for he counted on French support in his campaign for the papacy. He handled the discussions about various financial obligations between the countries that remained outstanding, especially the terms of the dowry for the promised marriage between the dauphin and Mary Tudor. Despite the lavish expressions of affection, deep suspicions, bred of centuries-long hostility between the countries, were hard to mask.

Wolsey relished his role, and England's role, as a mediator between France and the Empire. To prove himself a skilled diplomat and peacemaker might also advance his standing in the College of Cardinals. There was a growing sense that war between the Empire and France was inevitable. Soon enough, the question would arise as to which side England would take. Before the two kings could meet, the cardinal discussed his country's business directly with King Francis. At Francis's side stood another formidable player who would figure greatly in the events of the coming years. He was Charles de Bourbon, the constable of France, hero of the battlefield, the most powerful and the wealthiest man in the kingdom outside of the king himself. Bourbon had received his title and his lavish duchy through marriage. When two years after this conference his wife died, the king's mother, Louise of Savoy, herself a Bourbon, sought to disinherit Charles. This led to a lawsuit and ultimately to Charles's treason against the French crown. For now, however, he was still very much the constable of France.

On June 7, perfectly timed with salutes of cannon shot, and all orchestrated by Cardinal Wolsey, the royal processions left their respective redoubts at Ardres and Guines, and the kings came together in a field halfway between. Some five hundred horsemen and three thousand foot soldiers accompanied Henry. The kings, equal in luster, looked their parts, virile men in their prime.

Francis was twenty-six, a giant of a man, broad-shouldered, with a large head, aquiline nose, and narrow, squinting Gallic eyes. Graceful, athletic, and strong, he was the Frenchman's idea of the perfect prince. He loved jousts, fierce riding, and various racquet and ball games. In this latter category, besides tennis, his choices were many: an Italian game called *l'escaigne,* which featured a heavy ball studded with lead points and batted by a wooden paddle with a lead handle, or a game called *la soule* and *la crosse,* which was an early form of field hockey, or a stick-and-ball game called *pallemail,* which Francophiles claim is a form of golf that pre-dates the Scottish version. In his youth and early manhood Francis played these games ardently and roughly. He was also an avid cardplayer, and he often bullied his dukes and counts into high-stakes games that his courtiers could scarcely afford.

Hunting and women were his greatest passions. "No matter how old or ill I may be, I will have myself carried to the hunt," he had said, "and when I die, I shall want to go there in my coffin." Or to the bedroom. He was a sexual athlete. While he kept his teenage queen, Claude, in one pregnancy after another, he chased after a long succession of mistresses, viewing the chase playfully with the zest of a foxhunt. About his ladies he could wax poetic:

A court without women
Is a year without spring
A year without spring
Is a spring without roses.

After hearing once that a famously erotic Italian courtesan in the Mantuan court named La Brognina had given up her life of the senses and entered a nunnery, Francis had his scribe forge a papal order and dispatched a company of French soldiers to the convent to kidnap her and bring her to Paris. To his immense disappointment Spanish soldiers intercepted the kidnappers near the border and returned the victim to her pious seclusion. The only woman to whom the French king showed a doting respect and docility was his mother, Louise of Savoy.

Henry was three years older. He stood six feet four inches. While he was becoming solidly corpulent, he was still light of foot. In this early period of his reign, he still held his violent temperament in check. He was a genuine scholar who spoke fluent French and Spanish and enough Latin to converse with ambassadors and to read diplomatic dispatches. Music was his special passion. He was an accomplished lute player, a lusty singer, and avid composer who wrote hymns and romantic songs. He also tried his hand at writing plays and poetry. In the martial arts he was practiced in horsemanship and skilled with the sword, the lance, and the bow. He was also devout and well versed in the fine points of theology. As a youth, his practice was to begin his letters with the phrase "Jesus is my hope."

The royals shared a common bond. Neither had been born to kingship, but had acquired it through the accident of another's death. (For Henry, the death of his older brother, Arthur; for Francis, the death of the son of Louis XII.) They had never met. Dressed now in glittering gold and silver capes, black-feathered caps and jewels flashing, they embraced on horseback, then dismounted and embraced again. They took off their hats and strode arm in arm into a tent of golden cloth, Henry escorted by his privy councillor and Francis by the constable of France.

So began two weeks of banquets and balls and entertainments that sported much but meant little. Jousts, archery contests, fights at the barriers, and wrestling matches were plentiful, with the kings themselves taking part in these displays of knightly skill. The bills of fare for the royal banquets were enormous, including such exotic items as peacock, heron, egret, and crane, while for seafood, the royals dined on porpoise. In the two weeks of jousting, 327 lances were shattered, the kings themselves responsible for many. For the more delicate entertainments, music, dance, even architectural competitions, took place. It was a royal contest of manly skill and prowess, of feminine charms, of elegance and excess. A "view of earthly glory," Shakespeare called it. It was as well a constantly changing fashion show. To impart some measure of solemnity to the proceedings, Cardinal Wolsey interspersed the entertainment with a mass sung to the Holy Ghost.

Ten days into the festivities, things got testy when strong winds swept across the Field of the Cloth of Gold, blowing away tents and shattering some of the fragile and precious English glasswork in the temporary castle at Guines. The winds kicked up such a dust that the jousters could scarcely see one another across the field of mock battle. A day later, in a lighthearted mood, Francis I turned up in the early morning with only a few men at Henry VIII's castle. There, to jolly Henry out of his sullen mood, Francis said jovially, "I am come into your strong castle to offer myself as your prisoner." Henry was amused, and they cavorted languidly with the ladies for the rest of the day. If Henry's musical sensibility was more refined, Francis I seemed more adept at a public display of chivalry. In the balls and banquets, his brilliant maidens surrounded him, a number of whom were his mistresses, for it was said that he presided over the most lecherous court in Europe. At the Field of the Cloth of God, however, Francis I captivated the ladies with sentimental poems and comported himself gracefully on the dance floor. Henry protested his chivalry by wearing a motto on his jousting costume, "In love whoso mounteth passeth in peril." But the French seemed to be getting the better of it. The glittering French "all in gold like heathen Gods shone down the English," Shakespeare wrote later.

Then at a jousting tournament, Henry's dignity suffered a blow when he accidentally killed an innocent jousting partner. He recouped this faux pas somewhat by winning a spirited archery contest. Then came the wrestling. Both kings were skillful and athletic practitioners of this ancient sport. Despite his widening girth and puffy cheeks, Henry was quite agile. He easily bested a few French oafs who were put up against him. Then impulsively he grabbed Francis by the collar and challenged him to wrestle. This proved to be a mistake. Both men stripped to the waist. Henry charged. Francis stepped aside and treated his English counterpart to a *tour de Bretagne,* a kind of sneaky French flip, in which Henry was spun around, tripped, then slammed flat on his back. The ladies gasped. After he was helped to his feet, Henry asked for a rematch. Francis declined, as was his right under the rules as the winner. Henry stomped off in a huff.

Commentators later spoke of the "terrible consequences" of Henry's humiliation for Anglo-French relations. If that is so—that the loss of a wrestling match could undermine the whole purpose of the gathering—it only pointed to how little was at stake at the Field of the Cloth of Gold. All that came of it were slightly more generous terms for the proposed marriage between the House of Valois and the House of Tudor (a marriage that Catherine of Aragon would never permit), and that Henry VIII took notice of the young English girl in the French queen's court named Anne Boleyn.

The great event ended with overwrought flatteries and hollow promises that did little to disguise the frostiness between the sides and the personal pique of Henry. Francis called Henry his perfect friend and his brother. No sooner was Henry out of sight than the French began to fortify their border with the English pale and convert their tents and pavilions to military use. While Henry, in turn, promised to tell his French brother all about his coming meeting with Charles V, he was actually preparing to switch his allegiance to the emperor. Henry rode off to Gravelines in the Netherlands for his second meeting with Charles V, a meeting that would undo what little had been accomplished at the Field of the Cloth of Gold. With him was Catherine, happy and relieved now that the French farce was over. She was not the only one relieved. Many were ready for the historical enmity between the countries to be restored. One knight in royal retinue remarked, "When I meet those Frenchmen again, I hope it may be with my sword point."

Within a year he would get his wish.

5.

LET IT BE DONE!

On October 22, 1520, Charles V of Spain arrived on the outskirts of Aachen in northwest Germany near Belgium. The electors of Germany who had voted for him as the Holy Roman emperor and who were to figure so prominently in his rule in the next few years greeted him warmly. Charles was coming to pay homage to Charlemagne, the first and greatest Holy Roman emperor, the true champion of Christ who had defended Christianity against the infidels and who had established the kingdom of Christ in Europe. Charles had come to confirm his own election humbly as Charlemagne's thirtieth successor. With great ceremony the German princes escorted the king of Spain into the imperial city, with the hereditary marshal holding high the imperial sword ahead of him, and with knights and counts and Spanish cavaliers and the duke of Jülich (in whose province Aachen lay) trailing behind.

On the following day Charles was conducted to the imperial cathedral. The massive Gothic structure was the oldest church in northern Germany and had been built seven hundred years earlier. The famous and magical tomb of the first emperor resided in the place of honor in the church. In the jubilee year of A.D. 1000 Otto III, the Emperor of the Last Days, as he called himself, had opened Charlemagne's tomb. There, nearly two hundred years after his death, remarkably preserved, with only the tip of his nose fallen away, seated upright on his marble throne, and wearing a golden crown, was Charlemagne himself. Still dressed in his imperial robes, he held the scepter of temporal power in one hand, and the Gospels in the other. As the story is told, Otto III noticed that Charlemagne's fingernails had grown. Before he left the tomb, the Emperor of the Last Days took one tooth from the cadaver's mouth as a keepsake.

The ceremony of coronation had five essential elements. First there was the examination or scrutiny of the candidate. Two bishops brought Charles forward to the archbishop, who questioned the bishops about Charles's fitness for this high and holy post. He then took the oath of coronation: "In the name of Christ, I, Charles of Spain, the Emperor, promise, undertake, and protest in the presence of God that I will be the protector and defender of the Holy Roman Church in all ways that I can be of help, so far as I shall be supported by Divine aid, according to my knowledge and ability." His hand upon the holy Gospels, he then made a number of promises. He swore fealty to the pope himself. He swore to guarantee all the rights and possessions of the electors and German princes, to protect them against revolt, either by the nobility or the common people, to protect them against hostile alliances, to hold no diet outside the boundaries of the Empire nor to allow foreign armies on imperial soil. Lastly, he promised to increase the Empire by recovering lost lands.

Then, in perhaps the most dramatic moment, he prostrated himself before the altar. Mumbling their prayers of blessing, the prelates anointed him with the oil of catechumens on his arm and on his shoulders, thereby initiating him into the holy mysteries of the Church. The mass began. Now in the robes of his new office and seated upon Charlemagne's marble throne, Charles received the symbols of his new dominion: the sword of power, the crown of his empire, and the scepter with its distinctive orb.

Then the celebrant turned to the assemblage. Would they be obedient to this prince and lord "after the command of the Apostle?" The great church resounded with the loud chants, *Fiat. Fiat. Fiat.* Let it be done! With the singing of *Te Deum Laudamus,* the mass was ended. The new emperor greeted his people. At midnight, in Charlemagne's palace, a great banquet began in the magnificent coronation hall of the emperors. Just before the coronation, a solar eclipse had occurred, and this inspired a poet to tie together the galactic occurrence and the earthly celebration with a soaring encomium.

> *Not long ago Apollo scowled down from the height of the heavens*
> *And Daedalus himself concealed his light.*
> *Suddenly the divine star of Caesar arose,*
> *And Apollo cheering returned with the new Caesar,*
> *Henceforth he stood still and each one ruled by agreement,*
> *Apollo ruled over the heavens and Caesar on earth.*

Across the Rhineland, at about this same time, a very different ceremony was taking place. A few weeks before Charles's coronation, Luther's excommunication was published in the regions around Wittenberg. Luther's antagonist, Dr. Johann Eck, had brought the papal document to Germany. As the bull was published, students from Wittenberg University insulted Eck and threatened him physically. In various protests in Brandenburg and Meissen, the document was torn to shreds in public displays of anger. The universities of Wittenberg and Erfurt officially and collectively refused to accept the bull. Elsewhere, the bull's language was met with derisive laughter, especially the part about how Luther would be welcomed benignly back as the prodigal son into the bosom of the Church, if he would but desist in his errors. By the "bowels of the mercy of God, they shall find in us the affection of father's love."

Any pretense of respect and obedience now dropped away from the statements of Luther himself. Brazenly, he wrote a letter to the pope, dropping the salutation "His Holiness" and addressing him with an insultingly familiar greeting of "my Leo" or "my good Leo." He bore the pope no ill will personally, he proclaimed; he only pitied him, for he was like a lamb among wolves, like Daniel in the lions' den, like Ezekiel among the scorpions. The Church itself deserved no pity. It was more corrupt than Babylon and Sodom. "At one time the holiest of all, the Church of Rome is now the most licentious den of robbers, the most shameless brothel, the kingdom of sin, death, and hell." Elsewhere, Luther called upon all princes to oppose "the incredible madness of the Pope." In his formal answer to the bull of excommunication, he called himself Christ's evangelist and threw down his challenge not only to the pope, to the new Holy Roman emperor, and to the Christian world, but to Suleyman and the world of Islam as well. Contrition, retraction, abjuration, were impossible. About his central tenet of his new doctrine, justification by faith alone, he wrote:

"[It] shall remain untouched by the Roman Emperor, by the Turkish Emperor, by the Tartar Emperor, by the Persian Emperor, by the Pope, by all the Cardinals, Bishops, priests, monks, nuns, kings, princes, lords by all the world and all the devils, and may they have the fire of hell on their heads and not a word of thanks."

Then on December 10, 1520, a crowd gathered at the town gate of Wittenberg, where a pyre had been prepared for a public burning. Students and professors from the university bore placards and shouted antipapal slogans. To the cheering of the assemblage, the Evangelist appeared, dressed in his simple friar's cowl. The fire was lit. In a loud voice, Luther took the papal bull and proclaimed, "As thou hast saddened the holiness of the Lord, so may eternal fire sadden thee." And he cast the bull in the flames. Books of canon law and the works of Johann Eck followed. The spectacle mocked the auto-da-fé, the burning at the stake, that so many in Rome hoped for Luther himself. The next day, Luther took his challenge one step further.

"This burning does not say much," he lectured the students. "It would be better if the pope himself could be burned. If you do not renounce popery from your very hearts, you cannot save your souls."

Of this extravagant spectacle, Luther's colleague and biographer, Philip Melanchthon, calling him a "man of tender Christian temperament," wrote, "That Luther's words were true, no one can doubt, except those that are more stupid than a block of wood, as indeed the papists are to a man."

6.

THE SULTAN
OF LOVE AND WAR

I n the fall of 1520 word of the death of Selim the Grim and the accession of his son Suleyman to the Ottoman throne spread rapidly through Europe, and relief spread with it. It was widely understood that the fierce, war-loving Selim would soon have attacked the strategic Hospitaller bastion on the island of Rhodes in the Mediterranean. He was said to have designs on the Barbary Coast of North Africa. He might even have attempted to restore the glory of Islamic Spain. Now with the war-lover's death, those fears eased. His son seemed mild-mannered by comparison. "It appears to all men," wrote the contemporary chronicler Paolo Giovio, "that a gentle lamb has succeeded a fierce lion. Suleyman is but young and has no experience, and he is altogether given to rest and quiet." When Pope Leo X, the spurned crusader, received the news, he ordered that a litany of thanksgiving be sung throughout Rome, and men should go barefoot.

In the initial period of his sultanate, by no means was all of Suleyman's attention devoted to the affairs of state. He now had the privilege of exploring all the mysteries of the imperial palace: the expansive ostrich-filled gardens, the extensive stables, the lavish rooms and inner sanctums. These delights he shared with his great friend Ibrahim, whom the young sultan now promoted over others to head falconer, then assigned him to the privy chamber or throne room in the third courtyard of the Topkapi, as the master of the household. This throne room housed the mantle and the banner of the Prophet Mehmet, which had been brought to Constantinople from Cairo by Suleyman's father, as well as the swords of the first four caliphs.

Suleyman and Ibrahim seemed inseparable. They were often seen boating together around Seraglio Point. When they were not together, mutes passed frequent notes between them. Suleyman strolled the expansive grounds in the customary dress of the sultan: a heavy caftan in whose pockets were gold ducats and silver aspers* to be dispensed as favors during the day. In his quarters, he was attended by an army of pages, who served his meals on porcelain and silver dishes—Ibrahim was always present—while his Jewish doctor advised him on what to eat. Before he grew more ascetic in his later years, he enjoyed wine in moderation, even though the Koran forbade it. In cold weather he slept under a cover of sable fox and in hot weather between sheets of crimson velvet. His chamberlain stood guard by his bed as he slept, and Ibrahim slept not far away.

Of course, the harem was now his. The entrance to this inviting place was through the Carriage Gate beneath the Divan Tower, past the fearsome halberdiers-with-tresses and through the Courtyard of the Black Eunuchs. Some forty black eunuchs, hailing from darkest Africa, were known as "the generals of the maidens." They managed the harem, which consisted of a warren of some three hundred rooms, small and large. But the real power of the harem remained with Suleyman's mother, Hafsa, the daughter of Crimean Tartars and known as the Sultan Valide. She was accorded a lavish apartment and garden of her own. Now through her, her son was introduced to the pleasures of the place. About two hundred women resided there, organized into groups of ten and carefully schooled in music and dance, embroidery and courtly manners, as well as the principles of Islam. Many were the daughters of Christians.

From a Genovese slave in the sultan's court, we have a description of Suleyman's forays to this sacred place. He passed down a passageway known as the Golden Road, so named because when the sultan came on horseback,

---

* While a golden ducat was worth more than two dollars, a silver asper was worth less than a penny.

he would often throw golden coins to the maids of the harem who lined his way. "When the Sultan will go to the Seraglio of the ladies, either in disguise, or if he prefers on horseback, the chief of the eunuchs musters the inmates in the courtyard, all finely attired. When the Sultan arrives and the door is shut, he and the head eunuch pass along the line saluting them courteously. If there is one that pleases him, he places on her shoulder a handkerchief and walks on with the eunuch to the garden to look at the ostriches and the peacocks. Afterwards he returns to the ladies' apartments to sup and to sleep. Once in bed, he asks who has his handkerchief, and he desires that she should bring it to him. The eunuch calls the girl, she comes gladly, and the eunuch leaves the room. The next morning, the Sultan orders her a robe of gold and increases her family allowance by nine aspers and gives her two more waiting women to serve her."

Suleyman's father, Selim the Grim, mixed love and war with ease, then waxed poetic about it. In one poem he wrote:

While lions were trembling in my crushing paw
Fate made me fall prey to a doe-eyed darling.

Like his father, Suleyman was not overindulgent in these ready pleasures, though he certainly had his sensuous side. By the time of his accession, he had sired four children. His first love among the harem maidens was a Circassian beauty whose nickname was Rose of the Spring. (Most of the harem were Circassian, since the region of the Caucasus Mountains was famous for its exquisite women.) By her, beginning in 1515, he would have four star-crossed children, all of whom died at an early age. More important, in that same year another beauty, named Gülbahar, gave him a son named Mustafa. This was a serious event, for this son was the sultan's first and heir to the throne, and this, in turn, raised the status of his mother to queen mother. Rivalry in the harem was in the offing.

Shortly after his accession, Suleyman found the love of his life, Roxellana. The daughter of an impoverished Christian priest from Ukraine, she was probably brought into the Ottoman harem as a slave by Ibrahim Pasha.

Decades later, a Venetian diplomat related how Roxellana supplanted Gül-bahar in the young sultan's affections. Because Gülbahar had borne the sultan a son, she stood in an exalted position in the court and was naturally proud and protective of her special status. When she heard that Roxellana had "pleased" the sultan, she flew into a rage, insulting Roxellana, tearing her clothing, scratching her face, and pulling out some of her hair. "Traitor, sold meat," she was said to have screamed, "you think you can compete with me?" Several days later, Suleyman summoned Roxellana for his pleasure. But she told the black eunuch who came for her that she was not worthy to enter the sultan's presence, for she was "sold meat" and had a disfigured, scratched face. "These words were related to the sultan and induced in him an even greater desire to have her come to him," the Venetian wrote. Suley-man confronted Gülbahar with this tale of jealousy, and the Circassian con-fessed that it was true, saying that she had done less to Roxellana than she deserved. In anger, Suleyman sent Gülbahar away and transferred his affec-tion, quite permanently, to Roxellana.

Like his father and other sultans before them, the young sultan would write poetry. That tradition began with Mehmet the Conqueror, and a central theme was always the link between love and power. Mehmet II had written:

> We are in bondage to the sovereignty of love
> We beg for love's command.
> That's why we are the whole world's king.

Now the young sultan wrote saccharine lines about love both sacred and profane, most of which were directed to Roxellana. "I am the Sultan of Love," he began one poem. When he was not expressing his love for her, he could write about the temptations of power.

> Listen, my heart, don't crave silver and gold like a highwayman;
> Don't spruce yourself with satin and trinkets like a woman.
> Don't stand there stiff, chest puffed up like a wrestler's lion.

Never cherish wealth or high office. Don't brag: "I'm better than everyone."
Others have their own rights: don't stick out your tongue at them like an iris.

You might conquer far-flung lands and seas and rule them as their sovereign king:
Even if your reign on the imperial throne becomes everlasting,
Don't be taken in: one day, a hostile wind is bound to blow and bring
To your land of beauty heaven's misfortune and worst suffering.
Don't blow up your chest like a proud sail; shun arrogance and malice.

If you aspire to God's compassion, kindness should come from you too;
Be sure to offer your benevolence and mercy to people of virtue.
If you hope to reach the gardens of Paradise to find love and grace
Instead of terrifying destruction when the end comes to you,
Humble yourself like a skirt, bow at the sage's feet and rub your face.

The young sultan appreciated how important the symbolic first acts of a new reign were, and he set out immediately to enunciate his fundamental principles of justice, generosity, and great undertakings. The loyalty of the janissaries was his top priority. Though they were technically the sultan's slaves, they possessed the power to rebel against the sultan. Immediately, Suleyman announced a pay raise to every soldier and reassured his military elite that he understood his primary role as Commander of the Faithful. They could expect grand campaigns in the future, for he had not forgotten that the Ottoman Empire had risen from humble roots as a motley collection of nomadic Central Asian tribes to a great empire, chiefly through struggle against Christian infidels.

Second, Egypt commanded his attention, for it represented a conflict between Turk and Arab. His father had conquered the Mamluk kingdom of Egypt and brought the trappings of the caliphate from Cairo to Constantinople. The conquest in 1517 had been harsh, for Cairo had stoutly resisted with hidden trenches and forced the invaders to subdue the city district by district and house by house. Unlike in Aleppo and Damascus in Syria, which had surrendered without a fight to Selim, Cairo's resistance invited the invaders, with the sanction of Islamic law, to plunder the city ruthlessly. They stripped the jewels and gold and ornate carpets from the Mosque of Nafisa. Many of Cairo's treasures and monuments were shipped to the Bosporus. Five hundred of the richest Cairo families were forced to relocate to Constantinople.

Egypt remained restive and resentful. To deal with that, Suleyman wielded both the carrot and the stick. He released six hundred Egyptian prisoners from the war of conquest, but ordered the execution of a rebellious agha of Egypt and his five coconspirators. Then Suleyman wrote a veiled warning to his governor in Egypt:

"My noble orders act as fate and impose themselves as destiny. My order is that you rule rich and poor, townspeople and peasants, slaves and citizens, wisely. If some try to escape your rule, then you are to execute them, for retaliation against my rulers will not be tolerated. It is in this way that you shall bring order. By this just and effective governance, you will receive our mercy. Our grace will surround you. As long as you are grateful, I will grant you even more. And remember, gratitude is the mother of mercy. With grateful diligence, you shall execute the grand orders of the Sublime Porte whose purpose is to protect the big and the small of your territory with justice."

To this the bey of Egypt replied submissively, "The great news of your accession to the throne has been announced in all parts of my land, from Cairo to Tunisia. Through prayer and coin, Your Majesty is acknowledged and respected. All Arabian sheiks have sent their congratulations."

A vestige of Egypt's harsh conquest now became an irritant to the new sultan. During the conquest, an Egyptian emir named Ghazali had betrayed his Mamluk masters, and in gratitude Selim had rewarded him with the governorship of Syria under the Ottomans. With the news of Selim's death, however, Ghazali seized the opportunity to rebel against the supposedly shy and docile Suleyman, seeking to reestablish the Mamluk Empire in Syria. He captured the citadel of Damascus, occupied Beirut and Tripoli, sought to mobilize the Arabs, Bedouin, and Druze behind him, enlisted the aid of the Hospitallers in Rhodes, and had himself proclaimed the sultan of Syria.

Hoping for wider support, he sent word of his rebellion as well to the bey in Cairo. The bey, wavering between his duties to the Ottomans and his Mamluk sympathies, decided to play both sides. To Ghazali he promised his support if the rebel could conquer all of Syria, including Aleppo. And at the same time, he seized Ghazali's messenger and sent the rebel's letter to Suleyman in Constantinople.

Meanwhile, in northern Syria, the citadel in Aleppo resisted the insurrection for six weeks, long enough for Suleyman's vizier to arrive with a force of forty thousand janissaries and light cavalry, drawn from the eastern Turkish districts of Cilicia and Caramania. This forced Ghazali back to Damascus, where in desperation he massacred a contingent of janissaries in his midst. Outnumbered now nearly eight to one, Ghazali moved his force west of Damascus into the desert, where on January 27, 1521, it was crushed by the Ottoman forces. In the confusion afterward, Ghazali attempted to escape disguised as a dervish. But he was discovered and beheaded. His head was sent to Constantinople, where it was paraded as a relic of Suleyman's first military victory.

Suleyman's exuberance at his first triumph seemed a bit excessive. Of all the Christian powers of Europe, only Venice accorded the Islamic empire the dignity of a vigorous diplomatic presence in Constantinople. Now, as a gesture of deep friendship and gratitude at this show of respect, the young sultan proposed to send Ghazali's head to the eighty-five-year-old doge of Venice, Leonardo Loredan, as a gift. Fortunately, the most vigorous protestations by the Venetian ambassador turned this ghoulish idea aside.

At about the same time, another elemental crisis diverted Suleyman from the pleasures of his court. An Ottoman envoy who had been sent by Suleyman to Hungary to demand annual tribute as the price of peace staggered back to Constantinople and into the Topkapi with his nose and ears cut off. According to the story he blurted out, the Hungarians had been insulted at the demand of tribute from the infidel empire. At this barbarous and stupid provocation, Suleyman flew into a rage. When he calmed down, he surveyed the possibilities for his first grand undertaking. With the suppression of Ghazali's revolt and the apparent submission of his viceroy and the Arab sheiks of Egypt, the eastern portions of the Empire in Asia Minor seemed quiet enough. So, prompted by the Hungarian atrocity, he turned his attention north to the Balkans. He meant to teach the insolent Magyars a lesson.

But the road to Buda—and beyond to Vienna and the heart of Europe—was blocked by the formidable bottleneck of Belgrade. This great defensive city was located at the confluence of the Sava and Danube rivers, twelve miles from the current northern border of the Ottoman Empire. It was the southernmost boundary of the Hungarian state. Its tremendous fortress, Kalemegdan, commanded a high ridge overlooking the junction of the rivers and an island known as the Great War Island. This bastion had withstood three sieges by prior Ottoman sultans, including that of Suleyman's great ancestor the Conqueror, Mehmet II, in 1456 after thirty-nine days of assaulting the walls. For seventy years the stronghold had saved Hungary from Ottoman invasion.

Suleyman proposed to rectify that historical rebuff.

ACT TWO

Horsetails and Worms

✠

7.

A DIET OF WORMS

D uring his splendid coronation in Aachen, Charles V, the new emperor, had signed an important and portentous document, to which little attention was paid at first. It was the constitution of the Holy Roman Empire, and in it the young emperor promised never to send any accused person outside the borders of Germany proper for trial nor to punish a suspect without a fair hearing. Within days of his installation, Charles V would find himself embroiled in the Martin Luther affair, and the imperial constitution would become central to the coming debate.

Early in the new year of 1521 a diet of German princes had been announced, and already it was shaping up as a clash of titanic forces. The papal nuncio to Germany, Hieronymus Aleander, informed the Vatican that public sentiment in Germany overwhelmingly favored Luther. "Nine tenths of the German people cry 'Luther!'" he wrote. "The other tenth shout, 'Death to the Pope!'" Within two weeks of the coronation, the nuncio presented Charles V with a papal breve, a formal papal letter, in which Leo X berated himself for his leniency with Luther. The culprit's pride could not be "cured" with charity. The time had come for severity. The Vatican hoped that an imperial ban, issued by the emperor himself and not subject to the vote of the divided house of Germany, would follow Luther's excommunication by the Church. The emperor was reminded that not only was Luther excommunicated, but any location where the suspected heretic resided was placed under an interdict. That meant that in the cursed venue, Catholic sacraments, including proper Catholic burials, could not be performed. For the devout, the absence of a proper burial was a serious matter, for without burial the soul was denied access to heaven and consigned to everlasting limbo if not damnation.

The central player in the coming drama was Frederick the Wise, the elector of Saxony. Now fifty-eight years old, he was immobilized in Cologne with gout, but he was vigorous nonetheless in protecting his good relations with the young emperor he had helped to elect, just as he espoused his beloved cause of Catholic reform and nurtured his love for his German homeland. In late November Charles ventured to Cologne to discuss the Luther crisis with "Uncle Frederick." Before the meeting, Uncle Frederick consulted with the great humanist Erasmus of Rotterdam, who represented the middle ground between the warring parties.

"Luther has committed two crimes," Erasmus told Frederick. "He has attacked the crown of the pope and the bellies of the monks." At this, the jolly Frederick, himself a Falstaffian character of great girth, howled with laughter. To Charles, Frederick insisted that the German constitution be followed to the letter. He would not permit Luther to be sent to Rome for trial. If any trial was to be held, he insisted that Luther receive a fair hearing. Having no choice, Charles acquiesced in these demands, and on November 28 he issued a formal request:

"Beloved Uncle Frederick. We are desirous that you should bring Luther to the Diet at Worms, that there, he may be thoroughly investigated by competent persons, that no injustice be done nor anything contrary to the law."

Only a few days later, Luther held his ceremonial burning of the excommunication order in Wittenberg. When Uncle Frederick heard about it, he chose to ignore the provocation. On January 3, 1521, the new year opened with a renewal of the excommunication, with its provision of an interdict on the places "where he shall be."

Now the interdict itself presented a problem. If Luther came to Worms, the town would fall under interdict, and that was unacceptable. Moreover, the question hung in the air of whether a secular body of German princes and a mere emperor could examine a priest on matters of faith. The nuncio, Aleander, said emphatically, no, never. Only the pope was competent to judge Luther. "As for myself I would gladly confront this Satan, but the authority of the Holy See should not be prejudiced by subjecting it to the judgment of the laity. One who has been condemned by the pope, the cardinals, and prelates should be heard only in prison." Yet the nuncio was caught on the horns of his own dilemma. He wanted a secular punishment, yet he could not accept a secular inquisition to get it. Regretfully, Charles rescinded his invitation to Luther to appear. On January 28, the Diet of Worms formally opened with a high mass and an elaborate ceremony, in which Charles V contributed a few words of halting German. But with no appearance of Luther now scheduled, the princes were left to wonder what the diet would do.

At the safe remove of 250 miles in Wittenberg, Luther became more and more grandiose in his adoptive role as a martyr: "If Caesar calls me, God calls. If violence is used, I commend my cause to God. I must take care that the gospel is not brought into contempt by our fear to confess and seal our teaching with our blood." He compared his passion and suffering to Christ's passion and suffering. To a friend he wrote, "I burned the pope's book at first with fear and trembling, but now I am lighter in heart than I have ever been in my life. They are so much more pestilent than I supposed." But Luther was not the only one whose life might be at risk. In the overheated atmosphere of Worms, Aleander painted a bleak picture for the Vatican. Angry mobs controlled the narrow streets. Antipapal, pro-Luther pamphlets flooded the town: caricatures, parodies, cartoons, and diatribes. One cartoon pictured Luther holding up the Bible with the inscription "Champion of Christian Liberty." Another had the reformer holding a chalice with the words "The Ark of the True Faith." A parody of the Apostles' Creed was widely distributed:

"I believe in the Pope, binder and looser in heaven, earth and hell, and in Simony,* his only son our lord, who was conceived by the canon law and

---

* Simony is the buying and selling of a church office.

born of the Roman Church. Under his power, truth suffered, was crucified, died and was buried, and through the ban descended to hell, rose again through the gospel and was brought to Charles, sitting at his right hand, who in future is to rule over spiritual and worldly things."

In this volatile environment, Aleander feared for his life. "I cannot go out on the streets but the Germans put their hands to their swords and gnash their teeth at me. I hope the pope will give me a plenary indulgence and look after my brothers and sisters if anything happens to me."

With the two sides adamant in their opposition, it appeared that the much ballyhooed Diet of Worms would result in nothing more than a shouting match and a street fair. For his part, Frederick the Wise paid deference to the young emperor while he permitted his jester to make fun of cardinals before a cackling audience. Privately, the elector continued to express his admiration for Luther: "Our faith has long lacked the light that Martin has brought to it," he said.

Charles V was keenly aware that the first major event of his reign was fast becoming a fiasco. Conservative by nature, pious by instinct and upbringing, orthodox in his beliefs, cautious in these first months of rule, he was a worthy scion of the Spanish piety so identified with his grandmother Queen Isabella of Spain. In a fit of rage, he had torn up his copy of Luther's diatribe on "Christian Nobility," even though that very document had flattered Charles by proclaiming, "God has given us a young and noble ruler to reign over us and has thereby awakened our hearts once more to hope." Charles would gladly have consigned Luther's books and their author to the flames, were it not for the concern that he would alienate the very German princes who had supported his election and who were so important to his empire. He knew he must honor Frederick's demand that Luther receive a fair hearing. Luther's peril lay after his hearing.

In March, as matters approached stalemate, Charles took things into his own hands. When Luther heard of it, he was pleased, telling Frederick, "I am heartily glad that His Majesty will take to himself this affair that is not mine but that of all Christianity and the whole German nation." Despite the objections of the papal nuncio, who complained that Luther's appearance at Worms would merely give the devil a platform for his "godless doctrines," the emperor issued a new invitation, couched in terms that made the papal nuncio cringe. "Our noble, dear, and esteemed Martin Luther," the proclamation read. "Both we and the Diet have decided to ask you to come under safe conduct to answer with regard to your books and teaching. You have 21 days in which to arrive." The critical element was the safe conduct, but was it really safe? Others, including the "heretic" Jan Hus a century earlier, had been promised protection from injury and violence on a similar journey, only to be conducted swiftly into the flames. Luther's reaction was characteristically grandiloquent.

"If I am being invited simply to recant I will not come," he wrote to a friend. "If recanting is all that is wanted, I can do that perfectly well right here. But if he is inviting me to my death, then I will come. I hope none but the papists will stain their hands in my blood. Anti-Christ reigns. The Lord's will be done."

To another supporter, Luther wrote, "This will be my recantation at Worms: 'Previously I said the pope is Vicar of Christ. I recant. Now I say the pope is the adversary of Christ and the apostle of the Devil.'" Despite this posturing, he was eager to appear. If his suffering and his passion were akin to Christ's, there was one major distinction. Unlike Christ's silence before Pilate, Luther intended to be bold and loquacious.

For over two months as the delegates waited for a resolution of the Luther affair, the proceedings of the diet droned on with dilatory discussion concerning the governance of the empire. What were the powers of the imperial chamber? How would the land be governed in the emperor's absence? How would it be policed and by whom? Who would pay the astronomical cost of the young emperor's trip to Rome to be blessed by the pope? These bureaucratic questions were, from the Catholic point of view, quite beside the point. The diet had specifically been called to investigate "new and dangerous opinions that threatened to disturb the peace of Germany and to overturn the religion of their ancestors." In the hotbed of

Lutheranism that Worms had become, not all saw it that way. In any event, the religious issue could not be investigated until the Reformer himself stood in the dock.

However, one major new development did occur. Charles V, pondering the vast expanse of his Hapsburg dominion and the difficulties of its governance, had come to see that one man alone could not manage it. It needed to be divided. So he would cede the Austrian inheritance to his younger brother, Ferdinand, now eighteen years of age. This included not only Austria but the important German province of Württemberg. While Ferdinand showed promise as a leader, the farthest eastern extension of the Hapsburg dynasty, Hungary, the bulwark against the Turks, was in dire straits. His hapless brother-in-law Louis II, a Pole who was married to Charles's frivolous seventeen-year-old sister, Maria, ruled it.

Ferdinand arrived in Worms on April 2, and with him came the formidable royal ambassador from Hungary, Hieronymus Balbus. Balbus was a controversial, powerful, and eloquent figure. Now over seventy years of age, he had held professorships in Vienna, Paris, and Prague and had been discharged from them all for his arrogant manner, coarse poetry, and scandalous writings. But his skill in declamation was widely admired. In his middle age, he had been tutor to the royal princes at the Hungarian court. He also possessed a great crusading passion about the Turks and an appreciation of the vulnerability not only of Hungary but of Europe itself. He also came armed with intelligence from Constantinople that preparations were well under way for an Ottoman invasion of the Balkan Peninsula.

The day after their arrival, the two together raised the alarm about the advance of the Turks on the Balkan Peninsula. Before the skeptical German princes, they pleaded for the mobilization of ten thousand soldiers for the defense of Hungary and Europe and Christianity itself. Balbus rattled the windows of the Reichstag Hall with his rhetoric.

"Who prevented the unbridled madness of the Turks?" he thundered. "The Hungarians. Who checked their fury that overwhelmed our peninsula like the swiftest torrent? The Hungarians. Who warded off the Turkish darts from the throats of the commonwealth of Christendom? The Hungarians. Who finally preferred to turn against themselves the whole power and onslaught of the barbarians, rather than lay open to them an entrance into the lands of others? The Hungarians. Long, long ere now, a terrible tempest would have burst into the bowels of Germany and Italy were it not that, as if a wall had been set up against it, it was dammed in and kept from spreading by the Hungarians themselves, so that till recently it has only raged within the bounds of Pannonia.* But now the Hungarian kingdom is in such straits, and these people have been so continuously slaughtered, that it is not only unable to subdue its foes, but unless it is aided from without, it cannot any longer restrain or resist them.

"If Germany does not take action soon, one can not hope to reacquire Constantinople, but rather should fear the loss of Rome. While Christian dukes argue, the Turks seize lands around them. For bravery the Turks rely on Christians who would gladly join their fellow believers if they could. It behooves the Germans to come to the aid of Hungary now, while there is still time . . . and so that they will not have to fight this enemy on their own land."

The emperor listened politely, but his attention was elsewhere. Spanish nobles were again in revolt. The diet was quarreling over the powers of the imperial council. If the question was more troops, they would probably be more urgently needed in Italy where his chief rival, Francis I, was again threatening Lombardy. In what sense, the question was asked, was the defense of Europe solely a duty of the German nation? And there was this maddening Luther affair. The delegates began to grumble about Archduke Ferdinand's "Hungarian neurosis."

Along with the emperor's disinterest went the general skepticism of the assemblage. The religious question trumped all others, but beyond that, the sense was that the danger was exaggerated. Weren't the Germans warriors by nature? Could they not easily defeat these Ottomans in battle if it came to that? Moreover, an anti-Turkish propaganda campaign called *Flugschriften*

---

* Pannonia was the ancient designation for the territory of Austria, Croatia, Hungary, Serbia, Slovenia, Bosnia, and Herzegovina.

was under way. Its illustrated handbills contained slanted snapshots of Turkish history and embroidered accounts of supposed atrocities against women and children. While this propaganda was often a call to action against the infidel, it supposed the foe to be so corrupt that ferocious German soldiers would easily prevail in combat. Balbus was politely and ceremoniously dismissed.

The day before Balbus's bravura performance was Palm Sunday in Easter week. Theatrically, Martin Luther chose that day to leave Wittenberg for the long journey to Worms, repeating his analogy to Christ. "We see Christ suffer," he said. "Christ lives, and I shall enter Worms." His town had provided him with a two-wheeled covered wagon; his university with twenty golden ducats for traveling expenses; his order with traveling companions; and his emperor with an imperial herald to enforce the emperor's safe conduct. His route took him through Leipzig to Naumburg, and at each stop he received a hero's welcome. In Naumburg, an exuberant and somewhat dense supporter presented him with the dubious present of a portrait of Savonarola, who had also pointedly challenged a pope twenty-three years earlier and had been burned at the stake for his troubles. Through Weimar, the procession became increasingly triumphal. At Erfurt, a local priest greeted Luther at the town gate with sixty horsemen, and a poet extolled him for cleansing the "filth" of the town. The following day, he preached to a packed church whose balcony nearly collapsed under the weight of the throng, forcing many doting admirers to jump out the windows. He also preached at his next stops in Gotha and Eisenach. With each stop he seemed more and more in the grip of his imminent martyrdom. "I am lawfully called to appear in Worms, and thither will I go in the name of the Lord, though there are as many devils as tiles on the roofs there, and they are all combined against me." Overtly now, he compared his journey to Worms to Christ's journey to Jerusalem. He repeated his refrain:

"But Christ lives, and we shall enter Worms in spite of its gates of hell."

On April 16 he made his grand entrance into Worms.

In 1521 Worms was a walled town, with outer and interior defensive walls, and a broad thoroughfare called the Kämmerstrasse. This boulevard was alive with spectators now despite the earnest efforts of the papal nuncio and imperial authorities to keep them out. The imperial herald on horseback, the imperial eagle prominent on his bodice, escorted the triumphant procession through the town gate, lending an air of a state visit by a world leader rather than a simple monk in a rickety wagon. As Luther made his way to his lodgings with Hospitaller military monks, some two thousand people lined his passageway, holding aloft posters depicting him with a halo around his head and holding a dove, the symbol of the Holy Ghost. Others held up his pamphlets, for a press had been set up in Worms solely for the purpose of churning out his tracts and distributing them widely.

"I am ready to jump into the mouth of the Behemoth," he proclaimed. But he took solace in the knowledge that his principal defenders were less than a day's march away with their troops, if any harm was threatened to him. When he reached the house of the Knights Hospitaller, he greeted the crowd.

"God will be with me!" he said on the steps of his wagon.

Immediately, dukes and princes sought him out. One knight, from whatever prurient curiosity, asked him about his assertion in the most impassioned of his antipapal tracts, "The Babylonian Captivity," that a wife with an impotent husband was free to find one more virile. Luther waved the question aside as irrelevant and impertinent. Justification by faith alone and the villainy of the pope were the only issues here.

The following morning, briefly the simple village monk once again, he heard the confession of a sickly, aging elector. Then Luther fell to the ground in prayer and supplication and raw terror. He seemed momentarily to doubt his mission and to wonder whether his God had deserted him.

"O almighty and everlasting God, how terrible is this world! Behold, it opens its mouth to swallow me up. I have so little trust in Thee. My last hour is come. My condemnation has been pronounced. O God, O God, help me against all the wisdom of the world. For this is not my work, but Thine. I should desire to see my days flow on peaceful and happy. But the cause is Thine. Thou has chosen me for this work. Act then, O God . . . stand at my side." Then after a pause he continued, "Come, come. I am ready . . . I am ready to lay down my life for thy truth."

Later that day he was met at the appointed time and, to avoid the crowds, led through back alleys, to the auditorium next to the Worms Cathedral. The scene was extraordinary. The anticipation was electric. The young emperor sat on a raised dais, the symbol of his power, the imperial eagle, above his head. He was dressed in a velvet cloak and a soft hat, and he leaned forward, his distinctive Hapsburg jaw jutted out, as Luther entered the hall of one thousand five hundred expectant delegates. To a retainer, the emperor whispered, "This fellow will never make a heretic out of me."

Luther's supporters crowded around him as he came forward. The papal nuncio, Aleander, had been adamant in trying to limit the proceeding to two simple questions. A simple yes or no was all that was required to each question. Above all, this was not a disputation. The Diet of Worms was not to have the appearance of an ecclesiastical council. The "satanic dragon" was not to be given a platform to spew out his filth. The end was clear. The excommunication had condemned Luther the man; an imperial ban must condemn Luther the author. With a ban of the Empire following the excommunication of the Church, the Civitas Dei, the community of God, was affirmed. Sacred and profane authority would be joined in their condemnation. Justice could then be done.

Luther's works were piled on a side table. An inventory of the scurrilous oeuvre was presented to the emperor. "Let them read the titles!" someone shouted out in anger, and it was done, one by one. Calm was asked, and the inquisitor stepped forward to take charge.

"Martin Luther," he began. "His Majesty has ordered you to be called hither to retract the books that you have edited and spread abroad. I refer to all the books written in either German or Latin, and the contents of the same."

Then he asked his first question. Did Luther write these books? Suddenly, the witness seemed hesitant, uncharacteristically unsure of himself.

"The books are mine," he said softly. "And I have written more." He seemed overwhelmed by the princes who pressed close around him. He began to sweat profusely. Then the second question: Did he wish to revoke and retract their contents?

Finally, after a long pause, he spoke. The electors leaned forward to hear his barely audible, halting words. "This touches God and his Word. This affects the salvation of souls. Christ said, 'He who denies me before men, him will I deny before my father.'" Grumbles greeted this in the hall. "To say too little or too much would be dangerous. I beg you give me more time."

Astonishment greeted this plea. Was he not famous for his eloquence? Had he not had three weeks to consider his answers? He declined to answer just then. Was he wavering? Whisperings of disbelief filled the hall. Confusion reigned. The emperor had not understood his German. He was asked to repeat his answer in Latin. Most astonished, disappointed, and even angry were Luther's own supporters, who had invested so much in this man. The assembly was stunned as he was led out. He was granted twenty hours to consider his answer.

The following day, April 18, a larger hall was chosen for the encounter. Even so, it was so crowded with more people that only the emperor could sit. When Luther entered the hall this time, his demeanor was utterly transformed. Again, the electors pressed in around him. Again the emperor leaned forward, straining to understand a few phrases of the Reformer's guttural speech. Again, the inquisitor asked his question.

"Are you prepared to defend all that your writings contain, or do you wish to retract any part of them?" he bellowed.

"I ask pardon," Luther began, "if by reason of my ignorance, I am wanting in the manners that befit this court. I have not been brought up in king's palaces, but in the seclusion of a cloister." In this company of nobles, this preamble seemed to level the field. Their power came from inheritance and wealth; their manners from breeding. His power flowed solely from his conscience. Should he retract his writings? He joined the issue immediately and parsed the matter into three parts. Yes, he had written from the stance of a devout Christian and theologian. Even his adversaries, nay, even the pope himself, had acknowledged that his discussion of faith and good works had been constructive.

"What then should I be doing if I were now to retract these writings? Wretched man! I alone, among all men living, should be abandoning truths approved by the unanimous voice of friends and enemies, and opposing doctrines that the whole world glories in confessing!"

Secondly, yes, he had written against the Roman pope. He had attacked false doctrines, irregular and scandalous behavior that "afflicts the Christian world and ruins the souls of men. Is it not manifest that the laws and human doctrines of popes entangle, vex, and distress the consciences of the faithful . . . ?"

"No," shouted out the emperor in distress.

Luther was unperturbed. "If I were to revoke what I have written on that subject, I should strengthen this tyranny and open a wider door to many, flagrant impieties." Then turning to Charles V himself, he continued, "Not merely would the yoke which now weighs down Christians be made more grinding by my retraction, it would receive confirmation from your most serene majesty. Great God! I should thus be like an infamous cloak, used to hide and cover over every kind of malice and tyranny."

Turning then to the assemblage of princes, Luther said, "Let us have a care lest the reign of the young and noble prince, the Emperor Charles, on whom, next to God, we build so many hopes, should not only commence, but continue and terminate its course under the most fatal auspices." He invoked the pharoahs and the kings of Babylon who had been laid low by false measures. "'God moveth mountains,'" he said, citing Job 9:5, "'and they know not.'"

And third, yes, he had written against the supporters of the popish tyranny. Perhaps he had gone overboard in his invectives against them, but they had set out to destroy faith. "I can not sanction the impieties of my opponents, for they would crush God's people with still more cruelty."

For the papal representatives and the Catholic princes, this was nearly too much to bear. But they could say nothing; they had promised a fair hearing. How far would he go? How long would he go on? The nuncio's worst fear was being realized. The villain had his pulpit. And now he went further. He moved to associate himself with Christ himself, the ultimate arrogance and sacrilege.

"I am not a saint," he said. "As a mere man and not a god, I will defend myself after the example of Jesus Christ, who said, "'If I have spoken evil, bear witness against me'" (John 18:23).

He challenged the emperor, the high prelates, the illustrious lords, to prove to him from Scripture where he was in error. If they could do so, he would be the first to commit his writings to the flames.

"And so," he said, turning back again to the emperor, "I commend myself to your august majesty, and your most serene highnesses. I beseech you in all humility not to permit the hatred of my enemies to rain upon me an indignation I have not deserved."

The inquisitor could stand it no longer. "You have not given any answer to the inquiry put to you!" he bellowed. "You are not to question the decision of the councils. You do nothing but renew the errors of Wycliffe and Hus. How will the Turks exult to hear Christians discussing whether they have been wrong all these years? You are required to return a clear and distinct answer. Will you or will you not retract?"

"Since your most serene majesty and your high mightinesses require of me a simple, clear, and direct answer, I will give one," the monk responded calmly. "I can not submit my faith either to the pope or to the council, because it is clear as noonday that they have fallen into error and even into glaring inconsistency with themselves. If then I am not convinced by proof from Holy Scripture, or by cogent reasons . . . if I am not satisfied by the very text I have cited . . . and if my judgment is not in this way brought into subjection to God's word, I neither can nor will retract anything. For it can not be right for a Christian to speak against his country. Here I stand and can say no more. God help me. Amen."

Pandemonium broke out. The emperor was confused. He had understood little of what Luther had said in German. He called for quiet, and when it was given, he asked the witness to repeat his assertion in Latin. "If you can't do it, Doctor, you have done enough," a friendly voice shouted from the fringe. Luther was again sweating profusely, but he proceeded to repeat his discourse in Latin. As the convocation droned on, darkness fell over Worms. At last, Luther turned to leave. As he did, Spaniards fell in behind him, hissing and shouting out, "Into the fire, into the fire with him!" Luther turned on them gloatingly and raised his hands high in the air, in the manner of a victorious Teutonic swordsman. His followers did likewise and out they strode. But this show of bravado did not comport with Luther's true feelings of terror. To a supporter, he whispered sullenly,

"I am through. It's over."

That night, the adversaries huddled in various refuges in Worms. The prelates were furious. The ghost of Jan Hus had ascended from hell. Voices demanded that justice be done as it was in the Council of Constance in 1415 when the "safe conduct" given to Jan Hus was consigned to the flames along with Hus himself. When this notion was presented to Charles V that night, it was remembered that the king of Bohemia of Hus's time, Sigismund, had come to live in history's disgrace for betraying his promise of indemnity. The six electors met as well. The papal nuncio was told that they were in accord. Even Frederick the Wise wavered in his support. Of Luther's performance he said, "He was too daring for me." And Luther? Even though he was in the congenial company of the tough, protective Hospitallers, he trembled with terror over his fate. He could already feel the warmth of the flames. He mumbled Christ's words in John 16:17: "A little while and ye shall not see me, and again a little while and ye shall see me."

The next day, Charles V gathered the electors to ask for their opinion. Now they wavered. On the doors of churches around Worms during the night, posters with the symbol of peasant revolt had been tacked up as a warning. The electors needed time to deliberate. "Then I will give you my opinion," the emperor said calmly, and he pulled a speech from beneath his cloak. He read it in the French of his upbringing:

"You know that I am born of the most Christian Emperors of the noble German Nation, of the Catholic Kings of Spain, the Archdukes of Austria, the Dukes of Burgundy, who were all to the death true sons of the Roman

Church, defenders of the Catholic Faith, of the sacred customs, decrees, and uses of its worship, who have bequeathed all this to me as my heritage. According to their example I have hitherto lived. Thus I am determined to hold fast by all which has happened since the Council of Constance. For it is certain that a single monk must err if he stands against the opinion of all Christendom. Otherwise Christendom itself would have erred for more than a thousand years.

"Therefore I am determined to set my kingdoms and dominions, my friends, my body, my blood, my life, my soul, upon it. For it was great shame to us and to you, you members of the noble German Nation, if in our time, through our negligence, we were to let even the appearance of heresy and denigration of true religion enter the hearts of men. You all heard Luther's speech yesterday, and now I say to you that I regret that I have delayed so long to proceed against him. I will not hear him again. He has his safe conduct. But from now on I regard him as a notorious heretic, and hope that you all, as good Christians, will not be wanting in your duty."

From this speech sprang the Edict of Worms. Aleander, the papal nuncio, drafted it. "He has sullied marriage, disparaged confession, and denied the body and blood of our Lord," it read. "He makes the sacraments depend on the faith of the recipient. He is pagan in his denial of free will. This devil in monk's clothes has brought together all the ancient errors into one stinking puddle and has invented new ones." And then its damnation:

"Luther is to be regarded as a convicted heretic. When the time is up [the time of his safe conduct, due to elapse in nineteen days], no one is to harbor him. His followers also are to be condemned. His books are to be eradicated from the memory of man."

When Charles V signed it, he turned to Aleander and said, "You will be content now."

"Yes," the nuncio replied. "And even greater will be the contentment of His Holiness and of all Christendom."

On the same day that Holy Roman Emperor Charles V spoke with such passion to the electors about Luther, April 19, 1521, the Diet of Worms issued its decision about the Turkish invasion of the Balkan Peninsula. "The holy Catholic power and seat of sacred Roman power cannot presently promise troops or other assistance as aid against the Turks," the statement proclaimed officiously. The bombast of the Hungarian ambassador had fallen on deaf ears. Nothing was to be done at present, the delegates announced with mock regret. "We hope that with the goodwill of the Roman empire, and with the most esteemed king of Hungary undertaking an expedition against the Turks with the Lord's blessing and in keeping with Christian principles that the enemies of the Christian faith will be abolished," perhaps something would be done in the future. If the Hungarian king, Louis, could not defend his land, then the Empire approved of him making a truce with the Turks for a year, "provided always that it should be one not dishonorable nor injurious to himself, to the Catholic faith, or to the commonwealth of Christendom."

The provisos loomed large.

8.

THE SHADOW OF GOD
SPREADS NORTHWARD

Through the winter of 1521, as the princes of Germany dithered over Luther and hunted game in the woods around Worms, preparations for war were under way in Turkey. The logistics for Suleyman's first imperial campaign were staggering. The Ottoman quartermasters requisitioned thirty thousand camels, hundreds of elephants, and ten thousand wagons to transport grain and flour. Forty ships from the Black Sea fleet under the command of the Ottoman grand admiral were outfitted. Ceremonially, the imperial banners made of horsetails were placed in the sultan's court as a harbinger of the coming campaign. This was a tradition, harking back to the time when a heroic sultan lost his banner and replaced it with a horsetail.

In the days before his departure, Suleyman sought the blessing of his ancestors. He laid the first stone for the mosque dedicated to his father on the sixth hill of Constantinople. He prayed at the tomb of his grandfather Bayezid II and that of his great-grandfather the Conqueror of Constantinople, Mehmet II. In consultation with his governors and viziers, the objective of the campaign came into dispute. Suleyman himself leaned toward a plan to circumvent the daunting bastion at Belgrade by marching forty miles west of Belgrade to Sabac, crossing the Sava River there, and slicing directly to Buda. His third vizier, Ahmed Pasha, favored this approach. It was, after all, the king of Hungary who had delivered his insult to the Turks, and it was to the lair of the impertinent infidel king that the Ottoman army should go. But the grand vizier Piri Pasha, the wise elder who had served Suleyman's father, urged caution on the sultan. After the great Turkish victory at the Battle of Kosovo in 1389 and the collapse of the Serbian empire, Belgrade was the southern defense of the Hungarian empire and the bulwark of Christianity for Europe. It was dangerous, Piri Pasha argued, to leave an enemy stronghold untouched in the rear of a major campaign, for that would threaten their supply line. As the army prepared to move out, the objective remained in doubt.

On May 18, 1521, a grand procession marched out of Constantinople. In the lead were the heavy cavalry, the *sipahis*, riding single file on small, finely bred Syrian horses. The riders were clothed in scarlet, violet, and green silk cloaks, their heads wrapped in beehive white cotton turbans, festooned with a flute of purple silk. They were armed with a bow and brightly colored feathers, a scimitar studded with gems at their waists, a shield fastened to their left arms, and in the right, a green, short spear. A steel club dangled from their saddles. Behind them came the janissaries, the elite infantry. Their leader, the agha of the janissaries, was the third most powerful man in the empire, the only person who could approach the sultan and speak with him without first groveling in humility (and the only person, it was said, whom the sultan could not assassinate for malfeasance, unless he had appointed the agha himself). The symbol of the agha's power was a mace of stone crystal, which he held aloft now, sparkling with the rays of the spring sunshine. Behind him came the standard-bearer of the corps, who carried the large and much feared banner of the janissaries. Upon a green background, green being the favorite color of the Prophet, it depicted Mohammed's double-edged sword in flames, surrounded by the phrases of the Koran: "There is no God but God." "Mohammed is His messenger."

The agha's intimidating soldiers followed, marching in disciplined silence. They wore a long skirt of heavy felt and sported their distinctive flat-fronted hat with a square skirt that dangled over the back of the neck. On the front of these hats was a small emblem, studded with precious stones that also held colorful, curved feathers. They carried muskets and long axes known as halberds. After the janissaries came the dignitaries, the beys and viziers, followed by two hundred imperial bodyguards, chosen from the bravest of the Ottoman military.

And after them came the sultan himself, the "shadow of God" on earth. He rode a majestic charger and was dressed in a splendid embroidered robe with oversize sleeves and an undergarment of gold-threaded cloth. Diamonds and long, curved exotic-bird feathers adorned his high turban. Three pages followed the sultan's horse, carrying a flask of water, another cloak, and a chest that contained the mantle of the Prophet. Then came the sultan's eunuchs, and after them the irregulars: the light cavalry, called the *akinjis*, who were raiders and foragers, and the light infantry, called *azaps*, who wore distinctive pith helmets and carried a saber or a lance, and a strange shield with the left side higher to cover the soldier's face when he charged an enemy. The parade was extraordinary, and foreign dignitaries, especially the ambassadors from Venice and Vienna, watched it with awe and trepidation.

A week later, the Ottoman columns reached Adrianople, where the army camped in the traditional way. In the center was the sultan's spacious and sumptuous tent, and radiating from it were the tents of the viziers, then the janissaries and the heavy cavalry. Games and festivities were planned for the soldiers, but in camp, naturally, gambling and alcohol were strictly forbidden. Hygiene was a top priority. Ceremonial greetings for the sultan were arranged as villagers came forward with gifts. The sultan sat grandly on a hexagonal gold throne. The faithful approached the throne with arms crossed over their chest, bowing deeply in loyalty and submission. A lavish banquet took place, with the imperial gatekeepers first inspecting the sultan's food, then a six-piece orchestra with zither, tambourine, and clappers provided the music for dancers.

In early June the army proceeded to Philippopolis and Sophia, where the third vizier arrived with a Rumelian army from Greece that included another three thousand camels, packed with military equipment and gunpowder. In Sophia, the sultan partook of the famous hot baths and again greeted rapturous well-wishers. On June 20 the juggernaut reached Nis.

There, a divan was held to discuss strategy. The council was still divided over the ultimate objective. With no side giving in, Suleyman decided for both. He would split his army, sending the main force of janissaries under Piri Pasha toward Belgrade, while a contingent of heavy and light cavalry struck out on the western swing to Sabac on the Sava River. Suleyman accompanied the western force. If Sabac was easily taken, this contingent would race toward Buda.

Now in Serbia, Suleyman would be attacking a fortress that was ironically not Christian. Mehmet II had built the bastion of Sabac in 1470 as a staging ground for incursions into the Hungarian provinces of Bosnia and Croatia. The Conqueror had given the fortress the name of Bejerdelen, or "that which strikes from the side." So Suleyman would be testing the defenses of his own ancestor. A small but brave force occupied the fort now, under a legendary Hungarian champion named Simon Logodi. If he was to die heroically, he was determined to take as many Turks with him as he could. Before he was overwhelmed on July 7, he did exact a heavy price of seven hundred invaders. When Suleyman arrived the following day, the heads of the Hungarian defenders had been skewered on pikes and lined the gate to the fortress. A victory celebration was held in which the triumphant captains came forward to kiss the sultan's hand. "This is the first castle that I have conquered," Suleyman said effusively. "It must now be reconstructed, so that it serves its purpose." Its purpose was to help secure an Islamic dominion in the Balkans.

The sultan tarried there to supervise the reconstruction of the fort and the building of a bridge over the Sava River. To spur his men to greater effort, Suleyman pitched his imperial tent on the bank of the river for nine days, as the construction went forward. Then heavy rains came, turning the river into a torrent and destroying parts of the bridge; the army could not cross for another eight days. With this loss of time, and with reports from Belgrade about fierce opposition, Suleyman decided to give up his dream of reaching Buda on this first imperial campaign. Vengeance would have to wait. He turned east toward Belgrade, his commanders besieging other pockets of resistance. To send a message of terror, the Turks ordered prisoners to be trampled by elephants. When the sultan arrived on July 31, he found his eastern division arrayed across from the mighty fortress called Kalemegdan. Cryptically, he noted in his diary, "Before Belgrade, arrived to the jubilation of the army."

Kalemegdan was built on a high promontory where the Sava River empties into the Danube. Facing the bastion at the confluence of the rivers was a flat, thumb-shaped island, known as the Great War Island. Military men extending back to Roman times had appreciated the considerable defensive advantages of this strategic redoubt, surrounded by water on two sides and commanding both waterways. So vast were the battlements that for centuries the entire population of Belgrade had lived within the bastion's walls in closely packed domed buildings and amid defensive towers. Surrounded by crenellated walls, the complex was a citadel within a fortress, with its upper part presenting a further impediment, and its lower town defended by a massive tower known as the Daredevil Tower. Underground corridors honeycombed its grounds. Its storied past included attacks by Goths and Huns. Attila himself was said to be buried within its walls. At first glance, Suleyman could appreciate why three Ottoman assaults before this one had failed. He now realized the wisdom of Piri Pasha's position that no such fortress as this could be left behind his lines.

For the next twenty-one days the Hungarian defenders, with their Bulgarian mercenaries, turned back wave after wave of Turkish assaults. Suleyman watched the action in despair from his imperial tent. Turkish gunners kept up relentless cannon fire from the Great War Island. Eventually, this barrage crumbled the northern wall, allowing the Turks with their Serbian bond slaves to enter the lower town. But the defenders retreated into the impressive citadel and still held the Daredevil Tower. Despite numerous three-pronged attacks, they could not be dislodged. In one attack the agha of the janissaries was killed. In another, the grand vizier, Piri Pasha, was relieved of command after a particularly bloody and unsuccessful assault. Ahmed Pasha, Suleyman's third vizier, took over and was given a ceremonial robe and a golden saber to certify his promotion.

After three weeks of unspeakable carnage, the battle began to turn. A woman jumped from the wall and brought the intelligence that the Hungarians were short on ammunition and provisions. On August 25, a messenger arrived to request a ten-day truce. Suleyman saw this as a ploy to gain time to reconstruct the defenses and renewed his attacks, only to be repulsed yet again. Two days later, an assassin, dressed in Turkish garb, got within a few feet of the sultan before he was discovered. He was publicly buried alive in full view of the citadel's walls.

At last on August 29 two messengers arrived under a flag of truce and prostrated themselves in front of the sultan. They brought an offer to capitulate if the surviving Hungarians could depart with their families. This offer was accepted, and the messengers were sent back with honorary robes. As the Hungarians left, janissaries planted their green holy flag of Islam on the citadel's tower. The Belgrade Cathedral was stripped of its Christian relics and icons, including a miracle icon of the Holy Virgin. The casket of Serbia's Saint Petka, an eleventh-century nun, was removed and sent to Constantinople, where the Greek patriarch was forced to buy the body back. Once the building was so "cleansed," Suleyman entered it to celebrate Friday prayers.

"Thank you, All Merciful," he said, "for this victory on the night of holy destiny." The sultan remained for two weeks to supervise the reconstruction of the fortress. Two hundred more cannons were installed. He left Belgrade in the hands of twenty thousand Walachian mercenaries and three thousand janissaries under the command of his cousin Bali Bey. He would not return for another five years.

When the sultan arrived back in Constantinople six weeks later, he received a splendid reception for the success of this first imperial endeavor. But the inner sanctum of the Topkapi was in turmoil. Roxellana had borne a son and named him Mehmet, after Mehmet II, the Conqueror of Constantinople. So now the rivalry of royal infants between Gülbahar's son, Mustafa, and Roxellana's son, Mehmet, would have to be carefully managed by Suleyman's mother as the queen of the harem. Behind this competition hovered the grim Ottoman tradition of fratricide and infanticide in the imperial court, where rivals had routinely been executed to eliminate competition.

At this point, Suleyman was above such concerns. He was content to bask in his Balkan successes. The news of a terrible new conqueror in Constantinople spread rapidly across Europe, and with each telling, the dimensions of his ferocity seemed to grow.

"He slew the man who surrendered Belgrade," wrote one Christian chronicler, "in spite of his oath to the contrary, saying in providing him and others with a grave, he was giving them the land he had promised them."

A few months after his return, a peace treaty with Venice was signed, giving the Ottomans control of Cyprus and some Aegean islands, advancing Turkish commercial interests, and eliminating a potential enemy on the seas.

Satisfying as the agreement with Venice was, the Christian bastion of the Knights of the Hospitallers on Rhodes still threatened Ottoman interests in the eastern Mediterranean. Suleyman had now redressed one ancestral rebuff, the failure of his great-grandfather Mehmet II to capture Belgrade. Soon enough he would turn to the unfulfilled ambition of his father to capture Rhodes.

9.

HENRY'S HARANGUE

The virus of Lutheranism was spreading unchecked across Europe, and the kings and Catholic potentates of the Continent were powerless to contain it. Not that they did not try their best to suppress the contagion. In Paris, the Faculty of Theology at the Sorbonne published a condemnation of 104 Lutheran propositions and, six weeks later, made it a criminal offense to publish or sell any religious book without the faculty's stamp of approval. In the summer of 1521, with the approval of King Francis I, a decree was proclaimed "to the sound of trumpets" that all Lutheran books were to be handed in to the parliament within a week. But this measure did not stem the tide of Luther's works flowing into France and elsewhere. In his public posture, Francis I chose to be more patronizing than angry. He called Luther a *"triste personnage."*

In England, Henry VIII was more passionate than his French wrestling mate, for he was genuinely shocked at the reports from Worms. The English had an ambassador at the diet, who sent regular reports about Luther's impertinence. Conveying one of Luther's tracts to Cardinal Wolsey, the envoy wrote, "Burn it when ye have done with it." As matters moved to their dramatic conclusion in Germany, the same ambassador urged Wolsey to gather all the printers and booksellers of England and command them not to bring any more of Luther's books into the country, nor to allow any further translations, "lest there ensue great trouble to the realm and to the

Church of England, as there is here." Wolsey responded by ordering all existing copies of Luther's works to be delivered to the local bishop. On May 12, in London, Luther's books were ceremoniously burned at the bishop's residence.

But Luther's works had been filtering into England for four years. Wolsey's proclamation could scarcely sweep them all up. Lame anti-Lutheran efforts were made to keep up with the flood of Luther's writings. One such tract was called "A Little Handkerchief for Luther's Spittle." But the reformer had his English boosters. At Oxford University, several popular lecturers spread the new theology, and students embraced it eagerly. "What a pity it is," wrote the archbishop of Kent, "that through the lewdness of one or two cankered members of the faculty who are seducing the young, the whole university should run into infamy of so heinous a crime." Cambridge University was similarly infected. Still the archbishop thought that the less said the better.

By his education and temperament, Henry VIII was deeply interested in theology. He saw this crisis as an opportunity not only to exercise his considerable intelligence and display his theological uprightness, but also to ingratiate himself further with the pope. He was envious of the papal titles that had been conferred on both Charles V and Francis I. Was he any lesser a king or less a defender of the true faith than they?

As the Diet of Worms drew to a close, Henry VIII took it on himself to give the official English response to the contagion. With a little help from Sir Thomas More, he wrote a lengthy diatribe against Luther called *Assertio Septem Sacramentorum* (My Assertion of the Seven Sacraments). If it was not profound theology, Henry's *Assertio* was in the finest tradition of medieval insult. Luther was, wrote the king, "a venomous serpent, a pernicious plague, infernal wolf, an infectious soul, a detestable trumpeter of pride, calumnies, and schism, having an execrable mind, a filthy tongue, a detestable touch, stuffed with venom. This hideous monster having been caught, will become benumbed with his own vermin." Had he left anything out? In a letter to Charles V on May 20, 1521, Henry wrote of Luther as "this weed, this dilapidated, sick, and evil-minded sheep."

In the text itself, the king of England wondered, "Who is he, a single, insignificant friar, to challenge the majestic tribunal of the Saints, the Fathers, and the Popes? . . . How could Luther expect, I say, that anybody should believe that all nations, cities, nay kingdoms, and provinces, should be so prodigal of their rights and liberties as to acknowledge the superiority of a strange priest to whom they owe no allegiance?" The king held out no hope that one so stubborn would recant. "Alas, the most greedy wolf of hell has surprised him, devoured and swallowed him down into the lowest part of his belly where he lies half alive, and half dead. And while the pious pastor calls him and bewails his loss, he belches out of the filthy mouth of the hellish wolf these foul inveighings which the ears of the whole flock do detest, disdain, and abhor."

Perhaps this bizarre screed would have been quickly forgotten, had it not been written by a king, had eventually Luther not replied to it with equal vitriol and contempt, and had it not contained great ironies for this very king's future. In his diatribe, King Henry would make the assertions that, ten years later, when he was trying to solicit Luther's help in his own conflict with Rome, he would deeply regret:

"All the faithful honor and acknowledge the sacred Roman See for her mother and supreme [guide]." Then more pointedly, the king attacked Luther's view of the sacrament of marriage. "Whom God have joined, let no man put asunder," wrote Henry soberly. "Who does not tremble when he considers how to deal with his wife?"

By the summer Henry's *Assertio* was beautifully printed, stunningly illuminated, bound in golden cloth, and shipped to Rome, along with a note to the pope. Here was the "first offerings of his intellect," dabbed with "a little erudition," sent in the hope that "all might see that the King of England is ready to defend the church not only with his arms, but with the resources of his mind." His envoy requested an extravagant event for the book's presentation, and implicitly the conferring of a holy title. But Leo was in no hurry to make a lavish spectacle out of this modest book, for he too was of a mind to downplay the Luther affair. Still the English ambassador pressed his sovereign's case.

"I might hope that what the Godly Prince has writ against Luther's errors might compel Luther himself (if he had the least spark of Christian
piety in him) to recant his heresies and recall again the straying and almost
forlorn sheep. But what can be done when pharaoh's heart is hardened?
Where the wound stinks with putrification? Truly my most serene king is
so far from expecting any good from this idle and vain phantom. He rather
thinks this raging and mad dog is not to be dealt with by words."

Such words were intended to please the Medici pope, and he relented.
In October, the presentation took place. The words of flattery were
characteristically excessive. Someone compared Henry VIII to King Solomon. Leo himself went against his own best advice in praising Henry VIII
for having "the knowledge, will, and ability to compose this book against
this terrible monster." The pope extolled the "eloquence of his style" as well
as the king's wisdom. "We render immortal thanks to our creator who has
raised such a prince to defend His Holy church and this Holy See." Henry
VIII was proclaimed officially to be a "Defender of the Faith."

When the following year Luther's archenemy, Duke George of Saxony,
caused Henry's *Assertio* to be published in German, Luther felt compelled
to answer. It was not so much the king's insults that demanded a response,
as Henry's misrepresentation of Luther's theology and the charge of inconsistency. The king was in for a pasting. "What a fool!" the friar wrote of the
monarch. "One might suppose that a declared enemy of the king had written the book to bring everlasting disgrace upon him."

The charge of inconsistency was especially galling to the writer in Luther. Henry had written, "What avails it to dispute against one, who dis-
agrees with everyone, even with himself? Who affirms in one place what he
denies in another; denying what he presently affirms. Who if you object to
faith, combats by reason; if you touch him with reasons, pretends faith. If
you allege philosophers, he flies to scriptures; if you propound scriptures,
he trifles with sophistry."

These were fighting words. Was it not possible that one's thought
evolved over time? "Here the miserable scribbler has demonstrated with
poisonous words how well he can manage to soil a lot of paper, a truly royal

deed," Luther wrote. "From now on, no Christian can any longer improve himself or do penance, because the King of England would come along and say, 'Look, they confess as sin and error what formerly they maintained to be good and right.' . . . I wonder whether so clever a king keeps wearing his children's shoes, which after all are a contradiction of the shoes a grown man wears. How can he nowadays drink wine, considering there was a time when he was sucking milk?"

In this spirited disputation both sides had scored their points and taken their blows. Out of the contest, Henry VIII had received the title that he so coveted, while Luther had defended his beliefs, just as he had shown that no mortal, surely not a mere king, could intimidate him.

Inevitably the touchstone of the Turkish threat came into the debate, with a dab of irony. Henry VIII was now to Christianity what Suleyman was to Islam, a titled Defender of the Faith. Both were lauded as King Solomons. In his *Assertio*, Henry had asked how Luther could reject Christian doctrines that had existed for centuries. Luther replied that it was not the time of existence but the correctness of doctrine that sustained it. Had not Islam existed for nearly a thousand years? he asked. If the longevity of a faith sanctioned its correctness, how then could you reject that evil faith?

Thus, in 1521, even as the dominion of Islam spread north of Belgrade and threatened the heart of Hungary, the Turkish question in Europe remained the subject of academic quibbling. Suleyman's invasion of the Balkan Peninsula was a debater's straw man. More local rivalries commanded the real passion of kings.

10.

THE BLOOD SPORT
OF KINGS AND POPES

The year 1521 began poorly for the king of France, the vigorous, youthful, energetic, and randy Francis I. Wintering at his mother's royal place at Romorantin in the Loire Valley, he had made the mistake in the Christmas revels of hunting with an ill-shod horse on frozen ground, and he was badly thrown. From this he could recover, the damage less than an accident two years earlier when he was nearly blinded as he galloped by the wayward branch of a tree. Then in a royal game of hide-and-seek, he had hid in a straw hamper that was promptly set on fire by his pursuers. From this too he escaped, twice lucky, though a similar incident some years before had claimed the life of another royal sportsman. The mishap gave credence to his royal symbol of the salamander, a creature that can pass through fire unscathed. But in Epiphany festivities a mock battle with fathers and sons finally got him. This elaborate charade, conducted with eggs, apples, and potatoes as ammunition, was a favorite pastime in the French court, and the combat could involve whole towns and hundreds of competitors. As the king led an exuberant attack on a fortress wall, a young courtier on the opposing side saw the enemy below and dropped a burning log squarely on the head of the king. Francis fell unconscious with a serious head injury and was carried away to a bed, where he languished near death for two days. When he awoke, Francis was a good sport.

"I must take what comes if I want to play the fool," he said wanly.

Two full months would be required for his recovery. And not only his head needed to heal. Rumor spread through Europe that the king of France had syphilis. However his body was bruised and inflamed, his confinement concentrated his mind on larger questions. His reign had begun so gloriously five years before with his victory over the Swiss at Marignano in northern Italy. That had secured the prize of Milan, the wealthiest duchy in northern Italy, and extended French domain to the very frontier of Venice. Forget the Turks in the Balkans. In the narrow vision of the time, the control of northern Italy was regarded as the key to the control of all Europe. After the meeting at the Field of the Cloth of Gold, Henry VIII, Wolsey, and England seemed to support him, as did Pope Leo X, who, despite the election of Charles V as Holy Roman emperor, did not relish the presence of the Spanish in Naples, only a hundred miles from Rome. Francis's throne and his dynastic House of Valois were the wealthiest in Europe, and the most secure, far wealthier and more secure and compact than the diffuse and nearly ungovernable reach of the House of Hapsburg.

But then had come the rebuff at Aachen when instead of Francis, his rival Charles V was crowned Holy Roman emperor. Pope Leo X, however, had authorized Charles only to be called emperor "elect" until he came to Rome to receive the crown of Charlemagne personally from the pontiff. In that official blessing, Francis perceived a threat. If Charles went to Rome for his blessing, he would surely take an army with him, and that would threaten the French hold on Milan. Francis was determined to prevent that trip . . . or at least to delay it for as long as possible.

Between Charles's preoccupation with Luther at Worms, and the intelligence that certain Spanish towns had revolted against his Spanish rule, Francis saw the chance for mischief. He was not quite ready to challenge Charles openly. For now surrogates would have to suffice. From his sickbed in February, he encouraged the dissatisfactions of the Lord of Sedan, whose principality in the Ardennes was located just south of the Belgian border, abutting the ancestral Burgundian patrimony of the Hapsburgs in the Low Countries. After the payment of money, the Lord of Sedan invaded Luxembourg. Two months later, as the Diet of Worms was concluding its business, another Francis surrogate invaded Spanish Navarre. For both these actions Charles accused Francis of duplicity and conspiracy. The French king denied the obvious, and hot words were exchanged. Everyone knew of Francis's involvement. The English ambassador wrote of the Luxembourg caper, "Though it is called the act of the Lord of Sedan, it is done by Frenchmen and at the King's charge." Of the Navarre action, the king's denial was less vigorous. Navarre was French, he proclaimed, and if French allies asked for his help, he would give it. But not for long was it French. Imperial forces promptly threw the Lord of Sedan out of Luxembourg, and Spanish forces threw the French out of Pamplona by late June. These were, however, the opening shots of the coming four-year war between the House of Valois and the House of Hapsburg.

Francis I had every reason to feel slighted and claustrophobic and jealous. France was now surrounded by the imperium of the new Caesar. Flanders lay to the north, Spain to the south, the new Germany to the east. Francis's rival was piling up territories and accolades and titles. His newest was "King of the Indian Isles and the Oceanic Continent." As Charles was being crowned in Aachen in October 1520, Magellan, under a Spanish flag, was passing through his strait in South America into the Pacific Ocean. A few months before, the Spanish conquistador Hernán Cortés had defeated Montezuma in Mexico and was sending back vast quantities of gold to the mother country. Before long, Pizarro would be ravishing the Incas in Peru with Charles's blessing. Within a few months, Magellan's sole surviving ship, *Victoria*, would arrive back in Seville after circumnavigating the globe. Spain and the Empire were now truly global, and France, wealthy and compact and homogeneous as it might be, was hemmed in.

On April 22, only four days after Luther's defense at Worms, Francis I declared war on Charles V.

In Rome, the voluptuous Medici pope, Leo X, was faced with a choice. Ever since the French victory at Marignano six years earlier, the Vatican had thrown its hand in with the French, following the advice of his Florentine adviser, Niccolò Machiavelli, that between the Empire and France, France was the lesser evil. Precariously, the Vatican played the balance-of-power game, with the prize of Milan as its symbol. Of Leo's foreign policy, it was said, he played the game "with two hands at once."

"My cousin Francis and I are in perfect agreement," Charles V had remarked. "He wants Milan and so do I."

But the Roman Curia had been displeased with the threatening French posture in Milan and Genoa, which undermined papal independence and threatened Leo's beloved Florence. The alternative was no less inviting. Frustration was high in Rome over Charles's apparent coddling of Martin Luther. "If Charles is able to effect so little against one man who is in his power, what could the Church expect of him in the fight against the Turks and the infidels?" asked one Vatican insider. If the French in the north menaced Rome, the Spanish in Naples were no less menacing. But then came the Edict of Worms. It was now in the Vatican's interest to support Charles with all the vigor of the Holy See.

On May 29, Leo X concluded an alliance with Charles. In this switch of horses, elaborate, grandiose language accompanied the Machiavellian act. The two great powers, papal and imperial, were united "in purifying Christendom from all error, in establishing universal peace, in fighting the infidel, and in introducing a better state of things throughout." When on June 28 lightning struck an ammunition dump in the Milan castle, killing three hundred French soldiers, the pope declared it to be divine punishment for the French. Francis was having none of it. Promptly, he blocked all ecclesiastical monies from being sent to Rome. "Before long," he blustered, "I will enter Rome and impose laws on the pope."

Through the summer French and imperial troops tore up the fertile landscape of Picardy in northeast France in seesaw combat. By late summer the French reverses in Navarre, Picardy, and Rome had deflated the Gallic bravado. "For about half a year past they would by their words have overrun all the world," wrote the loquacious English ambassador of the French flagging spirits. "Now for all I can see, they would have peace with all their hearts." More important, the hold on Milan itself seemed increasingly precarious, for the Milanese had grown tired of the harsh rule of their French masters.

In the idyllic spirit of the 1518 Treaty of London, Henry VIII grandly stepped forward as peacemaker. Let the French and the imperials lay their differences aside with Christian charity and unite against the common foe of Islam. At Calais, Cardinal Wolsey convened a conference. The French attended, but they had good reason to be wary of Wolsey's motivations. Still the charade went forward as the respective envoys expressed lofty sentiments in public and schemed in private. In late August, Wolsey traveled to Bruges to meet Charles V, ostensibly to persuade him to make peace. Instead, in secret, they concluded an offensive alliance with the plan that, if no agreement was reached by November, England would enter the fray on the imperial side and invade France the following May.

Within a few days of this meeting, the fighting raged in northeast France with renewed vigor. Imperial forces sacked Ardres, the site of the famous Field of the Cloth of Gold, while the French took a handful of strategic castles, including Fuenterrabia on the Spanish frontier, which was called the "key to Spain." After this thrust into Spain, Francis was again ebullient. "I will soon live upon their country as they have done on mine," he said. Cardinal Wolsey was suddenly worried that England might be tilting toward the losing side. The French, however, missed a golden opportunity to capture the highly fortified bastion at Bouchain, widely regarded as "the key to the Netherlands."

"That day God placed the enemy in our hands, and our refusal to accept him cost us dear," wrote a French scribe. "He who refuses what God offers through good fortune can not get it back when he asks."

With this lost opportunity, the hostilities seemed headed for a stalemate. Francis was advised to conduct a *guerre guerroyable*, or dribbling war. Suing for peace now, he was told, would be the "wet nurse of a bigger war." As winter set in, armies were disbanded for the cold-weather recess, and the war in France dissolved into a war of words. Charles charged Francis with atrocities large and small, not only burning villages but cutting off the fingers of small children.

As all expected a lull, suddenly, in the all-important theater of northern Italy, disaster struck the French. On November 19, an imperial force broke through the walls of Milan and took charge of the city. The French fled across the Alps, and in rapid succession Lodi and Pavia, along with the episcopal sees of Parma and Piacenza, came under imperial control. At the head of the imperial army, dressed in his costume as a knight of Rhodes, was the unlikely figure of Cardinal Giulio de' Medici, Leo X's cousin and chief adviser and the odds-on favorite to succeed him as pope. The cardinal sent the glorious news back to Rome that the French occupiers had at last been driven out of Italy and the treasured papal cities returned to Vatican control.

As the story is told, Leo X received the wonderful news a few days later when he was at his villa in Magliana on the Tiber southwest of Rome. He was again enjoying one of his extravagant hunting expeditions. The word *hunting* does not quite describe the activity. Because he was immensely fat and half-blind, the pope was carried to these blood orgies in a litter. The battleground was often at the head of a ravine at a spot to which minions drove stags and boar from the hills with loud bells and horns, and the pope watched with his one good eye, transfixed, as the animals were butchered at his feet. He was also partial to aerial combat, when his papal falcons would be let loose to go after soaring vultures; if the party was lucky, an eagle might happen by and join the dogfight, sending the lesser birds plummeting to their deaths. After such invigorating "sport," the pope would often exclaim, "What a glorious day," and move on to an evening banquet. These feasts often featured ribald theater, deafening music, and up to sixty-five courses. The gorge was appointed with such exotic delicacies as a plate of peacocks' tongues or a huge pie from which an infant emerged to spout poetic greetings to the guests. Occasionally, the entertainment consisted of barrels filled with fat pigs rolled down a hill where starving peasants at its base fought with axes to secure some meat.

On this evening, the exertions of the day's hunt together with the excitement of the news wilted the pope. As he greeted his triumphant soldiers below and watched a celebratory bonfire being prepared, his body shook with a chill. His doctors downplayed the indisposition as a simple cold, no cause for alarm for the forty-six-year-old pope. He was taken back to Rome, where he died so quickly, it was said, that there was no time to administer the last rites. Inevitably in the conspiratorial hothouse that was the Vatican, poison was suspected. Days earlier Leo X was being extolled for his great contributions to the arts, for making Rome a center for culture and learning, for his patronage of Raphael and Michelangelo, for his charm and good nature, for his gay pageants and lavish banquets, and for his passion for defending Christendom against the Turks. With his death, the antipapal sentiment in Italy boiled to the surface. The late pope was abruptly ridiculed for the extravagance and indulgence and vulgar ostentation that had driven the papacy to penury and turned the Vatican into a pagan bawdy house. Wrote a Roman wag:

Without the Church's sacraments, Pope Leo died, I'm told.
How could he e'er receive again what he himself had sold?

ACT THREE

Ancestral

Aspirations

✠

II.

HOLY SMOKE

With the news of Pope Leo's death, Giulio de' Medici rushed back to Rome, confident that he would succeed his cousin and realize Leo's dream of Medici hegemony in Italy. His advantages were considerable. For Leo's entire papacy, Giulio had been his relative's right hand, skillfully handling the Machiavellian gyrations of Vatican foreign policy, while the pope lost himself in merriment. Giulio had proved himself not only an able prelate, but a stout military commander; he was officially a knight of Rhodes. Giulio was cunning and talented, experienced and well qualified. The only question was whether he could be as competent a pope as he was the first prelate. When the College of Cardinals convened, the Florentine cardinal had the most votes, fourteen out of thirty-nine. Cardinal Wolsey of England had seven votes, and he was offering one hundred thousand ducats for his election. His political manager in Rome saw a good chance to take advantage of the disarray. "Here is marvelous division, and we were never more likely to have a schism." Henry VIII was pushing hard for Wolsey's election, and the emperor's support was brazenly solicited. Wolsey even suggested that the emperor dispatch troops toward Rome to pressure the cardinals.

In the early going, the opposition held firm, and Cardinal Wolsey faded as a viable candidate. Still, the resistance to Giulio de' Medici was stout. Francis I let it be known that if the cardinals elected another Medici, "who is the cause of all the war, neither he nor any man in his kingdom would obey the Church of Rome." As an electioneering ploy and almost in jest, thinking he would break out more votes in later rounds, the Medici threw their bloc of votes to the most unlikely candidate of all, Adrian of Utrecht. Adrian was an apparition, utterly unknown in Rome, and not even present at the conclave in the Sistine Chapel. A foreigner from the Netherlands, he was now the cardinal in Tortosa, Spain, where he was the emperor's viceroy and the inquisitor-general. His personality and demeanor were the virtual antithesis of Leo's: frugal, intellectual, humble, and genuinely pious. Only once in recent centuries had there been a non-Italian pope, the Spanish Borgia pope Alexander VI (father of bloodthirsty Cesare Borgia and scandalous Lucrezia Borgia). The extravagance and corruption of his reign had nearly done the papacy in. Another "barbarian" pope from the outside seemed anathema to the Italian conclave. It was unthinkable that Adrian's candidacy would go anywhere. Moreover, years before he had been the tutor to Charles V in the Netherlands. Surely the conclave did not want a pope who was in the emperor's pocket.

Blithely, also in the spirit of political maneuvering, with an eye toward subsequent rounds, the other blocs also threw their votes to Adrian as well, and to the amazement of all, he was elected. Almost instantly after the holy smoke that signaled the election of a new pope dissipated over St. Peter's Square, the dismay was felt. This was a huge mistake and a terrible accident. One observer said of the looks on the faces of the cardinals as they left the Sistine Chapel, "I thought that I saw ghosts from limbo as white and distraught were the faces I looked on. Almost all are dissatisfied and repent already having chosen a stranger, a barbarian, and a tutor to the Emperor." A disgruntled cardinal was more cryptic: "One might almost say that the Emperor is now Pope, and the Pope Emperor." Rage gripped Rome. "Robbers! Betrayers of Christ's blood! Do you feel no sorrow in having surrendered the fair Vatican to German fury!" a heckler shouted. The rumor spread that the papacy would soon leave Rome. Someone posted a protest sign that read, "This palace to let." In Paris, Francis I scoffed at the new pope as a "creature" and as "the Emperor's schoolmaster."

If mortification was great, nowhere was it greater than in Adrian himself. When he heard the news on January 24, 1522, in Vitoria, Spain, he expressed profound sorrow. At sixty-two years of age and of uncertain health, he spoke of his personal weakness and inadequacy. His temperament was that of a scholar and a pastor, not a leader. Only in the emperor's camp was there satisfaction. Truly the choice of the Holy Ghost had been inspired, the Germans rejoiced (for the Holy Ghost was, by belief and conceit, behind the choice of every pope). Charles V wrote to the English ambassador that he was sure that he "could rely on the new Pope as thoroughly as on anyone who had risen to greatness of his service." The emperor was soon to be disabused.

The immediate question was whether the new pope would reaffirm the Vatican's place in the anti-French alliance. When the emperor's demand to that effect reached Adrian, the pope signaled a change. He would not follow the lead of imperial policy, and he announced the Vatican's formal withdrawal from the anti-French league. From that day forward, he would espouse a posture of strict independence and neutrality. His goal was to restore peace among the Christian princes, not to set one against the other. Christendom faced a grave threat from Islam. Ottoman power threatened strategic Christian outposts in Hungary and in Rhodes. The kings must unite against this threat. He pleaded with Francis and Charles to set aside their antagonisms in the interests of their faith.

"We take into consideration the dangers now threatening Christendom from the Turk," he wrote to Charles, "and are of the opinion that the greater dangers should be first addressed. If we protect and defend the interests of our faith, even at the loss of our worldly advantage, instead of meeting the evils of Christendom with indifference, the Lord will be our helper."

But the European monarchs were dismissive of this call for unity. Rhodes and Hungary seemed too far away to be threatening. Italy was the prize. "We are ready to make peace and to come with great power against the Turk," Francis wrote to Adrian, "provided Milan, which is our patrimony, is returned to us."

As Adrian urged the Christian kings to unite against the Turkish threat, so he argued passionately for them to confront the scourge of Lutheranism and to enforce the Edict of Worms. In a papal brief dated January 3, 1523, he wrote sadly that division and revolution had broken out in "our once so steadfast German nation." Luther's evil was spreading its poisonous tendrils far and wide. "We cannot think of anything so incredible as that so great, so pious a union should allow a petty monk, an apostate from that Catholic faith which for years he had preached, to seduce it from the way pointed by the Savior and His Apostles, sealed by the blood of so many martyrs, trodden by so many wise and holy men. We adjure you to lay aside all mutual hatreds, to strive for one thing: to quench this fire and bring back Luther and other instigators of error into the right way, by all means in your power. If however you will not listen, then must the rod of severity and punishment be used. God knows our willingness to forgive. But if it should be proved that evil has penetrated so far that gentle means of healing are of no avail, then we must have recourse to methods of severity in order to safeguard the members as yet untainted by disease."

Luther, he said flatly, had set a worse example than Mohammed.

Still, while he condemned Luther and longed for justice against the heretic, he became the first pope to acknowledge the abuse and corruption of the Church. Stoutly, he called for major reform. "We all, prelates and clergy, have gone astray from the right way," he said. "For long there is not one who has done good, no not one." This admission of collective guilt was greeted with dismay and protest by ecclesiastics, who argued that at the very least it undercut the case of the Church against Luther. No pope before Adrian had ever given so much publicity to the abuses of the Church. "When our Savior wished to cleanse the city of Jerusalem of its sickness, he went first to the Temple to punish the sins of the priests," Adrian proclaimed. "We know well that for many years things deserving of abhorrence have gathered around the Holy See. Sacred things have been misused, ordinances transgressed. Therefore we must promise to use all diligence to reform the Roman Curia."

This forthright admission marked the first step toward counterreformation.

With high-mindedness and considerable courage, therefore, Adrian set forth three great goals for his papacy: to unite Christendom against the menace of Islam; to confront the scourge of Luther; and to reform his corrupt Church.

It would take the new pope six full months to make his way from Spain to Rome. The sea voyage was perilous, for Turkish pirates infested the open waters of the Gulf of Lion. Adrian was loath to make the journey overland, for that would require special favors from Francis I, who was ridiculing him as the "emperor's schoolmaster." At all costs, he needed to avoid the battlefields of northern Italy. Not until August 1522 did a flotilla of fifty ships leave Tortosa. With the pope seated grandly on the prow of his flagship beneath a crimson awning embossed with the papal escutcheon, the fleet sailed north to Barcelona, across to Marseille and Genoa, finally arriving in Civitavecchia late in the month.

In these six months of interregnum, important events transpired without papal involvement or influence. On his way back to Spain after the Diet of Worms, Charles V had passed through England, met with Henry VIII at Windsor, and reconfirmed the plan for a joint campaign against France in the following year. Thus, Europe moved one step closer to continental warfare. On April 27 the French suffered total defeat at the Battle of Bicocca in Lombardy, and a month later they lost their hold on Genoa. This effectively ended the French presence in Italy for the moment. In Germany, meanwhile, Martin Luther widened his political campaign as, at the same time, he translated the New Testament into vulgate German, downgrading the Book of Revelation to an appendix. Another diet, this time at Nuremberg, again turned a deaf ear to the demands of the papal legate for the execution of the Edict of Worms.

And in France the duke of Bourbon, constable of France, defected from the service of Francis I and secretly made his way into the service of the emperor. This was a stunning development, one redolent with significance for both the French and the imperial sides. Bourbon was the eighth duke of Bourbon, a prince of Burgundy, whose ancestral lands of Bourbon and Montpensier were situated in the upper Loire Valley in the heart of

France. Through his inheritances, he was by birth and good fortune one of the most powerful men in France and, besides the king himself, the wealthiest man in France. His innate qualities as a military leader had been noticed early. Upon the accession of Francis I to the throne of France in 1515, Bourbon, then twenty-five years old, was appointed constable of France, the powerful post that gave him supreme command over the French army. Shortly thereafter, the duke had performed brilliantly at the great French victory at the Battle of Marignano, which handed Milan to France. Promptly, Francis I appointed Bourbon as Milan's governor and heaped upon him honors of the state. But tensions arose between the French king and his vassal over ancestral rights and over payment for services as constable. Secretly, Bourbon began to conspire with both Charles V and with Henry VIII about a possible partition of France. When Francis I caught wind of this conspiracy, Bourbon fled France and into the arms of the enemy. Now his military genius would be put to work in the service of the Empire as it had been in the service of France.

But most important of all, and yet seemingly far away from the center of action, Suleyman the Magnificent arrived in the vicinity of Rhodes with a massive force of over one hundred thousand soldiers. On the shores across from the island, this army joined up with a fleet of three hundred ships that carried another ten thousand men.

Facing them on the island was a battalion of the bravest and most capable soldiers in all of Europe: the military monks of the order of the Hospitallers. These fanatics, sworn to obedience, chastity, and poverty, numbered seven hundred knights and five thousand soldiers. To displace these utterly remarkable men from their fortress would be no small undertaking, despite their deficit in number of fifteen to one. Once before, in 1480, another sultan had tried it, and he had failed miserably.

12.

THE NEST OF
CHRISTIAN VIPERS

The island of Rhodes, the most significant island of the Dodecanese archipelago, which skirts the flank of Turkey, lies a mere seven miles off the southwestern coast of Asia Minor. Set on a northeast by southwest bias, this strategic real estate is forty-five miles in length, and at its widest, twenty-two miles across. Its spine is a range of high mountains, graced by its highest peak, Mt. Attairo, which rises nearly four thousand feet. Its location had made Rhodes a battleground for centuries, dating back to Homeric times. In Roman times it was famous for its school of philosophy, to which Caesar, Brutus, Cicero, and Tiberius had come for instruction. In 1309, the island had been captured by the Knights of St. John, known as the Hospitallers, after Arabs had driven these crusaders out of their Palestinian stronghold at Acre eighteen years before. The island acted as something like a bottle stopper between Constantinople and the outlying Ottoman province of Egypt, for the Christian knights controlled the 170-mile passageway between Rhodes and Crete, the island to the southwest then controlled by the Venetian Republic.

Over the succeeding two hundred years, the Knights of St. John became the last vestige of the Crusade era. While the Knights Templar and the Teutonic Knights had ceased to exist, the Knights of Rhodes had evolved from their founding mission of healing the sick into an organization of

Christian piracy. No longer could they assert that they existed to treat the casualties of holy war in the Holy Land, since Muslims now held all of Palestine. They justified their raids on Muslim shipping by claiming to liberate Christian slaves who were employed as rowers for Ottoman galleys, though they themselves used Muslim rowers for their own ships.

These rogues of a bygone era had built up their fortress on the northern tip of the island into the most formidable bastion in all of Europe. Their fortress embraced the semicircular commercial port and a town of some five thousand residents, the majority of whom were Greek Orthodox. High, crenellated, well-maintained walls, punctuated with thirteen daunting towers, surrounded the entire town. Two spits of land pointed out to sea, and at their end were the towers of St. Nicholas and St. Angelo. Between these outer defenses a great chain or boom could be raised across the port in the event of attack. Five gates led into the city. The defense of the bastion was organized into seven sections or "tongues," in each of which a distinct ethnic group held sway. The French and German knights guarded the northern approach, while the English had command of the southern flank. In between were the contingents of Auvergne, Aragon, and Provence, while the Italians and Castilians controlled the sections facing the sea.

Behind these formidable walls the knights-errant, up to seven hundred of them, resided in their national residence halls along a cobblestone street known as the Street of the Knights. There they lived in luxury, served by Turkish slaves, dining with silver engraved with their family crest, and sleeping on sheets of velvet and silk. When they strode the street like peacocks, if they were not wearing their simple black cowl with a white cross embroidered on the chest, they often wore a crimson cape with a white Maltese cross, or in preparation for battle, a red breastplate. At one end of this famous street was their hospital, the finest in the Middle East, and at the other end was the magnificent palace of the grand master. Its imposing entrance was appointed with two circular, fortified towers that led into a ceremonial courtyard. The knights prayed in their Church of St. John the Baptist, their patron saint and protector, the one who pointed the way to Christ. Outside of the defensive perimeter, the Hospitallers had built some

thirty smaller castles on the island, and one outpost on the Turkish main-
land, at Bodrum.

From this redoubt, sometimes joining up with other seaborne ruffians,
these monkish pirates put aside their black cowls, strapped on their armor,
and set out to interdict Ottoman trade and shipping. For decades they
operated with impunity in their brilliant red ships and enslaved pilgrims
on their hajj to Mecca. To the Turks this nasty lair of the infidel was known
alternatively as the "stronghold of the hellhounds," the "nest of Christian
vipers," and the "stick in the throat of Islam." It had been the goal of a handful of sultans to eliminate the galling irritant. In 1480, during the last year
of the reign of Mehmet the Conqueror, the Turks had staged their only
full-scale siege, only to realize how formidable this bastion was after they
were turned back ignominiously. Selim the Grim was well along in his preparations for another attempt when he died. Now Suleyman inherited this
insult to his empire, to his forefathers, to his faith. So long as Rhodes remained in Christian hands, the Ottoman Empire could never consolidate
its control over the eastern Mediterranean.

"These accursed infidels are the worst sons of error," wrote a Turkish
scribe. "Sent by the devil, they are noted for their cunning. They are expert
seamen and possess great fortresses whose defenses are incomparable in all
the earth. Their corsairs are noted for their energy and courage. They send
out their swift warships to the hurt and loss of Islam, permitting no merchant or pilgrim ship to pass toward Egypt unharmed by their cannon. How
many children of the Prophet have fallen prisoner to these people of error?
How many have chains put about their necks and their ankles? How many
thousands of the faithful are forced to deny their faith? How many virgins
and young women? How many wives and infants? Their malignity knows
no end."

In January 1521 as the Catholic world was focused on the excommunication of Luther and the opening of the Diet of Worms, the Knights of
Rhodes faced a decision. Their grand master had died, and two commanders
with proven military experience stepped forward to succeed him. Andrea
d'Amaral was a Portuguese nobleman from an ancient and distinguished

line. Noted for his valor and his haughty arrogance, he had the advantage of being in Rhodes as the election went forward, and the disadvantage of being broadly unpopular.

Opposing him, his name nailed to the door of the Church of St. John, was Philippe de Villiers de L'Isle-Adam, a Frenchman of equal pedigree. The Villiers family from Brittany boasted a long line of religious warriors, including Jean de Villiers, who had been the grand master of the order when the Hospitallers were expelled from Acre in 1291, marking the official end of the Crusade era in Palestine. Now fifty-seven years old, tall and lithe and graceful with snow-white hair and beard, Villiers had received his golden spurs in the order at an early age and had risen rapidly through the ranks from captain of the galleons to commander of the militia to Grand Hospitaller in charge of the hospital. Like d'Amaral he too had performed heroically in many sea battles. He was now the grand prior of France.

For years Villiers and d'Amaral had been rivals in both battle command and in politics. They had clashed often in disputes over naval tactics and strategy and had competed for the respect and affection of the knights. Quickly, the election turned ugly. When Villiers prevailed by only one vote, largely on the strength of his more attractive personality and the plurality of French knights in the order, the disgruntled d'Amaral proclaimed, as if prophetically, that the winner would be the last grand master of Rhodes.

Many weeks later, when the news of his election reached Villiers in Paris, his first step was to request an audience with his monarch, Francis I, no doubt to impress upon his sovereign the importance of supporting the last bastion of Christianity in the eastern Mediterranean, despite its great distance from the patrimony. After his requests for help were turned aside, the grand master–elect set out on his long and eventful journey to his new post. In Marseille he boarded the flagship of the order, the *Santa María*, the only ship of the order's fleet painted not red, but pitch-black. In the weeks ahead he was bedeviled by terrible storms, by ship fires, and by Turkish pirates, including an encounter in Syracuse with the most ferocious Turkish pirate of them all, Cortoglu, who had lost two brothers in battles against the knights, who had a third brother in captivity in Rhodes, and who was looking for revenge. With these travails and diversions the new grand master did not arrive in Rhodes until September 1521, only a few weeks after Suleyman had captured Belgrade.

In fact, Suleyman was keeping a close eye on Rhodes. He had been made aware of Villiers's election, and the Sublime Porte had a spy in the fortress itself, a Jewish physician who had been recruited and embedded in Rhodes by Suleyman's father, Selim the Grim. The mole was still active. He had inveigled his way into the good graces of the knights by performing well as a doctor, and he had allowed himself to be baptized. Meanwhile, he was secretly sending reports to Constantinople on the condition of Rhodes's defenses. With a section of the wall controlled by French knights under reconstruction, with the disarray caused by the death of the grand master, with serious dissension among the Italian knights in the fortress, the spy was suggesting that this might be a good time for an Ottoman attack.

Suleyman now initiated a series of taunts, as if he knew from the beginning that sooner or later Rhodes would be the focus of an imperial campaign. Back in Constantinople after the Balkan campaign, the sultan sent a boastful and menacing mock congratulation to the new grand master, laced with insulting cynicism:

"I, Sultan Suleyman, by the grace of God, king of kings, sovereign of sovereigns, most high emperor of Byzantium and Trebizond, most mighty king of Persia, Arabia, Syria and Egypt. Supreme lord of Europe and Asia. Prince of Mecca and Aleppo. Possessor of Jerusalem, and lord of the universal sea to Philippe de Villiers de L'Isle-Adam, Grand Master of the Isle of Rhodes, greeting.

"I congratulate you on your new dignity and your arrival in your dominions. I wish that you may reign there happily, and with more glory than your predecessors. It shall be in your power to have a share in our goodwill. Enjoy then our friendship, and as our friend, be not the last to congratulate us on the conquests we have just made in Hungary, where we have reduced the important fortress of Belgrade. I took many other beautiful and well-fortified cities and destroyed most of their inhabitants either by sword or

fire, the remainder being reduced to slavery. Now after sending my numerous and victorious army into their winter quarters, I myself have returned
in triumph to my court at Constantinople. Adieu."

Villiers had no illusions about the threatening tone of this communiqué.
He responded to it cryptically and with bravado: "To Suleyman, Sultan of
the Turks. I understand very well the meaning of your letter. Your proposals of a peace between us are as agreeable to me as they will be displeasing
to Cortoglu. During my passage from France, that corsair did all he could
to surprise me, but not succeeding in his project, and not caring to go out
of these seas without having done us some damage, he entered the river
Lycia and attempted to carry off two merchant ships belonging to our ports.
He had likewise attacked a bark belonging to some Candiots,* but the galleons of the order, which I sent out of the port of Rhodes, forced him to let
go his hold, and make off as fast as he could for fear of falling into our
power. Adieu."

The motto of Villiers's aristocratic family was Va oultre la main à l'oeuvre,
"Onward, hand to work," and it seemed especially apt as he took charge of
the Rhodes defense. During the fall and winter, preparations for war went
forward, for the new grand master had no doubt about the imminence of
an Ottoman attack.

In these preparations he had the services of a brilliant, visionary engineer, Gabriele Tadini da Martinengo. Tadini hailed from the mountains of
Brescia in northern Italy. A commoner, he had been trained initially as a
medical doctor. But early in his career he had turned his brilliant scientific
mind to the new art of military architecture and had served the Venetian
army with distinction in its various battles in the first years of the sixteenth
century. Better than any other military engineer in Europe, he understood
the implications of the invention of gunpowder to military defense. The
age of chivalry had passed. The engineer was now transcendent over the
valorous knight. The threat of explosive bombardment and mining had
rendered the traditional thin walls of medieval castles obsolete. Villiers

---

* Candiots refers to residents of Crete, which at this time was known as the Kingdom of Candia.

had secretly recruited Tadini from his Venetian masters in Crete and slipped him into Rhodes surreptitiously in the winter of 1522.

Il Bresciano, as Tadini was known, proceeded to remake the defenses of the Christian bastion. On the walls themselves, he reinforced the batteries and carefully calibrated their range with precise mathematical calculus. Beneath these walls, he constructed an intricate warren of tunnels and listening posts to detect any mining operations with a system of delicate bells and drums fitted with corks. Children, women, and elderly were trained as listeners. This subway system had to be carefully ventilated to prevent suffocations. Once an enemy mine was detected, the plan was to undermine it with mines of his own. Behind the walls he cleared large fields for transverse fire; he had the defensive ditches dug deeper, to a depth of forty feet; and he constructed palisades and retrenchments as a second line of defense in the event of a breach.

Through the spring of 1522, the bastion was provisioned for a long siege. Huge quantities of half-ripe wheat were shipped in from Naples and Romania. Ships heavy-laden with wine arrived from Crete and Cyprus. Great stores of ammunition, artillery, and other ordnance were stockpiled. All the wells outside the town's walls were filled in, to deprive an enemy of local water. Armed with his own intelligence, the new grand master dispatched envoys to Europe: Spanish knights went to Rome and to the Holy Roman emperor, and French knights to Paris. To all the message was the same: Christian princes must gather their resources to come to the defense of the most important outpost of Christianity in the eastern Mediterranean.

On June 1, 1522, Suleyman delivered his anticipated declaration of war in accordance with Koranic law: "The continual robberies with which you infest our faithful subjects, and the insult you offer to our imperial majesty, oblige us to require you to deliver up to us immediately the island and fortress of Rhodes. If you do it readily, we swear by the God who made heaven and earth, by the six and twenty thousand prophets, and the four *mushaf**

---

* *Mushaf* refers to the four "books" sent down from heaven by the prophets: the Torah, the Psalms, the Gospels, and the Koran.

that fell from heaven, and by our great prophet Mohammed, that you shall have free liberty to go out the island and the inhabitants to stay there without the least injury being done to you. But if you do not submit immediately to our orders you shall be all cut to pieces with our terrible sword, and the towers, bastions, and walls of Rhodes shall be laid level with the grass that grows at the foot of all those fortifications.

"Be certain that neither you nor your knights have slipped from my memory!"

Once again Villiers responded with brio: "I am pleased that you have not forgotten about me or my knights, since I also have heard about your grandeur. You remind me of your victory in Hungary of which you are so proud and you promise the same success in another enterprise though the war has not yet begun. Be cautious not to exaggerate. Of all the ambitions men can formulate, those that depend on the destiny of arms are the most uncertain!"

Eight weeks later, on July 26, a massive flotilla of 103 Turkish galleons and many more supporting vessels, perhaps 300 ships in all, appeared off the coast of Rhodes. The Christian knights watched as thousands of Turkish soldiers came ashore, along with their formidable cannons. Eventually, Suleyman himself was among them. A great celebration greeted his arrival, with huge imperial banners raised on the Turkish galleons and along their front line. The sultan set up his lavish, elaborate golden tent several miles from Rhodes and then rode onto the high hill of San Stefano, only a mile from the western walls of the city, to survey the scene. As more invaders poured ashore, Villiers gathered his knights in their Church of St. John the Baptist. After a pontifical mass was read, the grand master rose to address his brothers. He laid the keys of the city on the altar before an image of St. John the Baptist and commended the protection of the city to their saint.

"The hour for the last struggle has come," he said solemnly. "In a short time the enemy will encamp at our gates. Let us receive them with our ancient virtue and valor. Remember who you are. If you are determined to win or to die, put aside old quarrels and any hatred. Act like brethren. May unanimity reign amongst you. With unity, who can oppose your swords! If it is written in heaven that we should die, let us die. But it will not be in vain nor inglorious. On your tomb there will be the palm of martyrdom and eternity of fame. Now, with the help of God and of the Baptist John, let us wait for the enemy."

At the conclusion of this stirring speech, the knights turned to one another, embraced, and repeated their leader's charge softly: win or die. And then each knight came forward and swore his knightly and religious vows upon the cross-hilt of his sword.

13.

IN THE TRUEST SENSE

In mid-June 1522 plague broke out ferociously in Rome, and the contagion spread quickly. Bloated bodies piled up in the streets. With each passing week the epidemic grew worse until the death toll reached 150 a day. Some forty thousand Romans, including cardinals and ambassadors, fled the city in panic. For those who stayed the situation was dire. "One very cruel thing is that many people who fall ill with other ailments are abandoned and left to die of want," reported the Mantuan ambassador to Rome. "So people who have the plague in their houses often keep it secret, lest they should die of hunger. Sometimes as many as five or six corpses are found hidden away and are only discovered by the stench they cause." The devout joined processions in the streets with icons of the Madonna and wailed their prayers of supplication skyward. Miracles were reported. One devout woman, it was said, gave birth to an infected child, took it to the Church of San Agostino, a church just north of the Piazza Navona that is especially associated with motherhood, and laid the baby on the altar, where it was instantly and magically restored to health. The news of the siege of Rhodes and the continuing absence of the new pope added to the hysteria. Rumors were rife that the Turks would soon land in southern Italy.

In this environment of horror, the strange, "barbarian" pope, Adrian VI, finally arrived in Rome in August. His physical appearance alone was in sharp contrast to that of the obese Leo X, signaling that a new day had dawned. At age sixty-three, his face was long and pale, his body lean, his hands white and seemingly bloodless, and his demeanor reverent and serious. As he was conveyed to the Vatican, women wept with joy at the sight of this ethereal personage whose arrival had been so long anticipated. He gravitated to the poor. "I love poverty," he said to beggars along the way. "You will see what I will do for you."

But soon enough, men wept for different reasons. Adrian spoke no Italian and conducted all his business in Latin. More important, he evinced no understanding of or interest in the mores of Italian politics; indeed, he set out to violate treasured rituals immediately in his first week. Patronizing his cardinals as schoolboys, he evicted them from their plush Vatican apartments, instructing them to shave their beards and act like priests rather than potentates. When he was informed that Romans were building an arch in his honor at the Porta Portese, he proclaimed the enterprise to be heathenish and not in keeping with Christian piety, ordering the work stopped. Musicians and poets were sent packing. He saw classical sculpture and art as pagan and had much of it removed. Instead of taking charge of the glorious papal apartments, now luminous with Raphael's stupendous masterworks, he announced that he would live in a small house in the Vatican gardens, attended not by the hundreds who had served Leo X, but by four persons, including an aging Flemish woman who cooked his simple meals.

"What can the man mean?" wrote the imperial ambassador to Charles V. "When God has given him the finest palace in all of Rome?" The Venetian ambassador was more blunt: "All Rome is horrified at what the Pope has done in this one short week!"

Beyond his frugality and his reclusiveness, Adrian would quickly prove himself to be indecisive as well. He rarely granted audiences. "And when he does consent to see anyone," wrote the Venetian ambassador, "he says little and can not make up his mind. Whatever the request, big or small, his answer is always the same, We shall see." In sophisticated, pleasure-loving Rome the backlash was great. Adrian's Dutch advisers, wrote one Roman, were "stupid as stones."

If he was ungracious, dry, and austere, no one could challenge his courage. As other grandees fled the plague to the country, Adrian announced that he would stay in Rome. "I have no fear for myself," he said, "and I put my trust in God." His aides kept after him to leave, but he would not hear of it. By November the plague continued unabated. "Eight out of ten persons whom one meets bear the marks of plague," the Mantuan ambassador reported. "Only a few men have survived. I fear lest God should annihilate the inhabitants of this city."

In the midst of all of this, Adrian was receiving alarming reports from the island of Rhodes. The valiant knights of St. John were hard-pressed. They needed relief, but who would provide it? The Vatican was bankrupt. Only able to muster a few ships, it could scarcely finance a fleet or an army. But at every turn his urgent appeals to the Christian princes of Europe fell on deaf ears.

FOR 145 DAYS, in the late summer and fall of 1522, the siege of Rhodes went forward. During the first month the Turks set up their batteries and catapults along the land perimeter while the ferocious pirate Cortoglu positioned his galleons on the water. Suleyman's top commanders were his grand vizier, Piri Pasha, who was said to be a direct descendant of Abu Bakr, the companion of the Prophet Mohammed; he faced the Italian "tongue." His second vizier was his brother-in-law, Mustapha Pasha, who faced the knights of Provence; and the agha of the janissaries, named Bali, faced the Germans.

Then the shelling of the walls began. And it was awesome. "I believe verily," wrote a French knight in the town, "that since the creation of the world such artillery and so great quantity was never laid before any town as hath been against Rhodes in this siege." Stone projectiles, brass cannonballs, heavy mortars, rained down on the barbican from all sides. At horrendous cost, it took a full month for the Ottomans to creep close enough to the walls to begin mining operations. Despite the massive numbers of the Turkish force—some put the number as high as one hundred thousand—the invading army consisted more of cannon fodder than trained and experienced warriors. Only about eight thousand janissaries were available to spearhead a serious attack. Double the number of artillerymen supported them. Beyond that, an immense number of lightly armed irregulars and masses of Christian slaves had the terrible job of digging the trenches. Soon enough those trenches would fill with their own dead bodies. Since the Ottoman Empire had no real maritime tradition, their warships were flimsy and inferior and easily sunk when they sustained a direct hit. If the Turks outnumbered the defenders ten to one, so their casualties on land and sea rose in equal proportion.

On September 4 two mines exploded beneath the English section of the walls, opening a breach of twelve yards. Led by their agha, Bali, the janissaries stormed into the breach supported by waves of irregulars. But they were met by Villiers and a disciplined contingent of Hospitallers and driven back at the cost of two thousand Turkish dead. Six days later another section of the English wall tumbled down, followed by a similar assault, with the same result. Three weeks after that, the second vizier, Mustapha Pasha, led a coordinated assault against the Spanish, English, Provence, and Italian tongues. This time, the Turks opened their widest breach yet in the Spanish and Italian sections of the wall. Furious hand-to-hand combat took place in the rubble, directed by the agha of the janissaries on one side and Villiers on the other. At one point flags of the janissaries dotted the walls. The bastion of the Spanish changed hands several times. But in the end, yet again the Turks were expelled, their dead, numbering several thousand, filling the trenches.

From a distance Suleyman watched this mayhem in disgust. When he saw his best soldiers retreat, he was furious. He commanded that his second vizier and brother-in-law, Mustapha Pasha, the commander of his left flank, be brought before him, where he was chided for his prediction that Rhodes could be taken in fifteen to thirty days and relieved of command. In his fury the sultan threatened to have his brother-in-law executed in front of the whole army, but he relented the following day only after his other pashas persuaded him that such a spectacle would give aid and comfort to the enemy. The corsair Cortoglu was also dragged before the sultan and beaten with sticks for his missteps. As Mustapha Pasha was degraded and sent to Syria the next day as a governor, he was replaced by Suleyman's favorite, Ibrahim Pasha.

The conflict had reached a pivotal moment. Many in the Turkish camp were ready to give up the fight, for the slaughter had been unspeakable. The mines and the artillery had accomplished nothing. Winter would soon be approaching, when their batteries would sink into the mud. Some contingents, including all-important janissaries, could be seen retreating to their ships. But into the Turkish camp slipped an Albanian deserter who urged the Turks not to raise the siege, since the store of ammunition in the bastion was beginning to run low. Now in full awareness of his Homeric challenge, knowing that all of Europe and all of Islam were watching, Suleyman visualized the humiliation of the Turks at these walls in 1480 and its implications. Then the Turkish army had been half the size of the current army, and the great sultan himself had not been present as Suleyman was now. Thus, if he faltered, the disgrace would be his personally and twice that of 1480. His reign could not bear a repeat performance. Yet he had lost close to half of his invading force.

To abandon the fight or to redouble his efforts? Grandly he chose the latter course. Sending to Syria and Mesopotamia for replacements, he moved his command post closer to the walls, just beyond the range of Tadini's cannons. In a divan with his viziers, Suleyman announced his intention to continue the siege through the harsh, waterlogged winter months. As a show of permanence, he had his headquarters constructed of stone.

If the Turkish force was lagging, so too were the Christian defenders growing weary. The siege had lasted two months. Suleyman might lose half of his seemingly inexhaustible force, but Villiers could not bear the loss of half his knights. Surely, the Vatican, the Holy Roman emperor, Villiers's own king, Francis I, and European Christians generally were aware of his desperate situation. Was help on the way? Pathetically, in mid-October a brigantine with four Italian knights and a recruit slipped through the Turkish fleet. The recruit was admitted to the Order of St. John and killed the next day.

In October mining resumed. The Turks were now burrowing tunnels under nearly 80 percent of the perimeter, about sixty mines in all, and it was becoming harder and harder for the knights to repulse these efforts. Timber for countermining operations was running low. On October 11, the mastermind of the defense, Gabriele Tadini, was shot in the eye and put out of action. On October 17, breaches were opened in the English and French sections of the wall. The knights retreated to Tadini's retrenchments. Much of the English wall was reduced to rubble. A path to the town itself was opened, though few Turks wished to brave the withering flanking fire. Ammunition too was running low, and Villiers ordered that it be rationed and fired only upon the order of a commander. To the end of the month the mining and countermining, the breaching and the repairing of the walls, continued, and the Christians saw clearly that the Turks would not be deterred by the terrible slaughter they were suffering.

Still worse, treachery was in the wind. Late in October an alert lookout apprehended a Christian soldier cranking up his crossbow. On the tip of the crossbow's arrow was found a message, about to be shot into the Turkish camp: "The situation is critical. The knights are exhausted. The townspeople are revolting. Do not abandon the siege now. The fortress can not sustain another assault like that of September 24. If terms were offered, the Grand Master will have to accept." The culprit was the Jewish physician, assigned to the Castilian contingent under the command of the chancellor, Andrea d'Amaral. The traitor was expeditiously taken to the torture chamber. The rack was prepared, and when the "question" was put to him, he confessed that he was acting on the orders of d'Amaral himself, and that the chancellor had been in touch with the enemy for weeks.

Rumors of this high-level treason swept through the ranks. Given d'Amaral's unpopularity, it is not surprising that a number of witnesses came forward to testify to all manner of hearsay. More conspirators were arrested. One witness claimed to have heard the chancellor say, "I would sell my soul to the devil if I could accomplish the ruin of the order and Villiers de L'Isle-Adam." Promptly, d'Amaral was arrested and imprisoned in the battered Tower of St. Nicolas. He too was "put to the question," but, his iron will undented, he said nothing. With the constant din of Turkish bombs landing outside, an extraordinary trial before two grand crosses of the order was held. D'Amaral maintained his silence, except when his converso accuser was brought forward. D'Amaral called him a "poltroon." Despite the thinness of the evidence against him, the fallen hero of the order was found guilty. On November 8, he was stripped of his vows and the accoutrements of the order. Because he was lame from the exactions of the torture chamber, he had to be carried to the execution place in the courtyard of the grand master's palace, where he was beheaded and quartered, the parts of his body displayed at various places along the walls.

Two weeks later, Villiers wrote of the incident with satisfaction to his nephew in France. Of d'Amaral's guilt he had no doubt. "I have not only been at war with the Turks, but with one of the most senior members of our Council who, by reason of envy and a thirst for power, had long conspired to bring the Turk here and had promised to surrender this city to him. The matter has been divinely revealed and confirmed, and he has been executed."

On November 30, St. Andrew's Day, one final epic battle took place before the fate of Rhodes was decided. Neither the patron saint of Scotland nor his equivalent in Islam could have been pleased at the horrible scene. Rain poured down in sheets, mixed with pelting hail, and high winds, rain "so great and so strong that it made the earth sink," wrote a French soldier. As the Turks came through a breach in the Auvergne section in greater numbers than even in the great battle of September 30, "the artillery of the bulwark smote them going and coming, and made great murder of the dogs." The moat filled with the Turkish dead from the devastating enfilade crossfire. "The day might be called very happy," wrote that bedraggled knight, "and well fortunate for us, thanks be to God, for there was none that thought to escape that day but to have died all, and lost the town. The pleasure of our Lord was by evident miracle to have it otherwise, and enemies were chased and overcome."

When the rain stopped and the winds died down and the two sides surveyed the terrible carnage, the conclusion was inescapable that this siege had to end. In 120 days the Turks had not won a single battle, nor had they penetrated into the town or breached the second line of defense. Their dead numbered in the tens of thousands. The defenders, in turn, had lost 120 of the best and most precious men on November 30; few true warriors were left. The gunpowder was nearly depleted; their walls were undermined in countless places. The town was in ruins, and the townspeople on the verge of revolt.

During the first days of December several envoys from the Turkish camp presented themselves at the town's gates under a flag of truce. They were Christians in the sultan's employ and bore the message from the sultan himself to the grand master that if the fortress surrendered, all its defenders would be allowed to live and to leave freely without hindrance and with their property. These envoys were turned away rudely, one hastened along with a shot over his head. But word of the sultan's offer spread rapidly through the town and put "many folk in the thought," wrote the French chronicler, "to save their lives and those of their children rather than to uphold their honor."

At first, Villiers stubbornly resisted any talk of surrender. He proclaimed that all should be ready to stand and fight to the last man, as their vows commanded. But his advisers came back to him, pleading with him to consider the pitiful state of the town, the desperate state of their ordnance, and not to "make the enemy's victory the more splendid by our deaths." No relief from Europe was on its way. They should give up that hope. They were abandoned. "Wise men surrender to necessity," argued a Spanish knight. "No matter how glorious our death, let us consider whether it may not be more damaging to our religion than our surrender." While the high council engaged in this discussion, a delegation from the town pounded on the door.

Their spokesman, a Greek Orthodox merchant, told the grand master circuitously and then bluntly that if he would not surrender, they would surrender the town for him. At length, Villiers turned to his best expert, Gabriele Tadini, and asked for his opinion. Il Bresciano said the town was lost.

On December 10 formal surrender negotiations got under way, as the burgess of Rhodes traveled to Suleyman's stone pavilion. There, the sultan confirmed his offer and swore his sincerity "by his faith." The envoys were dispatched back to Rhodes, wearing a ceremonial robe of velvet and gold cloth that Suleyman had given to them as a token of his good faith. This led to a three-day truce. But in the midst of it, a Christian deserter slipped into the Turkish camp with the news that the lull was merely a gambit to gain time so that the defenders might repair their walls. Suleyman flew into a rage, broke off the talks, and resumed his bombardment. Perhaps not too displeased at the resumption of hostilities, Villiers was ambivalent, unable to fight capably or to surrender gracefully. A few days later, after more assaults were turned back, the grand master wrote a letter to Suleyman, invoking a decades-old promise from Suleyman's predecessor Bayezid II to a previous grand master of Rhodes in which the Knights of Rhodes were guaranteed free possession of the island so long as the House of Osman ruled over the Turks. Under the circumstances, the appeal was absurd, irrelevant, and insulting. Refusing even to show it to Suleyman, the sultan's vizier tore it up in a rage, trampled it in the dirt, and dispatched the messengers back to the fortress with their noses, ears, and fingers cut off. On December 18 the Turks broke through the walls of the Spanish bastion, and fighting took place in the streets of Rhodes for the first time. That was enough. On December 21, Villiers capitulated.

When the agreement was finalized and put in writing, the Turkish forces began to withdraw from the walls. The knights had twelve days to evacuate the city. If more days were needed, the vanquished could have them. Among the terms was the promise that if the knights did not have enough ships to withdraw all of their men and property, including their heavy guns, Suleyman would offer his own ships for the purpose. There would be no tribute for five years, and no attempt to seize Christian boys on the island and send them to Constantinople to be trained as janissaries. Relying upon Suleyman's word, the Knights of Rhodes began gathering their possessions. They fell back on the consolation that their fate was sealed by some mysterious divine plan. "It may be marveled at," wrote the French scribe, "how it was possible to have overcome our enemies in all assaults and skirmishes, and in the end to lose the town. It was the will of God, pleased in some cause to us unknown."

On Christmas Day, four hundred janissaries entered the town . . . and ran amok. They looted houses and entered the churches, smashing crucifixes, breaking relics, even opening the tombs of past grand masters in search of treasure. At the hospital they turned the sick out of their beds and gathered up silver vessels as souvenirs. By the account of the French chronicler, they "forced certain women and maidens." Somewhat languidly, their commander eventually stopped the pillage.

A day later, after the situation was in control, Philippe de Villiers de L'Isle-Adam strapped on his full body armor, including his red breastplate with the large insignia of the order on his chest, his helmet festooned with a large, curving feather, and with his red cape flowing in the breeze rode to the sultan's pavilion accompanied by eighteen knights. This show of proud men in shining armor, heads high, amazed the Turks, who expected to see an exhausted and bedraggled foe. At the pavilion the grand master and his entourage were greeted with honors and great respect. As Villiers entered the pavilion, Suleyman rose from his low, silver chair. He, in turn, was dressed in a long coat of brocade and golden thread with puffed sleeves and golden buttons. An egg-size emerald gleamed from the center of his immense, white beehive turban. They spoke only briefly. The sultan went to lengths to reassure the grand master that he would keep all his promises, and that Villiers should go with his people without fear.

When Villiers turned to leave, Suleyman said to him, "I am sad that you and your followers, who are so courageous and upright, are being forced from your home."

Later, Villiers would write of this encounter with great admiration for his Turkish foe: "He was a knight in the truest sense of the word."

They would see each other one more time when Suleyman himself entered Rhodes to tour the magnificent palace of the Christian grand master and to oversee the conversion of the Church of St. John the Baptist into a mosque.

On January 1, 1523, the Christians boarded some fifty ships and left.

14.

IN THE EXTREMITY
OF HIS AFFLICTION

With the fall of Rhodes not only was the Christian bottleneck between Constantinople and Alexandria removed, but a wedge was driven between the Venetian outposts of Cyprus and Crete. The Ottoman Empire now held sway over the entire eastern Mediterranean. The invasion of Italy itself by Islamic forces could not be far away. As the news of the calamity raced through Europe, the Turkish soldiers were reported to have shouted, "To Rome, to Rome!" as they entered the fortress walls. Rumors that Turkish spies had been spotted in Rome sent its residents again fleeing to the countryside in terror.

In his modest quarters in the Vatican, Pope Adrian VI received the full details of the catastrophe from the Venetian ambassador. When the briefing was over, the pope proclaimed through tears, "Alas, for Christendom. I should have died happy if I had only united the Christian princes to withstand the enemies of Christ." Again, Adrian sent urgent appeals to European kings. He reminded Francis I of the Asiatic sovereigns who had been conquered by the Turks after they were lulled into a false sense of security. To the king of Portugal the pope wrote, "Woe to Princes who do not employ the sovereignty conferred upon them by God and by defending the people of His election, but abuse it in internecine strife." It would not be long before this high-minded pope was himself promoting internecine strife.

But kings were not listening. Unfairly and outrageously, Charles V laid the blame on the pope. If only the pontiff had granted him the favors that his predecessors had never refused, the danger might have been averted. His sense of regret was perfunctory and, as usual, couched in high-minded rhetoric. Someday, the emperor promised, he would avenge the defeat of Rhodes "as a sacrifice to God, if such be needed, to aid and sustain our holy Christian faith as its true advocate and protector of its holy seat and temporal head of Christendom." At these empty words, Adrian was justified in his disgust.

The three central goals that Adrian had set for himself at the beginning of his papacy were fading into oblivion. In the north, heresy was rife and spreading; in the east the Muslim infidels were advancing; and soon enough, in the Christian heartland, war would break out among the Christian brethren. As he was ignored by kings, so he was scorned by the Roman people, who were confounded by his sanctimony, his indifference to Roman culture, and his indecisiveness. The story spread that on the very day that Rhodes fell, a piece of marble molding over the door of the pope's chapel had fallen and killed a papal guard, just as the pope was entering to pray. This was widely interpreted as a sign of God's wrath at the inability of the pope to protect the true religion.

Meanwhile, the sad flotilla bearing the displaced Knights of Rhodes made its way to Italy. In the lead ship, the grand master, Philippe de Villiers de L'Isle-Adam, eschewed flying the order's normal red flag with its distinctive Maltese cross and instead hoisted a white banner, bearing the image of the Virgin Mary with her dead son in her arms and the Latin inscription *Afflictis tu spes unica rebus* (In the extremity of my affliction, You are my only hope). In defeat, the grand master was flaunting his devotion to the Holy Mother, but also rebuking Christianity for abandoning its holy warriors. After some weeks the fleet of refugees dropped anchor at the papal naval base of Civitavecchia. There, the natives gawked at the remarkable figure of Villiers, tall and white-haired, proud and now famous around the Christian world as a great and courageous leader. But his fame was not enough.

To the Vatican the grand master sent word requesting an audience with the pontiff. He wished to know where the Holy See would designate the next home for its sacred militia. There was talk of Crete, Elba, Majorca, and Malta. But time passed without a summons to the Holy See. Villiers was put off indefinitely and inexplicably. He was instructed to settle his order in port patiently while other arrangements for the Knights of St. John were considered.

Only in the summer of 1523 did it become clear why Adrian was avoiding a meeting with this French hero. France and the Vatican were becoming enemies. Francis I had instructed French churches to send no more money to Rome. In August, Adrian dropped all pretense of neutrality and concluded a treaty with the emperor, Henry VIII, Venice, and several other Italian states to defend Italy against France. His last vow of neutrality among Christian princes was dead. In their narrow view, Italians cheered the scrapping of neutrality. "It is time to drink and dance," wrote one Roman observer. "I can not tell you how ardently the whole city rejoices at this treaty on which the salvation of our land and the whole of Christendom depends."

Shortly after this papal declaration of war against a Christian prince, Adrian fell ill, and only in his infirmity, perhaps with a guilty conscience, did he agree to see the grand master. The day appointed was September 1, 1523. Villiers entered Rome with great pomp, escorted by grandees of the papal court. Cardinals turned out as a group to greet their hero, who, by contrast to the Christian kings of Europe, had shown such courage in defense of the faith. When he came into the papal apartments, Adrian summoned his strength and rose from his sickbed to greet the Christian champion. Villiers prostrated himself before the cadaverous pope, kissing his feet. As the grand master shared the details of the Rhodes defense, the pope wilted and returned to his bed, his heart as well as his health broken. Before he left, the grand master was proclaimed to be an athlete of Christ and officially, like Henry VIII, Charles V, and Francis I, a Defender of the Faith.

Two weeks later, on September 14, Adrian VI died. Throughout Rome his passing was greeted with relief and even jubilation. Inevitably, in the grand tradition of papal deaths, the rumor circulated that his physician had poisoned him. "The city was never more glad of a Pope's death," the English ambassador wrote to Cardinal Wolsey. "Some light-brained fellow hung a wreath on his physician's door, inscribed with the words, 'To the deliverer of his country, of the senate, and the people of Rome.'" It was time to return the papacy to its mellow and sumptuous Italian roots. Adrian's epitaph emphasized the poignancy and even tragedy of his well-intentioned papacy:

"Here lies Adrian VI, who looked upon it as his greatest misfortune to be called upon to rule."

As Adrian was buried, Francis I invaded Italy.

ACT FOUR

THE CAPTURE
OF A KING

✠

15.

THE GREAT PLAN

In the fall of 1523 the advance of Islam through the Balkans to Belgrade and beyond seemed far away and out of mind to the potentates of Europe. Their attention was focused on Rome, where the death of the unpopular Dutchman Adrian VI brought new opportunities and new risks. At first, the pope's death seemed to favor Francis I. Now pressing his military campaign to regain control of Lombardy, the French king was determined to travel to Rome to advocate for a French candidate. But the imperial forces, now in control of Milan and commanded by the traitor to the French cause Charles, duke of Bourbon, blocked his way.

Giulio de' Medici emerged as the leading candidate. Tall and graceful, in excellent health, forty-five years old, a patron of the arts and literature, he was the cousin of Leo X, who had brought extravagance and permissiveness to the Vatican during his reign from 1513 to 1521. Giulio de' Medici had been his most trusted adviser and had been known for his steady judgments, his abstemious personal habits, his initiative, and his high-mindedness. Now he was vice-chancellor, second-in-command to the pope himself, and he controlled vast territory in the north of Italy radiating outward from his post as archbishop of Florence. With so vast an episcopal domain, containing many bishoprics and abbeys, he derived considerable income. If he was elected, he promised to spread these lucrative benefices generously among his supporters. Giulio de' Medici enjoyed a high reputation as a statesman in the Curia. Sentiment was strong for a lusty Roman pope who would return Rome to the relaxed times of Leo X, when there was a "flourishing Court and a brave Pontificate." Under another Medici the arts and science would blossom once again.

But he had powerful rivals. Henry VIII was promoting the candidacy of Cardinal Wolsey, lord chancellor of England, who was a major presence in Rome since his election as cardinal in 1514. After the exotic, austere papacy of Adrian VI, however, another foreign pope was unlikely. A more powerful competitor was the Roman baron Cardinal Pompeo Colonna, whose fiefdoms stretched across southern Italy and included Naples and who possessed an equal ability to spread his benefices among his supporters. In an effort to block Medici, Colonna fell into league with the French contingent and a group of older cardinals and controlled a bloc of nineteen cardinals in opposition.

On October 1, the thirty-five electors convened in the Sistine Chapel. As a symbol of his status as front-runner, Giulio de' Medici was escorted to Julius II's old cell, beneath the Perugino painting of St. Peter receiving the keys to Rome. He stood for election unabashedly as the candidate of the Empire and Charles V. Two years before as a Knight of Rhodes, he had ridden into Milan at the head of the imperial army displacing French forces, and thus he was known as a soldier as well as a priest. As a further gesture of support for the Medici candidate, the refugee grand master of the Knights of Rhodes, Philippe de Villiers de L'Isle-Adam, defeated by Suleyman in Rhodes only months earlier, was put in charge of security and secrecy for the conclave.

Days stretched out with no decision as the cardinals quarreled and jockeyed. Older cardinals set themselves up in opposition to younger cardinals. The French bloc was pitted against the imperials. Even when their food was reduced to one meal a day as an incentive, no decision was reached. Ambassadors and nobles cajoled to no avail. Days stretched into weeks as rival candidates were put forward and faltered. At last, in mid-November the deadlock was finally broken only when three latecomers arrived, bringing the number of electors to thirty-eight. This tilted the balance toward the

Medici candidate. Then Cardinal Colonna fell into a disagreement with his French cohorts. "Let each one act for himself," he declared, and withdrew from the bloc. Seeing this, Medici promised his rival the vice-chancellory and a fabulous palace in Rome if he came over to the winning side. Reluctantly, the unhappy Colonna did so. Later, with major implications for the future, Cardinal Colonna would not let the new pope forget who had been responsible for his election. The other holdouts soon fell into line.

On November 19, exactly two years to the day after he had entered Milan at the head of an imperial army, Giulio de' Medici was unanimously elected. Like Adrian before him, he wished to retain his own name as pope. But he was dissuaded from this course out of superstition. Since, as pointed out persuasively, every pope who had exercised this vanity before had been dead within a year. Consequently, he took the name Clement VII.

Upon the election the representative of Charles V wrote to the emperor, "Giulio de' Medici is your creature. Your power is now so great that it can transform stones into obedient sons." But once he took the throne, Clement would not be so obedient.

Jubilation greeted Clement's election, in Rome and across Europe. The French ambassador acquiesced in his elevation, and Henry VIII regarded him as an acceptable alternative to his temporary favorite, Cardinal Wolsey. Even Vittoria Colonna, the poetess of the rival family, sang his praises: "Praised be the Lord forever. May he further this beginning to such ends, that men may see that there was never wrought a greater blessing, nor one which was so grounded on reason." Another cardinal exulted as well, "Clement VII will be the greatest and wisest, as well as the most respected pope whom the Church has seen for centuries." The English ambassador was no less effusive: "There is as much craft and policy in him as any man on earth," he wrote home. The doge in Venice promised to send his noblest men to the coronation a week later to worship the new pope as "a divinity on earth." When the coronation took place, people noted with satisfaction that by contrast to the extravaganza of his Medici cousin's coronation, no outlandish spectacle and no jesters appeared at the coronation banquet.

First acts of a new pope always had an impact, and Clement seemed to appreciate their importance. He announced himself as a pope who understood world affairs by attempting to separate Switzerland from France. Immediately, he showed that he knew how to play the political game; he distributed a large number of benefices to his supporters. "He granted more favors on the first day of his reign than Adrian did in his whole lifetime," a beneficiary remarked. Better yet, unlike his predecessors, Clement asked for nothing in return for his generosity. His first masses were admired not only for their decorousness but for the fine, handsome figure that he presented to the world. (The Medici were generally homely.) "There is no one," wrote the Venetian ambassador, "who celebrates mass with so much beauty and piety of demeanor."

Not many weeks into the new papacy, however, opinions about the new pope began to change. His strengths as an adviser to the previous Medici pope did not easily translate when he was the holder of the office himself. For his two chief advisers Clement appointed champions of the competing French and imperial sides. Supporting the French side was Gian Matteo Giberti. Illegitimate by birth, deeply spiritual, and ascetic in his demeanor, a member of the mystical cult called Oratory of Divine Love, he was a sincere reformer by instinct. The pope immediately made Giberti the bishop of Verona, where in the coming years he instituted exemplary reforms for the clergy that might even have pleased Luther. Giberti both advocated for Francis I and had an instinctive sympathy for real reform in the Church. Giberti's counterpart was a Saxon, Nicholas of Schomberg, the archbishop of Capua, a Dominican and devotee of Savonarola, and a partisan of the Empire.

This competing counsel, of course, made it more difficult for the pope to pursue a confident, consistent course. He vacillated on whether he was responsible for the political alliances of his predecessor, especially Adrian's Holy League with Charles V, Henry VIII, the duke of Milan, and the princes of Florence, Genoa, and Siena, in opposition to the French incursion in the north. Because Clement set no firm commitment, the emperor quickly realized that the new pope was not his creature at all. Perhaps he was no one's creature, but merely a fatally indecisive Medici. The House of

Medici had risen to its vaunted status precisely by playing powerful sides off against one another and trying to offend no one.

Still, decisive or not, the issues facing the new pope were formidable. Luther's revolt raged in Germany. The war in Lombardy seesawed between the great powers, and the hostility between France and the Empire seemed intractable. Hovering above it all was the relentless advance of Suleyman and his Turks into the Balkans. The spiritual and the temporal authority of the Roman Church was under severe attack both from within and from without, making the future of the papacy uncertain. To Clement, the freedom and independence of the Papal States seemed to be the most pressing issue. To protect the papal patrimony was the first duty of all popes.

But how to do this? Ideally, Clement hoped to arrange peace between the powers. The Holy Father soon became aware, however, that the hostility between the powers was beyond negotiation. He must try to choose the winning side. If he chose France, he stood to undermine his influence with Charles on the Luther insurgency. If he chose the Empire, the independence of the Papal States themselves were at risk, for he certainly did not want to receive Charles V as the conqueror of Italy. If he could not unite the Christian powers, perhaps at least he could counterbalance them. Naples to the south belonged to Charles and the Empire. For the time being, Milan in the north was in the hands of the French. Clement tried at first to adopt strict neutrality between the warring parties in Lombardy. But maintaining neutrality in the months ahead would require the most skillful Machiavellian maneuvering, all the more so because the pope was operating from a position of severe weakness. That the pope was proving himself to be a congenital procrastinator made the Vatican's position all the more weak and desperate.

Early in the spring of 1524 the new pope's attention turned to the challenge from within. The Second Imperial Diet was gathering in Nuremberg. This would afford the pope an opportunity to proclaim his position on Luther. As his envoy, he tapped the estimable Cardinal Lorenzo Campeggio, an able and experienced papal statesman, and dispatched him north with considerable fanfare. His instructions were to mollify the obstreperous elector Frederick, to bring the diet to heel, and to reconfirm the Edict of Worms with its most important provision: to drag the heretic Martin Luther to the burning place. But once Campeggio passed into Germany, the ceremony of his journey dropped away dramatically. In Augsburg, his benediction to a crowd was greeted with jeers and insults. When he arrived in Nuremberg, the streets were cold and empty, with no official greeting.

Charles V too had sent his envoy to his imperial diet with no less forceful a set of instructions. Charles was furious that his edict remained unfulfilled. To him Luther was "worse than Mohammed." To the assemblage, Cardinal Campeggio dutifully expressed his wonder that "so many great and honorable princes should suffer the religion, rites, and ceremonies wherein they were born and bred, to be abolished and trampled upon." The imperial envoy recalled that these same princes had passed the Edict of Worms unanimously three years before. It must now be executed. Luther must be put to death.

These appeals met a chilly reception. Even the danger of the Turkish invasion did not seem to move the conclave. When the appeals were finished, the German princes turned the tables abruptly. Had they not sent a hundred grievances to the Vatican the year before, with demands for reform? What was the pope's answer? What reforms would be instituted? Feigning surprise at this impertinence, Campeggio at first pled administrative mix-up due to the death of Adrian, but then made the mistake of patronizing the assembly. True, the grievances had arrived in Rome, but "the pope and the College of Cardinals could not believe that they had been framed by the princes. It was thought that some private persons had published them in their hatred of the Roman Curia. Thus, he had no answer to their complaints." At this high-handedness, the hall erupted in indignation.

The German princes also faced a delicate problem. They could not repeal the Edict of Worms. But to enforce it, especially to burn Luther at the stake, would plunge the entire region into a bloody sectarian war. Predictably, they sought to compromise. The diet would carry out the Edict of Worms "as well as they were able, and as far as was possible." Theoretically,

that confirmed the edict and satisfied the Vatican's demand. But the diet
went on to propose that "so that the good not be rooted up with the bad,"
a general council be convened to consider these weighty matters in dispute.
(A general council, of course, was abhorrent to the Vatican, for by defini-
tion it would undermine papal authority.) During this "recess" the learned
doctors in German universities were to study the disputes in doctrine. For
the time being the old policy of exterminating heretics, especially Luther,
was abandoned. Quiet scholarly deliberation of the new ideas was put in its
place. To the papal legate the phrase about the good and the bad implied
approval of Luther, and Campeggio objected strenuously. To him the heretic could speak no good whatever.

Inevitably, the compromise satisfied no one. When the details of the
diet reached Rome, the pope was outraged. Rightly, he saw the diet as a
setback and an insult. Immediately he wrote a letter of complaint to Charles
V, enumerating four points to remedy the situation. Most important was
the first. The Edict of Worms must be strictly enforced. Second, a scholarly
examination of disputed doctrinal positions was, at all costs, to be prevented; matters of doctrine were the province of Rome alone. Third, no
council was to be convened. The Vatican would not be judged. However, in
a bone thrown to the German princes, a congregation of prelates in Rome
would take up their grievances. And last, the rebellious protector of Luther,
the elector of Saxony, must be deposed.

If, during the winter of 1524, the attack from within was deeply worrisome for Rome, the military situation in the north of Italy in that spring
turned even worse. In April, Lannoy, the imperial viceroy in Naples, forced
the French to abandon Milan and sent their troops scurrying over the Alps.
Now imperial dominions surrounded the fragile Papal States north and
south. The duke of Bourbon was firmly in control for the Empire in Lombardy. Driven by hatred, he was itching to follow up the imperial triumph
in Milan with an invasion of France itself, confident that would spark an
insurrection against Francis I. Vainly, the new pope attempted to forge an
armistice between the great powers, but his overture was brushed aside.

In Spain, Charles V laid out an ambitious plan for a coordinated attack on France. Bourbon was to come from Italy and conquer Provence before moving into Burgundy. Charles himself would cross the Pyrenees through Rousillon with eighteen thousand Spanish troops and ten thousand Germans and move into Toulouse. And Henry VIII was to cross the Channel to Calais and invade the province of Picardy. When these forces squeezed Francis I out of power, Bourbon would capture Lyon and move on Paris. Once there, he proposed to crown Henry VIII king of France in Reims. This would become known as the Great Plan, and it would hover over European politics for the coming few years.

In the summer the plan was launched, but not quite as it had been imagined. Bourbon entered France, crossed the Var on July 1, took Aix easily with the help of a compliant mayor, and laid siege to Marseille on August 14. Grandiosely, he proclaimed himself to be the duke of Provence. But Charles delayed his advance, and Henry VIII, wilting at the cost of this adventure, procrastinated in England to await developments. Meanwhile, Francis I, far from being the unpopular monarch that Bourbon thought, began to raise a tremendous army in Avignon. The bastion of Marseille held out heroically for over a month, and it gradually became apparent that Bourbon's force was insufficient for the job. The stout defense of Marseille caused a rift in the imperial ranks. The marquis of Pescara was the Spanish commander, and he began to see the futility of the siege, as well as the danger of the ballooning French army poised nearby. On September 28, he raised the siege and began a retreat. Bourbon followed with his force.

Suddenly, Francis I was in the ascendant. Hearing the reports of the imperial retreat, the French king gave the order to chase, and the pursued became the pursuer. His army was sixty miles to the northwest of Marseille in Avignon, but his initial way through the valley of the Durance was swifter. The race to Milan was on. The two armies marched in parallel. Bourbon moved to Nice, passed through the Tenda Pass at the western end of the Maritime Alps, and marched to Genoa. Francis I tarried briefly at Aix, long enough to behead the mayor who had let the imperial traitor into his town, before he moved to the formidable passes of the Cottian Alps. On this northern route the pass through to Italy was higher; at nearly ten thousand feet, the Col de la Traversette was already clogged with snow. Pulling the heavy artillery over this height was a Herculean task. Francis fretted at the delays. But the two armies were so close as they entered the plain of Lombardy that the French general, the duke of Montmorency, could harass the flanks of the imperial army.

In the fall of 1524, Milan, long the touchstone for political dominance in Europe, ordinarily the richest province in Europe, was no prize. For over a year, like Rome, the city had been in the grip of the plague. Wharf rats swarmed through the narrow streets. Thirty thousand people had died. The walls were in poor repair, and the city had no stock of food. So with the French army snapping at his heels, Bourbon bypassed the pestilential town to concentrate his forces in a crescent of river fortresses in the central valley of the Po: Pavia, Piacenza, Cremona, and Alessandria.

On October 28 Francis I entered Milan and was warmly welcomed by the remaining healthy citizens. Leaving four thousand men to garrison the town, he pushed on without delay to confront the enemy at Pavia. A year before, the French king had been beaten and harassed on all sides, his very kingdom at risk from hostile monarchs who surrounded him. Now he was transformed, brash and confident at the head of an immense army. Not only Milan but Naples seemed within his grasp. He stood on the brink of realizing the ancestral dream of his predecessors, the completion of a thirty-year effort to establish French dominance in Italy, and the satisfaction of the French claim to Milan that extended back to 1447.

The French situation, however, contained an element of illusion. From the hardship of the march, from skirmishes and from plague, the French army had been whittled down to about twenty-four thousand. A substantial portion of those were Swiss mercenaries who were there only for the pay and could disappear on the first day of lost wages. A Spanish commander wrote to Charles V that of the twenty-four thousand enemy, only about ten thousand were equal to the defenders. The opposing general, the Spaniard, the marquis of Pescara, looked out from his riverine bastions with satisfaction. Francis had made a strategic mistake.

"We were vanquished," said the marquis. "Now we are victors."

16.

THE LAST BATTLE
IN THE AGE OF CHIVALRY

Pavia was well suited for defense. A tributary of the Po, the Ticino River, protected the southern border of the town. To the north of the town lay a broad, triangular park. This huge ducal chase fanned outward from the town some three miles. The town's formidable fortress was built into the town's high walls and faced north to the park. A fifteen-foot wall surrounded the broad park and was fortified by towers, the most prominent of which was called the Torre del Gallo. In the middle of this park was a hunting lodge called Castello Mirabello. A hundred small canals striated this vast enclosure.

As the season moved toward winter, the park became a virtual swamp. Fog routinely covered the area until midday. The soft ground was covered with ferns and aquatic plants and dotted with massive black poplars. Francis approached the town from the north, took charge of a complex of abbeys and churches (the five-abbeys area) east of the city, then invested the park itself, making his headquarters in the Castello Mirabello. His soldiers dug trenches. As the October rains turned to November frosts, the ground of the park became a waterlogged quagmire, which made it impossible for the French to drag their heavy artillery pieces close to the city walls.

The imperial commander in Pavia, Antonio de Leyva, cut a most unusual figure for a heroic military commander. He weighed less than eighty pounds; his gout reduced him to a chair, for he could not walk; and he was constantly in pain. Yet in his determination, this bag of bones was as fierce as any strapping athlete. To his credit were a string of remarkable victories. But now in this era of the mercenary, perhaps his greatest challenge was how to pay his soldiers. He had famously succeeded in this by pillaging the strongboxes of churches and melting down the silver plate of religious altars, including the treasures of the famous Certosa, the Carthusian monastery outside the town walls, whose large and ornate façade was considered the highest expression of Renaissance art in Lombardy. In Pavia, de Leyva commanded nine thousand Swiss and German soldiers called landsknechts, professional soldiers all who expected to be paid for their pains.

The initial days of the struggle saw sallies and skirmishes, some fierce enough to cause considerable loss of life. Several times the French breached the walls of the town with their heavy artillery. But de Leyva had built earthen works behind, with killing fields in between, so nothing came of this. Soon enough heavy rain and frost made any significant attack impossible. On December 4, the defenders drove the French back into their trenches, and the invaders settled in for a long siege. Francis was in no hurry. He would be just as satisfied to starve out the town as to conquer it. By contrast, the imperialists were confident of their ability to hold Pavia for weeks to come, having provisioned the town for a long siege. The food supply was not luxurious, but adequate. In this stalemate, Bourbon left for Nuremberg to raise a fresh contingent of landsknechts, and Francis split off nearly ten thousand troops and dispatched them south toward Naples under the command of the duke of Albany.

Meanwhile, in Rome, Clement VII viewed these developments with satisfaction. Again a balance of power had been established in Italy, France versus the Empire, with the Papal States safely sandwiched in between. In Lombardy the French looked like sure winners. Perhaps it was time to make his choice. The lure of temporal power proved irresistible. Persuaded by the French victories and forgetting the much more serious threats of Luther and Suleyman, as well as his duty as the supreme spiritual leader of

Christendom to rise above the ambitions of mortal men, the pope abandoned his neutrality and forged an alliance with Francis. Yet again the Vatican had switched horses.

"What would you have me do?" he protested to the doubters. "The French are strong, and I cannot resist them. The imperial army needs money, and I have none to give. The emperor is far off and cannot help me."

On December 12, a new round of alliance was made in this scene of ever-shifting coalitions. As part of the agreement, the pope permitted a French expeditionary force to pass safely through papal territories to Naples. In an obsequious letter, the pope wrote to Charles on January 5, 1525, that "unwillingly and under pressure" he'd agreed to submit to the French.

Predictably, the emperor was appalled when he received the pope's apologia. "The pope thinks that I am but a youth, scarcely knowing what I do," he fumed. "I entered this war for him alone. I have lost money, men, and friends for his sake. I have risked my honor and even my soul. I could never have believed that he would desert me. However, I do not despair, nor will I yield. I will go to Italy to seek revenge on all who have wronged me, especially this poltroon of a pope." Then, almost as an afterthought, he added, "Perhaps someday Martin Luther will become a man of worth."

A dangerous personal grudge had been established. The pope had trivialized his office by becoming a mere profane leader of a small, weak state, and Charles would deal with him now as such. More than that, the behavior of the pope demonstrated Luther's point for Charles: perhaps Christendom could do without a pope.

Meanwhile, in Pavia, the days stretched into weeks, and the weeks became several months, and in this winter season, the siege went soft. In the broad park to the north, safely beyond the range of imperial batteries along the town's walls, the French set up stalls and markets. Peddlers and whores flooded into the French encampment, swelling the settlement by thousands. Laughter, dance, music, and wine replaced military discipline. Francis himself set up a lavish court whose warmth and high spirits attracted his nobles from their grim, damp command posts. By day the king hunted with his falcons, which he had brought along as an amusement, and by evening gloried in the convivial companionship of his childhood friends, the duke of Montmorency and Bonnivet, the admiral of France, both of whom he had elevated to supreme command over more experienced and skilled generals. This court feasted on the fat of Lombardy and imported famous ladies for entertainment, while behind the town walls the defenders ate mules and cats and burned the beams of churches to keep warm.

But the imperials were pursuing a wider strategy. While the French danced the winter weeks away in the park, the imperials were provisioning and reinforcing their strongholds at Cremona and Lodi, only a few miles to the north of Pavia. As these bastions became stronger, they would act as a band of containment for the French. If the siege of Pavia could be broken, the French army could be trapped between the garrison of Pavia and fresh imperial troops who were soon expected from Germany. Meanwhile, Bourbon had spent a productive month away from the battleground. In Innsbruck and Nuremberg, he had recruited an additional twelve thousand landsknechts, under the command of the old Swabian warhorse George von Frundsberg. They were now crossing the Alps into the Po Valley. Bourbon was there to meet them in mid-January. The race was now as much financial as military. Bourbon's funds to pay for these fresh troops were so minimal that he had pawned his family's remaining jewels in Innsbruck. As he prepared these reinforcements for battle, Bourbon wrote to Henry VIII and Cardinal Wolsey, urging them to invade northern France while the French king was out of the country. Bourbon had not given up his dream of a triumphal return to his homeland, where he longed to reclaim his ancestral lands and to settle scores.

By mid-January 1525 the imperial reinforcements, along with their provisions and guns, were in place at Lodi, fully expecting a quick resolution. The imperial force now numbered about twenty-five thousand, so the armies were essentially equal in strength. In the several weeks that followed, the imperial army maneuvered through the towns to the east of Pavia, hoping to lure the French army away from Pavia into a pitched battle, thereby lifting the siege. But Francis did not take the bait. His spies had informed him of the desperate financial state of the enemy. If he could hold out in place for only a few more weeks, he had every expectation that the imperial force would disintegrate.

Indeed this strategy of delay seemed to be working. The sides maneuvered and traded artillery fire among the five abbeys to the east of the city as the imperial force drew closer, but no strategic advantage was achieved by either side. Some funds arrived from Austrian banks, and this mollified the imperial mercenaries for a few additional days. But casualties were mounting with no gain, and disaffection was rising. The hero of the Spanish foot soldier, the marquis of Pescara, was forced back on his eloquence to convince his soldiers to persevere a little while longer without pay. Still, the great armies were now close and locked in an embrace.

In Rome, the pope fretted as the armies drew closer into a death grip. On February 19 his Francophile adviser, Giberti, wrote of the pope's mood: "I cannot tell you how great has been the Pope's anxiety and suspense, now that the armies are near one another. Though he has great confidence in the forces of the French king, still the love which he bears [Francis] cannot be without fear of the dangers which war brings with it." Still the pope and his advisers hung on to the pipe dream of peace.

"The desire which the Pope always had to bring about some peace or truce rather than risk everything on a battle has greatly increased," Giberti wrote. "Day and night His Holiness hugs this thought." The papal legate in Lombardy, Cardinal Salviati, shuttled between the camps looking for some form of accommodation and attempting to recapture a semblance of neutrality. To Francis, Salviati said, "As no sailor ever risks the storm of the open sea with one anchor only, so the pope, confident though he is in your strength, will not stake all upon the single throw."

Other commentators saw the situation more clearly. The papacy found itself between the perilous rocks of Scylla and Charybdis, the papal adviser Guicciardini wrote. Again seizing upon the anchor and the stormy-sea image, Guicciardini saw the pope as a sailor who kept more than one anchor in readiness. If the French prevailed, the pope would place his anchor there. If Spain won, he would anchor beside the emperor. But he would never be too firmly anchored anywhere. In fact, the pope would soon be anchored nowhere.

Nevertheless, a bet on the French side still looked good. Two days later, on February 21, the imperial commander, the marquis of Lannoy, made his desperation manifest. His commander inside Pavia had sent word that he was out of money completely. If relief did not come within a few days, he would have to surrender the city. "In three or four days," Lannoy said, "we must make contact with the garrison inside the town or all is lost." And if they did not join up with the garrison, they could not easily retreat either. With the French army now so close, an abrupt imperial retreat would invite disaster.

Money was driving the issue. This was a war of the poverty-stricken. The imperial commanders knew now that some dramatic thrust was required. In a council of war, with no thought that this would force the cataclysmic battle, but only satisfy the demand for action, they settled on a plan to breach the park wall on the north side, seize the Castello Mirabello, which they thought was the headquarters of the French king, then break for the town walls to relieve the hard-pressed imperial garrison. February 24 was settled upon as the day for the strike, a day that held symbolic significance. It was not only St. Matthias's Day,* but also the birthday of Emperor Charles V.

Toward midnight the imperial pioneers crept quietly to the extreme north end of the park and set about to undermine the fifteen-foot wall near a gate known later as Porta Pescarina (in honor of the Spanish commander the marquis of Pescara). They could not use explosives for fear of alerting the slumbering French, so the work was slow and tedious. As the sappers dug, the main force of the imperial army, some ten thousand soldiers, moved toward the demolition operation. They wore white cassocks over their armor or displayed white squares on their doublets for recognition in the dark and the fog. As the night proceeded, it began to dawn on the French that something was up at the north end. But the gloom prevented any exact

---

* Matthias took the place of Judas among the Apostles (Acts 1:26).

conclusion. Still, three thousand Swiss soldiers were detailed north from the Torre del Gallo. At 5 a.m. artillery fire erupted near the Torre del Gallo. This noise, along with the command to keep the campfires burning in the five-abbeys area to the east of the park, was intended as a diversion, and it proved effective.

As dawn broke, the breach was sufficient to allow a column of three thousand imperial forces to enter the enclosure. Once inside, rangers were dispatched to two gates in the north wall. When these were taken, the rest of the imperial army began to funnel into the park, with a vanguard of imperials, armed with rudimentary rifles known as arquebuses, moving south through woods toward the Castello Mirabello. The first engagements took place only a few hundred yards from the Porta Pescarina. In the fog and early-morning mist, line commanders could not determine the size of the opposing forces and considered these contacts mere skirmishes. By 6:30 a.m., however, the Spanish arquebusiers reached the castle. To their surprise, it was not the French headquarters at all, and it was lightly defended. They took it with ease. At about this time, upon a signal of three artillery shots, a party of ragged imperial soldiers stormed out of the garrison of Pavia and engaged the Swiss enemy in the five abbeys to the east of the town.

Without realizing it, the imperial movements had split the French army into three. Several days before, Francis I had moved his headquarters to the northwest quadrant of the park. The imperial thrust to the castle now separated him from his forces in the northeast quadrant. Meanwhile, the raid out of Pavia itself held down the Swiss around the Torre del Gallo on the east. At the breach in the north wall, the duke of Bourbon supervised the columns streaming into the park, which now included the disciplined landsknechts commanded by George von Frundsberg, batteries of light artillery, and cavalry under Lannoy, the viceroy of Naples, and the marquis of Pescara. Adding to the confusion of the weather were the hundreds of camp followers who had been leeching off the French army for two months. They were caught between the maneuvering forces now, and many were slaughtered.

By 7 a.m. the situation moved from scattered contact to the positioning of major formations for pitched battle. From a strategic standpoint, the imperial battalions now held the central position around the castle. Francis I, to the left, commanded some ten thousand soldiers, including his vaunted heavy cavalry. The king was now fully in command of the situation. He finally realized the danger of his divided force in the northern region of the park. But he was confident in the stoutness of his Swiss contingent to the south and completely unaware of the imperial thrust out of the Pavia garrison toward the Torre del Gallo.

Francis was most confident of his cavalry. It was his pride, his cherished "hares in armor," the heroes who had broken the Swiss ten years earlier at Marignano. These horsemen were more heavily armored than their Spanish counterparts, and the king deployed them now in a charge against a line commanded by Lannoy. The lines clashed in a terrible melee. Within a few minutes, the imperial line buckled and scattered. In disarray these Spanish horsemen fled into a dense wood to the east. "There is no hope left except in God," Lannoy is reported to have said. As the imperials were penned up in the dense eastern woods, Francis, in an equal apocryphal remark, gloated, "Now I am really the duke of Milan." But he neglected to notice that the charge of his heroic cavalry had taken place ahead of the French artillery. Therefore, the French cannons could not be brought into action without killing their own men.

As Lannoy tried to regain control of his routed cavalry, his fellow general, the marquis of Pescara, came to the rescue. On the open ground, the French cavalry, now completely unsupported, was regrouping after its successful charge. While they did so, Pescara brought up some three thousand arquebusiers, and they began firing on the French. Meanwhile, north of this action, the duke of Bourbon, near the breach, deployed a contingent of four thousand landsknechts to the south. They fell on the left flank of the French cavalry. And south of this action, Frundsberg's landsknechts fell on a Swiss force half its size and drove it backward toward the Torre del Gallo. From a distance Francis cried, "My God, what's this?" as he saw the Swiss force disintegrate in the distance.

By 8 a.m. the French cavalry was surrounded, and its annihilation commenced. One by one, its nobility was cut down, the very flower of France: its grand master, its admiral, its marshal, the master of the king's horse, even "the White Rose," the rebel duke of Suffolk. Large columns splintered into small bands and fought hand to hand with imperial pikemen . . . until it came down to the king himself. By all accounts, with his massive size and tremendous strength, a cloth of silver over his armor, a great plume flowing from his helmet, a caparison of fleurs-de-lis covering the flanks of his huge charger, Francis I fought well, until his great horse was finally brought down, and the king found himself engulfed by imperials ready to slice him up, steal his armor, and secure their rightful king's ransom. But then, the medieval annals tell us, Lannoy, the viceroy of Naples, who was fighting nearby, realized the situation and rode in chivalrously to rescue the French king. Once a circle was cleared around the monarch, it is written that Lannoy knelt before the king, took his sword with its signature salamander seal, then presented his own sword to the king as a mark of respect.

Then the marquis escorted the French monarch to safety . . . and captivity.

17.

My Honor and My Life

The Battle of Pavia was the pivotal battle in the Italian Wars of the early sixteenth century and the climax of the struggle between France and the Hapsburgs. Though it went uncelebrated by Shakespeare, it would be linked to the Battle of Agincourt more than a century earlier as a historic disaster for France. As at Agincourt, the nobility of France was essentially wiped out at Pavia, either through death or capture. If Henry V would celebrate St. Crispin's Day, so Charles V could celebrate the feast of St. Matthias, the replacement Apostle. That Charles's chief rival in Europe was now his prisoner made France's humiliation all the greater, a memorable birthday indeed for the young German monarch. For another century, the balance of power in Europe shifted away from France to Spain, Germany, and the vast domain of the Hapsburg family. For the foreseeable future, there would be only one superpower in Europe. But the Hapsburg empire would now be challenged by an empire far greater and more powerful than France: the oriental superpower, the imperium of Suleyman the Magnificent.

The battle had other consequences. The vaunted prowess of the Swiss as the most fearsome mercenaries of Europe was undermined. Demoralized by lack of payment, they had fought poorly at Pavia. Most were killed or captured by Frundsberg's landsknechts. Hundreds drowned in the Ticino River. From a geopolitical standpoint, European nations struggled to adjust to this extraordinary turn of events. Venice, the chameleon of Europe that was forever looking out for its commercial interests, had the best response to the capture of the French king.

"Being a friend of both sovereigns," said the doge of Venice, Andrea Gritti, "I can only say, with the Apostle: I rejoice with them that do rejoice and weep with them that weep."

With this titanic struggle, the nature of warfare changed. No longer was the armored man or force of armored men the most important factor in battle. Now artillery, both cannon and rifle, decided the outcome. The devastating impact of the Spanish arquebusiers against the heavy French cavalry was noted throughout Europe. The new weapon, the forerunner of the musket and the rifle, became a standard in European armies within a few years. Thus, the Battle of Pavia may be viewed as the last battle for heroic chivalry and the first battle of modern warfare.

The ferocious combat had lasted only about two hours. Francis I had been captured around nine in the morning. He had with him no clothes or purse, only his armor, and he was wounded in the final skirmish. But the imposing French king had fought boldly and chivalrously, surrendering only when he was defenseless. The news of the battle spread quickly. By noon, it was known in Milan, and within days much of Europe knew. Francis had, of course, anticipated no such catastrophe. In his royal tent, important papers were found, including compromising documents that proved his secret support of the dukes of Gelderland and Württemberg, German rebels who were seeking to undermine imperial rule.

On the evening of the battle, he was taken to a nearby monastery, where his wounds were dressed, and he was supplied with suitable clothes. A few days later he was moved to the imperial stronghold of Pizzighettone near Cremona, where he would stay for the next few months. Understandably, he was frantic about what would happen now. How long would he be kept? What was to happen in France? What terms would be offered for his release? What had happened to the mission of the duke of Albany to Naples? Would the emperor permit Francis to negotiate his own release personally? Within his own ancestry, he had an additional reason to fret.

His father, Charles of Valois, had been the count of Angoulême. A generation before him, the English had kept another prince of Angoulême, Jean d'Orléans, prisoner for thirty-two years, from 1412 to 1444. Was it conceivable that Francis would suffer the same fate?

Once he was able, Francis wrote two letters, one to his estimable and capable mother, Louise of Savoy, the other to Emperor Charles V himself. To his mother, he wrote the line that has come down through the ages as his most famous: "All lost save honor." What he actually wrote was "Madame, this is to let you know the full state of my misfortune. Not a thing remains to me but my honor and my life, which is secure. I implore you not to take this too harshly, using your customary wisdom, for I have confidence that in the end God will not desert me. I beg you to dispatch this messenger on his way to Spain, for he is going to the Emperor to learn how he wishes me to be treated. . . . Your obedient son, Francis."

His invocation of God in this first letter was revealing. In fact, Francis accepted his defeat at Pavia as the will of God. In his initial days of captivity, he fasted three times a week and even ate fish, knowing full well that sea creatures did not agree with his stomach. In due course he wrote sad poetry, lamenting his condition, prosaic, self-pitying, platitudinous rondeaux and amateurish attempts at lyric and classical poetry, one of which longed for the nymphs of the Loire. He vacillated between the suicidal:

> *I have no patience in my adversity*
> *As my pain is of such an extremity*
> *That I cannot hinder myself of staying quiet*
> *For all eternity*
> *So I beg, with great humility*
> *That death come to my calamity.*

And the upbeat:

> *I am joyful at the bottom of my misfortune,*
> *And miserable during my grandest of hours;*

Being cannot calm my thoughts,
Except, being the opposite of what I desire:
Deriving pleasure from tears and cries
Despite myself.

His letter to Charles V was more interesting, for its tone was sovereign to sovereign, brother to brother, as he appealed for fair play, high-mindedness, and mercy. "I have no other comfort in my plight but my estimate of your goodness," he wrote. "I have firm confidence that your virtue will keep you from imposing anything that is not fair. I beg you to decide in your heart what you are pleased to do with me, sure that the pleasure of such a prince as you are can only be linked with honor and magnanimity. If you are pleased to have this reasonable pity and to provide the security that the person of the King of France merits, which renders one a friend instead of a desperate man, you can be sure to have a benefit instead of a useless prisoner, and to make a King your slave forever." To refer to himself as a slave was the one false note, for it was beneath his dignity. But he repeated it at the end, signing the letter *votre esclave.*

Partly out of respect for his royal person, partly from admiration for the heroic manner in which he had fallen captive, his captors accorded Francis the dignity and some privileges of a reigning monarch. To be sure, he was deprived of his favorite avocations, hunting and the company of elegant women. There was no tennis court at Pizzighettone. Still, in his suite of rooms he was allowed visitors, before whom he could display his gallant and extravagant personality. Notably, these guests included two of his most mortal enemies, both of whom Francis himself had asked to see: his nemesis and betrayer, the duke of Bourbon, and the most formidable and effective imperial general at Pavia, the marquis of Pescara. As no record was made, one can only imagine how these virile warriors reprised their great battle and discussed what they might have done differently. One can suppose that Francis controlled his rage over the actions of Bourbon, as Bourbon controlled his anger over the confiscation of his ancestral lands. Later

Francis would write of Pescara that the imperial general was as "exquisite in peace as he was in war."

Soon enough, Francis's curiosity would be satisfied about what had happened to the Naples expedition of his commander the duke of Albany. The French detachment had never reached its destination. Organized quickly by the Colonna, an Italian force had blocked it. Thus repulsed, the French straggled back to Rome with their own Italian ally, soldiers of another great Roman family, the Orsini. But once there, Colonna's men fell on them again, and the soldiers of the two great families squared off against one another in the streets of Rome, fighting in the Campo dei Fiori, near the Orsini stronghold at Monte Giordano, near the Palazzo Colonna in the Quirinale, and along the Tiber in the Ghetto. Pope Clement VII shut himself away in the Vatican as the shots were fired across the river. The French under Albany did their best to avoid this internecine trouble, making their way to Civitavecchia on the coast and thence, on French galleys, to Marseille. So the last of Francis's pipe dreams—French glory in the south and rescue—fleeted away with the March winds.

Meanwhile, in early March, Charles V was suffering from his own melancholy in Madrid. He had been in Spain for three years now and was becoming more Spanish by the day. Spanish cavaliers had replaced his Flemish advisers, and the emperor was even learning the language. The choice of the Iberian Peninsula as the epicenter for the vast and ever-expanding Hapsburg dominion seemed to make sense, for the emperor not only had to look east as far as Vienna and Hungary, north to Denmark and the Netherlands, but also west to the New World. Charles could take great pride in his decision to authorize the historic voyage of Magellan seven years before when the explorer's own country, Portugal, had refused to do so. The decision was a worthy parallel to the decision of his grandparents Ferdinand and Isabella to authorize Christopher Columbus's voyage when similarly Portugal had demurred. After Magellan had been killed in the Philippines, the last of his five ships limped into Seville in 1522 after circumnavigating the globe, and thus the expanse of the world was known at last. And now

Hernán Cortéz was operating, however brutally, with the emperor's blessing in the area of New Spain known as Mexico. Soon, Francisco Pizarro
would ask the emperor's permission to conquer Peru.

But still the complicated exigencies of Charles's European domain, especially the war in Italy and the heresy of Germany, were hard to manage
effectively at the distant remove of Madrid. Venice had slipped away into
the arms of the French. Henry VIII had proved to be a slippery ally. Charles
owed his mercenaries in Italy six hundred thousand ducats and had no immediate way to pay them. While he had promised Henry VIII to marry his
daughter, Princess Mary, he was inclined to break that promise and marry
instead Princess Isabella in Portugal, for she would bring him an immediate
infusion of a million ducats in cash. Henry VIII was sure to be outraged if
the emperor took that step. And Charles's rage over the perfidy of his erst-
while "creature," Pope Clement VII, with his secret treaty with Francis, had
not slackened with time. The emperor had a lot on his hands.

Then, on March 10, he got the news of Pavia. "The king of France in my
power, and we have won the day!" he blurted out, then, embarrassed, seemed
to remember himself. He withdrew to his chamber, knelt before an image
of the Virgin Mary, and prayed. When he returned, sober and collected,
nobles surrounded him with their congratulations, but he called for quiet
and forbade any further noisy celebration. He asked for the full story.

The dispatch came from his viceroy of Naples, Lannoy, who praised
the individual heroes one by one: Pescara first and foremost, then Bourbon,
Frundsberg, and the bantam defender of Pavia under siege, Antonio de
Leyva. "God has given you your opportunity," Lannoy wrote. "Never will
you have a better occasion than now to take possession of your Crown.
Neither this land nor Navarre [a French enclave in Spain] will get more
help from France, and the heir of Navarre himself is your prisoner. In my
opinion you should come to Italy at once. Sire, you will remember that
the lord of Bersele used to say that God gave every man one opportunity
to reap a rich harvest. Should he fail to reap it, the occasion would not
come again."

Suddenly the supreme and unchallenged ruler of nearly all of Europe, the secular leader of Christendom, the emperor scanned the room. At this ultimate moment of triumph, instead of congratulation, recrimination was on his mind. First he scolded the Venetian ambassador: "I could have wished that the signory's forces had joined mine, as was becoming." Then he rebuked the papal nuncio: "They tell me that the pope gave passage to the duke of Albany, who marched into the kingdom of Naples." He would not be trifled with, and he would remember who had been with him in his hour of need and who had not. After this sober and restrained session, he went on a solemn procession to the Church of Notre Dame. He ordered there to be no outward signs of celebration, no bells rung, no fireworks, for it was suitable to celebrate victory only over infidels, not Christian princes.

Within a few days he wrote to Francis I at Pizzighettone, addressing him as *mon bon frère* and telling him that his terms would soon be on the way.

But what terms? A great debate, lasting for days, ensued. The bishop of Osma, Loaysa y Mendoza, was granted the honor of speaking first. Hailing from the noble Mendoza family, he was the emperor's confessor, a master general of the Dominican order, and a councillor to the Inquisition. In this "lower world," he began, it was rare to see the hand of God at work clearly. But in the victory at Pavia, especially in its completeness and its ease, that hand was manifest. "Therefore, the more manifest and greater his goodness, the more is Your Majesty obliged to acknowledge it and show the gratitude which you owe." So the emperor must direct the aftermath of his victory in service to God. Christendom, the bishop went on, had been reduced to a low state and faced "obvious ruin." On the one side were the Turks, who threatened Hungary, "the kingdom of your sister's husband," and who were making progress only because of the discord among Christian princes. "If they capture Hungary, as they will undoubtedly do unless the princes of Christianity unite, the road to Germany and Italy is open." On the other side was the Lutheran heresy, a "pernicious poison," "so dangerous to all Christian princes," "so great an enemy of God." "Unless provisions are made against it," the bishop said, "the whole world will be filled with heretics.

"How much more wicked, more poisonous, more foul is it, that so much Christian blood, which could be gloriously shed to strengthen faith in Christ, is being shed uselessly for our passions."

With the king of France, the emperor had three choices. He could keep the king imprisoned indefinitely and perpetually; he could free him without conditions in "loving and fraternal spirit"; or he could free him after extracting the most advantageous conditions, to the benefit of the Empire and the detriment of France. To imprison him forever or to force upon him harsh conditions as the price of his freedom, the bishop argued, would prolong and intensify future wars. Both would make the king an implacable enemy; indeed, to free him with a heavy burden was the most complicated and dangerous of all. If that course was taken, "he will not lack the company of all those who fear your greatness, with the result that we will have new wars, and more bloody and more dangerous than those in the past.

"If the king be liberated under conditions which are useful to you," the bishop of Osma continued, "he will not observe them, because no guarantee could be of such importance to him as the fact that his enemy should not become so great that later on he might oppress him. Thus we have either a useless peace or a perilous war."

Instead of this, a universal peace among Christian princes must be the emperor's goal. To accomplish this, the king of France should be released without condition. "If the king of France is treated with such generosity, he would remain more bound to you in his soul and more in your power than he is now in his body." There was glory in generosity. The true emperor must be as great in magnanimity as he was in military might. "It is to be marveled at that the Caesarian soul be capable of that which other men's minds cannot arrive at. For in the degree that he exceeds them in dignity, so much should he exceed them in magnanimity." The emperor now had the power to set the world at peace. He was in the position "to be no longer the enemy of any man, but to act as the common father for the safety of all." This was the "true and proper office" of the Christian prince. Once this peace was a reality, the emperor would be aided and followed by all, and the

Christian world could turn its attention, united, against the Lutherans and the Turks.

To this eloquent speech the emperor had listened attentively and stoically. He displayed no emotion and no indication of his agreement or disagreement. For a long time he sat silently in contemplation. Then he turned to another for a different perspective. That was the duke of Alva, a young warrior only twenty years of age, who had just returned from the battlefield of Pavia, where he had comported himself gallantly. He too had distinguished lineage as the scion of an important Castilian family, and with his youth and vigor he would soon become a favorite of the young emperor. In his presence Alva carried the authority of a battlefield warrior.

By contrast to the bishop of Osma, he invoked the traditional path of kings of the past, including Charles's ancestors. Yes, this great victory, "the greatest victory that any Christian prince has won in a very long time," came through the will of God. But it was also attained by the valor of the imperial captains and army. The fruits of that victory must be used well; not to do so was a greater infamy than not to conquer. It was prudent not to take decisions that would shame the emperor later, or to make errors that could not be corrected. Think, said the duke, what would happen if the tables were turned, if the king of France held the emperor as his prisoner. Could the emperor expect generosity and magnanimity?

If the king of France were precipitously set free, without lengthy and wise deliberation, the duke had his doubts that the king of France would regard it as an act of generosity for which he should be grateful. Rather he was likely to see lesser motives and to find greater excuses, such as the nuisance that was involved in his imprisonment. "Nothing has a shorter life than the memory of benefits received," Alva said. "The greater the benefits, the more are they repaid with ingratitude. Those who are ashamed of having been reduced to a condition where they need the goodwill of others are also angry and offended for having received it." More hatred and contempt than gratitude and love could be expected.

But Alva spoke most passionately and contemptuously on the character of the French. No people in Europe were more insolent and frivolous, he proclaimed. "Where there is insolence, there is blindness. Where there is frivolity, there is no awareness of virtue. What can one hope of a king of France, inflated with as much pomp and ostentation as might be expected in a king of the French, other than that he would burn with scorn and rage for having been made captive of the emperor? He would always have this infamy before his eyes. Nor, once liberated, would he ever believe that the way of extinguishing this disgrace is by gratitude. He will convince himself that you have let him go because of the difficulty of keeping him, not out of kindness or magnanimity. This is almost always the nature of all men. But it is always, without fail, the nature of the French. And anyone who expects seriousness from the French expects a new order and law in human affairs."

The price of a "profligate act of kindness" was high. The standing of the emperor would be lessened in the world rather than heightened. The army would feel deceived and lose its vigor. It would give comfort to those who hated and feared Charles. "It is in your power to hold all men bound and astounded," Alva said. "By such a frivolous act, you yourself will be the one who will unbind them and give them courage." More wars rather than fewer would result. Defeating the Turks and suppressing the heresy are "enterprises which need a prince so mighty that he should lay down rules for others." As for God's will, Alva did not presume to know it, for it was deep and mysterious. "But I believe He is favorable to your grandeur. I do not believe that His graces have been granted so abundantly that you should dissipate them yourself. Therefore, to lose so rare an occasion that God has sent you is nothing else but to tempt Him, to render yourself unworthy of His grace." True, Caesar and Alexander were liberal in their pardons, but they were not so thoughtless "as to put themselves back into those very difficulties and dangers which they had already superseded.

"Remember, O Emperor, that you are a prince, and that it is your office to act in a princely way. Remember how easy it is to lose great opportunities and how difficult it is to acquire them. While you have them, you must work at all times to retain them and not to depend on the goodness or wisdom of the conquered, since the world is full of wickedness and folly."

So Alva urged the emperor to reap as much fruit as possible from this great victory. These were worthy rewards and well in the tradition that great princes had always followed.

"You must not fail to increase your power as much as you can, not so much in the interests of your own authority and glory, but for the service of God and zeal for the common good."

This forceful presentation swept the court up in consensus, and the bishop of Osma receded into the shadows. The majority believed that the greatest advantage should be derived from the adversary's misfortune, and the emperor approved. In the days ahead, the terms were fashioned, and they were stiff. Francis was to give up all claims in Italy, including to Milan, Naples, Genoa, Asti, and Bournai. In France the vassalages of Artois and Hinault were to be turned over. More important, all of Provence and Dauphiné must be given to the king's tormenter, the duke of Bourbon, and his rightful claim to them recognized. Most important, the heartland of France, Burgundy, was to become imperial territory. Beyond these territorial concessions, the figure of two million ducats was set as the king's ransom. He was to promise not to provide any further aid and comfort to the imperial rebels in Germany, the dukes of Gelderland and Württemberg. As Francis's first queen, Claude, had died two years before, Francis I, upon his liberation, was to marry the emperor's recently widowed sister, the queen dowager of Portugal, Eleonore. As insurance that these demands would be satisfied, the king's two sons would replace the king himself as the emperor's prisoners. Once all this was accomplished, the emperor and the king of France were to join forces fraternally in a crusade against the Turks.

These demands were drawn up in an elegant document whose preamble described a litany of French villainies over the past twenty-five years and proclaimed that the Battle of Pavia showed God to be a just judge of all victories. The need now was for union among all Christian princes. The overriding imperative was holy war against the Turk. This document was then dispatched overland to Italy, where it was given to Bourbon and Lannoy, who in turn presented it to Francis I at Pizzighettone.

18.

I AM KING ONCE AGAIN!

When a few days later, the French king was presented with these stiff terms, not surprisingly he was horrified. Give up Burgundy? Impossible! He would stay in prison all his life rather than surrender this beloved piece of his patrimony. The liberty of France was at stake. He could not do it to himself or to his heirs. He did not have the power to do so. Give up Burgundy? Never. Theatrically, he drew his dagger from its sheath and raised it above his head.

"Better that a king should die thus!" he exclaimed as the generals rushed to restrain him.

In the lengthy deliberations over Francis's fate in Madrid, Charles V had been advised to move quickly and forcibly on a number of fronts. He must appear imperial, and the essence of that imperial policy must be leadership in a general war against the infidel Turk and the poisonous heretic. The new, transcendent imperial house needed to be put in order. Henry VIII could now be expected to demand that the Great Plan be put into effect, a plan by which he would go to France and be crowned the king of France. After that the allies would carve up Gaul to their liking. What Henry VIII wanted most were the ancient possessions of England in France: Gascony, Normandy, and Guienne. Central to that plan was Charles's old promise to marry Henry's daughter, Princess Mary. But Charles had been advised to resist this. Henry VIII should not be made any more powerful than he already was, especially since he had contributed money and little else to secure the new order. He would be told that Charles had done his part in the Great Plan while Henry sat idle. England was, therefore, entitled to nothing. There would be no Great Plan, Henry was told bluntly. Not only would there be no Great Plan, but Charles would marry not the princess of England, but the wealthier princess of Portugal.

Meanwhile in Rome, Pope Clement VII realized that he had now to make peace with Charles as the undisputed ruler of continental Europe. On April 1, yet another paper agreement was fashioned between the Empire and the papacy. It meant nothing, as Clement reverted to form. He was convinced that the emperor intended to subjugate all of Italy, no matter how forcefully the imperial ambassadors might deny it. But the pope vacillated about what to do about it. A noblewoman dubbed him "Pope I will and I won't," and elsewhere he was described by disgruntled Italians, tired of barbarians in their midst, as a man "very fainthearted and of little will." Desperately, the pope looked to Henry VIII as the man to moderate the emperor's imperial designs. The simple survival of the papacy as an institution was the pontiff's overriding concern.

Charles V dawdled. Had he acted swiftly, as he had been advised, he might have swept into leaderless France or crushed the remaining Italian resistance in Lombardy. Instead, he treated the victory at Pavia as the total and lasting annihilation of French power and resources. Through his inaction, a stalemate ensued, and a period of intrigues began. As the bishop of Osma had predicted, alliances began to form against the emperor. In the months after Pavia, Charles was in danger of losing the fruits of his great victory. Around this time Niccolò Machiavelli wrote a passage of which Charles might take heed:

"The ancient valor of the Italian soul is living yet."

Secret envoys passed in the shadows to unite Venice with Ferrara, Florence, and Urbino in a glorious new confederacy to drive the barbarians out and recapture the valor of the Italian soul, if only the pope would lead it. Agents went to London to sound out England, for England had to be the linchpin of any new counterforce.

"All Italy is at one in combining to defend the common interests and to resist any further increase of the power of Spain," wrote the imperial general Antonio de Leyva. "There is not a single Prince among them who thinks any longer of the favors received from Charles."

Meanwhile, Francis's mother, the queen regent, Louise of Savoy, had taken the reins of power in France and was acting forcefully, searching for anti-imperial alliances that might strengthen her hand in the negotiations to liberate her son. After the rejection of the English princess as the emperor's bride, Cardinal Wolsey was making overtures to Louise for a new anti-imperial alliance.

In Germany, in the meantime, a revolt of the peasants against their feudal lords was reaching its height. It had begun the previous fall as peasants, taking to heart Luther's teaching against spiritual authority, applied the same message to temporal authority. Luther was their inspiration. Over time he had called Emperor Charles V a "sack of maggots" and a tyrant and referred to the princes of Germany as "mad, foolish, senseless, raving, frantic, and lunatic." He had prayed to God that the German nation would be delivered from them.

"[The princes] know of nothing but flaying and squeezing and putting one tax upon the other, one rate upon the other. Here they send out a bear and there a wolf. No justice, no fidelity, no truth, is to be found in them. They act in a manner that would be too much for robbers and knaves. There are few princes who are not considered fools and knaves. In the long run people will not and cannot stand your tyranny and your arbitrary proceedings. The world is not now what it used to be, when you drove and hunted the people like beasts."

The peasants rose in bands. They were brutally crushed, only to rise elsewhere with a violence equal to their oppressors'. They protested against tithes and unfair rents, against arbitrary punishment, and against harsh game and forest laws. They demanded to choose their own ministers. At first, Luther found himself in the middle, for he despised the nobles while he espoused the importance of social order. He bade the nobles to stop their tyranny and deal reasonably with the peasants. Their revolt, he told the peasants, was taking the Lord's name in vain. As the butchery and arson continued—in Thuringen 70 monasteries were torched; in Franconia 293 castles were burned—he lost sympathy with the rebels altogether and dismayingly swung over to the side of the oppressors.

Luther did so with a brutality of language that was remarkable for a priest of the cloth, especially one who had inspired the rebellion. His writings became increasingly apocalyptic. "Remember that rebellion is irreparable, and the destruction of the world may be expected every hour." The "robbing, murdering peasants" were associated with the devil himself. They were guilty of every sin and "clothed their sins with the pretense of God's law. Let the nobles take the sword as ministers of God's wrath. Let him who can stab, smite, and destroy. If you fall, well is it for you; you could never die a happier death. Whosoever has it in his power to punish and spares the rod, is guilty of all the slaughter that he does not prevent. Let there be no pity. It is the time of wrath not of mercy.

"There is nothing more pernicious, nothing more diabolical, than a rebel," Luther asserted. "It is just killing a mad dog. If you do not kill him, he will kill you and a whole country with you."

He accepted that the blood of the peasants was on his own head, "but I put it all on our Lord God, for he had commanded me." It was a lot to take on his head, for in the final suppression of the Peasant's Revolt, some tens of thousands, inspired by Luther's "evangelical liberty," were slaughtered. With this acceptance, he seemed to invite his own martyrdom. Once again, but now from a different source, his life seemed to be in danger. "I see it clearly, the devil who has been unable to murder me through the Pope, is trying to destroy and to devour me through bloodthirsty prophets and spirits among you. Well, let him devour me. His belly will get narrow enough then, I know."

He wrote grandiosely, "I go home and with God's help will prepare for death, awaiting my new masters, murders and robbers. But rather than justify their doings I would lose a hundred necks: God help me with His grace. Before I die, I will take my Katharina to wife."

On June 13, 1525, he married Katharina von Bora. She was a runaway nun, one of nine apostate nuns who had escaped (in empty herring barrels) on Good Friday from their convent in Nimbschen and were sequestered in Wittenberg by Luther and his friends. This was an extraordinarily provocative act, taken not out of love for one he had protected from reprisal in his household but rather as an expression of inward completion for his individual self, as relief for the guilt he had felt as a monk over sexual temptation, and a manifestation of his thought. That thought had evolved radically since 1518 when he saw marriage as a sacrament, a most holy and noble thing, "the union of the human and divine natures in Christ." By 1521 he was denying the sacramental nature of the institution and saying that opinion had no scriptural basis.

Then in 1522 in his shocking sermon on marriage, "Increase and Multiply," taking his text from Genesis 1:28, he proclaimed marriage to be the natural state of a man and a woman. The vow of chastity for priests was an abomination, he said. Chastity was only possible in the married state. "As little as we can do without eating and drinking, just as impossible is it to abstain from women. The reason is that we have been conceived and nourished in a woman's womb, that of woman we are born and begotten, hence our own flesh is for the most part woman's flesh, and it is impossible to keep away from it. Chastity is not in our power. He who resolves to remain single, let him give up the name of human being. Let him prove that he is an angel or a spirit."

If these thoughts on chastity were not shocking enough, he uttered the phrase that would be most remembered of all in the sermon. On the subject of conjugal relations and divorce, he said, "If the wife refuses, let the servant maid come."

His marriage caused a great sensation. Catholics were scandalized, considering Luther's marriage to be a sacrilege. Luther responded characteristically. He took his marriage song from the seventh chapter of First Corinthians: "To avoid fornication, let every man have his own wife, and let every woman have her own husband." If the world was not scandalized, he said, he would be afraid that his work was not divine. With his marriage and his support of the nobles in the repression, however, he lost standing as both a social and a moral leader.

"If the monk marries," said an opponent, "the whole world and the devil will laugh, and he himself will destroy everything he has done."

In the period of intrigues after Pavia, during the spring and summer of 1525, no intrigue was more bizarre, more bold, and more Machiavellian than the one hatched by an experienced diplomat named Girolamo Morone. Morone was the chancellor of Milan for the duke of Milan, Francesco Sforza, a duke who bridled under the iron rule of the Empire and longed for liberation. The disparate and largely anemic Italian states—only Venice was strong enough to be independent—needed to bind together. But they had no leader, no forceful, charismatic grand personage around whom the petty rulers could gather and concentrate their frail forces.

Interestingly, rumors were rife that the most effective general at Pavia, the marquis of Pescara, was unhappy, feeling underappreciated for his heroic exploits and ill-used in the imperial court. Though he was proud of his Spanish descent, he was a Neapolitan by birth. Quietly, Morone approached Pescara, drawing out the marquis's rage about how he was being slighted. The conversation was steered toward far less worthy soldiers who were being rewarded more than Pescara. When the time was ripe, Morone launched his bold proposal. The Italian states were on the verge of uprising. Naples was tired of being dominated by strangers. If Pescara would lead them against the emperor, he could become the king of Naples. The pope himself had given his blessing to the scheme. Nervously, those around the pope waited for Pescara's response in the delusion that by one dramatic stroke, the whole situation might be changed.

"I see the world transformed," wrote the French-leaning papal adviser, Giberti, effusively, "and Italy arising from the depths of misery to the summit of prosperity."

Not so fast. Unfortunately for the conspirators, Pescara, Neapolitan or not, had a great contempt for Italians, and soon enough he reported the overture to the emperor. One last meeting between Morone and Pescara was arranged, while the imperial general Antonio de Leyva hid behind a tapestry. On his way home, Morone was arrested. The duke of Milan was charged with a felony and stripped of his power. The emperor once again had solid proof of the pope's efforts to undermine him.

In the fall of 1525 Francis I was no longer in Italy. In June of that year he had been transported to Spain. This had been his fervent request, and he even offered the galleys for the voyage. Undoubtedly, Francis thought that his Gallic charm and manly charisma could win over the dour Charles V more easily than the generals who held him captive in Italy. Those generals, Pescara and Bourbon, wanted Francis kept in Naples. The viceroy of Naples, Lannoy, took the French king to Genoa, but once at sea, he altered his course on his own authority and delivered the French king to Barcelona instead. (Pescara and Bourbon were furious at being duped, and Pescara even challenged Lannoy to a duel over his betrayal.)

The emperor, however, approved of having Francis closer at hand. Francis was locked up in the dank and musty alcazar of Madrid. Several months passed with no visit from the emperor, and the confinement was harsh. He was allowed no exercise, except to ride around the courtyard on a mule, surrounded by cavaliers on horses. This restriction began to wear on Francis, and eventually he lost his gay temperament, as he complained constantly of his undignified treatment. Gradually, he sank into dark melancholy. In October he contracted a severe fever and slid close to death. His physicians sent word to the emperor, then in Toledo, that they had no hope unless the emperor could raise the king's spirits. At last, although his counselors advised against it, he hastened to Francis's side. The meeting was brief. The emperor lavished his captive with pleasantries and expressions of concern and promises of better treatment. Francis was too weak to respond. Still, with these imperial words of encouragement, Francis rallied and soon returned to his old vigor. But his treatment did not change.

At about this time Bourbon came to Spain, and the emperor greeted his turncoat general warmly. They discussed the establishment of a new independent kingdom in southern France that Bourbon would rule. To cement the idea of Bourbon as new European royalty, the Constable Bourbon should marry the emperor's sister, the queen dowager of Portugal, Eleonore. Despite his exploits in behalf of the Empire, Bourbon was treated less royally by the Spanish nobility, who were contemptuous of traitors in general, no matter whom they betrayed and whom they favored. The emperor prevailed upon the marquis of Villena to provide his castle in Toledo as Bourbon's accommodation. "I could not refuse the emperor's request," said the marquis. "But he should not be surprised if the moment the constable departs, I should burn the home to the ground since it has been polluted by the presence of a traitor and has become unfit habitation for a man of honor."

To complicate matters, it emerged from the negotiation with Francis that he would be willing to marry Eleonore. The advantages of this were many, and Eleonore herself preferred the king Francis to the traitor Bourbon. The emperor was embarrassed. Then surprisingly, for he was only thirty-six years old, the marquis of Pescara died, and this provided a way out of the emperor's dilemma. Bourbon was offered the supreme command of imperial forces in Italy, as well as the duchy of Milan, since the duke of Milan, Francesco Sforza, had forfeited his rule with the Morone scandal. Off to Italy the chastened and unbethrothed Bourbon sailed, not yet a king but only a surrogate duke.

It was slowly dawning on both Charles and Francis that they must reach an agreement. The Morone scandal demonstrated to Charles that a confederacy of Italian principalities against him would only grow stronger with time. The soul of Italy was rising. Moreover, the queen regent of France, Louise, was inflaming the opposition in an effort to strengthen her negotiating position for her son. Then through the efforts of a sympathetic domestic, Francis nearly escaped, and Charles realized that in one moment of negligence he could lose the entire tournament. After this near miss, Francis devised a masterstroke. He informed Charles that he was now prepared to abdicate his throne rather than accede to the ignominy and disgrace of butchering his kingdom. He would proclaim his son, the dauphin, king of France. Name the place where I am to be imprisoned for the rest of my life, Francis wrote Charles, and let me appoint my attendants. If

Francis went forward with this plan, Charles would accomplish nothing from his capture. Scorn from the royal houses of Europe would be heaped upon him as petty rather than imperial. And an annoying Gallic thorn would be permanently in his side.

For nine months the stalemate had seemed intractable. Francis's "Burgundy, no, never!" had been met by Charles's "Burgundy, no more, no less." So stubborn were the parties that even Henry VIII had offered to mediate. But toward the end of the year the positions softened. Francis agreed in principle to hand over Burgundy if the parliament of France (such as it was) sanctioned the transfer, and the nobility of Burgundy acquiesced. All the other concessions were accepted, including his marriage to Eleonore, the royal domain for Bourbon in the south of France, and Francis's participation in a grand crusade against the Turks. For insurance his sons were to replace their father as hostages. When Pope Clement VII heard about the terms, he gave voice to the cynicism of the age: "If the French king has resolved to free himself from prison with the intention of using his freedom for the good of Christendom, that would be one thing. All this means is that the Emperor has the sons instead of the father. And the father can do more for the liberation of the sons than the sons can do for the liberation of the father." The treaty was a transparent sham. From his own behavior, as one who had put his name to many contradictory and empty treaties, the pope saw them as mere extravagant expressions, empty or real, to be kept or broken, depending upon the whim and convenience of the signatory.

Still, Charles V took the process seriously. On January 14, 1526, the Treaty of Madrid was signed. Its last clause elicited muffled twitters behind the drapery of the Spanish and French courts. "If Francis did not, within a limited period of time, fulfill the stipulations in the treaty, he promised, upon his honor and oath, to return to Spain and surrender himself again as the prisoner of the Emperor." Among the princes of Europe, only Charles V, in all his earnestness, seemed to believe in the honor of kings. It was he, not Francis, who often repeated his promise not to "cheat" his adversary.

Through the winter, Francis's release awaited the imprimatur of France's nobility. Charles and Francis rode around Madrid side by side, brother to brother, future crusaders-in-waiting, before Francis was returned to his comfortable prison. In April the requisite documents, decorous and worthless, arrived. The royal brothers bade one another farewell cordially, and a splendid entourage rode through Navarre to the border, with Francis in the control of the viceroy of Naples, Lannoy. On April 17, near San Sebastian, two barks waited on the opposite banks of the river Bidassoa, and another bark was anchored in the middle.

Lannoy turned to the king. "Your Highness is now free. Do not forget your promise."

"I shall fail in nothing," Francis replied.

Then together with eighteen attendants, they boarded the boat, as on the other bank eighteen attendants, with Francis's two sons and the French general Lautrec, boarded the other. In the middle of the river, Francis jumped in the anchored bark, gave his sons a brief embrace, then jumped in the French boat.

When he set foot on French soil, he exclaimed gleefully, *"Me voici roi derechef!"*—I am king once again!—then galloped off to Saint-Jean-de-Luz.

MORE WAS LOST AT MOHÁCS

✠

19.

THE GOLDEN-GRILLED
WINDOW

During his many humiliating months as a captive of Charles V in Spain, the moods of Francis I swung wildly between melancholy and hope. He looked in vain to any quarter that might offer an escape from his suffocating situation. Yet it seemed that all of Europe was arrayed against him. The eagle wings of the Hapsburg Empire now spread their giant shadow over most of the Continent, unchallenged, and in the New World, the emperor had a new spigot of fresh gold. Henry VIII growled like a greedy, salivating wolf, ready to devour hunks of northern France, while to the south, the traitorous lion, Charles de Bourbon, was ready to gobble up Provence and Burgundy. Where could Francis turn? He had to look farther east. Secretly, from his cell in Madrid's alcazar, he wrote a letter to Suleyman the Magnificent in Constantinople and dispatched two messengers across land to deliver it.

This overture came to the Sublime Porte as a welcome augury. After years of being snubbed and insulted, Suleyman was suddenly being courted by a major prince of the European unbelievers, beseeching him for help as a supplicant, lavishing praise upon his powerful empire and rich civilization. The invitation to confront his rival empire, led by the supposed temporal leader of Christianity, this "king of Spain," fit well with Suleyman's pride and intentions. With his mighty war machine, his glorious civilization, and his true faith, he demanded respect, even if conquest was necessary to secure it.

For five years, since he had captured Belgrade on August 29, 1521, all Europe lay open to him. Yet his attention had been drawn elsewhere, to problems in the east, in Egypt, in Persia, in the Mediterranean itself. After the capture of Belgrade, he had cleaned out the nest of Christian fanatics in Rhodes who were interfering with Ottoman trade to Egypt. In Egypt itself, a revolt against his rule, led by his previous third vizier, Ahmed Pasha, had to be quelled. By now Ibrahim Pasha had been promoted to grand vizier. At last, the sultan's confidant stood by the side of his boyhood friend as the second most powerful man in the empire. Suleyman now sent him to Egypt to take care of the trouble there. Then at the eastern extremity of the Ottoman Empire, tensions rose with Persia, the seat of Shi'ite Islam and the traditional enemy of Sunni Turkey. Shah Ismail had died in 1524, and a new shah, Tahmasp, Ismail's eldest son and still a mere youth, took over. In true oriental meanness, instead of sending a letter of congratulation to the new shah, Suleyman dispatched an abusive insult, in the most threatening language:

"If in your heretical nature there was but a sun-dust of honor, you should have perished long ago. Yet you have been kept alive only through our mercy. Your throat under the edge of our sword has been spared. I have decided to carry my weapons to Tabriz and Azerbaijan, and to put up my tent in Iran and Samarkand. My endeavor has been delayed only by my victorious campaigns against the unfaithful Hungarians and French, in Belgrade and in Rhodes, the biggest fortresses in the world, each conquest a miracle to the world. The house of the infidels has been transformed into the temple of Islam. The seat of the idols belongs to the rightful owner. The doctrines of the unbelievers were annihilated, their fallacy destroyed. Praise be to God who bestows this on us!

"Now consider that I am moving my victorious troops against you. Before I cover your land with armies, before our soldiers devour your family, withdraw the crown from your head and retreat, as your forefathers have done. Surrender and retreat into the chambers of humility. If you beg at my gate for a piece of bread, I will grant your wish, and you shall lose nothing but your land. But if you want to perish in the pharaoh's pride and Nimrod's delusion and embark on the path of fallacy, so your ears will soon perceive through the bridle's clang, the clash of spears and thunder of cannons the lore of your demise. Even if you were to crawl like an ant in the dust or to fly high in the air like a bird, I will not let go of you. Instead I will grab you with God's mercy and wipe your abject existence off the face of this world."

Within the tiled chambers of the Sublime Porte, it was unclear whether the sultan's next military adventure would be north through the Balkans or east to Shi'ite Persia. The great emporium of Tabriz, with its Citadel and its Blue Mosque of gold and alabaster, beckoned, as strongly as did the grim spires of Vienna. The sultan, seated unseen behind a golden-grilled window in the Topkapi Palace, listened to the debate of his imperial council over this question.

With Serbia as well as Bosnia now in the Islamic domain, Hungary stood as the last bulwark for Christendom in central Europe. If it was removed, the entire Continent lay open to this modern-day Alexander the Great. A wave of Christian fervor swept over Europe after the fall of Belgrade, but it was empty emotion. The Diet of Worms had voted twenty thousand troops for the defense of Hungary, but with war between the Empire and France in northern Italy, subsequent diets at Nuremberg in 1522 and 1524 had backed off and reduced the figure to six thousand. Well remembered in Germany was Martin Luther's proclamation that "to fight against the Turks is to resist the Lord, who visits our sins with such rods." The Turks, in Luther's view, should be seen as the Four Horsemen of the Apocalypse, coming to visit upon Christians only what they deserved for their corruption and decadence. Leo X had condemned the statement in a papal bull, but the power of Luther's statement lingered in the air. Resistance against the Turkish invasion was a papal affair. Moreover, Luther clearly admired the Turkish system of occupation.

"It is reported," he said, "that there is no better government on earth than under the Turks, who have neither civil nor canon law, but only the Koran."

For many years a series of Hungarian kings had appreciated Hungary's vulnerability to Turkish invasion. Under this relentless pressure the country had wavered between appeals for help to Europe and accommodation with the Ottomans. For the time being, the Ottomans tolerated Hungary's independence, so long as it prevented a Hapsburg from ascending to the Hungarian throne and so long as its foreign policy was essentially pro-Ottoman.

Between 1521 and 1525 a number of fortresses along the Hungarian border had fallen to the Turks, most significantly several that guarded the route up the Danube. An exception took place in 1524 when the warrior-archbishop Paul Tomori defeated a force of some fifteen thousand *akinji*, or lightly armed raiders. This was received in Constantinople as further provocation, in effect a pretext for another invasion. With France and the Empire locked in mortal combat in Italy, Hungary could scarcely hope for relief from those quarters. The papacy was paralyzed, caught in the middle of the Italian struggle. What meager funds the papacy had went to satisfy the extortionate demands of both the French and the Spanish for the protection of the Papal States.

An exchange between the archduke of Austria, Ferdinand, and the king of Hungary, Louis II, epitomized the desperate situation in the Balkans. Ironically, they were both related to Charles V in this vast and diffuse Hapsburg domain. Ferdinand was the emperor's younger brother, and Louis II was his brother-in-law, married to Charles's younger sister, Maria of Hapsburg. "We are both lost," Ferdinand wrote in May of 1523 to Louis. "It is impossible to resist so powerful an enemy as the Turks. As for assistance from the Empire, it is not worth a wooden penny." Ironically, though help was not to be forthcoming from any quarter, the pope steadfastly cautioned Hungary against making any compromise with the heathen Turks. Hungary must hold on to its feeling of belonging to a European Christian civilization.

In February of 1524 Turkish emissaries were secretly negotiating with Hungary in Buda. They demanded two things as the price of noninterference: tribute and safe passage for Ottoman troops through Hungarian territory. The latter could have only one purpose: an attack on Vienna and the heart of Europe beyond was a strategic goal for the Ottomans. Suleyman began to talk about the dominion of Islam stretching to the Rhine River.

Aggravating this dire circumstance was the pathetic state of the Hungarian royal house. The king, Louis II, was Polish by his ancestry—his father, Wladislas Jagello, had succeeded to the Hungarian crown in 1490 at Magyar invitation when a Hungarian monarch died without heir. Louis II became king of Hungary and Bohemia in 1516 at the age of ten. His birth had been a near miracle, for his mother had died when she was near term, and the doctors had hastily performed a medieval cesarean, removing the infant from his dead mother's womb and placing it in the cavity of a slaughtered pig for weeks to keep it warm. At the age of fifteen, with a full beard and mustache, he presented an odd appearance for a teenager, as if he were living on an accelerated calendar more suited to dogs than humans. This interesting physiology grew more bizarre at the age of twenty when his hair turned completely gray.

In 1521 he married Maria of Hapsburg. They seemed like a matched pair. Delighting in masquerade balls and elaborate tournaments, they disdained the weighty affairs of state. As one fortress after another on their southern border fell to the Turks, they left such annoying distractions to their military archbishop, Paul Tomori. They filled their palace with Bohemian nobles who were roundly disliked in Buda for their arrogant foreign manners. The king rose from his bed at noon and spent his day in various dalliances. When his court ran out of money, he was forced to beg from his nobles, who soon deserted him, to the point that the royal chairs at the feast table were largely occupied by royal hounds. In this mess the currency of Hungary lost half its value. What mercenaries could be hired refused to be paid in Hungarian coin.

Inevitably, a rival for the throne emerged. He was János Zápolya, the prince of Transylvania. He commanded an alliance of lesser nobles, while the nobility of Croatia, despairing of any help from the central government, put their province under the protection of the archduke of Austria, Ferdinand, and took their assets out of the fray.

Thus, the last bastion of Christianity against the mighty Ottomans was a soft underbelly altogether, rife with dissension, impoverished, ruled by a weakling, ignored by the great powers of Europe.

After the total victory of Charles V over Francis I at the Battle of Pavia in February of 1525, the news was soon reported to Suleyman. Its implication was clear. The Christian dominion in Europe was now consolidated under one head, this king of Spain, this Holy Roman emperor, this lord of the New World, who now ruled over an empire as vast as Charlemagne's. Suleyman's advisers predicted that it would not be long before the temporal head of Christianity heeded the plea of the Christian pope to unite against the Muslim challenge. Soon enough, the situation would no longer be state against state, but empire against empire, faith against faith, Europe against the Orient. From Suleyman's perspective his long-delayed push on central Europe should begin promptly, while the opportunity was ripe. His affairs in the east had quieted down. He made peace with Persia; he quelled disturbances in Syria, and Egypt was back under control. He recalled Ibrahim Pasha, his grand vizier, the *beylerbey*, bey of all beys, to make things ready.

In the spring of 1525 the sultan went west to Adrianople, the provincial capital of the Ottomans in European Turkey and the capital of the Empire before the fall of Constantinople. According to legend, the city was built by Orestes, the son of Agamemnon, and developed by the Roman emperor Hadrian. Adrianople, with its lovely mosques and palaces and its thick woods well suited to the hunt, was a pleasure center, and Suleyman went there to enjoy himself. Such indulgence left a bad feeling in the corridors of the Sublime Porte, however. Suddenly, trouble erupted in the most trustworthy and unique institution of the Ottoman court, the ferocious janissaries.

Because they were both slaves and aggressive soldiers, whose main rewards came from the spoils of war, the janissaries expected the sultan to sally forth in a new campaign at least every third year. Now, three years since the fall of Rhodes, when the sultan, instead of preparing for war, took himself off to the amusements of Adrianople, the janissaries revolted. This stunning act of treason cut to the heart of Ottoman traditions, and Suleyman rushed back to Constantinople to deal with it. Three days after his return, on March 25, 1525, the rebels ransacked the palace of Ibrahim Pasha and looted the Jewish Quarter. Dramatically, a contingent of mutinous janissaries burst into the very presence of the sultan and threatened his life. Suleyman killed three of them with his own hand before he retreated to safety. Thereafter, he had the agha of the janissaries and several other rebels executed. With the ringleaders of the rebellion exterminated, the sultan distributed two hundred thousand ducats to the remaining janissaries to mollify them. But the revolt prodded Suleyman into action on the military front.

It was in this environment that the captive French king, Francis I, dispatched his two messengers from Spain to Suleyman with his plea for help. One of them was killed when he crossed into Bosnia, but the other arrived in Constantinople in December 1525. Unless Suleyman acted quickly against Charles V, Francis's dispatch argued bluntly, the Holy Roman emperor would become the "ruler of the world." Suleyman thanked the intrepid messenger effusively, giving him two hundred ducats and a wedding dress and dispatching him back to Francis I with the following noble letter:

"I, the sultan of sultans, the leader of the lords, crown of the sovereigns of the earth, the shadow of God in the two worlds, caliph of Islam, the sultan and padishah of the Mediterranean, Black Sea, Rumelia, Anatolia, Karaman, Dulkadir, Diyarbakir, Azerbaijan, Iran, Syria, Egypt, Mecca, Medina, and all Arab lands that were conquered by myself, am Sultan Suleyman, the Son of Selim Han, the son of Bayezid Han.

"And you, Francis, the king of the province of France, have sent a letter to my court with an able man together with verbal communications informing me that the enemy has entered your country and imprisoned you. You ask for my grace and support, hoping for your freedom. Whatever you have said has been relayed to me. Now it is not befitting for rulers to cower and to be imprisoned. Keep your spirits high, do not be heartbroken. Our glorious ancestors have never refrained from expelling the enemy and conquering lands. I also follow in their footsteps, conquering nations and mighty fortresses with my horse saddled and my sword girthed night and day. May God bestow charity on you. You will learn our decision from your man."

Preparations for a major offensive into Europe in the new year now got under way.

20.

THE HIGHWAY
OF HOLY STRUGGLE

On April 17, 1526, Francis I was released from his captivity. Scarcely had he set foot on French soil than he flamboyantly disavowed the severe terms of the Treaty of Madrid. The unconscionable, outrageous terms were signed under duress, he proclaimed, and no king could abide such harshness. The treaty therefore, was null and void. Potentates of Europe, including the pope, were not surprised; indeed, they agreed and approved. Within a month, Francis forged a new anti-imperial alliance with Venice, Florence, and the Vatican and called it the Holy League of Cognac. In the background of this new continental alliance, if only in the imagination of Francis I, was the hope for an alliance with Suleyman the Magnificent and his mighty Ottoman Empire. When he heard about the betrayal of his former captive, Emperor Charles V was furious. Yet his ire was even greater against the pope than against Francis I. For the pope to ally himself with the French monarch who had broken his solemn word was scandalous. By the summer Charles V and Clement VII were trading the sharpest of insults.

Little noticed in this preoccupation with Italian affairs were events along the Bosporus. Only nine days after the release of Francis, Suleyman the Magnificent marched out of Constantinople at the head of a large contingent of janissaries and turned north toward Hungary. Engineers were sent ahead through the Ottoman vassal states in the Balkans to build bridges on the northern fringe across the treacherous waters of the Sava and Drava rivers, two tributaries of the Danube in Serbia. The sultan's push toward central Europe had begun.

To outside observers, his objective was unclear at the outset. Did the sultan intend to conquer and occupy Hungary as an extension of his empire? Or something either grander or more modest? If he intended to conquer and occupy Hungary, he might need to contemplate forcibly converting the country to Islam, a practice expressly forbidden by the Koran.* Or did he merely intend to make Hungary a buffer state against the Holy Roman Empire? Perhaps his plan was even more ambitious: to make Hungary a staging ground and safe transit route for a push into Austria and the heart of Europe. The truth was elusive. His objective would evolve during the campaign.

On May 3, Suleyman and his force of janissaries arrived in Adrianople on the western edge of Turkey proper. There, the army rested for four days, as the sultan convened a divan to discuss strategy with his beys and viziers. On May 8, the force moved out on narrow western roads into the vassal state of Bulgaria. Bulgaria had been Ottoman territory for over 150 years, ever since Philippopolis, the country's second city, had been captured in 1364, to be followed by the capture of the capital, Sophia, twenty years later. But the pivotal event in Turkish domination of the Balkans took place in 1389 at the Battle of Kosovo. In that legendary battle, resented and remembered especially by Serbians six hundred years later, the Turks crushed a combined force of Bosnians, Serbians, and Croats, and the entire Balkan Peninsula fell under Turkish rule.

So Suleyman was entering friendly ground. In the early decades of the Turkish occupation of Bulgaria, Turkish rule had been harsh. Towns were sacked. Vast numbers of Christians fled, their towns resettled by Turks. The Christians who remained were subjected to a heavy "capitation" tax. The Christian families of Bulgaria became a rich source for the enslavement of janissaries, the flower of Balkan youth who were seized from their families between the ages of ten and twelve, sent to Constantinople for

---

* Sura 2:256: "There can be no compulsion in religion."

training, and were now returning to their native land as an invading force. As the janissaries provided the Ottomans with first-rate soldiers, so their recruitment undermined the ability of annexed territory to resist. The Ottomans replaced the feudal system with their own administration, dividing the country into *sanjaks* or districts, to be ruled by a commander or *beyleybey* in Sophia. Many nobles had converted to Islam and were rewarded for it with fiefdoms. Most Bosnians converted as well.

But after the initial suppression and reorganization of Bulgaria, the lot of the subject peoples, especially the peasantry, improved under Ottoman rule. Aside from the brutal enslavement of janissaries, Christians were not required to perform military service. Aside from voluntary and self-serving conversions, no systematic effort at enforced conversion to Islam was undertaken. Aside from the capitation tax, Christian churches were permitted to function as before. Commerce thrived as the Ottomans built new roads. Strategic towns designated by the Turks as "warrior villages" prospered especially. The basis was laid for a patchwork of Christian and Muslim communities, living side by side under an efficient and relatively benign Ottoman administration.

After a relatively easy march across the golden grasslands of the Maritsa basin in central Bulgaria, the sultan's force reached Philippopolis on May 19. There, the army grew exponentially with the addition of two other divisions, one from Anatolia, the other from the European provinces of Turkey and Greece called Rumelia. The Anatolian army had mustered in Bigaz and crossed the Dardanelles at Gallipoli, following the sultan's vanguard through Adrianople. The Ottoman strength was now close to one hundred thousand men, and this did not yet comprise the entire force. For, as the sultan's forces had marched out of Constantinople, simultaneously a huge flotilla of some eight hundred riverboats, including transport boats and biremes with their two banks of oars and heavy cannons, had sailed into the Black Sea, moved to the mouth of the Danube in Romania (whose Walachian and Transylvanian princes were also vassals of the sultan), and headed upriver toward Belgrade.

With so many soldiers massed in the small town of Philippopolis, the logistics of quartering and resupply were monumental. Ferocious storms with hail as big as walnuts complicated these efforts. Besides the needs of the soldiers, hundreds of camels, artillery pieces, and transport wagons had to be organized and secured. Again, a divan was held, and the commander, Ibrahim Pasha, then ordered the Rumelian division to move out on the road north to the Balkan range. This leg of the march would be the most difficult. The sultan divided his army, sending the janissaries and their artillery through the pass known as the Gate of Trajan, while the Rumelian and Anatolian divisions passed farther west through the pass connecting Zlatitsa with Teteveni. Discipline was strict. Guards were set up along the way to protect local fields; villages were spared. "Whoever damaged but one blade of grass received a thousand blows of punishment," wrote an observer.

On May 29 the armies joined up in Sophia. The weather was oppressive, with high temperatures, slackened only by the occasional heavy downpour. As resupply was carried out, the grand vizier preoccupied the armies with parades, even as they had to slog through mud. Within a few days the army was on the march again. On June 5, Suleyman noted in his diary, "Two soldiers beheaded because they let their horses loose on grained soil."

Now on the more welcoming Danubian Plain, the armies reached Nis in Serbia on June 9 and moved quickly north toward Belgrade, which was regarded by all as the key to Hungary. There, the Sava River joins the Danube, and the crossing was a formidable obstacle. If the Hungarians were to arrest the advance of the invaders, it would be here. For months Hungarian generals had pleaded with their king to deploy troops along the Sava to hinder the Turks at this most vulnerable point to prevent them from reaching the north bank. But Ibrahim Pasha had sent engineers ahead to build a bridge under the management of the Ottoman bey in Belgrade. By the end of June the bridgehead was completed over the Sava.

A defeatist attitude infused the Hungarian communications. "Suleyman always brings along a large army," wrote one Hungarian commander. "He cannot be detained or prevented from crossing the Danube or the Sava by any means at our disposal." Lamely, the Hungarian king, Louis II, gave the order for the people in the border areas to take up arms and rise up against the Islamic invaders, as if farmers with pitchforks could stop the Ottoman advance. "If it is still possible, prevent the Turks from crossing the Sava. If this is no longer possible, confront the Turks on this side of the river."

The Turkish army crossed the Sava on July 9, ferrying thirty thousand troops across the river in less than three hours and entering Belgrade. Its vanguard moved swiftly north in the Srem region in northwestern Serbia and took up positions near the border of Hungary.

One last obstacle remained along "the highway of holy struggle," as Suleyman's jihad was being called. This fortress, called Petrovaradin, was an immense bastion, commanding a bluff at a bend in the Danube some eighty miles south of the Hungarian border. (Not far from the current Serbian city of Novi Sad.) Dating back to Roman times and considerably expanded by Cistercian monks in the thirteenth century, it was sometimes called the Gibraltar of the Danube. With the reports of an impending Turkish invasion, its formidable walls had recently been reinforced, and its nether portions were crisscrossed with a warren of underground tunnels. The Turkish armies could easily bypass it, but not the Turkish flotilla, the main source of supply for the vast army, that was rowing upriver from Belgrade. The Turks would leave this fortress behind their front lines at considerable peril.

On July 14 the Rumelian division began the siege. Three days later, the Anatolian army joined the assault. The galleys of the Turkish flotilla added heavy cannon fire from the river. But bombardment alone was insufficient. The defense was stout, and it included several sallies out of the fortress by brave defenders who inflicted over a thousand casualties on the Turks. Repeated assaults were turned back. Across the river, Archbishop Tomori, "the accursed priest" as Suleyman called him, watched the action helplessly, unable to deploy the two thousand troops he had with him. The siege lasted for two terrible weeks, before the Turkish engineers finally undermined a portion of the wall, and the Turks poured through the breach. Petrovaradin fell on July 28.

The door to Hungary was now open.

21.

SQUABBLING AT SPIRES

If Charles was concerned about this massive Muslim force moving relentlessly north toward the kingdom of his sister, he gave no indication of it. He was far away in distance and temperament, absorbed by his spat with the Vatican. There was trouble again in northern Italy. If he was oblivious to the threat from without, he seemed indifferent to the threat to Roman Catholicism from within as well.

On June 23, as the Turkish army approached Belgrade, another diet convened at the town of Speyer on the Rhine River in the Lower Palatinate in southwestern Germany. Speyer, the city of spires, had been an episcopal see since the fourth century, and its history was bound up with the construction of the Romans and the destruction of Attila the Hun. A Romanesque cathedral dating to the eleventh century graced its center. Since the twelfth century it had been a free imperial city. Charles proclaimed himself too busy to attend the diet and delegated its leadership to his brother, the archduke of Austria, Ferdinand I.

Ferdinand, of course, was far more attuned to the Turkish danger. His country lay directly in the path of the Turkish terror. But he was also harried by the problems of the Reformation. Peasant revolts still raged in Austria against both temporal and Church authority. During the Peasants' Revolt of the previous year and a half, scores of Lutheran ministers were hanged with his approval. The revolt was not over. Ferdinand was a firm believer in the necessity to enforce the edict of Worms, but the mood had shifted in recent times. Two years earlier, at a diet in Nuremberg, the principle of enforcement had been watered down. "Each prince should enforce the Edict of Worms in so far as he might be able." This was the germ of a new principle of territorial control of religion, known as *Cujus regio, ejus religio:* each region shall have its own religion. If that principle took hold officially, the authority of Rome was shattered.

By mid-1526 no one could have any illusions about the spread of Lutheranism. As the princes gathered at Speyer, nearly all of northern Germany had come under its spell, as had all of Swabia in the south. The Catholic liturgy was everywhere scrapped; Catholic masses were forbidden; Catholic cloisters were being abandoned. The word *popish* had become a slur. Grimly, in a witting exaggeration, Ferdinand reported to his brother, Charles, that Lutheranism infected 999 out of 1,000 in Germany. Martin Luther furthered this German contagion with a steady stream of antipapal tracts. The advances in printing, seventy years after the Gutenberg Bible, made wide dissemination ever easier. That Luther wrote his propaganda both with passion and in the vernacular made these pamphlets all the more popular. And his barbed wit was irresistible.

"The world is too wicked and does not deserve many wise and pious princes," he wrote in 1523. "Frogs don't need storks."

In addition to his emotional pamphlets were his stirring hymns. In another year, he would write his greatest, "A Mighty Fortress Is Our God," which would, centuries later, be alternately described as the "Marseillaise" and as the battle hymn of the Reformation.

Beyond tracts and hymns Lutheran propagandists began to employ ridicule, sarcasm, and parody as tools of struggle. In one cartoon Christ on a donkey disarms the pope, who sits astride a great warhorse with the devil riding behind him. In a burlesque, a dialogue between Christ and the pope put the pope in a bad light.

"I have no place to lay my head," says Christ.

"Sicily is mine," replies the pope. "Corsica is mine. Assisi is mine. Perugia is mine."

"He who believes in me and is baptized shall not perish," says Christ.

"He who contributes to my church and receives indulgences will be absolved," replies the pope.

"Feed my sheep," says Christ.

"I shear mine," replies the pope.

"Put up your sword," says Christ.

"Pope Julius killed sixteen hundred in one day," replies the pope.

Lamely, Catholic promoters answered with their own cartoons. These often featured the devil perched on Luther's shoulder and whispering in his ear. But in the war of lampoons the Catholics were outclassed.

The opening day of the diet in Speyer on June 23 set the tone. Philip of Hesse, a young, bold, and impulsive renegade in the reform wing, rode into Speyer with a brigade of two hundred soldiers who guarded a contingent of defrocked Lutheran ministers. These breakaway priests climbed to the balconies of inns, where they preached to a throng that grew into the thousands. As a further provocation, the insurgent from Hesse staged a barbecue of ox on Friday of the first week, only to incense the Catholic conservatives at this sacrilege on their holy fast day. In the conclave itself Hesse joined his like-minded believers from such imperial cities as Augsburg, Nuremberg, and Strassburg, along with delegates from northern Germany. But the Catholic wing was equally strong. Beyond the Hapsburgs, it included princes of Bavaria and Brandenburg. Hoping to shock the assemblage, Luther's chief antagonist, Duke George of Saxony, wrote out the most inflammatory of Luther's statements in his own hand ("I took the rogue's cloak off Roman knavery!") and distributed them to the delegates. With the two wings exercising almost equal power, only compromise was possible.

As Catholics and Lutherans debated fine points of dogma, the Turkish army moved purposefully northward. On August 21, it was at the Drava River, the border between Croatia and Hungary, and crossed over the bridge that Ibrahim Pasha had ordered built at the town of Osijek in eastern Croatia. The river was little more than a hundred yards wide at this point and presented no extraordinary impediment. But it took two days for the massive force to cross.

For two months in Speyer, seemingly oblivious to this juggernaut creeping north in the Balkans, the factions haggled over the dominion of papal authority, with the reformers professing their Lutheranism more openly and brazenly than ever before. Was the Church to be that of St. Peter? Or Luther's church of the redeemed, answerable only to God? If it was the former, the Edict of Worms must be enforced. Luther must be seized and burned. If the latter, central Europe was moving toward a patchwork of independent provincial religions. The squabbling was interminable.

During these two months, if only as a respite from the inflexible positions in an intractable debate, the delegates at Speyer took up the Turkish question. They had heard that the Ottoman sultan was marching toward Hungary with an army as "large as the Black Sea," but this menace still seemed remote. Luther himself had softened his apocalyptic stance on the Turks. Six years earlier, in a statement condemned by Leo X, he had argued that the Turks were the instruments of God's wrath against sinful Christians. The true "Turks" were internal and all on the Christian side, he argued. The Turks were metaphorically the sins of greed, usury, unfaithfulness, tyranny, and especially arrogance. But the state of the world had changed since that initial provocation. After the Peasant's Revolt, partly to save the Reformation, Luther had thrown in his lot with the princes rather than the peasants and espoused the principle of obedience to the orders of rightful authority. For this shift, he had been criticized as a "flatterer of princes."

In the summer of 1526, Luther was preoccupied with his domestic arrangements. On June 7, his first child, Hans (John) Luther, was born. But given the war in the Balkans, the reformer was also concerned about the moral posture of the soldier in combat and was working on an essay entitled "Can Soldiers Too Be Saved?" His essay addressed the question of service versus conscientious objection.

"Suppose my lord was wrong in going to war?" he wrote. "Then I reply, 'If you know for sure that he is wrong, then you should fear God rather than men and you should neither fight nor serve, for you cannot have a good conscience before God.' 'Oh, no,' you say, 'my prince would force me to do it. Besides, I would be despised and put to shame as a coward, even worse, as a man who did not keep his word and deserted his prince in need.' I answer, 'You must take that risk and with God's help let whatever happens, happen.'"

He opposed aggressive war, especially any war fought in the spirit of a crusade or holy war. He had not departed from his opinion that the Vatican's repeated calls for crusades against the Turks were merely ploys to raise money. "The popes never seriously intended to make war on the Turks," he wrote, "but used the Turkish war as a conjurer's hat, robbing Germany of money by means of indulgences." He had torn off the conjurer's hat, exposed the papal fraud, and blocked the flow of money to Rome. "If they had seriously wished to fight against the Turk, the pope and the cardinals would have had enough from the pallia, annates, and other unmentionable sources of income so that they would not have need to practice such extortion and robbery in Germany.

"What moved me most was this: They fought against the Turk under the name of Christ and taught men and stirred them up to do this, as though our people were an army of Christians against the Turks who were enemies of Christ. This is straight against Christ's doctrine. It is against his doctrine because He says that Christians shall not resist evil, shall not fight or quarrel, nor take revenge. It is against His name."

Still, if Luther heaped contempt upon the pope, he doled out no less scorn for the Turks and their faith. He could not resist doing some stirring up himself. The Turks were evil incarnate, he proclaimed. The Koran was a "foul and shameful book," and Mohammed was a destroyer of the Lord Christ and His kingdom. Especially loathsome was the Muslim belief that Christ was a mere prophet, not divine, and lesser than Mohammed. The sword, Luther said, was the essence of the Turkish faith, "in which all abominations, all errors, all devils, are piled up in a heap.

"Thus in truth the Turk is nothing but a murderer or highwayman. Never has any kingdom come up and become so mighty by murder and robbery as that of the Turk. . . . All fanatics, when the spirit of lies has taken possession of them and led them away from the true faith, have been unable to stop there, but have followed the lie with murder and taken up the sword, as a sign that they were children of the father of all lies and murder."

And so war itself was a necessary evil when it was fought as a defensive measure, he now felt. In that spirit, war had a rightful place in the world. Disavowing the pacifism of the Anabaptists, he did not now oppose resistance against the Turks, so long as it was interpreted as defensive war rather than crusade, and so long as it was not led by either the pope or the emperor. A united front of all Christian forces was acceptable to him, and it would not be long before Luther's hymn "A Mighty Fortress Is Our God" would be used as a rallying cry against the Turks.

As he pondered these lofty questions, Luther was also keeping his eye on the proceedings in Speyer, which held grave consequences for him personally and for his movement generally. His old friend and supporter Wenceslas Link, the former vicar-general of Augustinian hermits in Wittenberg and a fellow professor, provided his eyes and ears at the diet. Link had moved to Altenburg, where he preached and introduced the Reformation. He too had married. As the diet was drawing to a close, Luther wrote a note to Link expressing his low expectations for the conference. "Germans assemble wreathes as a custom, in death and in celebration. That is how it happens and it is being played out now, nothing more."

Toward the end of its proceedings, the diet reluctantly took up the Turkish question. Only Archduke Ferdinand appreciated the grave danger. "Save our neighbor's house, in order to save your own house from the oncoming fire!" he cried. But the delegates saw the threat through the lens of their religious disagreements. The Catholics called for a "dogged" defense and accused the Protestants of trying to thwart a plan for military help to embattled Hungary. The conciliators thought that a military defense could be mounted only after religious unity was established between the parties. Twice, on June 30 and July 7, the archduke had tried to focus the debate on the invasion, only to be dismissed by the electors.

At last on July 31, as far to the east the Gibraltar of the Danube fell to the "infidels," the question was put on the agenda. Like all divided deliberative bodies in history, the diet fell back on the time-tested evasion of

appointing a commission. More days were lost in fights over who would
be on the commission, and still more in fights over what to do and the size
of a military force . . . if any. Some electors worried that if the force was too
large, it might defect and join the enemy in an invasion of Germany. At
last, they settled on a paltry force of ten thousand. But who would lead it?
More discussion. The Turks could well be on their way to Vienna, the archduke warned. Finally, on August 23, the assembly issued a tepid double
negative:

"As a Christian nation, the Crown and the Hungarian Kingdom are not
to be left without help."

Four days later, on August 27, the Diet of Speyer produced its unanimous proclamation. Against Vatican objections, it endorsed the notion of
a general council to settle differences between Catholics and Lutherans, but
set no timetable for its convocation. Until that council of reconciliation was
convened (perhaps in another twenty years), "every state should live, rule,
and believe as it might hope and trust to answer before God and his imperial majesty."

This weak and vague assertion was, in effect, a declaration of independence. It gave each provincial ruler the right to act as he pleased. It was a
further endorsement of the principle of local rule; *cujus regio, ejus religio* was
confirmed as the operative principle. The prince of each province could
decide the religion of his realm, based upon the preference of his subjects.
If the people of a certain province were largely Lutheran, it would be a Lutheran province. The consequence of this compromise was far more sweep-
ing than the delegates intended. The door was opened for the rapid growth
of official Reformist states. Soon after the diet of Speyer, Saxony, Hesse,
Prussia, Anhalt, Lüneburg, East Friesland, Schleswig-Holstein, Silesia, and
the imperial cities of Nuremberg, Augsburg, Frankfurt, Ulm, Strassburg,
Bremen, Hamburg, and Lübeck all became officially Lütheran. Only Bavaria in the south remained stoutly papist.

Soon enough the Diet of Speyer became known as the recess of Speyer.
Luther himself viewed its decision as a reprieve, or even stronger, as a de
facto acquittal of heresy. The Edict of Worms was virtually dead, all the

more so because the pope and the emperor were at each other's throats and neutralizing one another. Indeed, by virtue of his split with the pope, the emperor had independently decided, on July 27, that the penal provisions of the Edict of Worms, especially the proviso of burning Luther as a heretic, should be abolished. The conclave at Speyer had immensely advanced the cause of the Reformation. The history of Protestantism had begun.

Six hundred miles away on that same day, the army of Suleyman the Magnificent massed on the plain of Mohács in southern Hungary.

22.

THE GAME PACK OF JIHAD

Through July 1526 the much belittled, gray-haired, youthful king of Hungary, Louis II, had remained in Buda, intently aware of the looming danger in the south, yet unsure of his course of action. The spies of his commander in the south, Archbishop Tomori, provided nearly hourly intelligence on the movement of the enemy. The king had given up hope of arresting the invasion at the Sava outside Belgrade and then at the Drava at Osijek. But he still anticipated the arrival of reinforcements from Croatia in the west and from his rival János Zápolya, the prince of Transylvania, in the east. The issue was whether to remain in Buda for these reinforcements and thereby give up the southern part of his country without a fight, or to move south with the insufficient forces he had, making a stand around Mohács and risking probable defeat.

The insufficiency of his forces was not his only problem. So unpopular was he with the Hungarian people that an uprising was possible with the least setback to the royal enterprise. "It can not be denied that His Majesty's life is in danger," wrote a Hungarian chronicler. "If he does not go down to the battlefield, he will fall into the hands of his own subjects, and that could only end badly. But if His Majesty does go down to fight all the way to the Drava, he would be poorly equipped and ill-prepared. I daresay that his own subjects would also present a threat, because everyone is dissatisfied with him. Especially Zápolya and his followers are against him. It is strongly suspected that they are in cahoots with the Turks. So His Majesty will have no other recourse than to flee the country."

Indeed, the option of fleeing was prominent in the king's thinking. His most loyal supporters resided in the western province of Slavonia, including the archbishop of Zagreb and the warlord of Croatia. Louis had a number of strong castles there, as did his brother-in-law, Archduke Ferdinand of Austria. In Croatia, the threat of a rebellion against him was smaller.

In early August, he struck a compromise, moving with his retinue to the town of Tolna, north of Mohács. A great debate with his nobles ensued over what to do. The nobles bickered not only about strategy but also about their privileges and duties as royal lords. Clearly uncertain of the king's commitment and skeptical of his courage, the nobles proclaimed that they would fight the Turks only under the royal flag, meaning that the king himself had to be present on the battlefield. The wrangling went on for two weeks. While they argued in Tolna, the Ottoman forces crossed the Drava and were a mere five-day march away from Mohács.

Finally, the king adopted a heroic pose. "I can see that everyone is using my person as an excuse," he told the diet. "I accepted this great danger personally, exposing my own life to all the fickleness of fortune, for the sake of the country and for your welfare. So that none may find an excuse for their cowardice in my person and so that they would not blame me for anything, tomorrow, with the help of God omnipotent, I will accompany you to that place where others will not go without me." Tomori was appointed commander in chief (unless János Zápolya should turn up) and instructed to take up battle positions in Mohács.

The Ottomans too had excellent intelligence. On August 19, the Turkish force was camped at Osijek, and Suleyman's clerk brought the sultan the following message: "A scoundrel came here from Buda and brings the news that at the fifth stage after crossing the Drava, you will meet with the evil king." The Turks also knew that the Transylvanian and Croatian reinforcements were on the way. In fact, a Croatian brigade of four thousand soldiers arrived a day before the battle.

No sooner had the Hungarian king announced his bold decision to make a stand than he regretted it. Soon after the diet of nobles broke up, he received a message from Zápolya, criticizing the decision to confront the Turks before he could arrive with his excellent Transylvanians. Zápolya was still at least two days march away. His soldiers were exhausted, having already covered over two hundred miles in a forced march. An additional argument for delay came from intelligence about Turkish military custom. By tradition, it was important to Suleyman to be back in Constantinople by the end of October for the traditional feast known as *kassim gunu,* which always marked the beginning of winter for the Ottoman Empire. He needed to complete his mission expeditiously, whatever precisely that mission was, in order to begin a timely march home. The Hungarians were well aware of this constraint.

Coupled with the news that Suleyman had crossed the Drava, these considerations changed the king's mind, and he tried frantically to reverse his call to battle. One of the king's counselors, the bishop of Vesprimic, prophesied disaster: "The Hungarian nation will have twenty thousand martyrs on the day of battle, slain for their belief in Jesus Christ, and it would be well to have them canonized by the Pope." But the Hungarian troops were now primed and eager for combat. The opposing armies were already locked in close proximity, and a safe retreat was fast becoming impossible. Moreover, the psychological priming was under way. The eager Hungarian warriors were being told that while the Turkish force might be large, it was composed of young and inexperienced soldiers "because the Turks lost the flower of their military at the battle of Belgrade [in 1521] and in the island of Rhodes." Tomori did his best to disabuse his soldiers of the wild estimates that were being tossed about concerning the size of the enemy: one report put the Turkish force at three hundred thousand. Tomori's own estimate was probably correct, about seventy thousand. Still, that put the Hungarians at a three-to-one disadvantage at least. Significantly, the Turkish army also had about three hundred artillery pieces.

When Tomori attempted to obey the royal order and pull back his forces, he was met only with scorn and disobedience. "Cowardly priests" and "war dodgers" were deceiving the young king, the knights complained.

"They are bent on softening the king, so outstanding in body and in spirit, whom they wanted to spoil with their cowardice and their unmanly advice, in order to turn the brave youth into their own image." But another contemporary wrote that when Tomori tried to pull the soldiers back, they were "blinded by their eagerness to fight in the vain expectation of victory." Their leaders "dared not dissuade the troops, who were hell-bent on fight." It was too late to pull back.

On August 28 the immense Turkish army crossed the Drava under the personal supervision of Suleyman. Once his entire force had crossed, the sultan ordered the bridge destroyed to scotch any idea by cowardly soldiers that they might flee the battle. The Turkish army now found itself faced with yet another natural obstacle: a swampy floodplain of the Danube that stretched five miles north to the Karasso River. Here, the Hungarians missed yet another opportunity to compensate for their disadvantage in troop strength. "The terrain is so swampy that it can carry neither man nor horse," a Turkish chronicler wrote. "Wherever one steps, you are bound to sink. If the miserable [Christian] king with his dogs comes to the edge of the swamp, sets up his batteries, and fires against us, he can prevent the soldiers of the true faith from entering the game pack of jihad." But the game pack of the Hungarians was different, and the Ottoman army slogged across the bog unhindered. On the eve of August 28, the Turks camped on the north side of the Karasso. On that evening, the imams fanned out among the troops to give rousing sermons on the eve of a great battle.

The Turkish bivouac stretched across a seven-mile line east to west and was organized in its order of battle: the Rumelian army on the left, the sultan and his janissaries in the middle, the Anatolian army on the right. At dawn, after morning prayers, this phalanx moved forward toward the plain of Mohács. An Ottoman chronicler celebrated the mood of the departure: "As soon as dawn began to smile announcing victory, and the breeze of salvation began to rise, the troops, burning from the desire to fight, went into motion like the sea, raising the banners and the horse's tails." The Rumelian army, commanded by Ibrahim Pasha, left first. Under a bright and cloudless sky, the line moved slowly, for it had to be constantly adjusted and rectified so that the huge columns would stay abreast of one another. Suleyman noted in his diary, "A young soldier is beheaded when he advanced without permission." As the line moved, it tilted slightly northeasterly to face the north-south Mohács road and beyond that a bend in the Danube in the distance and another swamp in front of it. If the Turks were victorious on the battlefield, the Hungarian force would be squeezed against the swamp and the river.

In due course, the line came onto an extensive terrace, dotted with fields and vineyards. At the northern end of this plateau, the ground sloped down sharply to a band of woods to the plain of Mohács itself beyond, where the Hungarian army lay in wait. The terrace put the Turks at a tactical disadvantage, for the rains had been heavy and steady in previous weeks, and the slope was muddy and slippery, scarcely the kind of footing from which either man or beast would want to spring forward in attack. Indeed, on the plain itself the remnants of the heavy rain were so visible in extensive pooling in the low-lying areas that one commenter wrote, "The waters of the Danube spread out like the sea."

The Hungarians surmised that so immense a force could never arrive all at once in an orderly line. So the sensible strategy was to take the Turkish units on one by one as they arrived sporadically. The most impressive asset of the Hungarian force was its armored cavalry. Both sides understood that a determined charge by this mounted force could cut through any Turkish line. The success of these Magyar cavalrymen was central to Archbishop Tomori's battle plan.

But Louis II was still wavering. Tomori's guess proved right: the Turkish force did arrive in pieces. Though the Rumelian army on the left had to march the farthest, it arrived at the northern slope of the terrace first at about noon; Suleyman arrived two hours later, and the Anatolian division an hour after that. They all arrived exhausted. And they looked down on the plain to find that the Hungarians had dug a formidable and nearly impassable trench at the base of the slope.

Suleyman gathered his viziers, known now by such monikers as "young lion" and "old wolf," to decide what to do. "O Padishah, who are the refuge of the entire world, the hope of all Muslims," began one counselor, "before we attack the infidels, we must have recourse to reflection, because the infidels number in the thousands and have formidable cavalry, much artillery, and many muskets. Moreover there is this trench. It would be most risky to attack without plan and foresight. It would be entirely appropriate to consider whether the Majestic Lord has indeed decided in favor of our salvation." The decision was made to postpone the battle to the following day.

Beyond the timing lay the question of strategy. The viziers acknowledged that an assault by the enemy cavalry, covered as it was "with steel from head to toe," could not be resisted no matter how stout the defensive line. Experience had taught them that a charge of heavily armored knights could destroy a whole line of infantry, creating panic and confusion throughout the ranks. Why not, suggested the "young lion," Ibrahim Pasha, open up the line and let the enemy charge through into the rear where artillery could be positioned, then let the ranks of the true faith close in around it? This idea was received as divine inspiration, a "plan of profound wisdom" conceived "in the lucid mind of the pasha blessed with a talent for military leadership."

As this discussion over strategy took place on the terrace, the Rumelian army moved gingerly down the slippery slope and began to set up their tents on the plain before afternoon prayers. When the divan was over, the sultan strode to the brow of the terrace, surrounded by his beys and aghas, to see the daunting Hungarian cavalry in the far distance. Suleyman got down from his steed and fell to the ground in public prayer. "My God!" he cried. "All force and power are with you! Support the people of Mohammed!" As the sultan rose, excited shouts and cheers greeted this display of piety. Ibrahim Pasha rode off to oversee the settling of his army for the night.

From afar, the Hungarian high command had watched the approach of the Turkish horde carefully through the afternoon. A few skirmishes had occurred between light cavalries on the plain, but nothing of significance, and the Hungarian barons were still itching for battle. They had seen the glint of steel in the afternoon sun. They watched the Rumelian flank descend and begin its bivouac in front of the tree line in the plain. The king too had witnessed this and took it as a sign that he could live to fight another day. He ordered Archbishop Tomori to return to camp. Tomori burst in on him in a frenzy. They should immediately attack the exposed Turks on the left flank, for they were certainly exhausted. Indecisive as always, the king vacillated, but finally, dilatorily, acquiesced and ordered an attack. Valuable time had been lost. Tomori rushed off, leaving the king to strap on his armor at his own pace and leaving him without a guard in force.

The initial charge of the Hungarian cavalry was brilliantly successful. It achieved the shock it expected. The Rumelian division, disarmed and busy with its tents, fled into the woods in disarray. The screams of terrified men mixed with the bellowing of camels and the braying of mules in the mad dash for safety. "Since the Rumelian army was dispersed," Suleyman wrote in his diary, "it was unable to resist, and part of it fled in the direction of the ruler." In this chaos, elements of mounted Hungarians got perilously close to the sultan himself. Two knights actually got within striking distance before they were cut down. Tomori was jubilant. To the king he sent a message that "victory is ours."

But if there was shock, there was no longer surprise. As the Ottoman left flank scattered, so in the center, the disciplined janissaries of the sultan began to descend en masse onto the plain. "The padishah ruling the world was approaching in battle order and with unfurled banners," wrote the triumphal Ottoman scribe. "At the sight of this, panic seized the infidels. Seeing their life in the mirror of death, they turned upon their heels and joined the troops that remained on the banks of the Danube." At this point the banks of the Danube were not a good place to be, not at least if your back was toward the river.

Tomori's horsemen saw the janissaries pour down the slope, kneel, and lay down a withering fusillade of musket fire. Shortly afterward, this enfilade was supplemented by the thunderous cannon fire from some 150 Ottoman artillery pieces that the janissaries had hastily pulled into position in the center of the line. The sultan noted in his diary:

"The division of Janissaries attacked the contemptible infidels three or four times with musket fire and tried to force them back."

This hailstorm blunted the advance of the Hungarian horsemen, and Tomori found it impossible to turn his line to face the threat. Somewhere in this furious and well-coordinated musket fire, a bullet found Tomori himself, and he fell mortally wounded. Briefly, infantry of Hungarian mercenaries came into play, fighting bravely in the center. Tough and professional though they were, they were soon overwhelmed by superior numbers as the Anatolian army now entered the fray. The long Ottoman line began to bend and envelop the Hungarians, until the Magyars were desperately fighting in a large, confining rectangle, completely surrounded. Under the withering and concentrated cannon and musket fire, the Hungarians were mowed down by the thousands. Gradually, relentlessly, the Hungarian force was swallowed up, with the tough mercenaries in the center wilting last. Suleyman the Magnificent watched from the terrace.

Only with darkness did the slaughter begin to slacken. As rain began to fall again on the plain of carnage and scattered baggage, the Muslim army fell into the mud for an evening prayer of thanksgiving, invoking the victory sura from the Koran (sura 48):

"We have given you, O Mohammed, a manifest victory."

In the morning the grim task of taking stock got under way. Mass graves were dug for the Hungarian dead. Of the entire Hungarian force of perhaps twenty-five thousand, only two thousand prisoners remained. They were paraded in front of the sultan before he gave the order for their execution. Afterward, their heads were speared on pikes and stuck in the mud in front of the sultan's tent. Of this "blood-call" he wrote diffidently in his diary, "The Sultan, seated upon a golden throne, receives the homage of the viziers and the beys. Massacre of 2,000 prisoners. Rain falls in torrents." The following day, his diary entry was even more matter-of-fact: "Rest at Mohács. 20,000 Hungarian infantry and 4,000 cavalry buried."

The accuracy of those figures must be questioned, but without doubt the Hungarian army was completely annihilated. Among the dead was the flower of Hungarian nobility: twenty-eight magnates, five hundred knights, and seven prelates. Tomori's head was placed upon a pike and paraded around the Turkish camp. Of him, the triumphal Turkish scribe wrote with grudging admiration and many mixed metaphors: "He was like hammered iron. The more blows he received the harder he became. Had he been smitten to death like a rabid dog, he might still have revived. When he launched a charge, like the flooding Nile, braying like an enraged elephant, even tigers and lions would have stayed clear."

The Hungarian king, Louis II, had disappeared from the battlefield when the right wing of his army disintegrated and the artillery barrage began. In the light of next day, the body of the king known as the Unfortunate was discovered in a ditch and identified only by his signet ring and a golden, heart-shaped locket that he wore around his neck. No mark of violence was on his body. A peasant found him, took the ring and the locket, and buried the body. It was surmised that in the darkness during his frantic attempt to escape, the king, weighted down with his heavy armor, had fallen from his horse into a brook and drowned.

"May Allah be merciful to him and punish those who misled his inexperience," Suleyman noted in his diary when he got the news in Buda twelve days later. "It was not my wish that he should be thus cut off, while he had scarcely tasted the sweets of life and royalty."

23.

THE SOW AND HER PIGLET

In the coming days Suleyman tasted the sweets of life, royalty, and military victory. It was military victory medieval-style, Turkish style, with terror and memory at its core. Two days after the battle, Suleyman toured the horrific battlefield with two of his viziers. During this reconnaissance, he came upon a wise elder.

"And now what should we do?" the sultan asked.

"Beware that the sow does not give birth to a piglet," the elder warned. Suleyman smiled and handed the old man a gold ducat.

With the sultan's blessing, his vast army went on a wild, three-week rampage. In this extended blood-call, villages were burned; infidels were slaughtered by the hundreds; and everything from the valuable to the worthless was looted. An army once so tightly disciplined now ran completely amok. The village of Mohács was the first to be burned, though no village in the march north to Buda and Pest was spared. The light cavalry known as the *akinjis* led the way and established the pattern. When it was over, scarcely a piglet could be found.

The news of the catastrophe in the south soon reached Buda and Pest, and panic ensued. Queen Maria of Hapsburg hastily gathered a few of her most precious belongings and fled the capital through the Logod Gate in the company of her ladies, her treasurer, and fifty German knights. The populace followed, leaving, as one report said, only "the poor, the lame, the blind, and the Jews" to await the predators. Hope that the Transylvanian prince, János Zápolya, would arrive to defend the capital quickly faded. His army was camped sixty miles to the east on the Tisza River. The prince, no fool he, had no intention of mounting a challenge.

On September 11 Suleyman arrived at Buda and was handed the keys to the city by a Jew named Joseph B. Solomon. Joseph was lavished with gifts and rewarded with relief from the poll tax that was normally levied on Jews under Ottoman rule as a "protected" people. (This tax, the *jizya,* as it is called in the Koran, implied submission to the superior believer and acknowledgment of second-class status. But it guaranteed comfort, security, and protection from discrimination.) Not all the Jews of Buda were so lucky. Despite this general attitude of tolerance, Suleyman's diary indicates that he banished some Jews and forced them to flee south.

The sultan took up residence in the royal palace on the palisade above the Danube. There, he entered the premises of the fabled Corvinian Library, the most magnificent collection of illuminated manuscripts and beautifully bound leather books in all of Europe outside of Italy, rivaled only by the libraries of the Medici, the Sforza, and in Spain the House of Aragon. This fabulous library that graced the first floor of the palace was a feast of leather, gold embossing, velvet, decoratively carved wood shelves, and gold cloth. It had been developed by King Matthias Corvinus, a predecessor of Louis II, who died in 1490. It was the highest expression of the Renaissance in Hungary. Suleyman gazed at this treasure in awe, then ordered that it be packed up and shipped to "the capital of the true believers," along with the munitions in the castle. Ibrahim Pasha also had his eye on special spoils for himself: three giant statues of Hercules, Apollo, and Diana that were status symbols of the European Renaissance. When the statues arrived in Constantinople, Ibrahim Pasha had them installed in front of his palace on the Hippodrome. His purpose, he said, was to communicate the superiority of the Ottoman Empire over the declining cultures of Christian Europe. As we will see, their display had a very different effect.

Once these treasures were safely on their way down the Danube, three hundred arsonists fanned out across the city to set their fires. "All the nations of the world needed to remember that the emperor of the Turks was here," wrote a chronicler. Suleyman watched the city burn from the royal palace high above the Danube. In certain aspects he was displeased.

"A large church with belfries is destroyed against the Sultan's orders," his secretary wrote. "The Grand Vizier wished to extinguish the fire, though that was not possible." When it came time to leave, Suleyman looked with favor on the royal palace itself. "The Sultan found it unworthy to burn down the King's castle, since he had received company there, and therefore ordered for it to be guarded by Janissaries," so his scribe wrote, as if this were a question of good manners.

As Buda smoldered, Suleyman and his entourage withdrew to the outskirts of the city for four days of victory celebrations at the hunting castle of the Hungarian kings. The festivities were a mix of stirring martial music, banquets, courtly dances, loyalty processions, and religious devotionals. The sultan sat on his golden throne, a crown of diamonds on his head, as his minions came forward to kneel and kiss his hand as a gesture of allegiance. It was the month of Dhull-Hijja in the Muslim lunar calendar. It was time, after Ramadan, for the religious ceremony marking the willingness of Abraham to sacrifice his son to God. As if their military campaign had been a kind of hajj, they marked the time as an end of a pilgrimage. Goats and camels were symbolically slaughtered in the spirit of sacrifice and in the name of Allah, the Greatest and Most Merciful.

On September 13 a bridge across the Danube was built, and the Ottoman army crossed into Pest. It too was stripped and gutted before it was burned. The only resistance to the Ottoman juggernaut was mounted north of the capital near Esztergom on the Austrian border. There the refugees with their women had holed up in a fortress at Pilismarot. Ottoman artillery soon reduced this last refuge to rubble. Only the women were spared.

So, it would seem, Suleyman's five-month Balkan campaign had been brilliantly successful. Hungary had been completely subdued. Its Hapsburg, Christian leadership was wiped out. A great and historic victory had been won at Mohács, a victory so total that it would be remembered centuries later, as a complement to the Turkish victory at Kosovo in 1389. Mohács became a standard against which all Hungarian misfortune, ancient or modern, personal or collective, would be measured. When disaster strikes today, a common saying in Hungary is "No matter, more was lost at Mohács." The northern border of the Ottoman Empire was extended. Great treasures including a world-famous library and priceless artworks were shipped to Constantinople. Suleyman stood transcendent, the most feared emperor in the world. His path, and the path of Islam, lay open to the Rhine River.

Only Vienna stood in his way.

YET IN THE VERY completeness of the triumph lay its central problem. In its wake it exacted an enormous political price. A vacuum of leadership now yawned over Hungary. Suddenly, it was no wonder why Suleyman so mourned the passing of the ineffectual Hungarian king. The emperor had lost his toady. The alternatives were more formidable. For the moment, with Louis II dead and the chivalry of Hungary virtually wiped out, Suleyman had no authority with whom to negotiate a graceful exit and subservient rule over his conquest.

Indeed, Ferdinand I, the archduke of Austria and Charles V's brother, had learned of Louis II's death before Suleyman did. Wasting no time, on September 8, only ten days after the Battle of Mohács, he began to circulate a petition among the surviving nobles and towns of Hungary, laying his claim to the Hungarian throne by virtue of both inheritance and treaty. (His wife was the daughter of a prior king of Hungary.) Ferdinand was, as Suleyman was well aware, a far more substantial character than his weak, little-mourned brother-in-law, and he was the blood brother of Suleyman's most formidable adversary, the king of Spain and the Holy Roman emperor, Charles V. If Ferdinand's claim was accepted, a Hapsburg Austro-Hungarian empire would formally be established and extended southward into the newly acquired Ottoman territory. Instead of extending and securing Ottoman control over Hungary, the consequence of the Battle of Mohács would be to strengthen and consolidate Hapsburg control over the strategic Hungarian plain. Instead of pushing the Hapsburgs back, the Turkish victory had sucked them farther in.

The sow had produced the piglet.

The elusive, opportunistic prince of Transylvania, János Zápolya, was Suleyman's best hope to fill the vacuum. As the great columns of the Ottoman army prepared to leave Hungary, Zápolya was tapped to be the next king of Hungary. Under the watchful eye of Turkish agents, diets in the eastern city of Tokay and in the royal city of Székesfehérvár to the southwest of Buda elected Zápolya king. He was crowned on November 11, 1526. The following month a different diet in the northern city of Pressburg (Bratislava) elected Ferdinand I king of Hungary, after the archduke had also acceded to Louis II's throne of Bohemia. Before Suleyman arrived back in Constantinople on November 23, two Christian princes were vying for the crown of Hungary. In France, Francis I saw this competition as another way to sow mischief for the Hapsburgs. He sent his representative to János Zápolya to offer French aid in his struggle for the Hungarian crown.

A year later, the matter was resolved to the Ottoman and French disadvantage when Ferdinand defeated Suleyman's vassal at Tokay and had himself crowned at Székesfehérvár as the sole monarch of the land. It was as if the Battle of Mohács had been for naught. Suleyman had left behind no garrison authority, no occupation force. If the Ottomans were to rule Hungary, they would have to slice still deeper into the Hapsburg dominion.

"The time when this province should be annexed to the possession of Islam had not yet arrived," wrote an Ottoman apologist. "The matter was therefore postponed to a more suitable occasion." Suleyman had left behind unfinished business.

ACT SIX

THE SACK
OF ROME

✠

24.

ALAS, POOR ITALY

In the spring of 1526 the Medici pope, Clement VII, was feeling emboldened. Francis I, the fickle king of France, had at last been released from captivity in Madrid. No sooner had he crossed into French territory than he disavowed the harsh terms of his release in the Treaty of Madrid and declared his intention to have his revenge on his captor, Charles V. Once again, the pope had a powerful sovereign in his camp, one who bristled with a passion for war. The time had arrived to renew the campaign to liberate northern Italy from the Spanish occupiers who now held substantial territory in Lombardy, including the episcopal sees of Parma and Piacenza, and who threatened Milan. The people of the north reached out to the pope for help. They were being abused and exploited by the foreign marauders and were suffering under heavy taxation and other exactions. Upon the fate of Milan hinged the very independence not only of the papacy but of Venice. Clement VII might be the spiritual leader of the Christian world, but his first priority was as the leader of the Italian people. He would be the last pope to claim this right.

"Hunt down these wild beasts who have only the faces and voices of men," wrote a prince of Florence about the Spanish in the north. That was the fading voice of Niccolò Machiavelli, now only a year away from death, but still active. His great works were behind him. He ventured forth still from his contemplative villa in Percussina outside Florence at the behest of the pope for readings of his works to select audiences in Medici Rome and for diplomatic missions. During the spring of 1526 the pope asked him to inspect the fortifications of their beloved Florence. There was premonition in the request: the defenses would soon need to prove themselves.

If Machiavelli was passionate in his hostility toward the foreigners in his beloved land, an Italian poet at greater distance was wistful. "Alas! Poor Italy, whither hast thou fallen? Thy glory, thy fame, thy strength, have perished." By its fracture into petty principalities, Milan, Venice, Florence, Siena, Ferrara, Urbino in the north, Naples, Apulia, and Sicily to the south, each tasty morsels for outsiders, the peninsula had ceased to be a player on the greater stage of Europe. Instead, it had become the victim of the larger powers who feasted on its wealth. It was no mystery why Machiavelli had focused his mind and talents on the problem of survival for the Italian prince under these fragile conditions. In the past two decades, he had seen his Florence overrun by the French, attacked from all sides by various provincial dukes, ruled by the wealthy Medici, by weak democrats, by the Borgias. In this disastrous situation, his paragon for the effective prince had become the unscrupulous and brutal Cesare Borgia. In this last year of his life, the great writer was still writing his history of Florence, deducing from that history certain principles for effective political behavior in adverse situations.

"Let the Emperor rule Italy and he will rule the world," a Roman diplomat wrote at this time. *"Vae miserae Italiae et nobis viventibus."* (Woe to wretched Italy and to our livelihood.) That was the view from the other side, and so Charles V himself must have thought. He was the Holy Roman emperor. It was his ancestral right, nay, his duty, to rule Italy. Let the pope have dominion over souls. He would rule the land and its people.

With the freeing of Francis I, there was hope for the papacy, if only the other kings of Europe would ally themselves in a coalition against the emperor. In secret, that alliance came into being on May 22, 1526. On that day, in Cognac, the Holy League of Cognac was formed between the Vatican and Venice, France, Florence, and the beleaguered Sforza clan of Milan. The pope longed for Henry VIII to bring England into the league soon.

Then the anti-imperial alliance would be complete. By the terms of the alliance, Milan was reaffirmed as the possession of its traditional rulers, the Sforza. All the possessions that had been taken by the imperialists were to be returned. Florence was to be protected. Most significant, war was to be declared on Emperor Charles V, and his vassal state of Naples was to be wrested from him.

The immediate goal of the new league was to relieve the siege of Milan, but a far broader, bolder plan was envisaged for the liberation of the entire peninsula. It had been crafted by pope's great statesman and general (and later historian of Italy) Francesco Guicciardini. It was to be a war for all of Italy at once, with the result of "universal celebration." The papal naval commander, Andrea Doria, was to capture Genoa; the province of Siena, which lay strategically between Florence and Rome, was to be retaken from democratic upstarts for papal exiles; Venice was to invade the boot of Italy, ancient Apulia or Calabria. The dream was grand: the fate of all Italy was at stake.

Still, the situation in Milan was dire. The town itself had already fallen into the hands of imperial forces, but the great castle of the Sforza, Castello Sforzesco, held out. The immense entrance tower of the four-sided behemoth had been restored after its destruction five years earlier when the French were driven out. Now the pope imagined a reversal of fortune. In 1521, as Giulio de' Medici, he had entered Milan as the victorious general over the French enemy. Now, as Pope Clement VII, he would return as conqueror over the German and Spanish enemy with the French as his ally. His own Italians did not figure significantly in the picture.

An army of eleven thousand imperialists besieged the castle, and they had built imposing trenches around their outer perimeter. But they were isolated and disgruntled, for they had not been paid for several months. When Guicciardini and the pope added up the forces of the new coalition, including Swiss and Venetian soldiers, they expected a superior force of some twenty thousand. If these forces moved quickly, success was assured, especially if French and Swiss reinforcements could arrive promptly.

Far away in Granada, Spain, Charles V soon caught wind of this league, and his reaction was swift. He appointed a fearsome commander for his

Italian operations, Don Ugo di Moncada, who had once been a Hospitaller knight at Rhodes and had served in the Spanish navy in the war against the Moors. A disciple of Cesare Borgia, he had been appointed viceroy of Sicily, where he had been reviled for his cruelty. He was well known as belonging to the school of thought known as the *exaltados*, who wished to put all of Italy under Spanish rule. The emperor dispatched Moncada to Rome to meet the pope and see if he could exact a favorable accommodation. If not, Moncada was to proceed to Naples to conspire with the powerful Colonna family on the next step.

On June 16 Moncada and the pope sparred testily. Awkwardly, they talked past one another, offering impossible things. Moncada suggested that the siege of Milan could be lifted if the pope and the Italian powers would pay the impecunious imperial army for its troubles. Clement said he would agree if all foreign troops left Italy and the captive sons of Francis I were freed.

A week later, on June 23, Clement VII wrote a long and intemperate "brief" to Charles V, rejecting Moncada's overtures. In it the pope reviewed his relations with Charles from the outset of Clement's papacy and described them as a "long tragedy." He listed a litany of grievances: reasonable overtures spurned, efforts to keep the peace of all Christendom met with invasion, conspiracies to undermine the authority of the papacy, secret intrigues, broken promises, quartering of imperial troops on papal soil in violation of treaties, failure to repay monies that had been advanced, relentless insults and calumnies and indignities. This had engendered a deep distrust of the emperor in the pope and had forced him into alliances with other European monarchs to counterbalance the "insatiable ambition" of the emperor. His duty, wrote the pope, was to prevent the servitude of Italy and of the Holy See, and therefore, he was forced into a war of self-defense.

Characteristically, the insecure pope immediately regretted the violence of his language in the June 23 brief and two days later dispatched a shorter, more diplomatic message to Charles. But the damage was done. Two weeks later, in the palatine chapel in Rome, the Holy League of Cognac was made public with great pomp and ceremony.

In July the wider war in northern Italy began.

But events did not go well for the papal forces. The duke of Urbino, Francesco Maria della Rovere, was the commander of the Venetian army, and he refused to move until a promised contingent of Swiss soldiers arrived. When he finally moved west on Milan and reached the imposing trenches of the imperial army, he hesitated, then retreated. Contemptuously, the papal general Francesco Guicciardini said of the duke, "He came, he saw, he fled." Meanwhile, in central Italy, after the overthrow of the aristocratic government in Siena by popular rebels, a counterattack by papal forces faltered, and Siena remained friendly territory for the emperor. Finally, the tardy five thousand Swiss soldiers had turned up, but it was too late. On July 24, unrelieved and starved, the castle of Milan surrendered.

Frantically, the pope looked to Francis I. Where were the French? he asked, reminding Francis of his obligations under the league. But, as a historian wrote, "The fickle king had repented of his martial zeal and was squandering his time and his revenues on the chase, gambling, and women." Henry VIII was standoffish and incommunicado. There were reports of an army of Germans forming in the Tirol.

The pope was disconsolate, deserted, and betrayed. "I never saw a man so perplexed," wrote the French ambassador in Rome. "He is half-ill with disappointment and says plainly that he never expected to be so treated. You have no idea what things are said about us by persons of high standing in the Curia, on account of our delays and our behavior. The language is so frightful that I dare not write it. His ministers are more dead than alive. You can well imagine what the enemy will make of the situation."

In Rome itself, the pope was losing the support of his own citizens, who grumbled about the heavy taxation from the war effort. To make matters worse, plague was raging again in the Eternal City.

Meanwhile, per his imperial instructions, Don Ugo di Moncada had repaired to Naples after his unproductive meeting with the pope in June and there, with the powerful Colonna family, had began to conspire against the pope. Since the eleventh century, the Colonna family had been prominent in Rome and had supplied several popes, including Martin V

(1417–31), who had vastly expanded the family dominion in southern Italy, as he resisted reforms for the Church. In the two decades that Naples had been a vassal state of the Spanish throne, the Colonna had been the emperor's representatives. The feud between the Colonna and Clement VII dated back to Clement's election as pope, in which Cardinal Pompeo Colonna had been a pivotal supporter. But when Clement had turned against the emperor and in favor of Francis I, and when the pope refused to appoint Cardinal Colonna as ambassador to Spain, the cardinal's anger had grown exponentially. For the harshness of his dissension from papal authority, he had been placed under a papal admonition. Now he imagined a scenario in which, with the emperor's help, Clement would be dislodged and he himself would don the tiara.

"If you are unsuccessful in gaining Clement," Moncada's instructions from the emperor read, "speak secretly to Cardinal Colonna, so that he may set in hand, the matter recommended by his agents. Give him all your support in private." The matter recommended by his agents was to raise a fighting force quietly and then, at just the right moment, to move on Rome, from "whence all the mischief springs." If Colonna's troops invaded the Romagna, perhaps that demonstration would compel the pope to withdraw his soldiers from Lombardy and Siena. In the emperor's mind it was to be a demonstration only, not an invasion and occupation. In Cardinal Colonna's mind, he was soon to take a new name and title.

In mid-August Ugo di Moncada sprang his trap. Venturing to Rome as if he were bearing an olive branch, he persuaded Clement VII that he was there as an agent of reconciliation between the pope and the Colonna. With an air of contrition, he promised that Colonna's soldiers would be withdrawn from papal territory. Hearing these comfortable words, the gullible Clement VII fell haplessly into the trap. Summarily, he pardoned all the past transgressions of the Colonna family and lifted his admonition against Cardinal Colonna. With the threat from the south having miraculously disappeared, the pope felt he could now look to his budget. The cost of maintaining a garrison of six thousand soldiers and six hundred cavalry was a burden on his treasury. Despite howls of protest from his advisers, he dismissed the greater part of Rome's defenses, reducing his palace guard to a mere five hundred men.

With the pope thus so easily duped and disarmed, the plot was ready for execution. Several weeks of surreal calm fell over Rome. "Here all is quiet," wrote the Florentine ambassador. "No suspicions are aroused." His Spanish counterpart wrote with glee to the emperor that the treaty had lulled the pope into a false sense of security, while among the local populace dissatisfaction with the pontiff was rising. For his part, Emperor Charles V felt compelled to consult with his moral advisers before the plot was hatched. Was it acceptable in the eyes of God for him to withdraw his obedience to the pope and for his agents to attack Rome? By such actions would he not subject himself to excommunication? The pope had initiated the war, his confessor responded, so it was lawful to take all necessary measures in self-defense.

Both moral and military preparations proceeded quietly. In Naples, under the watchful eye of Ugo di Moncada, the Colonna mustered a force of three thousand soldiers and eight hundred horsemen. Across the water in Granada, Spain, Charles V prepared his formal response to Clement's brief of June 23. Its language was no less energetic than had been Clement's, and later it would be described as the "most violent document addressed in that century by a Catholic sovereign to a Pope." The pope's brief, wrote the emperor, had filled him with "astonishment," for such sentiments were unbecoming for the Vicar of Christ and the Chief Shepherd of Christendom. Clement had lent himself and his office to intrigues and alliances against the emperor. It was contrary to Scripture that a pontiff should gain possessions through bloodshed. Did he not remember that Christ had commanded Peter to replace the sword in its sheath? Despite his noble expressions in his brief, the pope's conduct did not protect Italy or the Holy See. Instead, by his actions, he had squandered both the loyalty of Christians and the treasure of the Holy Church.

He, the emperor, by contrast, had always shown "filial devotion" to the papacy. He was a lover of peace and wanted only peace and freedom for Italy. He reminded Clement that most of the papal revenues came from the emperor's dominions, and that therefore Clement owed the Empire much. His tenuous papal authority was thus dependent upon imperial favor. He should lay down his arms. By so doing, he would make it easier to combat the errors of the Lutheran heretics. By starting war on the Holy Roman Empire, he was forcing the emperor to employ Lutherans in self-defense. How could Charles uphold the Edict of Worms, with its ban on Martin Luther, when the pope was making war on him and endeavoring to deprive him of his empire? Rather than act like a partisan, the pope should act as the shepherd of the Christian commonwealth. Instead of quarreling, insulting one another, warring on one another, they should join together in a common effort against the heretic within and the Turkish menace without.

So with this apologia Charles V tied the war in Italy to the wider question of the internal rot in Christianity. The war in Italy was linked to the Catholic Reformation.

Within a day of Charles's apologia, the other great theme of European Christian history forced its way into the minds of the players. From the east came the shocking news that the prince of the Turks, Suleyman, had crushed the Hungarian army at the Battle of Mohács. The young and foolhardy king of Hungary, Louis II, had been killed as he led a suicidal attack into the center of the invading force; his body was found in a swamp and identified only by the jewels in his helmet.

Francesco Guicciardini, the pope's chief lieutenant, saw the disaster as the will of God. So distracted by their internal divisions and quarrels were the Christian kings of Europe that they had overlooked the greater threat from the outside. Clement VII had been among the most distracted. He had certainly been made aware of the advance of the Turks northward through the Balkans, to Belgrade and beyond. He had trusted that as in the past the stout Hungarians would blunt the advance. Now he learned that this last defense of Europe was gone, the Christian army decimated, Buda and Pest burned to the ground; the heart of Europe exposed. Gathering his cardinals together, he spoke eloquently of this threat to the bulwark of Christianity. He would appeal to all Christian kings of Europe to conclude a universal peace. He would convene a conference in France with Francis I, Charles V, and Cardinal Wolsey, Henry VIII's powerful prelate. The Christian sovereigns must lay aside their differences and face the threat of Islam, lest the forces of Mohammed come to Rome itself. He, Vicar of Christ and Defender of the Faith, would lead the crusade against the infidel.

They should "pray to God that He be favorable to so holy a work," Guicciardini wrote of the pope's appeal to his cardinals. "If this could not be carried out successfully because of the sins they all shared, that it please Him at least to grant the Pope grace that he might die during such negotiations, before all hope was ruled out. For no unhappiness, no misery, could be greater to him than to lose hope and the possibility of being able to lend his hand to quench so pernicious and pestilent a fire."

The pope and his cardinals had about a day to wallow in these grand and noble sentiments concerning universal peace. On September 19, 1526, a more immediate problem presented itself.

25.

SETTING THE STAGE

O n the morning of September 19, 1526, an army of nearly four thousand Spanish troops, under the command of Ugo di Moncada and the Colonna, appeared before the gates of Rome. To maintain the element of surprise, the soldiers had marched at a furious pace from Naples; oxen pulled their artillery. After they crashed into the city through the Gate of St. John the Lateran, they moved quickly to the Tiber River, stormed across the Ponte Sisto into Trastevere, then raced along the Lungara to the high ground of the Janiculum, where they looked over to the Borgo and St. Peter's. The Romans offered no resistance to the invaders. They were fed up with papal war taxes and especially the tax on wine, and they regarded this as a family spat, Medici versus Colonna. "This is not our affair, but the pope's," one resident was heard to say. Others were more vocal. With their great palace in the Quirinale, the Colonna were viewed as Romans rather than Neapolitans, and now their name was shouted in celebration. "Empire, Colonna, freedom!" The Spanish dispatched the few guards at the Porta San Spirito and poured into the Old Borgo.

Then the plundering began. The marauders raced through the corridors of the Vatican, into the papal apartments, even into the pope's very bedroom, stripping whatever could be removed: relics, crosses, chalices, pastoral vestments, even the pope's tiara. A soldier was seen dancing drunkenly through the streets wearing the pope's white vestments, the tiara half-cocked on his head, dispensing mock papal blessings. Raphael's tapestries were taken, and the cross of St. Peter itself was stripped of its ornament. Only a bribe for drink money saved the Vatican Library. "There was no greater respect for religion nor horror of sacrilege than if they had been Turks despoiling the churches of Hungary," Guicciardini wrote later. The price tag for the plunder was put at three hundred thousand ducats.

At the first sign of the threat, Clement had proclaimed that he would clothe himself in his full pontifical garb and meet the rebels as a martyr of Christ at the altar of St. Peter's, just as his predecessor Boniface VIII had greeted another Colonna renegade heroically two hundred years earlier. Clement's cardinals quickly talked him out of this insane posturing and hustled him through the covered passage to the bastion of Castel Sant'Angelo. From there, he could hear the rabble wreaking their havoc in the distance, beyond the range of the papal cannons. Unfortunately for the pope, the papal bastion had not been provisioned with food and water, and this sapped the pope's appetite for resistance. He called for Ugo di Moncada.

The Spanish *exaltado* presented himself as an obedient and contrite (if totally hypocritical) supplicant, throwing himself mawkishly at the feet of the pope, offering his apologies, and returning the despoiled tiara and the vicar's dented silver staff. Once he brushed away his crocodile tears and was on his feet, Moncada's demands were stiff. There was to be a four-month truce; papal troops were to be withdrawn from Lombardy, and the pope's fleet, under Andrea Doria, was to be withdrawn from Genoa. A full pardon for the Colonna was required. In return, Moncada would withdraw his troops to Naples. With them would go a Medici hostage, the husband of Clarise de' Medici, as security for the pact.

The pope was frantic. He fumed about the disloyalty of the Romans. "I will let them see what the absence of the Pope means to Rome," he said, scowling. He railed against Moncada's terms and against the Colonna, but he had no choice but to agree. Whatever his dismay at his humiliation, his hysteria was matched by that of Cardinal Colonna himself. The cardinal had come to Rome with his soldiers to be installed as pope and to have the current pope hung from the rafters. He was returning home empty-handed. Contemptuously, he told Moncada that he would not abide by the treaty. It was left to Moncada to explain why the Colonna had not followed up on their victory.

"They couldn't have done less," he said, "and it appeared to them that they had already done too much. Had they not made an agreement with Our Holy Father, it would have been necessary for them to leave Rome ashamed, having achieved nothing." Indeed, nothing had been achieved, except a little shame.

Nevertheless, the renegade troops did withdraw. As they were returning to Naples, Moncada wrote with satisfaction to Charles V. Their point had emphatically been made: the pope had been humbled and insulted. He exercised no control whatever over Rome. Their action had detached the Vatican from this so-called Holy League. That the pontiff was subservient to the emperor's whim had been made abundantly clear. Now, Moncada advised the emperor, for public consumption, to act as if he disapproved and disavowed the action of his unruly agents.

"It seems to me that your majesty ought to show great regret at what has befallen the Pope, and especially at the sack of his palace. You should give complete satisfaction to the nuncio and write to the Pope so as to cheer him in his misfortune. It would be well to write to the Cardinals also, and to assure all Christian princes that what has happened was contrary to your will and intentions. And you should do this in such a way as to ensure wide publicity."

In succeeding weeks, some papal forces were gradually pulled out of Lombardy, though a number were redeployed to Florence to protect Medici interests there, and still others remained in the vicinity of Milan under the ruse of their being in the pay of the French. Soldiers from the northern front poured into Rome itself, some seven thousand of them, filling the Eternal City with a newfound military spirit. By osmosis, their presence seemed to instill new confidence in the beleaguered pope. When Venetian soldiers captured Cremona, midway between Parma and Piacenza, from imperial forces, the pontiff was buoyed still further.

He still seethed with resentment against the Colonna, although he remained terrified of a second assault. Desperately, he appealed again to Francis I to meet his obligations to the Holy League, to follow his empty promises with a real commitment to enter the fray in northern Italy. The pope felt secure enough now to issue a citation against Cardinal Pompeo Colonna and the other leaders of the raid. Formally, the family, including the cardinal's brothers and nephews, were deprived of all their dignities. The catastrophe in Hungary seemed far away, almost like an afterthought. To his cardinals the pope still talked about traveling to Nice to affect a Christian peace between Charles V and Francis I and then to lead a holy force against Suleyman and the Mohammedan scourge. But inevitably, the troubles close to home took precedence.

To the north in Lombardy the illusion of a tilt back toward the pope lasted through October. Though the duke of Urbino, as papal commander, had been woefully slow and had missed important opportunities, his Venetian and Swiss soldiers now encircled Milan and were pressing hard against the imperial defenders. And the defenders were now in a bad way. Faced with the new privations, the citizens of Milan were on the verge of revolt against their occupiers. The imperial troops were unpaid and increasingly falling prey to sickness. The commander of imperial Milan, Charles de Bourbon, reported to Charles V that some three thousand of his soldiers, close to half of his garrison, had been taken ill. If the imperial forces in Lombardy received no reinforcements from overseas or from Germany, the duke of Urbino felt that he could starve out the enemy in a month or two.

But Charles V acted quickly at this call of distress. At the age of twenty-six he had developed into a mature, if austere, global leader. The Venetian ambassador described him at this time as a man "of serious character, very religious, with an ardent love of justice. He was a stranger to the light pleasures common to men of his age. He gave himself over rarely to the distraction of the chase, although he was a splendid athlete, the equal of any of his nobles in joust and tournament. He was constantly occupied in the government of his immense dominions and in the management of his affairs. He delights in negotiations and in presiding at his councils. In this he is most assiduous and spends most of his time." He would need all of these qualities as this struggle between spiritual and temporal authority heated up.

In Spain he equipped a fleet to transport some ten thousand Spanish and German troops to the Italian front. In command of this force he placed the viceroy of Naples, Charles de Lannoy. His orders were to land south of Rome (but north of Naples) on the coast near Gaeta, thereby simultaneously threatening Rome and stifling any ambitions the Colonna might still have toward further mischief. Simultaneously, the emperor ordered a similar number of troops to be levied in Germany and chose as their commander the venerable veteran of Pavia, George von Frundsberg. If Lannoy could bring his convoy safely across the water and Frundsberg could make it over the Alps, the imperial pincer would be formidable.

In the defender of Milan, Charles de Bourbon, and his rescuer, George von Frundsberg, the coming conflagration featured two of the most interesting characters of the period.

George von Frundsberg was a veteran warhorse, sixteen years older than Bourbon. His glorious service to the Empire was a study in loyalty rather than treason. He had fought in the Netherlands and in Bavaria, against the nobles of France and the peasants of Germany. Like Bourbon, some of his more heroic exploits had revolved around the competition between France and the Empire in northern Italy. In 1509, 1513, and 1514, he was engaged with the Venetians and the French. In the imperial invasion of Picardy in northern France from the Netherlands, which resulted in much of Lombardy devolving to the Empire, he had been an important commander. And he too, side by side with Bourbon, had been a general of great distinction in the imperial victory at the Battle of Pavia. Interestingly, he was also a convert to Lutheranism and had spoken in support of Martin Luther at the Diet of Worms five years before. With this extensive experience in field command, he became a visionary in military science. He had ushered in a new era of military discipline, military organization, order of battle, and esprit de corps.

He was best known as the "father of the landsknechts." These were the fearsome and colorful soldiers of southern Germany who came into existence as a corps d'elite during the reign of Maximilian I in the 1490s and who were recruited from the farms and towns of Swabia, west of Munich. Distinguished by their discipline, by their rectangular battle formations, and by their military organization along regimental lines, their preferred weapon was the eighteen-foot pike, which was especially effective in repulsing a cavalry charge. Their ranks also included halberdiers, whose weapon, shorter in length than the pike, was a combination of the battle-ax and pike, but which also had a hook at the base of the ax, better to pull an armored horseman from his steed. Sprinkled amid the pikemen and the halberdiers were arquebusiers, who carried a rudimentary musket, and still others who carried a twenty-eight-inch short sword known as the cat ripper. But at least from a distance, the landsknechts were more distinguished by their motley uniforms rather than their weapons. They sported wildly colorful doublets, quilted jerkins, garish stockings, leather pants, and spiked helmets or plumed berets. Frundsberg encouraged this sense of fun along with his strict discipline. By the mid-1520s these rowdy Swabian soldiers were known as the best in Europe.

The fates of these very different men, Bourbon and Frundsberg, were now to become intertwined.

In October 1526 Frundsberg mortgaged his Swabian castles in Mindelheim, raised thirty-five thousand ducats to pay for his army, and proceeded to the Tirol. There he recruited thirty-five companies, or twelve thousand troops. These landsknechts were mainly Lutheran. In his recruitment Frundsberg pointed to his encouragement of Martin Luther at the Diet of Worms five years before and waved a golden rope, promising that with their help and God's he would go to Rome and hang the pope. In this new threat, the struggle took on a new shape. Beyond the conflict between Christian and Muslim, between spiritual and temporal authority, it had become a struggle between Catholic and Protestant.

"There are many enemies and much honor to be had," he told the assembled recruits. "With God's help we will succeed in saving the emperor and his subjects."

The path over the Alps was not easy. The perilous high passes were well defended and fortified by the soldiers of the Holy League. So, instead of taking the more direct route toward Verona, Frundsberg marched his soldiers east to Trent and from there attempted a near impossible route over wild mountain gorges and across precipices where occasionally the stout Frundsberg had to be supported by soldiers who straddled him with their pikes. Despite the odds, this remarkable army did make it across, descended into Italy between the lakes of Garda and Idro, and came upon their first astonished opposition near Brescia.

Now pivotal was the status of Alfonso I, the duke of Ferrara, whose fiefdom held a strategic location in northern Italy and whom the pope had courted through the fall in the hope that the duke would join the Holy League. The duke had wavered between the sides. In the imperials' favor was the resentment that Alfonso I still harbored about prior interference in the affairs of his principality by previous popes, especially the warrior pope, Julius II. In his courtship Pope Clement VII was occasionally brusque. "If the duke wishes to make the emperor master of all Italy, let him do so," he told the Ferraran ambassador. "Much good may it bring him."

With Frundsberg's fiery landsknechts in the country now, Alfonso I swung over to the imperial side, and this freed Frundsberg to cross the Po River. Opposing him on the other side of the river, however, was the duke of Urbino, who, in an effort to block the Germans from joining up with Bourbon's Spaniards, had divided his forces between Milan and the Po. At Governolo a fierce fight ensued. "The landsknechts stood with their muskets like a wall," wrote an observer; "when the enemy drew near, the Germans showed their faces and drove the enemy back." At this engagement, Giovanni de' Medici, the leader of the so-called Black Bands, was killed. (The black bands they wore were originally in honor of the late Medici pope, Leo X.) He was the best field general of the Holy League. Indeed, the very hopes of the papacy and the Medici rested with him.

Confidently, on November 28, Frundsberg crossed the Po and faced no opposition. The duke of Urbino remained idle in the face of the exotic, highly skilled landsknechts. His strategy now became to follow Frundsberg's columns at a safe distance and occasionally to snipe at the invaders' rear guard. When the pope's statesman, Guicciardini, heard about Urbino's timidness, he remarked, "The good fortune of the emperor is boundless, but it achieves its height in the circumstance that his enemies have neither the wit nor the will to use their forces."

Frundsberg pressed on to threaten Parma and Piacenza, bolstered now with money and supplies from Ferrara. On this open ground, he paused to contact Bourbon:

"In the face of great dangers, I have crossed high mountains and deep waters, have spent two months in the country enduring poverty, hunger, and frost. Owing to the great patience of my soldiers and with the help of God, I have divided and driven back the enemy. I lie here in the enemy's country, attacked every day. I need further instructions."

Meanwhile, three days later, far to the south, the viceroy of Naples and imperial plenipotentiary, Charles de Lannoy, landed his fleet at Gaeta. On the shore he was greeted by the Colonna, Cardinal Pompeo Colonna and the general Ascanio Colonna. They urged Lannoy to march immediately on Rome, which was less than a hundred miles up the coast. Lannoy chose instead to move inland against the papal fortress of Frosinone. The defenders of this papal stronghold were the Italian mercenaries of the Black Bands. It is a commentary on the chaotic Italian history of this period that Lannoy had commanded these very troops only three years ago in the Battle of Bicocca, when they were allied with the landsknechts, commanded by George von Frundsberg. But in a pay dispute, the Black Bands had switched their allegiance back to the pope.

The concatenation of reverses . . . the advance of the landsknechts, the defection of the duke of Ferrara, the death of Giovanni de' Medici, the timidity of the duke of Urbino, the indifference of the Vatican's allies Venice and France, and the landing of Lannoy with his Spanish troops at Gaeta . . .

dawned on Rome and the Vatican in early December. The joy of only a few weeks earlier turned again to gloom. Romans panicked and started to hide their possessions.

"We are on the brink of ruin," wrote a papal adviser. "Fate has poured all its evils upon us and has nothing more to add to our misery. We have already received a sentence of death and only await its execution." Characteristically, Clement VII was hysterical. Of his demeanor, an adviser said, "The Holy Father is in such a state that he does not know where he is."

26.

PAY! PAY!

The year of 1527, the year of penultimate misfortune for the papacy, began with ominous signs. Leaving his siege of Frosinone, Lannoy turned up in Rome to present his demands. Predictably, they were harsh and unrealistic: the papal enclaves of Parma, Piacenza, Pisa, Leghorn, Ostia, and Civitavecchia were all to be surrendered to the Empire and two hundred thousand ducats paid to satisfy the bounty-hunting landsknechts. Again, the privileges, lands, and titles of the Colonna were to be restored. A few days later, the pope received the envoy of Francis I. After months of silence, the pope hoped this meeting would bring good tidings of a renewed French commitment to the Holy League; perhaps relief troops were on their way to Lombardy. In this fantasy, the pontiff was disappointed. Instead, the French ambassador brought an additional demand: the price of French support in the Italian war was the kingdom of Naples. The son of the king of France should be proclaimed the king of Naples and marry Catherine de' Medici, it was suggested. The pope, of course, was in no position to provide large sums of money to Lannoy or to convey the hostile kingdom of Naples (now virtually an integral part of Spain) to France or anyone else.

"The pope does not have a penny left," the Venetian ambassador wrote home. The pontiff was being urged to sell cardinals' hats to raise money. For the time being, out of "honorable conscience," he was turning this suggestion aside. "I would rather sell the property of St. Peter's," he said theatrically. Could not Frundsberg be bribed with Venetian money? the pope wondered. Not likely, the Venetian ambassador replied, for one who had mortgaged his own estates in Germany to raise his Lutheran army of invasion.

Before the month of January was out, a different sort of danger surfaced. Lannoy and the Colonna had become impatient with the advance of the armies and decided to try a more direct approach. They recruited an abbot who was close to the pope as the linchpin of a plot to assassinate the pope and eight of his cardinals. The plot was foiled before it could be hatched, but it put the pope on notice about just how desperate his situation was and just how severe were the dangers that lurked around every drape. As January turned to February, Clement had a brief respite from his travails. To the surprise of all, news arrived that Lannoy had miraculously been defeated at Frosinone by the stout Black Bands and was retreating. From the doldrums, the pope soared into glee.

"I do not know when His Holiness has ever experienced so much pleasure," his amanuensis reported. The pope's happiness would be momentary. Lannoy was retreating and regrouping.

In early February Charles de Bourbon left a sizable garrison at Milan and took his remaining force east to join Frundsberg at Piacenza. Bourbon was bringing with him an unruly horde that was already in open mutiny. His Spanish soldiers had not been paid for months, and they were frantic. The situation had disintegrated to the point where the men were threatening their officers and demanding money. They had resorted to outright robbery in Milan. In November Bourbon had written to the emperor that his men "were so mutinous and disobedient as to be becoming unmanageable." The duke had sold his own jewels to pay a pittance of what he owed, and he had given many speeches. But the only thing that Bourbon was really offering was the dream of great plunder in Florence or Rome.

In joining up with the landsknechts, the Spanish contingent was temporarily mollified. The weather was bad and the roads were impassable, and the wretched soldiers shivered and groused at Piacenza for twenty days. Still their numbers were formidable. The union brought the imperial force to a strength of over thirty thousand soldiers. But whether they were an army or a mob was open to question.

On March 7 the joint force was on the move south along the ancient Emilian Way, crossing over the Panaro River north of Bologna and into the traditional territory of the Papal States. Francesco Guicciardini, the pope's leading statesman, had come to Bologna to assess the situation. To him Bourbon applied for safe passage through papal lands to Naples. At so transparent a trick, when Florence and Rome were clearly the targets, Guicciardini demurred. This was a hollow gesture of resistance, however. As with the imperial soldiers, the papal soldiers had also not been paid for weeks, and they began to melt into the countryside. The weather remained horrid, with torrents of rain soaking the soldiers on both sides and turning the ground to rivers of mud. Nevertheless, this wavering serpent that the imperial army had become was within striking distance of Florence and the wealth of the Medici. Through their moist lips the imperial soldiers could almost taste it.

In Rome the Medici pope was nearly apoplectic. With virtually no choice, he made one last desperate effort to save his papacy and his beloved city. He called for Lannoy, whom he had been calling "the greatest enemy of the papacy," hosted him lavishly at the Vatican, and showered him with worthless honors. Then the pope acceded to the viceroy's terms: the cities in the north to the Empire; the restoration of the Colonna; disbanding of the papal army; Naples to remain imperial; Milan to the displaced Sforza; and sixty thousand ducats for the Spanish and German invaders in return for an eight-month armistice and the withdrawal of the imperial army from Italy. Despite the skepticism of his aides, Clement was sure that the terms of his agreement would be accepted. "What is written is written," he said. Quietly, the pope dismissed all his forces with the exception of one hundred cavalry, two thousand Swiss guards, and two thousand Black Bands, congratulating himself on saving thirty thousand ducats a month.

Within a few days the rumor of this dubious treaty reached the sopping, hungry soldiers outside Bologna. The wretched imperial troops saw their predicament starkly. They had come all this way, endured unspeakable hardship without pay; they were within reach of the enormous wealth of Florence and Rome; and it would be all for nothing. On the strength of an evil deal with the Antichrist made by another commander, not even their own, they were meant to turn around and slink home empty-handed like beggars.

On March 13, the revolt was immediate. Mutineers stormed into Bourbon's quarters while the estimable eighth duke of Bourbon discarded his dignity and hid with the horses in a nearby stable. Later, his splendid ducal coat of gold mail was found in a ditch. The mutiny spread quickly to the landsknechts, who also rampaged through the camp and the countryside, threatening to string up their superior officers. "Pay! Pay!" they shouted as they sloshed through the mud.

At this appalling scene of mayhem the chivalrous general George von Frundsberg, the most distinguished commander of his generation, hero of Picardy and Pavia, Bicocca and Milan, stalwart of the Hapsburgs, stepped forward to quell the tumult and to restore order. He pleaded with his "children" to have patience for another month, and then all their magnificent efforts would be rewarded. By the account of his secretary, his oration was "so earnest" that it "would have moved a stone." But the stone was immovable. His men shouted him down. "Pay! Pay!" they shouted furiously. Disciplinarian that he was, Frundsberg was shocked and heartbroken at their defiance. He was suddenly seized with an attack of apoplexy and sank down on a drum, suffering a stroke. His lieutenants carried him from the scene, took him on a donkey to his tent. His physicians ordered that he be placed in a bath of warm oil, in which a fox had been boiled, but it was to no avail. In grief his secretary called his affliction the sickness of Hercules and compared his hero to Romulus and Caesar. Eventually he was transported to his estates in Swabia, where he died a year later.

Now the command of the mob fell to Bourbon, who emerged from his malodorous hiding place and attempted to exercise a measure of control. To mollify his soldiers, now described as "raging lions," he promised to enforce the "law of Mohammed" when they reached Florence or Rome: three days of unrestricted plunder upon the victory over a resisting foe. To Lannoy and the pope himself, he conveyed his rejection of their nefarious treaty and demanded not 60,000 ducats but 150,000. He admitted candidly that he was powerless to control his troops and was, therefore, compelled to advance. After reading this, the pope's right-hand man, Guicciardini, told the pope that three things remained to him: to yield everything in a new treaty, to take flight, or to defend himself to the death. "The most honorable is to perish like a hero," he proclaimed.

With an infusion of supplies from Ferrara, the horde moved south on March 30. Bourbon's scouts in the upper Arno Valley reported that snow still covered the Apennines and that the passes into Florence had been beefed up by papal forces. Florence or Rome? Bourbon delayed his decision as the imperialists proceeded down the Emilian Way. Mutinous soldiers rushed forward, shedding their baggage and their artillery in anticipation of easy plunder. The duke of Urbino followed with his army at a safe remove twenty-five miles behind.

Meanwhile, the pope faced a rebellion within his own court. Both generals and cardinals complained that by disbanding his local defenses, the pontiff was sacrificing Rome to save Florence. Francesco Gonzaga, the marquis of Mantua and a papal ally, wrote on April 11, "The imprudence and carelessness [of the pope] is too great. Before the armistice has taken effect the Pope has entirely disarmed himself. All this has been done only to save a little money. Everyone is astonished at such proceedings. But without doubt, God's will has so ordered this, that the Church and its leaders may be destroyed."

By April 20 the imperial horde was in Florentine territory at the Pieve of San Stefano in the upper Arno Valley and envisaging "the glorious plunder of Florence." To his commander in Milan Bourbon wrote that he would not delay a single hour in his advance, "for in consequence of the treaty with our good viceroy the enemy is unprepared and can scarcely find time to take precautions. The distress of the army is indescribable, but it is willingly borne, since the soldiers think it a thousand years until this

accursed sack of Florence. We shall therefore march straight toward it."
Bourbon took the occasion as well to raise his monetary demand to 240,000
gold ducats. The pope appealed to England, France, and Venice to help; all
demurred. "To produce 240,000 ducats," wrote a papal aide, "is as impossible as to join heaven and earth together." In hearing this response, Bourbon, now a professional extortionist, raised his demand still further to
300,000.

Rome took on a surreal air. In the streets around St. Peter's, a wild and
terrifying apparition from Siena roamed about, prophesying the end of the
papacy. This was Bartolomeo Carosi, known as Brandano, suggesting the
firebrand that he was. He had reputedly repented after a youth of dissipa-
tion through severe acts of penance. His words were regarded by some as
lunacy and by others as prophecy. Barefoot, with long, disheveled red hair
down to his shoulders, he was clothed only in a skimpy leather apron. His
body was strong but emaciated from extreme fasting. His green-yellow eyes
blazed from his drawn cheeks. In his right hand he brandished a cross, and
in his left a skull. Rome, he proclaimed, would soon suffer the fate of Troy,
for he had seen the signs of its destruction in the planets. He had come to
proclaim the truth, as Jonah had preached to Nineveh, the ancient city of
Assyria, before its destruction.

"I cry out from the belly of hell," he cried. Rome was the "proud mistress
of crimes" and the "bastard of Sodom." "For thy sins, Rome, you shall be
destroyed. Repent! They shall deal with you as God dealt with Sodom and
Gomorrah! Turn away from your sins." The tempest was coming, he predicted. "If you do not believe me, in fourteen days you will see it!" Then he
mumbled incomprehensibly, as if to himself, "He has robbed the Mother of
God to adorn his harlot, or rather his friend."

These ravings unsettled the population considerably, so much so that
the pope felt compelled to lock the prophet up. The prophet spoke blasphemy. Still, graffiti about the forthcoming doom were mysteriously
scrawled on the walls of the Vatican.

If the atmosphere in Rome was surreal, the mood in Florence was rebellious. Toward the end of April Bourbon's dangerous rabble was camped at

Arezzo, famished and insubordinate and desperate for the spoils of Florence, only twenty kilometers away. Yet to the papal forces, it was unclear
whether the serpent would strike Florence or Rome. Suddenly, disgruntled,
armed youths, angry at the dictatorial Medici rule in Florence and terrified
of the imperial army close by, stormed the Palazzo Signoria in an attempt
to overthrow Medici rule and reestablish a more conciliatory republic. This
drew the duke of Urbino with his Venetian army into the city to quash
the rebellion. Only after a difficult and subtle negotiation, conducted by
the pope's lieutenant general, Francesco Guicciardini, were the rebels persuaded to leave the palazzo peaceably, avoiding bloodshed. A byproduct of
this maneuver was that papal forces now blocked the road to Florence.

When news of Urbino's presence in Florence reached Bourbon, he
scrapped his designs on Florence and decided to move on Rome. This decision further infuriated his hungry soldiers, who were by now surviving as
roving bands and eating unripe almonds off the trees. Rome, they felt, was
a more challenging military target than Florence; it enjoyed an aura of im-
pregnability. Bourbon tried to mollify them, promising to "make them all
rich" and adopting the slogan "Victory or death!" But they were suspicious
of him now and insolent to his face. Once they got close to Rome, they
feared that Bourbon would cut an unholy deal with the pope that would
avoid plunder of the city.

In fact, Rome was far from impregnable. For years personal weapons
had been banned in the city, and the walls had been neglected for centuries.
It was essentially a city of priests and their servants, and it had been rendered even more docile during the years of luxury and indulgence under
Leo X. The Roman citizens despised the papal government with its heavy
taxation and grandiose airs, and they saw in the emperor a preferable governor. The city's garrison consisted of about two thousand Swiss guards and
the remnants of the Black Bands.

In early May the unruly imperial horde surged south, laying Montepul-
ciano and Montefiascone to waste, shedding its remaining artillery and baggage, and covering as much as eighteen miles in a day. Its commanders were
powerless to control the savagery of the plundering. "If God does not

punish such cruelty and wickedness," wrote one of Bourbon's associates, "we shall infer that He does not trouble himself about the affairs of the world." From the rebels of Siena the imperials received some supplies, but only enough to deter them from falling on Siena itself. It was enough to reinvigorate them for the final push.

When the force reached Viterbo, they were greeted by the grand master of the Knights of Rhodes, Villiers de L'Isle-Adam, for Viterbo had now been granted to the military monks as a refuge after the disaster at the hands of Suleyman four years earlier. With this special dispensation, Viterbo was exempt from pillage and off-limits to the invaders. True to their mandate as Hospitallers, the Knights of Rhodes fed the invaders as a courtesy.

27.

RABBLE AT
PORTA SAN SPIRITO

I n Rome, meanwhile, Clement VII at last comprehended his desperate need for a quick influx of money to raise a defense, and repugnant as it was to him, he sold three cardinal's hats for forty thousand ducats each. Of course, armies do not spring up overnight, and this maneuver came far too late to make a difference. The pope turned to the elite of Rome in an appeal for money, but they were indifferent. The richest member of the nobility offered to lend the pope one hundred ducats, while the others were gathering up their valuables and fleeing the city. Again the pope appealed to Henry VIII and Francis I both for cash and for troops. They should put aside their differences and come to the defense of Christianity. This time, the appeal seemed to have an effect, at least on paper, as England and France made a treaty in late April, the core of which was a promise of marriage between the reigns. Henry VIII joined the Holy League, but it would be months before either his money or his soldiers could arrive in Italy. Francis I, in turn, was secretly more interested in seeing Charles V exhaust his resources in the Italian campaign than in meeting the imperial forces on the battlefield. So this conclave too was an empty gesture.

Still, the pope seemed to have an infinite capacity for self-delusion. He seemed to expect League soldiers to appear out of thin air. To his cardinals he supposed that the invaders would turn west and satisfy their appetites in Siena. When they did not, he opined that the "barbarians" were so bedraggled and wasted from famine that they would have no strength for combat. When he received news of a minor victory by his forces in a skirmish at Ponte Molle, a bridge over the Tiber just north of Rome, he was elated and supposed it to be a turning point. "The Pope is in the best of spirits," the envoy from Mantua reported. Grandly, the pontiff rode around the city offering encouragement and declined to flee to Civitavecchia on the coast, where the navy of Andrea Doria waited offshore. Even when the invaders could be seen pouring over the Neroian Hills and approaching the walls of the city, he was confident, for he had heard that they had shed their artillery.

His delusions were encouraged by the fantasy of his own commander, Renzo da Ceri, a once heroic but now incompetent leader, who felt that the several thousand defenders, recruited from local tradesmen and the grooms of cardinals, would be sufficient to turn back the horde. With this confidence, he fortified the Borgo and Trastevere but declined to destroy the bridges over the Tiber, even as the imperials began to appear on the Janiculum. Soon enough the invaders were camped in the vineyards behind St. Peter's.

On May 4, the pontiff made himself look further ridiculous by donning his papal vestments and grandly proclaiming a crusade against the imperial army, against all Lutherans, and against "sons of Moors" who were then threatening his sacred city. For those who stepped forward, he promised eternal bliss, but few stepped forward.

At dawn, two days later, under the cover of a thick fog, the attack began. Bourbon still exercised enough control to concentrate his forces at the weakest points along the Leonine Walls, the stretch between the Porta San Spirito and the Porta del Torrione. He rode from point to point on a great horse with his silver coat of mail covered by his signature white surcoat. The Spanish troops massed at the Porta San Spirito, while the landsknechts attacked farther south at the Porta del Torrione (or Porta Cavelleggeri). Without artillery the attackers were at a decided disadvantage, reduced to scaling ladders and hand weapons. But the thickness of the fog allowed them to get close to the walls before they could be seen. At first they were repulsed with heavy losses.

Seeing this, Bourbon, in his glistening silver armor, rushed forward rashly and began to climb a scaling ladder at the Porta del Torrione. Above him among the papal soldiers was Benvenuto Cellini, later famous as a preeminent artist of the post-Renaissance. He would later claim for himself a heroic role: "Directing my arquebus where I saw the thickest concentration of the enemy, I aimed exactly at one who was higher than the rest. The fog prevented me from being certain whether he was on horseback or on foot. When we had fired two rounds apiece, I crept cautiously up to the wall. Among the enemy there was a most extraordinary confusion. I discovered afterward that one of our shots had killed the constable of France. He was the man whom I had first noticed above the heads of the rest."

Mortally wounded in the thigh, Bourbon was taken to an adjoining chapel, where he died within a half hour. It would go down in legend that his last words were "To Rome! To Rome." Eventually, his body was carried to the Sistine Chapel, where it lay in state, and this probably saved that magnificent chapel from ruin.

Now completely leaderless, the assault was renewed with a vengeance. Within an hour the invaders broke through both gates and poured into the Borgo. Despite the heroic efforts of Swiss guards, the defenders for the most part took flight in total rout. As the imperialists swarmed into the City of Rome, Clement VII prayed in his apartments. His cardinals and his pathetic commander, Renzo da Ceri, burst in on him with news of the calamity and hustled the weeping pontiff along the covered passage toward the papal bastion of Castel Sant'Angelo. When they came to the open bridge across the moat, someone threw a purple velvet cloak over the pope's white vestments so he would not be recognized by the enemy below. His escape was narrow. Had he tarried further as long as it took to say three Apostles' Creeds, wrote a Spanish observer, he would certainly have been captured.

Castel Sant'Angelo quickly became the sole place of refuge. As smoke mingled with the fog, its denizens, including now fourteen cardinals, two ambassadors, and three thousand others along with the pope, peered helplessly down on the scene of devastation. Their heavy cannons were now worthless. "We stood there and looked on at all that passed as if we had been spectators of a *festa*," wrote one artilleryman. "It was impossible to fire for had we done so, we should have killed more of our own people than the enemy. Between the church of S. Maria Transpontina and the gate of the castle more than four thousand persons were crowded together pell-mell, and as far as we could see, hardly fifty landsknechts behind them. Two standard-bearers of the latter forced their way through the turmoil with uplifted banners as far as the great gate of the castle, but were shot down at the head of the bridge."

Only pockets of resistance remained in the Vatican. Swiss guards died to the last man around the obelisk next to St. Peter's. When the remaining resistance was quashed, the landsknechts repaired to the Campo dei Fiore to set up camp, not far from the national church of Germany, Santa Maria dell'Anima. The Spaniards camped in the Piazza Navona across from their national church, S. Giacomo. Matter-of-factly, a German knight wrote, "On May 6 we took Rome by storm; put 6,000 men to death, took everything that we could find in the churches and on the ground, and burnt a great part of the city."

After midnight the pillaging of the richest city in the world began in earnest.

Driven by pent-up privation and greed, the invaders fell upon the city with no less a vengeance than the Goths had exhibited 980 years earlier. They stripped churches and palaces and monasteries, stealing relics and paintings, lifting all things of value until an estimate of the loss could later be put at one million ducats. A German soldier replaced the point of his spear with the sacred lance head from Calvary. The Handkerchief of Veronica, which had supposedly wiped the brow of Christ, imprinting his image on the cloth, was passed around in taverns. The busts of the Apostles from St. John Lateran were affixed to spears and sported through the streets. The Cross of Constantine was dragged through the Borgo and lost. One soldier paraded a limp rope, which he claimed was the rope that had hanged Judas. Raphael's tapestries were stolen and sold, along with other masterpieces of the Renaissance. The grave of St. Peter was profaned, along with the coffins of Popes Julius II and Sixtus IV. Landsknechts and Spaniards divided up jewels using shovels. Parodies of sacred ceremonies were performed in the squares. Landsknechts shouted up to the Castel Sant'Angelo that they would make Martin Luther the next pope. Priests were forced to give asses Communion. According to one report, "some who resisted were suspended naked from their own windows by a sensitive limb." Dice were rolled on the high altar of St. Peter's as the invading soldiers drank holy wine with prostitutes from sacred chalices. Only through vigorous appeals to his own soldiers was Philibert of Chalon, the prince of Orange, able to save the Vatican Library, but from other precious archives papers of great historical value were thrown to the winds. And the prince of Orange, to whom nominal command of the mob had devolved and who was only twenty-five years old, was himself gravely wounded before the Castel Sant'Angelo as he tried in vain to control the plundering.

More lucrative even than the theft of property were the ransoms that could be extracted from ecclesiastical and temporal notables. They were forced to pay immense sums to one group for their freedom, only to be detained and bilked by another group. "In the whole of Rome," wrote an observer, "there was not a living soul over three years of age who was not obliged to pay a ransom." Cardinals and bishops were a favorite target, especially by the Lutherans, who seethed with hatred for the Roman Church. Some of these were paraded on asses through the streets in their clerical robes and mocked, while their palaces were singled out for special destruction. Even the palace of their supposed ally Cardinal Colonna in the Piazza SS. Apostoli was not spared. Cardinal Cajetan, who had questioned Martin Luther severely in Augsburg, was dragged through the streets, then paraded, wearing a porter's cap, on the shoulders of landsknechts.

Women too were violated. Husbands were forced to pay money to redeem their wives. "Hearing the cries and miserable shrieks of Roman women, and of nuns led in droves by the soldiers to satisfy their lust," the pope's statesman, Francesco Guicciardini, wrote later, "one could not but say that God's judgments were beclouded and concealed from mortal men, inasmuch as He allowed the renowned chastity of the Roman women to be so miserably and brutally violated." Some women hurled themselves from balconies to escape their fate. Another account said of the noblewomen of Rome, "Marchionesses, countesses, and baronesses now served the unruly troops, and long afterward the patrician women of the city were called 'the relics of the sack of Rome.'"

Weeks before, when he'd struggled to maintain control over his forces, Bourbon had promised to exercise the law of Mohammed when they captured Florence or Rome. This law accorded to a victorious army three days of unrestricted plunder in the cities and homes and lands of a resisting foe, and in this era it seemed to be accepted as a rule of war in Christian countries as well. The spoils of war were the warrior's reward on earth for his struggle in the highest duty against the infidel, just as paradise was his reward in heaven. In the Koran, plunder belonged to Allah, not to the individual. It was Allah's gift, and one fifth of it, the "holy one fifth," was supposed to be given for charity and to the poor. "Eat ye the spoils of war," runs the Koranic verse, "for they are lawful and pure." With this, the conscience of the plunderer was relieved.

But the occupiers of Rome were no longer an army in any sense, nor were they bound by any Islamic laws. They were leaderless in their unbridled ravaging. So after three days, when the prince of Orange tried to call a halt, he was ignored. On the fourth day Cardinal Pompeo Colonna arrived in Rome. Horrified at the devastation and at the spectacle of the dead moldering everywhere in the streets, he sought to quell the raging fever. Some days later, the treacherous cardinal was ushered into the Castel Sant'Angelo for an audience with Clement. Colonna was like the lance of Achilles, someone remarked, he wounded and healed at the same time. The two rivals faced one another warily, tearfully. It was almost difficult to remember whether at that moment Colonna was deprived of or restored to his "dignities." But with his own Roman palace in ruins, Colonna was now

Constantinople
Library of Congress

Suleyman the Magnificent,
tenth sultan of the Ottoman Empire
Hungarian National Museum

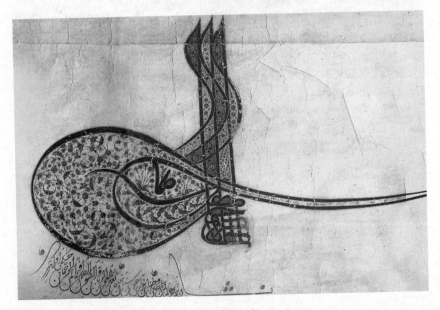

The seal of Sultan Suleyman I
Museum of the Topkapi Palace

Charles V, Holy Roman emperor and leader of the Hapsburg Dynasty
Library of Congress

The double-eagle seal of the Hapsburg Dynasty

Francis I, king of France
Library of Congress

Henry VIII, king of England
Gelman Library, George Washington University

Clement VII, Medici pope
Library of Congress

Luther burns his excommunication order, 1520
Library of Congress

Leo X and Clement VII,
Medici popes
Library of Congress

Ibrahim Pasha, Suleyman's
favorite and grand vizier
Library of Congress

Roxellana, the first lady
of Suleyman's harem
Library of Congress

The fortress at Rhodes
Library of Congress

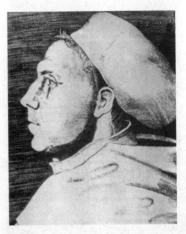

Martin Luther in 1521
German Historical Institute

Luther confronts Charles V at the Diet of Worms, 1521
Staatsgalerie, Stuttgart

The capture of Francis I at Pavia, 1525

Gelman Library, George Washington University

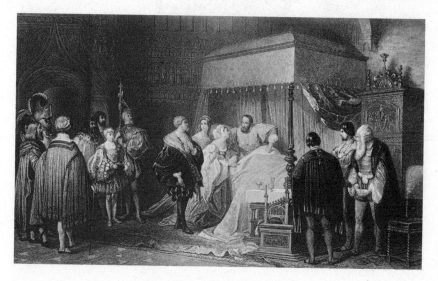

The captivity of Francis I in Madrid

Gelman Library, George Washington University

Suleyman at Belgrade
Library of Congress

The imperial coronation of Charles V by Clement VII, Bologna, 1530
National Gallery of Art Library, Gift of Lessing J. Rosenwald

Janissary
Library of Congress

Landsknecht
German Historical Institute

LEFT: European galley
Library of Congress

BELOW: Barbary pirate galliot
Library of Congress

Kheir-ed-Din Barbarossa, Barbary pirate
and Suleyman's admiral
Turkish Naval Museum, Istanbul

Andrea Doria, Charles V's
imperial admiral at Tunis
Library of Congress

Muley Hassan, dissolute king of Tunis
Gelman Library, George Washington University

Older Charles
Library of Congress

Older Suleyman
Library of Congress

Suleyman and Roxellana

Gelman Library, George Washington University

Mosque of Suleyman
Library of Congress

a victim as well as a perpetrator. Together they bemoaned the fate of Rome, even though clearly Colonna's insult to Rome the year before had set the stage for the devastation outside. He expressed regret; the pope asked for his help and offered new honors. Empty promises and flatteries were exchanged, and the bizarre meeting broke up with nothing accomplished. Meanwhile, in the streets, Spaniards and landsknechts began to turn on one another in dispute over dividing the spoils from the richest palaces, and this had a greater effect on bringing the situation under control. The tension between the two camps provided an opportunity for commanders to step in and mediate. But not until eight days had passed did the fury begin to spend itself.

With the sounds of mayhem constantly in his ears, Pope Clement VII sat in his bastion amid his fourteen cardinals and wept. He was paralyzed into inaction, vacillating between one course and another about what to do, delusional about the relief that he felt was imminent. He made no effort to rally his few supporters or to come to terms with the situation. In an initial contact with a representative of the mob outside, instead of trying to stop the pandemonium, the pope sought to buy time, hoping that the army of the Holy League under the duke of Urbino would soon arrive and lift the siege. Urbino and his army, however, were far away. Several days before the attack on Rome, they were still in Florence. Urbino, as usual, was slow in moving. He tarried for three days in Perugia to satisfy an old grudge. His army did not arrive in Isola, eight miles north of Rome, until May 22, two weeks into the sack of the city. He had no appetite for confronting this wild Lutheran rabble.

The pope again turned to Lannoy, the viceroy of Naples, to intervene, even though Lannoy had already shown his perfidy. The viceroy was in Siena, but even if he was open to an accommodation, he had no influence over the Spanish and Germans in Rome. They saw him as a traitor and dealmaker who would only short-circuit them from taking their just deserts. When Lannoy turned up in Rome on May 28 to consult with Clement, imperial soldiers threatened to kill him, and he quickly fled. Meanwhile, the landsknechts were still demanding three hundred thousand ducats as the price for desisting. The pope replied that he had no more than ten thousand ducats in his coffers.

The soldiers had released the wild-haired prophet Brandano from confinement, and he now turned on his liberators. "Now is the time. Rob and take all that you can find," he said to cheers. But then he deflated them: "You will have to yield everything up again. The property of priests and the spoils of war come and go."

The command of the marauders had nominally passed to the prince of Orange, who had formally been designated the successor by Bourbon before the attack on Rome began and who now occupied the papal apartments, while his horses were stabled in the Sistine Chapel. After eight days of unchecked plundering, he asserted a small measure of control. He warned the mob of Urbino's large army to the north of the possibility that if they did not reorganize themselves into their proper military units, the looters could lose all their loot. With no progress toward a resolution, the invaders prepared to besiege the Castel Sant'Angelo. As the pope watched the enemy dig a deep trench around the castle for the siege, this seemed to concentrate his mind. On May 18 he was prepared to surrender, but then a day later, he wavered, asking for a six-day delay. "I wish to deal fairly with you," he told the enemy's plenipotentiary. "I have made a capitulation that holds little honor for me, and I would gladly escape from this disgrace. The army of the League is close at hand, so I ask for six days to see if I am relieved." Such a tactic would only increase the wrath of the besiegers, the imperial envoy replied. If the castle fell, the Apostolic See would forever be destroyed.

The duke of Urbino was now close enough to appreciate the scope of the catastrophe. "The destruction of Jerusalem could not have been worse than that of Rome," the Venetian ambassador informed him. Hardly a house in the city had been spared. Pestilence had begun to set in. Provisions in the pope's bastion were growing short. In his councils of war Urbino heard only what he wanted to hear: that the situation was impossible. To his lieutenants he announced that the Castel Sant'Angelo was provisioned for three months, and he would not attack until he received reinforcements from Switzerland. On June 2 he ordered his army to retreat to Viterbo. This craven retreat would forever after be remembered in Ariosto's famous epic poem, *Orlando Furioso* (canto 33, stanza 49):

> Loe here the wofull murder and the rapes
> That Rome doth suffer in cruell sacke
> Where neither thing profane nor holy scapes
> But all alike do go to spoyle and wracke
> The League that should relieve sits still and gapes
> And where they should step forward, they shrinke back.
> Thus Peter's successour by them forsaken
> Is straight besieged and at length is taken.

On June 5 the pope surrendered. Ignominiously, he placed himself and his cardinals in the hands of the imperial generals. He promised four hundred thousand ducats would be paid in installments to the imperial army. The papal cities of Ostia, Modena, Parma, Piacenza, and the naval base of Civitavecchia were surrendered. He restored the ever-restored Colonna to their "dignities," and he revoked all his recent excommunications. Two days later, the papal garrison vacated the papal castle as German and Spanish soldiers marched in. The pope and his cardinals became the prisoners of Alarcon, the jailer a year earlier of Francis I. A landsknecht found the pope and his cardinals cowering "in a narrow chamber, making great lamentation and weeping bitterly. As for us, we all had become rich." Still the spectacle of the pope's final humiliation touched even this stoic Teutonic warrior. "Even if we are forced to say that they have brought this misfortune on themselves, it is still heartrending to see the chief ruler of the Christian church in such distress and humiliation."

Within a few weeks, news of the Italian developments reached Charles V in Spain, and he reacted with the most deplorable hypocrisy. Feigning overweening remorse, he put his court into mourning, while he gathered his inner council together to discuss what his public reaction should be. It was generally agreed that he should express his regret for the awful fate of Rome and identify it as an unforeseen and unintended act of God. That was public relations. In a letter to the pope on July 25, after these obsequies, he said his most fervent hope after the liberation of Francis I had been that Christian princes would unite against the Turk. But then the pontiff had arranged alliances against him and had attacked imperial interests in Italy, indignities and insults against which the emperor was compelled to defend himself. That his troops had run amok and his commanders had been killed and had blundered, he regretted, and if he could, he would shed his own blood to repair the disaster. By this circular reasoning, he laid the blame for the sack of Rome on the pope himself.

To the Christian princes of Europe, in a letter from Valladolid on August 2, Charles summoned all his propagandistic resources to shift the blame to the pope. "Since they wished to wage war on us, against all reason and justice, we were forced to take up arms in our own defense. But first we protested not only to the Pope but also the College of Cardinals, so that no one might complain if, as a result of this war, which we did not seek, the Apostolic See should suffer some harm. Indeed we pointed out that they could only blame themselves for the consequences since they had been the cause of it all. Our protest availed nothing. . . . So we committed our cause to God and sent more troops from Germany into Italy in order that we might at least achieve through force what we had been unable to accomplish through love and virtue." As if these crocodile tears were not enough, the emperor also argued that God sanctioned the sack: "This has been the will of God, who in His infinite goodness allows great evils in order that even greater good may come."

Of course, the real focus of his council was on how to take advantage of an opportunity so rich in possibility. Perhaps the emperor should go to Italy and personally set the pontiff free in a great and charitable show of unity between the Empire and the papacy. Perhaps this was the occasion for his formal coronation as the Holy Roman emperor, the secular leader of all Christians. Perhaps there should be a great ceremony that would consecrate his duty to the Holy Church, the Bride of Christ. At so fulsome and solemn an occasion, it could be made clear that only the Holy Roman emperor had the power to turn back the infidel Turk, the Ottoman emperor Suleyman.

The summer passed into the fall with no decision. Gradually, the Lutherans left Rome, partly because there was nothing more to rob, partly because the plague again became virulent. (The pestilence claimed the life of Charles de Lannoy, the viceroy of Naples; he was replaced by Ugo di Moncada.) The city was a shambles. "There will be no business done at Rome for a long time," read a letter that came to the emperor's chief adviser, Mercurio Gattinara. "The city itself is so destroyed and ruined that until 200 years hence, it will not be Rome again."

The pope remained a captive in the Castel Sant'Angelo until early December, when he escaped in a slouch hat and rags, laden with baskets, in the disguise of a peddler. In Orvieto, he took up residence in the tumbledown house of the local archbishop, and he sought to reclaim his dignity and that of his office.

His apologists manfully tried to see the situation in a positive light. The lieutenant general of the tardy papal army and later historian of note, Francesco Guicciardini, had watched the humiliation of the pope from a distance. "Never in the history of the Church has something like this happened," he wrote. "That a pope is fallen from such power and reverence, is held in captivity, loses Rome, and the entire domain falls into the power of others. And that this same pope, within a space of a few months, is restored to liberty, much of what was taken from him is restored to him, and he is returned to his former greatness. So authoritative is the papacy among Christian princes, and the respect which all of them have for it."

In his simple cell in Orvieto, Clement VII, deprived and melancholy, cold and with feet swollen from gout, might not have seen the situation quite so rosily through the next six months of his exile. Bitterly, he remembered Guicciardini had been among those who advised him to declare war on the emperor. Another observer, an English ambassador who came in March 1528 to Orvieto to ask the pope's permission for Henry VIII to divorce Catherine of Aragon, gave a more objective picture.

"It is a fall from the top of the hill to the bottom of the mountain," the Englishman wrote. "Indeed, the Pope can hardly be said to be at liberty, for hunger, scarcity, bad lodging, and ill air keep him as much a prisoner as he was in Castel Sant'Angelo."

His bitter confinement at Orvieto was also a time of reflection. Had his detractors been right? Had the culture of ecclesiastical Rome contributed to the ruin of the Holy City? Was the Curia really so corrupt that it deserved God's punishment? Was the sack of Rome a version of the Apocalypse? Even some of his top advisers thought so and sounded almost Lutheran in their condemnation. A Croatian bishop and important adviser in the Roman Curia railed against Rome's corruption: "Why did such horrendous calamities fall upon us? It is because the sins of the flesh corrupted the mission of Rome. We were no longer citizens and inhabitants of the Holy City of Rome, but of the harlot-city of Babylon. And our day has seen fulfilled the word of God as it appears in Isaiah." Even the pope himself, on Palm Sunday in 1528, called upon his cardinals and prelates to change their ways, do penance for their sins, for the "scourge" that befell Rome.

What the pope could not know was that the glorious Renaissance of Italy was coming to an end. The great age of Italian history was dying in a bathos of collective guilt, an acceptance of divine punishment and self-flagellation, a desperate need for healing, and a longing for order, even if only the Caesar who had caused the catastrophe could provide that order.

The End of
the Renaissance

✠

28.

SINGLE COMBAT

The sack of Rome and the captivity of the pope were momentous events whose blessings were decidedly mixed for Emperor Charles V. With his counselors he discussed how to make the most of the situation, "since God has brought this to pass." But revulsion spread across Europe, and as the year 1527 drew to a close, the enemies of the Empire bound together in their determination to confront the domination of the Hapsburgs. Under the skillful hand of Cardinal Wolsey, England and France formed an anti-imperial alliance. Among the motives of Henry VIII in this new alliance was the desire to please the pope and appear to be the catalyst for his liberation. He would soon be asking of the pontiff a big favor. By the end of 1527, Francis I was again contemplating an invasion of Italy, to be supported with England's money.

In Spain, the emperor continued to issue his public apologies for the desecration of the Eternal City. He sent a contrite envoy to Italy, bearing expressions of fulsome regret for the outrageous and unwanted actions of his unruly and disobedient soldiers. He wished nothing more than to go to Rome, to kiss the feet of the Holy Father, and to set him free. What he really meant was that he wished to go to Rome to thank God for the unexpected victories that had been granted him, and to be crowned at last, officially, as the Holy Roman emperor. He had convinced himself that his good fortune was God's plan, and he was his Lord's chosen instrument to unite Christendom to face down the infidel.

By year's end, the emperor had concluded that the pope's further captivity in Castel Sant'Angelo was counterproductive. Quietly, the pope's "escape" to Orvieto was arranged with the emperor's connivance. But the pontiff was no more free in Orvieto than he had been in Rome. In the rundown, drafty archbishop's house he shivered through the winter in poverty and squalor under the watchful eye of imperial minders, while he pondered the ruin of the Church. Foreign mercenaries were everywhere in Italy. The Church's doctrine and authority was disrespected in more than a third of the Church's wealthiest provinces. The infidel Turks threatened Vienna. Luther continued to hold court as a hero and a prophet in Germany as the Edict of Worms was ignored. And Henry VIII was making uncomfortable suggestions that challenged past papal decrees and threatened the authority of the Roman Church in England.

On January 22, 1528, the wages of the previous year came due. In Burgos, envoys from France and England presented Charles V with a formal declaration of war. A litany of complaints about the emperor's behavior poured out of them. Beyond the sack and the captivity, the emperor was charged with allowing inhumane treatment of Francis I's sons, who were still held hostage in Spain in place of their father. The emperor had laid siege to Rome, held the Holy Father captive, despoiled the churches, and humiliated cardinals. He had allowed Belgrade and Rhodes to fall to the Turk and allowed the infidel into Europe virtually unhindered. Though more important personal problems aggravated Henry VIII, he still seethed at the emperor's marriage to Isabel of Portugal instead of to his daughter, Mary Tudor, as had been promised long ago.

The emperor listened to these complaints with regal dignity and courtly decorum, until he could stand it no longer. Then he expressed his astonishment at his very own prisoner declaring war upon him. Francis I was nothing less than a coward and a knave, the emperor blurted out. Francis I had broken his word and trampled his pledges. He was a liar, a stranger to honor, and no gentleman. To the amazement of the proper envoys, the Holy

Roman emperor drew himself up in moral outrage and threw down the gauntlet. Instead of Christian blood being further spilled, let the kings fight, man-to-man, in hand-to-hand combat.

This challenge was no ordinary invitation to a duel. Duels were common in Europe. The law sanctioned them in disputes over property or women when a wronged party sought satisfaction that no statute could provide. But Charles's challenge was to single combat over a quarrel of sworn promises between monarchs representing their respective nations. These were fought not with the sufferance of a mere magistrate, but before the Supreme Being himself.

Two months later, after a French army followed this declaration of war with an invasion of Naples, Charles again summoned the French and English envoys for a round of talks. Thinking himself reasonable, Charles offered to moderate the terms of the Treaty of Madrid. He would accept two million ducats in lieu of the province of Burgundy, and he would set Francis's sons free if the French army withdrew from the environs of Naples. But the French envoy was unmoved. The situation had changed. With the English alliance, France was emboldened and cheered by the progress of its army in the south. Not only was Naples on the verge of falling, but the French had seized large sections of Apulia and Calabria.

At this defiance, Charles again flew into a rage. The following day, he summoned the French envoy again and presented him with a written challenge. "The King, your master, has behaved in a cowardly and treacherous way. He has not kept his solemn pledges. If he wishes to say the contrary, I will maintain what I say to his face, man-to-man." Out of spite, Charles had Francis's sons removed to a dank castle in Segovia and denied them their French attendants.

By Charles's putting the challenge in writing, the matter became more serious. Two weeks later, on March 27, 1528, Francis rose to the notion of a royal combat with sporting gusto. The court was gathered with great circumstance, and a herald read out the imperial pronouncement. Then Francis covered it with contempt. "I do not remember ever having seen or encountered him in any war where I have been," he said to the cackles of his courtiers. The Treaty of Madrid had been signed under duress and was therefore void, as the royalty of Europe, including the pope in Rome, all agreed. "If you say we did not behave as a gentleman should, you lie in your throat," he hissed. Grandly, his response, known as a cartel of defiance, was drawn up. Officially, the challenge was accepted. Charles need only name the time and place for the single combat.

Weeks later, Charles proposed the banks of the Bidassoa River, so that the broken faith of the French king would be avenged on the very spot where Francis had been set free. By early June more official exchanges took place that brought the duel closer. When Francis officially accepted the challenge, Charles informed the nobility of Castile and asked for its official sanction, as the only way that further bloodshed between Christians could be avoided. Meanwhile, he chose his seconds and began daily training for the fight.

Soon enough the news of the duel became delicious gossip in the courts of Europe. "I was greatly amused to hear of the challenge between these two monarchs," remarked a prince of Transylvania. "It is quite a tragedy, although I expect the result will be more comic than tragic. People talk of nothing else. When kings go mad, the people suffer." In Spain a Spanish nobleman wrote, "It will be a rare sight to witness a duel between two such monarchs. One wonders if it will really come to pass. In any event, it will supply the world with a topic of much conversation during the next few weeks." The papal nuncio to the imperial court in Spain, Count Castiglione, thought the matter had become deadly serious, indeed far too serious, especially as he watched Charles receive the French envoy graciously and speed him back to Paris with further details, along with costly gifts including a velvet robe lined with gold thread from his own wardrobe. "His Majesty is so eager to fight that I shall not be surprised if the duel actually takes place. Indeed, unless the King of France makes difficulties, I think nothing can prevent it." Charles had asked the papal nuncio to be one of his seconds.

"When kings go mad, the people suffer." Perhaps by July 1528, Charles and Francis had received this caution from the Transylvanian knight and realized how ridiculous their challenge to single combat was appearing to the world. Francis put an end to the farce when he refused to receive Charles's envoy with his gold-embossed ultimatum and velvet robe.

Suddenly, other matters seemed more important. Charles had developed a new obsession. Desperately, he wanted to go to Rome to be officially crowned by the pope as the Holy Roman emperor. To his brother, Ferdinand, he wrote that spring that he "desired nothing in the world so much" as to go to Italy. He desired it as much for Ferdinand's sake as for his own, both so that he might "reform" the Church in Germany, and so he might be crowned—a ceremony from which both stood to gain. He only lacked money.

But perhaps there was a solution to his penury. During this period, Charles received Hernán Cortés, the conqueror of Mexico, and bestowed on him every honor, making him marquis de la Val de Oaxaca, a knight of Santiago, and captain-general of New Spain. Then word came that another Spanish conquistador, Francisco Pizarro, was asking permission to conquer Peru. With no question about Pizarro's methods, Charles gave his hearty approval to proceed. Rivers of gold from the New World would soon be flowing his way.

Francis too had more serious matters on his mind. In Italy there had been a dramatic reversal of fortune. Andrea Doria, disgruntled at neither receiving the money nor the dignity he required for his service to the French king, abruptly removed his blockade of Naples just as the city was about to fall to France. Supplies poured into the beleaguered town, suffusing it with life and vigor once again, as Doria sailed north and promptly switched his allegiance to the emperor. As a consequence, Genoa, Doria's home port, reverted to the imperial side. Still worse, plague broke out in the French army. Within weeks it had been reduced to a third of its size. The French force had become "not so much an army as a walking pestilence."

The collapse of the French invasion was as surprising as it was total. By September the commander of the imperial forces, the prince of Orange, reported that only a few pockets of French resistance remained in the south and in Lombardy. By October the entire Ligurian coast from the French border was in imperial hands. With this astonishing development Pope Clement VII finally gave up the pretense of neutrality.

"I have quite made up my mind to become an imperialist, and to live and die as such," he said.

29.

SHOWDOWN
AT BLACKFRIARS

While kings traded insults and their armies traded fortunes in Italy, another drama was being played out in parallel: the divorce of Henry VIII from his queen, Catherine of Aragon. Since their marriage in 1509, Catherine had had six pregnancies, which included two princes. All but one had ended in miscarriage, stillbirth, or nearly instant death, and it began to be rumored that these tragedies were God's punishment for some moral defect in the marriage itself. Only her daughter Mary had survived, and this put the survival of the Tudor dynasty itself at risk, for up until this time, no woman in England had served as monarch. It might have been considered that the House of Tudor could follow the Spanish example, where Queen Isabella, Catherine's mother, had been the dominant partner in her glorious reign with King Ferdinand. But Mary was no Isabella. Moreover, Henry had tired of his wife and had his eye on another. The other was Anne Boleyn, a spry and manipulative courtier who possessed no royal lineage and whom Henry had at first considered a "foolish girl." By the spring of 1527 paternalism had changed to infatuation. She appealed, it was said, to the baser side of Henry's nature.

As early as the spring of 1527 the pretext for a change of circumstance presented itself when the bishop of Lincoln questioned the fundamental basis of Henry's marriage to Catherine. Catherine had initially come to England in November 1501 to marry Henry's older brother, Arthur, the prince of Wales and heir to the English throne. But the marriage lasted only six months; Arthur died in April 1502. Thereupon, Pope Julius II issued a special papal dispensation that permitted Catherine to marry Henry. At the core of this papal permission was the representation that during the six months of its existence, the marriage between Arthur and Catherine had never been consummated. Of course, only Catherine could testify on this point.

Now, charged the bishop of Lincoln, Henry's union to his brother's wife was "not good but damnable." The royal couple were living in sin, and the issue from their cohabitation was illegitimate. An ecclesiastical court, he insisted, must be convened to consider the matter. This was done in secret in May 1527 before Cardinal Wolsey at the archbishop's palace at Canterbury. Nothing came of this hearing, but the idea of an annulment took hold. Cardinal Wolsey, ever the international schemer, had his own agenda. He was conspiring to cement an alliance with France as a counterbalance to the Empire, and he had a visceral dislike for Catherine's nephew Emperor Charles V. In the wake of the sack of Rome and the pope's captivity, Wolsey hoped that Henry's marriage might be dissolved, and that his king would then marry a French princess. While Wolsey pushed for an annulment, he was adamantly opposed to Henry marrying Anne Boleyn, who brought with her no value whatever in international affairs. In this manner, geopolitics and dynasty and religion became intertwined with personal grudges, ambition, and love interest.

In the latter months of 1527, while Pope Clement was still kept captive in Castel Sant'Angelo in Rome, the campaign for a divorce began. Given the pope's dire circumstance, where he was weak in power, desperate for allies, and victimized by the emperor, Henry wagered that the pope would easily grant his wish. Graciously, England offered four thousand soldiers for the pope's personal defense. But when he escaped to Orvieto with the connivance of the emperor, the matter became more complicated. On January 1, 1528, English envoys did pry a document out of Clement that countenanced Henry's divorce from Catherine and remarriage to Anne, but only if his original marriage was found to be unlawful under canon law. The qualifier was the rub.

Then three weeks later, Henry joined Francis I in the declaration of war against Charles and provided English treasure to support the French invasion of Italy. Now Henry's brief for divorce became bound together with the progress of that war. So long as the fortunes of the French army were high, the prospects for Henry's cause looked promising. The French were in high feather during the first six months of 1528.

Meanwhile, the prelates and papal advisers looked with amazement on Henry's lust for Anne. "This passion of the King's is a most extraordinary thing," wrote a papal legate. "He sees nothing. He thinks of nothing but his Anne. He cannot be without her for an hour, and it moves one to pity to see how the King's life, the stability and the downfall of the whole country, hangs upon this one question." An English commentator wrote wryly, "It is a wondrous thing to consider the strength of Princes' wills when they are bent on having their pleasure fulfilled. Among other things there is nothing that makes them more willful than carnal love."

The letters that Henry VIII wrote to Anne Boleyn during this period demonstrated his lusty appetite. "I beseech you now with the greatest earnestness to let me know your whole intention as to the love between us two. I must of necessity obtain this answer from you, having been for a whole year struck with the dart of love." He promised to make her "his sole mistress, casting off all others who are in competition with you." He lavished her with gifts including the meat of a stag he had killed in the hunt. It was "some flesh representing my name, the hart's flesh for Henry, prognosticating that hereafter, God willing, you must enjoy some of mine which if He please I would wish were now. When you eat of it, I hope you will think on the hunter." Eventually, these letters would come into the possession of the Vatican, where they remain to this day, in a locked cabinet deep within the bowels of the Vatican Library, in a drawer next to the original trial transcript of Galileo Galilei. Over the centuries these letters must have mystified many a curious ecclesiastic.

In March 1528, in dismal, rainy weather on the butte of Orvieto, English envoys were again closeted with the pope for several days of discussion about the legal process. Would the pope appoint a commission that could render a swift, final, and definitive decision? Clement VII, later called Pope I Will and I Won't, vacillated. He feared the wrath of Charles V over any decision adverse to Charles's aunt, and though the forces of the English ally Francis I were making good military progress in Italy during that spring, he was none too sure of the ultimate outcome of the war.

At length, the pope agreed to a commission, but its proceedings would be open and its mandate was only to investigate the legality of the marriage, not to issue a final, actionable judgment. When the envoys returned to England with this mixed report, Henry was ecstatic and proclaimed victory, rushing to his beloved to announce the good news. Upon sober reflection, however, he realized the emptiness of the pope's action. Crestfallen, he sent his envoy back to Orvieto in mid-May to pressure the pope to upgrade the commission by giving it the power to issue, in secret, a final decree of annulment. The pope procrastinated, and soon enough the frustrated envoy dubbed the pontiff "the great delayer." Eventually, Clement VII did agree to a so-called decretal commission. But he left himself the loophole of revoking or nullifying its decision if he so chose.

Henry, in turn, tried his best to sound moral and high-minded. He lavished his wife with praise. "There was never a thing more pleasant nor more acceptable to me in my life, for Catherine's qualities of mind and body are evident. If I were to marry again and if the marriage were good, I would surely choose her again." But he professed to be troubled by the nightmare that for twenty years, "to God's displeasure," he had been living in sin. "These are the sores that vex my mind. These be the pangs that trouble my conscience. And for this grief I seek a remedy." Should the papal legate find their union to be unlawful, he would regretfully have to leave her, lamentable as it would be to part from "so good a lady and so loving a companion."

Meanwhile, Cardinal Wolsey seized on a simple solution to the difficulty. Catherine should find religion, enter a convent, and renounce her marriage. Much taken with the brilliance of their idea, Cardinal Wolsey and the papal legate, Cardinal Lorenzo Campeggio, traveled down the Thames to present their proposition to the queen. They were an impressive pair. Campeggio was a noted professor of canon law and officially the "protector" of the English Church in Rome. They had three sessions with the queen. How great would be her name if she saved herself, her king, and her nation the trouble of divorce and scandal, they argued. This was the solution for her to avoid the hostility of her people and to secure the affection of her God. They promised that if Catherine were to enter a nunnery, her daughter, Mary, would not lose her dynastic right of succession. They reminded her of the example of a pious queen of France who had taken this admirable course so that Louis XII might remarry. (This was scarcely a persuasive argument, since Louis XII was a disastrous king; his queen had been his second cousin, saintly but misshapen.) At one point the immensely fat Cardinal Wolsey dropped to his knees and begged Catherine to do this for the good of England and Christendom.

Catherine listened stoically. At length, she replied that she was a loyal and obedient daughter of the Church. She would consult with counsel, with her confessor, and with her God. She wished them to know only that she had come to her marriage with Henry as a virgin and that she had been a good and obedient wife to him. If she was stubborn, she had no illusion about how damaging her position could be to her Church and her country. Her road ahead would be lonely and difficult, yet she did not doubt the righteousness of her course. The cardinals went away empty-handed and exasperated. They were, in turn, followed to her door by King Henry himself. He presented the case more violently. All the world knew that their marriage was unlawful, he shouted. Unless she entered a convent voluntarily, she would be forced to do so against her will. Catherine stood firm, unmoved and unintimidated by his bluster. She may even have become more adamant in her decision after his undignified harangue. It would later be written that she was as certain of her moral rectitude as Luther was at Worms.

In a letter that she wrote to her nephew Charles V during this ordeal, she also stood on precedent. "For the present Pope to undo what his predecessors have done, would reflect on his honor and conscience, and bring grave discredit to the Apostolic See which should stand firmly on the Rock which is Christ. Were the Pope to waver now, in this case, many might be led astray into thinking that right and justice are not with him."

A trial seemed inevitable.

In the summer of 1528 the tide turned against Henry. In Italy, his ally the French army faltered at Naples, as the plague sapped its vigor, and Andrea Doria deserted to the other side. As the news of the divorce campaign became known, public opinion turned against Henry, and Catherine's popularity soared. An epidemic of the mysterious sweating sickness swept across England, killing thousands, halting business, and breaking up the royal court. Henry fled to the countryside, changing his residences frequently, heard mass three times a day, and downed a number of quack medicines obsessively. Then Anne Boleyn came down with the disease. Frantic, Henry kept his distance at first, writing to her frequently, with the comfortable words that the disease did not seem to affect women as virulently as men. "Whoever strives against fortune is often the further from his end," he wrote ponderously. But then he could bear it no longer and fled to her side. At length, she passed the danger point and survived.

It is left to speculation how English history and Church history might have been different if Catherine had acquiesced in the demand to renounce her marriage, or if Anne Boleyn had succumbed to sweating sickness.

With the collapse of the French army in Italy, Clement swung over to the imperial side. His policy of delay in Henry's case had worked. He no longer needed Henry's support. In June, gaining confidence, the pope left Orvieto for Viterbo, and in October 1528 he returned at last to Rome. To his advisers his whole appearance had changed. He had aged dramatically and had grown a long and hoary beard, as an outward sign of inward penitence.

After sack and plague, he found his beloved city to be "a pitiable and mangled corpse." Nevertheless, he was home with a semblance of dignity restored. He could now openly express his sympathy for Catherine's cause and speak of Henry's case as feeble. Hearing this, Cardinal Wolsey resorted to threats. To a friend in the pope's inner circle, he wrote that Henry was being treated unfairly and inhumanly. Unless Clement VII acted like a true vicar of Christ and did his duty, the price might be the ruin of the Church and the destruction of papal authority in England. For the first time the notion of a breach with the Roman Catholic Church was hinted. "I close my eyes before such horror. I throw myself at the Holy Father's feet," Wolsey wrote. "I beg him to look on his royal majesty's holy and unchangeable desire, his most just, most holy, and most upright desire."

For another seven months the sides jockeyed. More insults were delivered; more lofty rebuttals were tendered, while the papal legate, Cardinal Lorenzo Campeggio, did his best, under instructions from the pope, to delay the final confrontation as long as he could. Privately, Catherine had gone to Campeggio to swear again before her God that her marriage to Arthur had had "no effect." Moved by her nobility, Campeggio wrote privately to the pope supporting the validity of her marriage to Henry. Not until June 17, 1529, did the case finally come to a head and be heard in central London at Blackfriars. With Cardinals Wolsey and Campeggio presiding, Queen Catherine swept into the court, accompanied by four bishops and a retinue of court ladies. Outside the court a huge, angry crowd, made up of both men and women (and undoubtedly turned out and paid for by the Spanish ambassador), protested the proceeding. Like a seasoned politician, Catherine knew how to play to her supporters. After making her way through the cheering throng, she came to the window to wave to them. Henry's proxy sat glumly to the side as the impressive woman entered the courtroom. Referring to herself as a poor, ignorant woman, she made a solid legal case that Rome, not England, had jurisdiction over the matter.

Three days later the court met again, and this time Henry appeared. Catherine went to him in a show of conjugal obedience and knelt at his feet. When the testimony began, Henry went first, again covering his lust with the most lofty motives, presenting himself as a man tortured by conscience. "I most heartily beseech you to ponder my mind and intent, which is to have a final end for the discharge of my conscience. Every good Christian man knows what pain and what disquiet he suffers when his conscience is grieved."

Catherine dropped her pose of obedience and confronted him squarely, even though she remained on her knees. "I take God to witness," she said, "that I have been a true, humble, and obedient wife. When you had me first, I take God to be my judge, I was a true maid, without touch of man. Whether this be true or not, I put it to your conscience."

Henry stared blankly forward. Seeing him unmoved, she rose and made for the door, ignoring the commands of the judges to remain. "On, on," she waved to her ladies with a flick of her hand. "It makes no matter. It is an indifferent court to me. Therefore I will not tarry."

For her breezy exit, the judges proclaimed the queen to be "contumacious," stubbornly disobedient, and willfully in contempt of court. The proceeding, of course, had no power to do anything about regal contempt that was common enough. For weeks the matter dragged on with witnesses and speeches and sharp exchanges. Outside the court an unruly mob milled around the building, women shouting their praise of Catherine, while men extolled their king obediently. In fact, it was all a sham. In Rome, Pope Clement VII, pressured by Charles and persuaded by Campeggio of the marriage's validity, had resolved to supersede the Blackfriars court and bring the case to a Vatican court.

By the pope's revoking the London court and remanding the case to Rome, Cardinal Wolsey's religious and diplomatic policy lay in ruins. In assuring Henry that he could secure the desired result and that Campeggio was merely a neutral observer, Wolsey had oversold his power to his king. When the two commissioners disagreed, Wolsey for the king, Campeggio for the queen, there could be no judgment and no sentence. In a Rome now dominated by the Empire, Wolsey would have no influence to undermine the marriage of Charles's aunt and do Henry's bidding. Within six months the king sacked him, and the hatred that he inspired poured out, again covering with scorn his humble roots in York as a butcher's son.

Of the proude Cardinall this is the shelde
Borne up between two angels off Sathan.
The six bloody axes in a bare felde
Sheweth the cruelte of the red man,
Whiche hathe devoured the beautiful swan,
Mortall enemy unto the whyte lion
Carter of Yorcke, the vyle butchers sonne.

The once all-powerful chancellor receded into self-pity over his cruel fate. "If I had served God as diligently as I have done my King, He would not have given me over in my gray hairs. But this is the just reward I must receive, for in my diligent pains and studies to serve the King, I looked not to my duty toward God, but only to the gratification of the King's wishes."

While the surrogates of the king and queen squabbled in Blackfriars, far to the south in Barcelona, on June 29, 1529, the pope and the emperor joined hands in a treaty, "out of grief at the divisions of Christendom, to beat off the Turks, and to make way for a general peace." The pope acknowledged the hegemony of the Empire in Italy, while the emperor guaranteed the protection of the Papal States. To make matters worse for Henry, a month after that, his ally Francis I signed a truce with Charles V in the so-called Ladies' Peace.

By the pope's public pronouncement that he would now live and die as an imperialist, Henry knew that in his troubled marriage he would receive no relief or succor from Rome. In European politics Henry VIII was now left as the man out, and England's breach with Rome came one huge step closer.

30.

More Than Table Talk

Since the First Diet of Speyer in 1526, in which a "recess" had been declared in the hostilities between the Catholic and Lutheran provinces of Germany, Martin Luther had led a quiet, productive life in Wittenberg. In the Catholic provinces to the south and the north, the Edict of Worms was still in effect. If Luther strayed into these hostile regions, he was subject to be burned in the Inquisition's holy fire. But in the benign, ever-expanding evangelical enclaves in the center of Germany, his person was safe, and he was treated as a hero and a prophet.

In Wittenberg, he plied his scholarship, wrote his letters and his diatribes, gave the occasional sermon, and taught his theology classes at the university. Occasionally, he paid attention to his wife and two children. But nearly every evening, except on Sundays and festival days, he beat a steady path to the local tavern called the Black Eagle, where he held court among his friends and drinking companions. They bought his beer, and it was dark and thick. The brew came from a dirty little town in the north near Hannover called Einbeck, in a region where Luther dared not venture himself. This syrupy brew, called *eimbockbier* or bock beer, was the favorite of princes as well as wayward priests, and pewter mugs of it slid down the oaken tables of the Black Eagle to the lusty clientele that talked and sang and told off-color jokes until closing time at ten o'clock.

Mainly, Luther himself supplied the entertainment, but it was of a particular kind. With jovial wit and sarcasm, good German that he was, he would expound upon topics as diverse as witchcraft, astrology, celibacy, bigamy, and the Turkish infidel. His tongue was always sharp; his fascinating ramblings were filled with anecdotes and metaphors; and his patter was tinged with irony and guttural humor. These evenings were later recorded and came to be known as Luther's *Tisch Reden* or Table Talk.

The conversation might begin straightforwardly. "And so, master," a comrade might say, "of what shall we speak first tonight?"

"Honor to whom honor is due," Luther might reply. "Let us speak of the devil." And off he would go on a long discourse about who the devil was (a skillful murderer who had more poisons than all the world's chemists), where devils reside (in the dark edges of clouds, deep in the forest, or underwater), what shapes they can take (such as a fly that leaves its mark on the white pages of a book and, when it finds a pure and innocent heart, settles on, sullies, and corrupts it).

Or on another evening once the mugs brimmed full, someone else might say, "Doctor, can those who believe in God be enchanted?" and off Luther would go on the subject of witchcraft. Yet the conversation always seemed to return to two core subjects: the Babylon called Rome and the future of his Reformation movement. In his refrain about the corruption of the Vatican, its priests, its bishops, and especially its pope, the Turks were often used as straw men, usually in the role of the lesser evil. "Every animal is composed of a body and a soul," he said once at table. "The soul or spirit of Antichrist is the pope. The Turk is his body or flesh. The Turk troubles, torments, and lays waste the Church of Christ bodily or materially. But the pope does so all at once, both bodily and spiritually, by his satellites, his executioners, and murderers. In the days of the apostles the Church triumphed over the spiritual power of the Jews and the sword of the Romans. In our time it will become victorious over the superstitions and the idolatry of Rome, and over the tyranny of the Turks. . . .

"Cursed be the pope who has done more harm to the kingdom of Christ than Mahomet!" he continued. "The Turk kills the body, devastates and pillages the goods of Christians. But the pope is more cruel than the Turk with his Koran, for His Holiness forces Christians to deny Christ. Both are enemies of the Church, and servants of Satan."

In another aside, Luther seemed to anticipate the importance of the decretal commission that had been convened to consider the validity of Henry VIII's marriage to Catherine of Aragon. "Do you know what a decretal is?" he asked rhetorically. "It is the excrement of His Holiness."

The fame of these sacred and profane ramblings spread far and wide, and it was not long before he was being called the Beer Pope. Characteristically, he was less than humble about the explosiveness of his table talk. "My idle conversation in the tavern shook the papacy more effectively than the princes and the emperor could have done with all their iron-mailed knights."

In fact, the three years of the Speyer Recess had enabled the Lutheran princes of central Germany to consolidate their gains and to expand the reach of their revolutionary new doctrines. The movement that had begun twelve years before with a conscientious protest by a single man had been transformed into a political entity, with territorial expanse, backed by powerful princes and buttressed by powerful armies. Not surprisingly, the Catholic provinces viewed this consolidation with intense alarm. The innovations had to be stopped or at least circumscribed. If the contagion could be contained, perhaps it would wither and die. The Recess, wrote one Catholic scribe, had been used "as an excuse for all sorts of shocking new doctrines and sects." The truce had come to mask "apostasy, strife, dissension, and wickedness." In the Catholic provinces repression of Lutheran beliefs was carried out vigorously. It was time, the emperor concluded, to convene a Second Diet of Speyer to undo the damage of the first.

Beyond the need to check the Lutheran expansion, another important matter needed to be addressed. A Turkish fleet had been sighted off Sicily. The memory of the sack of Otranto by a Turkish fleet in the year 1480 was still fresh. Did Suleyman intend to follow his capture of Rhodes with the occupation of Otranto, thus establishing an Islamic base in the boot of Italy? Or were his ambitions larger, to reclaim Sicily for Islam as it had been for 263 years around the turn of the first millennium? Or worse, were the cries of Suleyman's warriors at Rhodes real? "To Rome, to Rome!" they had shouted. Or was Suleyman's focus to be on the heart of Europe? To move past Buda, to capture Vienna, to threaten Germany itself? Signs of preparations for a major Turkish offensive somewhere were being reported from Constantinople. The infidel again threatened Christendom.

In March 1529 the delegates arrived for the Second Diet of Speyer. For this all-important convention the Catholics came in force and were fated to be in the clear majority. Charles V remained in Spain, preoccupied with his Italian problems, and deferring once again to his brother, Archduke Ferdinand of Austria. The emperor now delegated authority to the younger Hapsburg to deal with the knotty problems of the eastern portion of the Empire. Widely considered to be less able and imaginative than his older brother, Ferdinand now held the titles of king of Bohemia, Austria, and Hungary as well as the honorary title of king of the Romans. Ferdinand rode into town, resplendent in shining armor, accompanied by three hundred knights as a show of force. The dukes of Bavaria followed with an equally large contingent, then came the spiritual electors of Mainz and Treves and the bishops of Trent and Hildesheim. Their purpose was clear. "They had come to bury the Reformation," a scribe wrote later.

The Lutheran princes arrived afterward more modestly. The most important, John of Saxony, was accompanied by a single companion, Luther's associate Philip Melanchthon. John of Saxony, known as John the Constant, had succeeded his brother, Frederick the Wise, as elector; Frederick had died four years earlier. Only the flamboyant Lutheran renegade Philip of Hesse (who would soon be asking Luther to sanction his bigamy) came grandly, with two hundred soldiers. His first act was to organize a Lutheran worship service, which more than a thousand worshippers attended, and to follow it with a great feast in which meat was served in abundance, even though Ferdinand had expressly forbidden meat to be consumed during the diet.

If the arrival of the evangelicals was modest, their entrance was also troubled. Not only were they in the minority, but they were split. A rival reformer had burst upon the scene to challenge Luther. He was Huldrych

Zwingli, a Swiss reformer who was to Switzerland as Luther was to Germany. Starting in Zurich a few years after Luther, Zwingli had confronted the Catholic order with some of Luther's essential complaints: the celibacy of the priesthood, the need for liturgical reform, the primacy of Christ over terrestrial authority, the removal of images and icons from the Church, the return to a simple Communion service. But Zwingli and Luther differed profoundly on the symbolic nature of the bread and wine. Both rejected the Catholic concept of transubstantiation, where the bread and wine are miraculously transformed into the actual body and blood of Christ. But they disagreed on the symbolic presence or absence of Christ in the Eucharist. Zwingli's movement had spread rapidly through the cantons of Switzerland in the early 1520s. But its adherents had come into conflict with Lutherans in southern Germany over doctrine. Their rivalry weakened the evangelical side now at the Second Diet of Speyer.

On March 15 the diet opened with a bang. A herald stepped forward and read a curt imperial decree from Charles V. Sonorously he proclaimed, "The numerous misinterpretations and errors of previous edicts have inflicted great harm on our holy belief and the Christian religion. This has led to a deteriorating situation in our Holy Empire, to violence and misunderstandings between clans. Thus, the Turks have remained without challenge and have not been stopped." The duty of the diet was to declare the religious tolerance of the First Diet of Speyer null and void. The Edict of Worms was to be reinstated and applied throughout Germany without waiting for a general council. Any further expansion of reformist doctrines was to be prohibited beyond the status quo. There were to be no further innovations in Catholic doctrine. The emperor expected the diet to ratify these imperial measures within a few days and disband.

At the high-handed, imperious tone of the decree, the Lutherans reacted in shock and horror. The emperor's demands meant nothing less than the demise of the Reformist movement. It would reestablish the authority of the old religion throughout Germany. It would pave the way for a papal restoration in Lutheran provinces. The prohibition against further expansion would snuff out the movement's vigor. Reinstituting the Edict of

Worms meant a return to a policy of the extermination of heresy. It would spell the death of Martin Luther himself.

"Christ is again in the hands of Caiaphas* and Pilate," one Lutheran delegate remarked.

On April 12, the Catholic majority voted the imperial demands into law. The reaction was swift. Led by Philip of Hesse, the evangelical delegates united in appealing to the emperor and all impartial Christian judges against the tyranny of the Catholic majority. This "appellation" was motivated solely by conscience and out of concern for the salvation of their souls, they argued. They could not be party to executing the dreadful Edict of Worms.

"In matters concerning God's honor and the salvation of our souls," the appeal read, "each man has the right to stand alone and present his true account before God. On the last day no man will be able to take shelter behind the power of another, be it small or great."

Despite the howls of the opposition the majority pressed on. On April 19, the imperial commissioners formally ratified the decision in the emperor's name and requested the opposition to submit and desist.

Instead, the evangelicals walked out. Their first concern now was an actual military invasion by the Empire or its Catholic surrogates. Again instigated by Philip of Hesse, the Lutherans and Zwinglians met secretly and entered into an agreement for mutual military defense. They agreed to resist with arms any attack that might be made upon them. What before had been scattered opposition was now organized into a unified force. The new order of things in Germany was solidified. If the Catholic contingent came to Speyer determined to bury the Reformation, they left with it stronger than ever.

Three days later, on April 25, the dissidents went a step further. They issued the formal legal version of their appeal and demanded that it be entered into the official record of the diet. They called the document their

---

* Caiaphas was the Jewish high priest who charged Christ with blasphemy, then handed him over to the Roman court and Pontius Pilate, the Roman governor of Judea, for trial.

Protestation. It protested all the measures of the diet that, they said, violated their conscience, the word of God, and the promises of 1526.

"What would our assent be but a public denial of our Lord and Savior Jesus Christ and His sacred Word which there is no doubt we now possess in all its purity, simplicity, and justice?" the protest read.

Blithely, Ferdinand and the commissioners ignored this upstart proclamation and refused to include it in the official record of the proceeding. The archduke packed up and left. The majority ruled and was intent to enforce its ruling on the minority. Yet that minority now comprised a virtual nation-state in the heart of Germany: Saxony, Brandenburg, Lüneberg, Braunschweig, Hesse, Anhalt, and fourteen imperial cities. These dissenters were bold enough to believe that the Catholic majority had neither the stomach nor the force to pursue a sectarian civil war against them. Indeed, a few among them, such as Margrave George of Brandenburg, proposed to organize an offensive force and to attack the Catholic provinces of Mainz, Bamberg, and Würzburg. In this saber rattling, the hotheads reached out to the enemies of the Hapsburgs, including Francis I and János Zápolya, Suleyman's vassal in the east.

"We fear God's wrath more than we fear the emperor," said one prince.

Ironically, when the news of the diet reached Martin Luther, he approved of the Protestation, but strenuously disapproved of any military action or alliance to defend the Lutheran dominion by force. His conscience could not countenance bloodshed in defense of his gospel. He especially abhorred the idea of an alliance with the Zwinglians. They represented a new form of heresy: deviation from Luther's own evangelical doctrine.

The Second Diet of Speyer broke up in disarray and confusion. The sides were further apart than ever, and their differences were now committed to writing. As the Protestants seceded from the Catholic union, the Catholic majority had no way to impose its will. As Rome had its doctrine, now Protestantism had its organizing principle, its official credo, and its essential constitution in opposition. The protest of conscience at Speyer became the collective expression of Luther's individual declaration of conscience at the Diet of Worms eight years earlier.

Loosely, the new order could, for the first time, be called the Protestant Church. John the Constant supplied the Protestant motto: "The Word of God abideth forever."

Still, if the Protestants were unified in a negative sense against Rome and united militarily against attack, they were passionately divided in doctrine, especially over the interpretation of the Last Supper. Zwinglians resented the arrogance of Luther. "You will never convince us," wrote one Zwinglian, "that the Holy Ghost is confined to Wittenberg any more than to Basle, in your person any more than in that of any other." "They cry out," wrote another, "that we are heretics who should not be listened to. They proscribe our books and denounce us to the magistrates. Is this not to do as the pope did formerly when truth endeavored to raise her head?" Earnest efforts to form a Protestant Union in the next year failed.

THE RELIGIOUS QUESTION was the text of the Diet of Speyer. But a subtext was nearly as important: the desperate danger of the Turkish threat to eastern Europe. In fact, text and subtext were intertwined, yet they stood in opposition. Catholics, especially Archduke Ferdinand I, wanted to solve the religious question quickly and definitively, even if it had to be accomplished by fiat, so that he could secure immediate aid from the German estates to defend Hungary and Austria against the Turks. But Protestants, by withholding their aid, might extract concessions from the Catholic side on the question of religious tolerance. In the spring of 1529 the Turkish menace and the Protestant challenge were for Ferdinand interrelated. He was threatened with invasion from without and rebellion from within. By contrast, the Catholics threatened the Protestants. So long as the Catholic world was under grave threat from Suleyman, the Protestants had a measure of mobility and safety.

Neither side in the religious dispute could have any illusion now about how serious the Turkish threat was. For eight years, from the Diet of Worms forward, Ferdinand had hectored diet after diet about the peril to Christianity in the Balkans. Routinely, his appeals had been ignored. Either he was exaggerating or the religious question took precedence or the Italian war took precedence or the Balkans were simply too remote or his timing was wrong. His cry for help had been an exercise in futility. Even after the fall of Belgrade, the battle of Mohács and the death of Louis II, and the burning of Buda and Pest, the reaction of the European princes, including his own brother, Charles V, had been detached or perfunctory, empty and token, too little or too late.

So Ferdinand of Austria had been thrown back on his own meager resources and his own modest diplomatic skill. He had sent ambassadors to Constantinople with a conciliatory message, offering peace and cooperation and even deference. In the court of the Sublime Porte, his envoys had been abused and imprisoned, then dispatched home with a stiff rebuff. Sultan Suleyman, sultan of the sultans, leader of the lords, the shadow of God in two worlds, the padishah of the Mediterranean Sea, would discuss the matter personally with the Archduke Ferdinand—in Vienna. With that chilling threat, Ferdinand rode off to the Diet of Speyer.

Through the days of the Second Diet of Speyer, discussion had alternated between the two great issues. Ferdinand had made his choice. There would be no concessions to the heretics; a solution to religious wandering would be imposed. The rot from within was more dangerous than the menace from without. The Protestants had made their choice as well: no concessions, no aid. Ferdinand's desperation was their leverage. To aid Ferdinand with troops for his defense against the Ottomans was to strengthen his ability to repress the new teaching.

Ironically, at this critical juncture when the Protestants held their trump card, Luther himself seemed to undercut their position. With the situation in Austria more dire than ever, the threat of Islam to Germany, and indeed to Christian civilization in Europe itself, ceased to be an abstraction. As a result, Luther's attitude experienced a tidal change. He did not alter his opinion that the Turks stood alongside the pope as the Antichrist. God could and did use heathen nations as His instrument of punishment. The Turk was the destroyer and the enemy of the Christian faith. His holy book was a "foul book of blasphemy," and he was a whoremonger because he sold women like cattle. As such, he was like the fourth king in the book of Daniel 7:19, whose "teeth were of iron, and his nails of brass; who devoured, broke into pieces, and stamped the residue with his feet." Austria and Germany and Europe deserved him. "Because Germany is so full of evil and blasphemy," Luther wrote in 1529 as the Diet of Speyer convened, "nothing else can be expected. We must suffer punishment if we do not repent and stop the persecution of the Gospel."

In this debate Luther propounded a novel theory to flatter his own movement. The power of the Turks was regenerated largely because the power of the Gospel had been regenerated in his Reformation. As the truth of his teaching had reinvigorated Christianity, so the devil had reinvigorated his forces in opposition.

So resistance to the devil, to the Antichrist, to the whoremongers of Islam, was now acceptable to him. "If you go to war against the Turks," he wrote, "you can be sure that you are not fighting flesh and blood, i.e., against men, because the army of the Turks is actually the army of the devil."

But Luther remained clear upon one essential point. Resistance to the Turk was the duty of the citizen but not the Christian. One could go to war in good conscience against the Turk in defense of temporal law and civil order and to protect home and family. But not to defend the faith or the Gospel, and never in the spirit of a crusade. A crusade to Luther was blasphemy. Holy war was the antithesis of Christ's message. A citizen's protection of his homeland, however, was right and appropriate. In turn, the duty of princes, especially Emperor Charles V, was to protect their citizens from outside threat, and their power was derived from God.

Luther's newfound call to resistance may have had another motivation. In the face of the resounding Turkish victories, the advance of Islam seemed unstoppable. Many were ready to give up. Germany was doomed. Islam was the future. Perhaps life under the sultan would be better than that under petty, thieving Christian princes. Many in the Ottoman provinces in the Balkans held that opinion. "What should we do?" Luther asked. "Throw up our hands? Let the Turks rob us blind without lifting a finger? No, by God! I only have one word of advice for you: You should not give up. As much as

God frowns upon bloated self-confidence, He does not want us to give ourselves over to despair."

To the satisfaction of Archduke Ferdinand, the Diet of Speyer, with its Catholic majority, had voted to authorize the contribution of sixteen thousand soldiers to the defense of Hungary and Austria. With Luther's changed attitude, his Protestant princes could now, in good conscience, contribute to that force.

Pleased though he was at this action, and facing imminent attack, Ferdinand had his doubts as to whether these troops would, in fact, be sent. On April 24, 1529, he wrote to his sister, Maria, the widow of the king of Hungary, Louis II, that due to the intense arguments and conflicts at the Diet of Speyer, his hopes for significant military help might be wishful thinking: "It will be difficult to obtain these soldiers in their entirety. Nonetheless, I hope to receive the majority of them." Predictably, after the troops were voted by the diet, interminable wrangling began over who should command the force.

To some extent, the safety of the Reformation depended now upon the strength of the Turkish army. That was true only in a narrow sense. So long as Ferdinand was hard-pressed militarily, he could scarcely devote his full energies to repressing the religious novelties. In a larger sense, Luther now realized that if the Turks invaded Europe and conquered Germany to the Rhine River, Europe as a Christian civilization, either Catholic or Protestant, would cease to exist.

At his table in the Wittenberg pub, he learned that Suleyman had expressed a casual interest in him and had even inquired about his age. When the sultan was told, he reportedly said, "Pity. I wish he were even younger. He would find in me a gracious protector."

Luther sighed when he heard this and made the sign of the cross. "May God protect me from such a generous benefactor," he quipped.

31.

HIS MOUTH RAINS PEARLS

In the year after the great Ottoman victory at Mohács, Ibrahim Pasha became the most influential figure in the Empire. During the campaigns against Belgrade and Rhodes, he had merely been the sultan's friend and favorite. At Mohács he became a general, second-in-command only to the sultan himself, and after the victory Suleyman accorded to him the lion's share of credit. Spouting oriental extravagance, the sultan's citation read, "The leopard of strength and valor, the tiger of the forest of courage, the hero filled with a holy zeal, the lion of the restoration of dominion, the precious pearl of the ocean of all power, the champion of the faith, the grand vizier, beylerbey of Rumelia, Ibrahim Pasha." With this sanction, Ibrahim Pasha married Suleyman's sister and took charge of a magnificent palace near the old Byzantine hippodrome overlooking the Bosporus.

The relationship between Ibrahim and Suleyman was close, but not without occasional tension. Indeed, only a few months after their return from Hungary, they had a public disagreement over a court case. A member of the *ulema,* the company of distinguished religious scholars, had been accused of openly professing the superiority of Jesus Christ over the prophet Mohammed. At this serious charge, the scholar was brought before two young and inexperienced judges, convicted of heresy, and sentenced to death. But Ibrahim Pasha, with his sway over the courts and his concern for Ottoman jurisprudence, reviewed the case and determined that the proper procedures had not been followed. He reprimanded the judges and ordered a new trial. Before the royal divan, Ibrahim defended his actions forcefully. Deeply interested in the case, Suleyman had listened to the debate behind the grilled window. So outraged was he at Ibrahim's arguments that he burst into the meeting.

"Why has the heretic who dared to show preference for Jesus over Mohammed not been punished yet?" he demanded.

"Because the judges dealt with this case not out of reason but out of blind anger," Ibrahim responded confidently.

"The law is not solely administered by these judges," the sultan replied. "The heretic will be tried tomorrow before the grand mufti."

Predictably, the trial the next day concluded with the same verdict, and the scholar was hanged. But word of the case and its uncivil procedures had reached the large Christian community of Constantinople, sparking outrage. In reprisal, a Muslim family that resided not far from the memorial mosque of Suleyman's father, Selim I, was murdered. The killers were rumored to be Albanian. As a result, Suleyman rounded up some hundreds of Albanians and had them summarily executed.

On the wider stage, in the post-Mohács period, a sense of unease swept eastern Europe. Ferdinand ruled warily and unsteadily in Buda, with dominion over western Hungary. He was not a popular monarch, for his brazen German ways provoked distrust and hate among his Hungarian subjects. Meanwhile, his rival, Zápolya, had returned from Poland to hold sway over large portions of eastern Hungary, bolstered with support from Francis I and promises of assistance from Protestant forces in Germany, and waiting, as a good and dutiful vassal, for the second coming of Suleyman to the region. Consorting with the infidel had cost Zápolya his Catholic faith. The pope, Clement VII, had excommunicated him.

As Ibrahim Pasha rose in influence, so his arrogance grew great. He dressed even more lavishly than the sultan, his fingers laden with jeweled rings. According to a contemporary, he "bought almost every fancy object he could acquire" and became the intermediary for the court's purchases of fabulous gold artifacts from Venice. Appealing to the Sultan's education as a goldsmith, he persuaded Suleyman that the display of precious jewelry and gold treasures was promoting an ideal of magnificence akin to that of Hannibal and Alexander the Great.

And he cultivated a close relationship with a shadowy Venetian alien named Alvise Gritti. Gritti was a fascinating blend of European sophistication and oriental exoticism. The illegitimate son of the Venetian doge, fluent in Italian, Turkish, and Greek, Gritti presided over a sumptuous court of his own in his Italianate palace overlooking Seraglio Point. Known as the prince's son, he wore an Italian beret to display his Christian faith. His fantastic banquets and balls were famous and attended by the high society of Constantinople. These diversions included dance and song and even lengthy productions of classical drama, such as a saucy comedy based on the Greek legend of Cupid and Psyche. Because Gritti straddled two worlds and could command the attention both of Ottoman grandees and Western dignitaries, he became an important diplomatic adviser to Ibrahim Pasha, as well as his agent in commercial transactions with the West. Through his good offices Ibrahim Pasha acquired a gold and jeweled helmet for Suleyman worth 144,000 ducats from the goldsmiths of the Rialto in Venice.

Ibrahim Pasha began to describe himself openly as the real power behind the Ottoman Empire, and he threw his weight around brutally. When the deferential envoy of his vassal János Zápolya paid a call, the grand vizier treated him with contempt and taunted him. Why had his weak master not been able to defeat Ferdinand? How had Zápolya dared to enter the royal castle of Buda when it had been spared and sequestered only for the return of the sultan? Did he not know that kings are not kings because of crowns and gold and precious stones, but because of sharp metal? Did he not know that the Ottoman emperor was powerful as the sun and reigned over heaven and earth?

"We will soon launch an attack against each of our enemies larger than we have done in the past," he boasted. "We will transform Buda into another Constantinople. I haven't spoken to you in Turkish terms, meaning words not short enough. Turks say little but act grandly. You are surprised to see me laugh. I laugh at you trying to claim for yourself something you lost a long time ago." Contemptuous though he was of Zápolya's envoy, he formalized an alliance with the Transylvanian prince in anticipation of a return visitation. When the envoy was brought to the sultan to put the final stamp on the deal, Suleyman was gracious.

"As a reward for your master's loyalty, I will not only bequeath the king of Hungary to him, but I will protect him from Ferdinand so effectively that he can rest and sleep on two ears." On January 27, 1528, the Sublime Porte announced that Zápolya was now under the protection of the Empire and was recognized as the king of Hungary. His representative in Constantinople was to be Alvise Gritti, the Venetian fixer for the Ottoman court.

In Vienna, Archduke Ferdinand was shocked at the formal agreement between Zápolya and the Sublime Porte. Its meaning was unmistakable. Thus, he too dispatched envoys to Constantinople in the hope that they might reverse the sultan's decision. To their regret later, they were not so deferential. Initially, the Austrian envoys were received with great ceremony. They were lavished with gifts and engulfed in flowery words. Brought before Ibrahim, they professed a desire for peace among "neighbors" and asked the Sublime Porte to recognize Ferdinand's right to the throne of Hungary. When the envoys spoke of Hungary as a Hapsburg domain, Ibrahim had had enough.

"By what right do you claim this when Sultan Suleyman has subjugated Hungary?" he said, and invoked a Turkish proverb: "Wherever the hoof of the sultan's horse has trod, that land belongs to him."

"I can only say no more than that my king holds Buda," an envoy replied.

"Why has he sent you to ask for peace and friendship if he holds Buda, which the Sultan has conquered?" Ibrahim responded.

The ambassador changed the subject. He derided Zápolya and pointed to the many merits of Ferdinand.

"You have talked of many virtues of your lord," Ibrahim said. "Very noble if they be true. If you have served him for such a short period of time, how do you know he is so wise and virtuous and powerful?"

"Because when he has won great victories, he ascribes the glory to God. In our books and in yours, the beginning of wisdom is said to be the fear of God."

What great victories? Ibrahim might have asked. Instead, he took the presumptuous envoys into the presence of Suleyman himself. The sultan sat silently to the side, as Ibrahim continued the interview.

Glancing at the formal letter from the archduke to the sultan, Ibrahim barked, "With what false audacity does your master call himself 'all-powerful' in the presence of the Sultan under whose shadow the other Christian princes take refuge?"

Name the princes, the envoys challenged. The demand was an insult to the sultan, who had regularly seen the princes of France, Poland, Serbia, and Venice kowtow to him. At this lack of respect, Suleyman rose and left the room. Taken aback, the Austrian envoys protested their king's desire for peace.

"If the Sultan is not willing, what then?" Ibrahim replied.

"Our master forces no man's friendship," the ambassador said.

"Your king has seized our land, and yet he asks for friendship? How can that be?"

The envoy was not intimidated. He went on brazenly to request the return of twenty-seven fortresses that Suleyman had subdued in Hungary.

"I am surprised that your master does not ask for Constantinople," Ibrahim quipped sarcastically. If the sultan returned the castles he had conquered, the grand vizier continued, would he be compensated for the cost of capturing and maintaining them?

Their master would certainly consider a fair payment to the sultan, the ambassadors replied.

"Do you think the Sultan is so poor that he needs to sell the castles he conquered with his own saber?" Ibrahim shouted. By this time, it must have dawned on the Austrian diplomats that their mission was not going well.

"You know the arms of the Turks, how sharp they are, and how far they can penetrate, for you have fled before them many times," Ibrahim continued contemptuously. It was time to get down to the essence. "There is no other way but for your king to abandon Buda and Hungary, and then we will treat with him about Germany." The envoy protested this provocation. Ibrahim brought it down to his own accomplishment:

"I conquered Louis and Hungary, and now I will build the bridges of the Sultan and prepare a way for His Majesty into Germany."

Ibrahim's patience thus came to an end. Again he brought them into Suleyman's presence for a final rebuke.

"Why does your master travel so extensively?" Suleyman asked idly.

"Our master is very young, sire. He cares deeply for the well-being of his people while he tries to prevent war through friendship."

"How is it then that your master, as well as his brother, the Emperor, are so devoid of friends? Apparently, they are utterly incapable of keeping peace."

His enemies were constantly provoking him, the envoys replied, and did not abide by their treaties.

"What about your poor priest, the highest in rank?" Suleyman asked, referring to the pope. "Why has he been treated in such a disrespectful manner? In my Empire, the highest priest has a place at my highest council and is well treated."

Before the envoys were dismissed from the sultan's presence, the audience concluded with Suleyman promising to give his answer to the archduke in Vienna. The ambassadors were led away and were soon called spies rather than diplomats. They were detained for another five months, then dispatched back to Ferdinand with their bleak message, just before Ferdinand departed for the Diet of Speyer.

THE PREPARATIONS FOR the assault on Vienna commenced in the fall of 1528 with the traditional ceremonial that always preceded an Ottoman move to war. A grand council convened, and the Sheik-ul-Islam, the supreme religious head of the Islamic world, stepped forward to deliver his *fetva*. Theoretically, the sheik's moral power exceeded that of the sultan himself, and Suleyman bowed in perfunctory deference. Then the sheiks and imams of the imperial mosques gathered in the Hall of the Divan in the Sublime Porte to listen reverently as the verses of the Koran relating to war and fighting were read aloud: "Fight in the way of Allah but transgress not the limits. For truly, Allah does not like transgressors. And kill them wherever you find them, and turn them out from where they have turned you out. . . . And fight them until there is no more disbelief and worshipping of others along with Allah" (sura 2:190–93).

The next step was the investiture of the commander. At last, Ibrahim Pasha officially took his place at the pinnacle of power, as the sultan appointed him to the supreme command of the army with absolute authority. In a brilliant, colorful spectacle, nine richly caparisoned horses were brought forward for him, and a bejeweled sword was presented to him, along with a quiver of arrows that were inlaid with precious rubies and stones. Three honorary double-breasted fur robes were offered, and he would carry six horsetail flags into battle. Then Suleyman stepped forward to proclaim, "I command Ibrahim Pasha to be from today and forever my grand vizier and chief of my army, named by My Majesty in all my estates. My viziers, beylerbeys, judges of the army, sheiks, my dignitaries of the court and pillars of the empire, my generals of cavalry or infantry, all my victorious army, all my slaves, high or low, my functionaries, the people of my kingdom, my provinces, citizens and peasants, rich and poor, in short all, shall recognize my grand vizier as chief of the army and shall esteem and venerate him, regarding all that he says or believes as an order proceeding from my mouth which rains pearls. If any member of the army (which Allah forbid!) shall rebel against the order of my grand vizier, let my Sublime Porte be immediately informed, and the guilty, whatever be their number or station, shall receive the punishment which they shall merit."

Grand processions through the capital followed, as various ambassadors came to the Topkapi to deliver their congratulations to the grand vizier. As each did so, Ibrahim Pasha answered with a bow and a stock reply: "Marching under divine protection, under the influence of the sacred banner, under the auspices of the grandest, most powerful of monarchs, I hope to gain brilliant victories over the enemies of the empire and return triumphant."

On May 10, 1529, a huge army departed from Constantinople. Suleyman boasted that he would not lay down his arms until he had erected a monument to his campaign and to Islam on the banks of the Rhine River. When Ferdinand's agents reported the arrival of the Turks in Belgrade in June, he wrote a last desperate appeal to his brother, Charles, for help:

"The Great Turk, with a force larger than has ever been seen before, has arrived in Belgrade with full intentions to march straight for Vienna. May God come to rescue us! I will do as much as I can with the little force that I have to fight him off. I hope, sire, that you will not abandon me, for otherwise Christianity will be in grave danger. I can not say what the outcome will be. I have every intention to act in your honor and glory."

At these frantic pleas, Charles, as usual, remained indifferent. Once he cleared up his business with the pope and the French king, he wrote languidly, he would try to help.

ACT EIGHT

THE GATES OF
VIENNA

✠

32.

THE BANKS OF
THE RHINE RIVER

The Turkish army that left Constantinople in May 1529 was considerably larger than the previous imperial invasion force in 1526. It consisted of at least seventy-five thousand men, and the force was so impressive that some chroniclers put the figure outrageously at four times that number, ballooning the figure from one hundred thousand to two hundred thousand and finally to three hundred thousand. Again the logistical side of the operation was daunting and Hannibalian, with thousands of camels and mules and hundreds of elephants to haul the supplies, including three hundred heavy cannons. Leading the procession was the sultan himself, with his horsetail banners fluttering in the wind and with his high expectations for his next imperial triumph.

Almost immediately, the grand expedition was dogged by terrible weather. Spring rains were even worse than in the previous campaign. Rivers were swollen; plains were flooded; roads were washed out; temperatures fell to record lows; and the winds were high. At the first way station of Adrianople, the bridges had been destroyed. Several weeks later, near Philippopolis, the Maritsa River raged over its banks, drowning a number of soldiers and horses, and forcing soldiers to climb trees to escape the flooding. Inevitably and perhaps critically, the weather slowed down the march north through Sophia and Nis. For this holy war against the infidel Suleyman must have wondered what was going through the mind of the

All-Powerful and the Most Merciful One. The arrival in Belgrade was a month later than had been planned. In the midst of a hurricane, the crossing of the Drava River took six days, and lightning killed nine men.

Not until August 18 did the army finally come to the glory fields of Mohács in southern Hungary. There Suleyman greeted his vassal, János Zápolya, who had brought six thousand reinforcements with him. Zápolya was treated grandly and superficially. Around the imperial tent the Rumelian and Anatolian armies were mustered in formation. Janissaries surrounded the tent itself. The agha of the army brought Zápolya forward. When he entered the tent, Suleyman rose to receive his kiss of submission. For his homage, the vassal was rewarded with four ceremonial robes, one on top of another, in the Ottoman tradition, and officially proclaimed to be the king of Hungary. He was accorded the singular honor of having a bodyguard of janissaries. An iron crown was placed on his head, for the sacred crown of St. Stephen, the crown of every king of Hungary since A.D. 1000, was still missing. Behind the pomp lay a certain reserve, however. To Suleyman, Zápolya was little more than a glorified slave.

A few days later the massive force stood before Buda. There a brave force of a few thousand Austrians put up only light resistance. After a dilatory five days of siege, the city fell to the Ottomans for a second time, and for a second time janissaries ran amok with looting. Once again Suleyman entered the royal palace above the Danube, which had supposedly been held pristine for his return though it had been defiled upon occasion by the presence of both Ferdinand and Zápolya. There another installation ceremony was held for Zápolya. Interestingly, by this time, under the direction of Ibrahim Pasha, Ottoman soldiers had recovered the stolen crown of St. Stephen as Ferdinand's soldiers tried to sneak it out of Hungary. Though the relic was now in hand, Zápolya again received a stolid iron crown. Importantly, neither Suleyman nor Ibrahim Pasha attended this perfunctory ceremony. Zápolya could have no doubts about his place.

To the west Ferdinand continued his frantic efforts at recruitment through the Austrian provinces of Styria, Carinthia, and Tirol. Having given up on help from his brother, Charles, his ambassadors canvassed other European states. With his English counterpart, the Austrian ambassador pointed out that Vienna was more than halfway between Constantinople and London. When he encountered the usual indifference, he responded by saying that without English help, the Turks might soon be watering their horses in the Thames. Within the confines of his own domain, the Archduchy of Austria, the Kingdom of Bohemia, and the Margravate of Moravia, Ferdinand had more success. He laid down the requirement that every tenth man in his archduchy step forward to defend Vienna. He levied a war tax that was especially steep on the wealthy Catholic clergy. His realms of Moravia and Bohemia promised nine thousand foot soldiers and eight hundred cavalry. While by no means did he get the sixteen thousand soldiers that the Diet of Speyer had authorized, he did get perhaps a third that number, and they were the fearsome German pikemen who had wrecked Rome two years earlier.

Most significantly, a formidable commander, Nicolas von Salm, arrived with a thousand pikemen and seven hundred Spanish musketeers. Seventy years old, a veteran of the siege of Rhodes and a minor hero of the Battle of Pavia and the commander who in the service of Ferdinand I had defeated János Zápolya at Tokay, Graf von Salm hailed from a small fief on the Rhine River in southwestern Germany, not far from Speyer and Worms. Apparently, von Salm took seriously the threats of Suleyman to extend the dominion of Islam to the Rhine River. Already, the skeptics who felt it was hopeless to resist the Ottoman juggernaut and who were already contemplating the nature of life under Islamic rule had begun to hum the following ditty about Suleyman:

> *From Hungary he's soon away*
> *In Austria by break of day*
> *Bavaria is just at hand,*
> *From there he'll reach another land,*
> *Soon to the Rhine perhaps he'll come.*

Ferdinand put Graf von Salm in operational control of the defense, ably to be assisted by an estimable soldier, Wilhelm van Roggendorf, a Dane, who had distinguished himself in the Italian Wars and was now the marshal of Austria. When all the soldiers from various quarters were counted, they amounted to a motley garrison of about seventeen thousand. Small though this force was by comparison to the horde it would soon face, it was stout and professional.

The city they were to defend presented daunting challenges. Vienna in 1529 remained a small medieval town of narrow streets, cramped houses with shingle roofs, a few Gothic towers, and a magnificent cathedral, St. Stephen's, at its center. Its circular, three-mile long wall, called Ringmauer, was of antiquated design and had been built in the thirteenth century on the ruins of the old Roman fortifications. Following the line of what today is the famous Ringstrasse of Vienna, the walls were dilapidated and thin, pockmarked, and crumbling. The trench around them was piled high with years of garbage. The northern perimeter was perhaps the most substantial, as it followed the line of the Danube and contained a number of towers. The citadel of Vienna scarcely deserved the term; it was merely an old building, with no particular defensive attributes, built into the southwestern wall. The city had nine gates, the most important being the Scottish Gate, the Stuben Gate, the Carinthian Gate, and the Salz Gate, which funneled into a bridge over the Danube.

Immediately, von Salm put his mind to the sorry state of Vienna's defenses. The wall was thickened and raised in height to twenty feet. The ditch behind it was cleaned out and deepened. Houses with flammable shingle roofs, both near the walls and in the suburbs outside, were razed. Within four days, some eight hundred of these structures, including convents and nunneries and the city hospital, were burned down to create clear fields of fire. The berm along the bank of the Danube, previously little more than a thick hedge, was heightened and fortified. Elder citizens, children, and priests were evacuated. In anticipation of a long siege, after the manner of Rhodes, large stores of wheat and water and other staples were laid in. All the gates of Vienna were bricked up, except one, the Salz Gate, facing the river.

Meanwhile, on September 15, Suleyman prepared to move north. Before he left Pest, he issued a directive to the Hungarian people: "Whosoever in Hungary should withhold obedience and subjugation to the Count of Zips, János Zápolya, whom the Sultan has named king, will be punished and exterminated with fire and sword. But those who submit themselves will be stoutly protected and able to possess their property and privileges."

On September 18, Turkish raiders swept across the Austrian border. The reputation of these mounted irregulars, known as the *akinjis*, preceded them—they were the Turkish terror incarnate—and the Austrian towns in their path emptied. To the Italians these marauders were known as the despoilers, but to Germans, more pointedly, as sackmen. With their sacks hanging from their saddles, ready to be filled with the spoils of war, they stormed forward, looting and burning everything in their path. The peasants who fled to the forests were pursued and slain. Women and children were not spared. The roads were clogged with refugees. When they heard of the fall of Pest, the burghers of Vienna were the first to flee with their women and children. When the sackmen finally reached the outskirts of the city, their sacks would have to remain empty: the perimeter around the walls was still smoldering with the embers of the houses that had been burned down.

By crossing into Austria, Suleyman's soldiers were crossing more than a state border. They were leaving the orbit of Constantinople and entering the orbit of Rome, trespassing for the first time onto the dominion of Western rather than Eastern Christianity. Suleyman's great ancestor and mentor, Mehmet the Conqueror of Constantinople, had consciously avoided this trespass, for he understood the political and military aspect of this dividing line. In annexing Serbia in 1459 and Bosnia in 1463, Mehmet II was arguably consolidating the realm of the patriarch in the Ottoman Empire. What belonged to the Orthodox Church of Constantine after the Great Schism of 1054 should rightfully belong to the Ottoman Empire, and Mehmet II promised to these natural citizens of his empire tolerance for their religion and stability in their civil affairs. As the Church of Serbia and Bosnia had their leader in Constantinople, so too they should have their secular leader there also. Vienna was a different matter. By transgressing the restraint and moderation of his forebear, Suleyman was violating an important precedent. He might defeat opposing armies. But unless he planned to repopulate Austria with Turks, he would have difficulty in holding on to his conquered territory in the long run.

On September 28, a day that the defenders celebrated as St. Wenceslas Day after a Bohemian saint, Suleyman himself arrived before the gates of Vienna in a driving rain. South of the city walls in the suburbs of Simmering and Wieden, a great sea of white, distinctly Turkish tents sprang up, as far as the eye could see even from the perch of St. Stephen's spires. In Simmering, Suleyman took charge of his own royal tent. From a far distance it was easily distinguished, its multiple pinnacles topped with knobs of gold. Its interior was appointed with fine carpets, cushions, and jeweled divans. Delicate gossamer tissues hung from its ceiling to separate its many compartments. Outside, some five hundred royal archers guarded the tent. The camp of Ibrahim Pasha extended west of this tent, across the high ground of Wienerberg to Wieden.

The sultan soon fell into deliberations with Ibrahim Pasha about the battle plan. Graf von Salm's hasty reinforcements could not disguise the fact that the city was wholly unsuited to defense. To veterans of the sieges of Belgrade and Rhodes, the challenge seemed minor. Nevertheless, the Turks suffered from one liability. Due to the soaking rains, they had left their heavy artillery behind in Hungary. The siege would therefore have to rely on mining operations.

As the troops massed south of the city facing the Stuben and Carinthian gates and several hundred Ottoman boats were positioned on the rivers, boasts and threats were issued to the defenders. If they resisted, the sultan promised to breakfast in St. Stephen's Cathedral on St. Michael's Day, only a few days hence. If the resistance was fierce, he would level Vienna as if it were Carthage, pour salt into the earth, and ensure that the city would never again exist. He would spare no one, including "the child in the mother's womb."

To his own soldiers, he promised handsome rewards and instant promotion for the first soldiers to breach the walls and enter the city. Ibrahim Pasha, in turn, offered handfuls of gold to the hero who brought him the head of an important enemy commander. Where was Ferdinand, Suleyman asked, this supposed "all-powerful" king his ambassadors had spoken of? When he was informed that the Hapsburg king was somewhere in the mountains—he was actually in Prague, still trying to drum up more troops—Suleyman promised to follow him to wherever he was hiding.

For several days brave and provocative talk was exchanged between the sides. The sultan sent a Bohemian prisoner into the city with the message that the sultan had a few more Bohemians available to strengthen the weak garrison. The Austrians sent him back with two Turkish prisoners, saying that they had quite enough Bohemians for a stout defense of the city, thank you very much. A day later, four more Christian prisoners were sent in, richly robed in oriental garb, with threats of terrible vengeance if the resistance continued. Hours later, four more Turkish prisoners came out, lavishly dressed in Western garb, but without a reply to the sultan's threats and promises.

But soon enough reality replaced this bravado. In the first days Suleyman realized that he had underestimated the strength and the passion of the defenders. Steady rain by day and unseasonable frost at night favored the defenders, as the Turks shivered in their light tents. Suleyman quickly regretted having left most of his heavy cannons back in Buda, for his light cannons of small caliber were having little effect on the refurbished walls. The first efforts at undermining the walls, especially by a Bosnian contingent, were turned back handsomely by von Salm's pikemen. The Austrians had good information about where the Turkish sappers were working, for they had placed peas on drums or tubs of water in the cellar corridors along the walls and took note when the peas or the water vibrated. Even when a few breaches were successful, the Austrians repulsed the assaults.

Adding to the indignity, the Austrians roared out of the Salz Gate in almost daily sorties that inflicted heavy casualties on the Turks. With clever disinformation, the Austrians led the Turks to believe that the defenders were more numerous than they were, and that their camp included the important nobility of the country. In his diary, a duped Suleyman noted on October 7, "It is said that all the important nobles of the Kingdom are behind the walls." In the rain the colorful tents began to droop, and the meadows turned to mud. Before long, instead of relying on the incentives of gold and promotion, Turkish commanders were whipping their soldiers into action. Some soldiers in turn responded sorrowfully by saying they would rather die by the Turkish whip than by the Austrian firepower.

After a third unsuccessful assault, Suleyman's confidence in victory began to wane. According to a legend told afterward, the sultan had a dream in a night of restless sleep in which the Prophet Mohammed himself appeared to him and delivered this message: to appease an angry God and save his army from disaster, he must sacrifice forty thousand sheep. When the sultan awoke, he gathered Ibrahim and the other advisers, told them of the dream, and ordered the sacrifice. His advisers objected. Supplies were short; the men were hungry and cold; few sheep were available after the ravages in the countryside by his raiders. Moreover, said his viziers, the dream must be seen as metaphorical, not literal. Perhaps the Prophet's message meant that forty thousand Muslims would have to die a martyr's death as the price of victory. Reluctantly, Suleyman relented.

On St. Michael's Day, it became the Austrians' turn for insult. They sent a messenger to Suleyman informing him that his breakfast was getting cold in the cathedral and that he would have to content himself with gruel from the Austrian guns. Yet again, a company of Spanish cavalrymen stormed out of the city and killed a number of Turks before they were driven back with only light losses. In his diary, Suleyman noted cryptically, "One mine explosion, but the breach is not large enough." Halfway through the siege, Graf von Salm announced a message from King Ferdinand that he was expected within a week with considerable reinforcements. This news was greeted with a roar of celebration from the troops, a noise that confused the besiegers into imagining a formidable force. Trumpet blasts from the spires of St. Stephen's celebrated each successful Austrian operation. Meanwhile, von Salm enforced tight discipline over the defenders. Strong Austrian wine was rationed. Two landsknechts who became drunk and deserted their post were publicly hanged. Two weeks into the siege the defenders had lost only 625 men.

Late in the evening of October 12, the sultan convened a divan to review the situation. Ibrahim Pasha spoke up for the majority. The Turks needed to face facts. The janissaries were complaining. Morale was flagging. Supplies were running low. The animals were mired in the mud, and fodder was running out. Their light cannons had accomplished nothing, and their mining operations had been repulsed. The enemy was apt to be reinforced at any time. Vienna was not Rhodes. Their soldiers were summer soldiers, not accustomed to the nip and the damp and the mud of the Viennese autumn. Three main assaults had failed, and by Islamic law this magic number fulfilled the obligation of the faithful. They had begun this effort too late, Ibrahim said. Winter approached. They faced a long and difficult march home. The grand vizier counseled withdrawal.

One last, desperate assault was agreed upon. Gold was promised to any soldier who got within the walls. A thousand aspers were promised to every janissary. To the first man to mount the walls thirty thousand aspers or six hundred ducats were promised. But money no longer motivated the Turkish soldiers. Reluctant and exhausted, they had to be whipped and beaten with sticks into action. The effort failed at a great cost. When the casualties for the two weeks were counted up, more than four thousand Turks had been killed.

The first siege of Vienna thus ended in humiliation for the Turks. The retreat was to be as brutal. In disgust and beneath incessant rain, the invaders burned their camp. The janissaries were the last to pack up, and they ended their stay at Vienna with horrendous atrocity, tying together a large number of their prisoners, including women, children, and elders, and throwing them into the flames of their burning camp.

And yet on October 16, the propaganda for domestic consumption in Constantinople began. Ibrahim Pasha, the secondary viziers and aghas, and the important generals gathered around the sultan in a great divan to congratulate him on a successful campaign. Each came forward to kiss Suleyman's hand in the traditional ceremony of fealty. The infidel Ferdinand had been shown to be more cowardly than "all-powerful." Skulking somewhere in his hiding place he had been taught an important lesson. The Ottoman hold over Hungary was consolidated, and the boundaries of the empire extended. Solemnly, Suleyman distributed rewards and gifts to his many heroes. The janissaries received their aspers. And Ibrahim Pasha was presented with a jeweled saber, a long, fur-lined coat, and five purses containing six thousand ducats each. The sultan protested that he had no real intention of capturing Vienna anyway. The mission of the great campaign had been to evict Ferdinand from Hungary and to show him that the great Ottoman army could penetrate the infidel dominion at will. The mission had been accomplished. The following bulletin was issued:

"An unbeliever came out from the fortress and brought intelligence announcing the submission of the princes and of the people, on whose behalf he prayed for grace and pardon. The Sultan received his prayer with favor and granted them pardon. Inasmuch as the German lands were unconnected with the Ottoman realm, that henceforth it would be hard to occupy the frontier places and conduct their affairs, the faithful would not trouble themselves to clear out the fortress or purify, improve, and put it into repair. Security being established, the horses heads were turned toward the throne of Solomon."

No one wished to state the obvious. This siege was a stunning first defeat for Suleyman. A much inferior force had turned back the great and righteous Ottoman army. The Spanish and Austrian musketeers and pikemen had shown themselves to be at least equal if not superior to the much vaunted janissaries. European artillery had outdueled the Turkish cannons. The Turkish Empire had overreached its natural limits. Vienna was indeed not Rhodes. For the moment at least there would be no Empire of the West within the Ottoman dominion.

When the Ottomans disappeared over the horizon, the celebrations began in Vienna. Throughout the siege the bells of St. Stephen's Cathedral had remained silent. Now they tolled joyously for the great victory for Austria and for Christianity, as within the church the *Te Deum* was sung exuberantly. The residents gazed at their great cathedral and its magnificent spires and gave thanks that these spires would not become minarets. Hans Sachs, the most famous of the German Meistersinger, composed a ballad of thanksgiving that included the line "Except the Lord keep the city, the watchman waketh in vain." Ironically, Sachs was an ardent supporter of Martin Luther. The celebrations had one bittersweet element. Their heroic leader, Nicolas von Salm, had been killed in the fray.

In all the euphoria, however, a certain dread lurked in the background. Was this truly the end of the Islamic threat? Perhaps the victory was temporary. Suleyman would certainly be back.

As with the previous campaign, the journey home was treacherous for the Turks. Again the swollen rivers, including the Danube at Györ, were crossed with great difficulty and with considerable loss of artillery and provisions. Heavy snow began to fall. By the time the army arrived at Buda, it was bedraggled and hungry, scarcely the conquering, victorious army it professed itself to be. Nevertheless, appearances had to be kept up. János Zápolya rode out to greet the sultan and to congratulate him on his successful campaign. Unsatisfying though he might be as a true king, Zápolya was the only possible caretaker of Hungary. Ceremoniously, his iron crown was removed and replaced with the sacred golden crown of St. Stephen. Again, neither Suleyman nor Ibrahim Pasha attended the ceremony.

On December 16 Suleyman arrived in Constantinople to a sumptuous welcome. The festivities celebrating the magnificence of his victory over the infidels lasted five days.

33.

CORONATION IN FAT CITY

Through the terrible crisis for Christianity in Vienna, Charles V had remained oblivious, for the two main strands of his imperial reign were being tied up elsewhere to his great satisfaction. In late June as the Turkish cavalcade was moving toward Hungary, the representatives of the emperor and the pope signed the Treaty of Barcelona, which put their harsh differences and insults of the past to rest. The way was at last clear for Charles V to realize his dream of traveling to Italy for his splendid official coronation as Holy Roman emperor. Clement VII, ever mindful of his family interests, was asking only that imperial soldiers invade Florence and restore the Medici to power there. (After Charles put his army at the pope's disposal, this was accomplished a year later when Florence surrendered and became Medici once again, and Clement's illegitimate nineteen-year-old son, Alessandro de' Medici, became the duke of Florence.)

Meanwhile, ladies had taken over the stalemate between France and the Empire and did what men could not. The mother of Francis I, Louise of Savoy, had suffered much through her son's captivity in Spain and was suffering as much through the captivity of her grandsons there. The aunt of Charles V, Margaret of Austria, the Hapsburg regent of the Netherlands, could identify with this feminine agony, so these two estimable dowagers, with the tacit support of their brood, took it upon themselves to end the seven-year strife between the two principal powers of Europe. After weeks of negotiations through the summer of 1529, agreement was reached on August 3. Called the Peace of the Ladies, it marked the official end of the seesaw, draining Italian Wars. France gave up all her claims in Italy and, by so doing, ended the thirty-five-year quest of French kings for hegemony in Milan and Naples. In addition France gave up suzerainty over Flanders and Artois. At the price of several million gold pieces, however, France retained its beloved Burgundy, and the sons of Francis I were to be returned to the bosom of their family.

Between his peace with the Vatican and with France, Charles V could achieve two fundamental objectives. He could get his coronation, and he could finally turn his attention to the heresy in Germany and the threat to Austria. Officially now, the Empire stood alone as the superpower of Europe. Luckily for him, Suleyman had faltered at the gates of Vienna with no help from Charles. But the emperor could have no illusions that Suleyman's first campaign against the heart of Europe would be his last.

Only a few days after Suleyman ordered his retreat from Vienna, Francis I welcomed the ambassadors of Charles V effusively in the great hall of the Louvre. Where a year before he was leveling insults and declaring war, now he proclaimed himself to be his rival's brother and undying friend. He stood ready to join Charles and his brother, Ferdinand, in a glorious crusade against the infidel Turks. France would provide sixty thousand troops for the noble effort. Rightly, Charles should be the supreme commander, and Francis would be the emperor's general in the field. He stood ready to meet the emperor at his coronation to sketch out their war plans. In praise of the ladies, a mass was held in the Cathedral of Notre Dame to ratify their peace treaty.

By this time Charles was already on his way to Italy. He had sailed from Barcelona at the end of July in the flagship of his admiral, Andrea Doria, and was in Genoa on August 12. Traveling across the suddenly peaceful countryside of Lombardy, he tarried for three weeks at Piacenza. There, he met the admiral of France and solemnized the Peace of the Ladies. In mid-October he moved on for another three weeks in Modena. There, on October 19, he received a letter from Ferdinand with the glorious news of Vienna:

"Sire, after the Turk has made every possible effort to take Vienna, where he made fourteen large and furious assaults that have all been repulsed and where he has lost a great amount of men without inflicting great damage to the Viennese troops, he has, through divine intervention, lifted his siege on Vienna. I do not know what he will do next, whether go back to his country or stay in Hungary or if he intends to return next spring to invade all of Christendom, though I very much suspect the latter. Thus, sire, Your Majesty's presence is very much desired to hear more on the Turkish matter and the need for his repulsion."

Meanwhile, the way was being prepared for the emperor's entry into Bologna. Bologna had largely escaped the turmoil of the last few years in Italy. Known as the Fat City for its love of food and life, for its two leaning towers, its joy in art and learning, it was here rather than in Rome that the coronation would have to take place. The decision was mutual between the pope and the emperor, although to both it was a disappointment. Charles V had longed for a grand spectacle in St. Peter's Basilica, and so too had the pope been eager to assert his papal prerogative at the spiritual center of Western Christianity.

But the bitterness of Romans toward the emperor was still great. Rome remained a pitiable and mangled corpse from its sack two years before, and it was advisable that the ruin of the Eternal City by the emperor's own soldiers be kept from the emperor's eyes. There were also narrow political considerations. The pope was eager to keep the emperor close to Florence, so that Clement could emphasize the need to recapture the city for the Medici. Charles accepted the downsizing of the celebration stoically, rationalizing that after his glorification he could more quickly hurry to Germany to deal with the heretics.

While the emperor languished in Piacenza and Modena, papal and imperial advisers debated how best to aggrandize the second city of the Papal States. If they could not have Rome, then Bologna had to be made over to look like Rome. "We have found an ingenious way to overcome the differences in the two locations," wrote a papal adviser. "Bologna will take on a Roman décor." If the event was not a grand enough spectacle, the outside world might question its validity. They settled the symbolism first. The allusion must be to ancient Rome, not to the present day. This was to be the union of St. Peter and Caesar. The spiritual and the temporal were joined at last. The coronation must suggest the coronation of the first Holy Roman emperor, Charlemagne, on Christmas Day A.D. 800. If Bologna was to be romanized, so too was the Hapsburg emperor to be romanized.

And so Bologna became faux Rome. Triumphal arches spanned the streets. Façades of buildings were hung with garlands. Renowned painters and sculptors and architects were put to work to refashion the landscape. Epic medallions of the great emperors of ancient Rome—Caesar, Octavian, Titus, and Trajan—adorned the Gate of San Felice, the entrance to the city. Beneath these huge medallions were statues of Roman generals: Scipio Africanus the Younger, the hero of the Third Punic War; Quintus Caecilius Metellus Pius, who won great victories in Spain in the first century B.C.; and Marcus Claudius Marcellus, the conqueror of Syracuse. Along the parade route of the imperial entry were figures of the Roman gods Janus and Apollo and an equestrian statue of Caesar Augustus. Several of the allegorical statues possessed an element of irony. One depicted Numa Pompilius, the legendary Roman king who was responsible for nearly all the pagan religious institutions of ancient Rome; another represented Marcus Furius Camillus, who confronted the Gauls in the fourth century B.C after they had sacked Rome, and who persuaded the Romans to rebuild their city.

The coronation was set for February 24, 1530, the emperor's thirtieth birthday and the feast of St. Matthias, and the anniversary of his triumph at Pavia. The extravaganza was to be held at the Basilica of San Petronio on the Piazza Maggiore in the historic center of the city.

Flushed with the news that the Turks had been turned back at Vienna (no thanks to him), the emperor made his grand entrance on December 6, 1529, into Bologna. His cavalcade included musicians and pages, three hundred light horsemen in red uniforms, ten artillery pieces, a company of sappers, twenty-four young gentlemen of Bologna in yellow velvet, and a huge contingent of German foot soldiers. Preceding the emperor was the hero of Pavia, Antonio de Leyva, who was carried in a chair because his gout was severe. He would be in charge of security for the imperial visit. On the emperor's head was the helmet of Caesar, sprouting a golden imperial eagle, and he wore complete body armor, iron inlaid with gold. In his hand he held the scepter of power.

At the entrance of the city at the Gate of San Felice, he dismounted and was greeted by Cardinal Campeggio, fresh from his deliberations in England over the Henry VIII–Catherine of Aragon matter. The cardinal held a crucifix to the lips of the emperor. Then atop a white charger, Charles rode grandly down the processional route as the people along the way shouted, "Caesare, Caesare, Carlo, Carlo, Imperio, Imperio!" The bells of the city pealed; trumpets blasted fanfares; and cannons thundered salutes. French and Spanish nobles held a magnificent gold brocade canopy over his head, and Alessandro de' Medici, the pope's nineteen-year-old illegitimate son, rode by his side. (Alessandro de' Medici was known as the Moor, since his mother was a North African serving girl.) At the Palazzo Pubblico the pope greeted him.

Clement VII had come some days before to oversee the arrangements, and he waited for Charles V now in a grand temporary structure, appointed with blue and white draperies, the colors of the Medici, that had been built at the top of a flight of stairs. The enclosure for the papal audience was meant to replicate the Hall of the Consistory in the Vatican. The pope sat on a throne, his tiara on his head, surrounded by twenty-eight cardinals. When the emperor approached the pontiff, he knelt and kissed his feet. "I have come where I have long desired to be, to the feet of Your Holiness," Charles said in Spanish, "that we may take measures together to relive the needs of afflicted Christendom. May God grant my coming may prove to be for the good of His service and that of Your Holiness, and useful to the Christian world."

"I thank God that I see you here safe after your long journey by sea and land," the pope replied, "and that affairs are in such a state that I need not despair of seeing peace and order reestablished."

For the next three months the emperor and the pope resided in adjoining apartments in the Palazzo Pubblico on the Piazza Maggiore, while their supernumeraries fought over protocol. The two potentates had many intimate conversations during the period, and no doubt many elaborate meals, for during this period Charles's gluttony was especially out of control. His confessor warned him about both the quality and quantity of what he was eating. "Remember that your life is not your own," the confessor wrote, "but should be preserved for the sake of others. If Your Majesty chooses to destroy your own property, you should not endanger what belongs to us." Especially he was to stay away from the highly spiced fish and eel pies that were his particular fancy. "I once wished Your Majesty to do some penance for old sins," the confessor continued, "but if you will change this injunction into a firm resistance against gluttony, it will be to you as meritorious as flint and scourge." Nevertheless, the emperor was accustomed to a breakfast before dawn of fowl prepared with milk, sugar, and spice; at noon a hearty lunch; at six an evening repast of anchovies; and at midnight, a dinner of twenty courses. His confessor must have found some consolation in the emperor's moderation when it came to drink.

When the potentates could find time to talk between meals, their conversation concerned the complexities of Italian politics, the peril from the Turks, and the dangerous quandary of the German heresy. With an eye to the future, the emperor issued an invitation on January 21, 1530, to the German princes to gather at a diet in Augsburg in April. Its purpose, the summons stated, was "to settle disputes, to commit previous errors to the mercy of our Savior, to hear, understand, and weigh the opinion of each man with love and charity, and thus come to live again as one Church and one State." This was a noble and quite unattainable goal.

The closeness of the two men's circumstance, however, could not overcome the grievances of the past and the suspicions of the present. Reluctantly the emperor had acquiesced in the pope's determination to end the republic in Florence and restore the Medici to power there. But he suspected that the pope was also soliciting the help of France in the endeavor.

The pope, in turn, could not overcome his worry that the forthcoming coronation was merely the pretext for a permanent occupation of Italy. At one point the pope manifested his paranoia by remarking to a French ambassador,

"I am being betrayed, but I must act as if I am unaware of it."

Meanwhile, the time was filled with many diversions: tournaments, horse races, cane fights. Once a bull was let loose in the Piazza Maggiore for the amusement of the grandees, who watched from their windows above. The emperor became a tourist, visiting castles and grand churches in the surrounding area, wandering through the university that was among the oldest in Europe, and conferring honors on the Knights of Santiago and of the Golden Fleece. These diversions were suspended in January when the emperor came down with an attack of quinsy, but he recovered within a few days. The time of festivities was not altogether happy, for German and Spanish soldiers were often out of control, committing robberies and other mischief. The citizens of Bologna quickly tired of the long delay before the coronation, and many began to conclude that the honor was decidedly a mixed blessing. It was as if the prediction of a well-known astrologer was coming true. In early 1530 as Mars aligned with Saturn, the seer predicted "famine, various tumults, clash of arms, thefts, robberies, fires, crushing and murder of human bodies."

Finally, the time for the ceremony approached. On February 22, 1530, in the great hall of the Palazzo Pubblico, Clement crowned Charles with the iron crown of Lombardy, whose ring of gold contained a nail from the True Cross of Christ. As Charles knelt at the feet of the pontiff, he once again expressed his remorse for the sack of the Eternal City. It was the last time for sorrow and for dwelling on the past.

Two days later came the long-awaited day of pageantry. The pope emerged from the palace first. On his head was the distinctive triple crown of his holy office, and around his shoulders a magnificent white embroidered cope, drawn at the neck with a broach encasing an immense diamond. Gingerly, in the company of cardinals, he passed over a wooden bridge that had been constructed to link the palace with the basilica and was draped in priceless tapestries and blue velvet. The emperor followed, wearing the crown of Lombardy and a magnificent royal mantle that displayed an immense imperial eagle. Just as he passed into the church, there was a loud bang. A gallery had collapsed on a formation of pikemen. Several spectators were killed instantly as general panic ensued. But the show had to proceed. Charles remained cool until order was restored.

Again the ritual of Aachen was followed: the kiss of peace, the anointing with holy oil, the presentation of the sword, orb, and scepter. Along with the traditional sung texts of *Kyrie Eleison* and the *Gloria,* soaring music featured fanfares and kettledrums and Charles's much beloved carillon, whose bell ringers always accompanied his retinue. Charles swore on the Gospels to be a faithful champion of the Holy Roman Church. At last, Clement presented him with the imperial crown. "Receive this symbol of glory and the diadem of the Empire in the name of the Father, of the Son, and of the Holy Ghost, that you, despising the ancient enemy and guiltless of all iniquity, may live in clemency and godliness. And so one day may receive from our Lord Jesus Christ the crown of His eternal kingdom." When the ceremony was over, the pope and emperor passed down the aisle hand in hand, as the crowd shouted, *"Evviva Carlo Imperatore!"*

"Under the same golden canopy these two great luminaries of the world shone like the sun and the moon," wrote one observer. Not everyone was so smitten. A wag would write, "When Caesar shakes hands with Peter, human blood oozes from the grasp."

Having been crowned in a church that was ersatz St. Peter's, the two moved on to the Church of St. Dominic, whose décor was meant to suggest the basilica of St. John Lateran in Rome. There, following the tradition of the previous thirty Holy Roman emperors, Charles was invested as a canon of the Church. Then the majestic procession repaired to Palazzo Pubblico for an extravagant banquet. Wine flowed from a fountain in the middle of the Great Hall, and over an open pit was roasted the carcass of an ox whose cavity was filled with smaller animals and birds, such as turkey and geese and suckling pig.

This was to be the last time in history that a pope and an emperor would join in a union of spiritual and temporal power in Christendom. With this ceremony a seven-hundred-year-old tradition came to an end. Charlemagne and Charles V were to be the brackets of a dying ideal, the ideal of a universal empire joined with a universal religion.

The end of the ceremonies could not come too soon for the people of Bologna. When Charles V prepared to leave their city, a resident remarked, "He may do as he likes. We are certain that we shall have more mirth on his departure than we had on his arrival."

Far away in Constantinople the pageant was watched closely, with annoyance. Through Venetian emissaries, Ibrahim Pasha was briefed on the magnificent spectacle. "How can there be any true emperor other than my grand signor?" he asked contemptuously. Charles's claim to be Caesar elicited special scorn. Hereafter, Suleyman referred to Charles disparagingly as "the king of Spain." Just as there was no other God but God, there could be only one true emperor of the world. Suleyman planned to demonstrate soon who that was.

Diplomats in the Ottoman court began to report the anger of the sultan over the claims of universal empire joined with universal religion. It was predicted that Suleyman would soon lash out with another assault on the Christian world. In Paris, Francis I, now consigned to the second rank and playing both sides against one another, made a breezy prediction to a Venetian emissary who had reported the disgust of Constantinople: "The Turk will make some naval expedition and may ravage Puglia, going as far as Rome. Sultan Suleyman always says, 'To Rome, to Rome,' and he detests the emperor and his title of Caesar." Detest he might, but Suleyman would soon seek to imitate and surpass the splendor of the imperial coronation.

All this was far from the mind of Charles V. He left Bologna in late March for Germany. Difficult disputes at his diet at Augsburg lay just ahead. At long last, he was in a position to turn his full attention to the heresy.

34.

THE CREED OF PROTEST

Since the Diet of Speyer the year before, the Protestants had scarcely been idle, for Speyer had imparted a sense of urgency to the evangelical cause. The draconian provisions of the Diet of Worms had been reinstated, including the reaffirmation of Luther as an outlaw. It was well appreciated that if the Turks were turned back and with the Italian Wars ended, the emperor might well turn the full force of his military might on the rebel estates of Germany, with the pope and his cardinals cheering from the side pews.

Philip of Hesse now assumed the role of de facto leader of the evangelicals on the political front. He felt it imperative that the Protestant princes negotiate a formal military alliance that would span both Saxony and the Protestant cantons of Switzerland and form a deterrent to any nefarious imperial designs. But in this early stage of the Reformation, the Lutheran and Zwinglian factions were in passionate disagreement over points of dogma, and this weakened the overall cause. Philip felt that, for practical political reasons, the factions must attempt to reconcile their differences, so as to present a united front to the new Caesar. He offered to be the facilitator. The papists, as he called them, had made much about the discord of the Protestants at the Diet of Speyer.

And so in June 1529, Philip had issued an invitation to Luther and Zwingli to come to Marburg in his province to thrash out their disagree-

ments and come to an understanding. Luther was suspicious and went reluctantly. "I can not give ground," he said characteristically, "because I am
certain that they are in error." Before setting out, the Reformer asked Philip
to pressure the Swiss faction to soften their positions.

Philip hoped for a "friendly private discussion" when the sides gathered
at Marburg Castle on September 29, and the audience was kept to a min-
imum. To maintain calm and avoid fireworks, Luther and Zwingli were
kept apart in the first discussion. When they were finally brought together,
the scene was remarkable. They sat at a table facing Philip, as if he were a
stern schoolmaster. Zwingli wore a black tunic, a sword strapped to his side,
and a fur pouch dangling across his loins. Luther wore his simple friar's
cowl. It would be the only face-to-face meeting of the rivals in the early
Reformation.

In the four days of the Marburg Colloquy the two firebrands for the most
part behaved themselves. As they debated the sacraments in Latin, the par-
ticipants were alternately acerbic and cordial. "I want your friendship, not
your enmity," Zwingli said in one breath, and called Luther "prejudiced" in
the next. Luther said at one point, "I pray God that you will come to a right
understanding," and soon after, "I apologize if I have been harsh to you." The
Reformer could be at once pious—"Christ gives himself to us in preaching,
in baptism, in consoling our brethren in sacraments"—and at another moment shockingly crude—"If He were to order us to eat shit, I would do it."

In its process the Marburg Colloquy found its significance. Philip had
asked Luther to prepare specific articles that defined the agreements and
the disagreements between the sides. Luther had the help of Philip Melanchthon, a professor of Greek at Wittenberg University, who had been
Luther's second-in-command throughout the past decade. Where Luther
was precise, uncompromising, and confrontational, Melanchthon could be
conciliatory and flexible. By forcing Luther to be specific, the sides discovered that they agreed on many things: marriage of priests, original sin, the
nature of grace, baptism, the role of the state versus the church. Indeed,
they agreed on thirteen of fourteen articles that Luther and Melanchthon
had penned.

But Lutherans and Zwinglians disagreed passionately and profoundly about the Eucharist. To onlookers their dialogue about the Lord's Supper was esoteric. What was Christ's presence in the bread and the wine? Was it spiritual or carnal? What had Jesus meant when he said in John 6:53ff: "Except ye eat the flesh of the Son of man and drink his blood, ye have no life in you. Whoso eateth my flesh and drinketh my blood, hath eternal life. . . . He that eateth my flesh and drinketh my blood dwelleth in me, and I in him. . . . It is the spirit that quicketh. The flesh profiteth nothing: the words that I speak unto you, they are spirit, and they are life." The disagreement over this passage scuttled Philip's plan for unity. After four days the rivals went their separate ways, confident in their own righteousness, and their factions diverged accordingly. But a process of defining essential articles of faith was established. The Marburg Colloquy became the first draft of the theological basis of Lutheranism.

On his way home, Luther learned that the Turks were at the gates of Vienna, and he was sorely troubled.

Seven months later, in early April 1530, Martin Luther set out on another political journey, this time to the diet that Emperor Charles V was summoning to the free German city of Augsburg in Bavaria. Accompanied by Melanchthon and several other monks, the Reformer preached at various stops along the way, finally arriving in the town of Coburg in southern Saxony. There the evangelicals met with Elector John to discuss strategy. John greeted his holy men warmly, bristling with optimism for the apparent reasonableness of Emperor Charles. His talk of unity encouraged the Protestants, especially his evident acknowledgment that the reformers had been treated unjustly in the past. Inspired by the example of Marburg, the elector had ordered the reformers to begin writing a synopsis of the Lutheran faith for the convocation. Luther and Melanchthon had already drafted a number of points, which were later called the Torgau articles after the town where the two began their work.

But the elector had one stiff demand. Luther would not be permitted to proceed to Augsburg. The route to the independent imperial city would take them through 150 miles of hostile Catholic Bavaria, where Luther was in danger of being seized at any point as an outlaw and a heretic. According to the Diet of Worms he should be burned as a sacred duty in obedience to papal decrees. Moreover, the presence of the excommunicant at the imperial diet might be personally offensive to the emperor. And so the Reformer was deposited in the comfortable surroundings of the twelfth-century Coburg castle, overlooking the town, and his colleagues moved on without him. Luther would write wistfully "I live like a Lord," but soon enough he came to view his splendid confinement as his wilderness and his Sinai.

At the same time, Charles V converged on Augsburg from the south in even grander fashion. From Bologna, he went to Innsbruck, where he was joined by his brother, Archduke Ferdinand, and learned the full story of Vienna's defense. At long last, Charles understood the full implications of the Ottoman assault on Christian Europe and realized how close they had come to disaster. The heart of Christendom had only survived through sheer luck. Had the Ottomans arrived at their destination six weeks earlier and with their heavy cannons, the result would surely have been different. The Holy Roman Empire could not expect to be so lucky next time.

From Innsbruck the royal procession moved on to Munich, seeing first-hand the signs of Lutheran influence everywhere along the way. On June 16, the vigil of Corpus Christi, the cavalcade entered Augsburg, accompanied by two thousand foot soldiers in a display of Hapsburg military might. If Elector John bristled with optimism over Charles's ostensible moderation, Charles bristled with confidence over his ability to restore religious unity. He was now in a position to impose his will on his rebellious German lands. After his coronation, he felt his duty keenly as the temporal leader of Roman Catholicism. He came as their sovereign and as the vicar of all Christendom. If the Protestants appealed to conscience, he would remind them that he too had a conscience, and his conscience could not permit the ancient Christian faith to be trampled underfoot. He was intent to "tear the heresy out at its roots," as he wrote his wife.

While the emperor had not changed his views in the nine years since the Diet of Worms, he was pragmatic enough to realize that he faced now not a single obstreperous monk but a collection of determined, militant states. He could accommodate the rebellion or he could seek to crush it. In light of the Turkish menace, the prospect of raising another army to fight fellow Christians was dispiriting. Negotiation was the wiser course. There was a third way. Together with the Protestant side, they could insist on an international council of Christian leaders to be convened promptly to debate dogma and discuss reforms for the Church. He had discussed that possibility with the pope in Bologna. Clement VII was adamant in his rejection of the idea.

In its initial days the diet seemed to go the emperor's way. He exhibited some flexibility, showing the evangelicals respect and allowing them wide latitude to express their opinions. At the same time, he insisted that the electors submit to imperial authority and that innovations be suspended until a general council was convened. When he forbade Lutheran chaplains to preach in Augsburg during the conference, the electors agreed.

But five days into the conference the Protestants seized control of the agenda. Their carefully planned strategy had been two months in the making. Initiated by Elector John's order, Luther and Melanchthon had begun writing their articles of faith in Torgau in April. They had discussed their first draft with Elector John in Coburg in May. Once in Augsburg, Melanchthon had taken charge, sharing the articles with Lutheran princes, including Philip of Hesse, and asking for their comments. He kept in constant correspondence with Luther about developments. After further refinements, the text was signed by the princes, approved by both Elector John and Martin Luther himself at a safe remove in Coburg.

This was now as much a political as a religious process. The Protestants laid their groundwork deftly. Instead of the spacious city hall of Augsburg where the plenary sessions were held, they chose a small chapel in the bishop's palace as the venue for the presentation. The text was prepared in Latin as well as German, and the document was addressed to the emperor deferentially "so that His Imperial Majesty might see that we have not acted unchristianly and blasphemously in this, but only as being forced to

God's commandment." A day before the main event, the emperor was informed of what was coming.

On June 25 the Augsburg Confession was read out. The document constituted the fundamental sacramental beliefs of the evangelicals. Its text would become the most important statement of faith during the Reformation, and it would later form part of the Lutheran Book of Concord. Melanchthon had gone to considerable lengths to show respect for the Apostolic See, and deference to the Holy Roman emperor. In his preface he wrote that Lutherans "are neglecting nothing that may serve the cause of Christian unity." The first articles emphasized beliefs held in common with Roman Catholicism, with several glaring exceptions. The Lutherans agreed with Rome on the Trinity, original sin, baptism, and repentance. But the doctrine of justification by faith alone was boldly enunciated without qualification. Works might be good, but they counted for nothing before God. The Lutheran view of the Real Presence of Christ in the Eucharist was laid out starkly.

These twenty-one articles formed the first part of the Confession. The second part, consisting of seven additional articles, addressed the wrongs of the Church and the way in which evangelical doctrine corrected these wrongs. On the right of priests to marry, the Confession argued the scriptural basis for it. Confession was regarded as voluntary rather than mandatory for the devout. And in a point that was bound to offend Charles after his glorious coronation in Bologna, the Lutherans called for a separation between political and theological power.

For the next three months the Diet of Augsburg debated this extraordinary credo. Increasingly, the diet took on the feel of an ecclesiastical court, with prosecution and defense, call and response. Into July and August, Charles V listened to this discourse with rising frustration, alternating between saber rattling and negotiation, hoping against hope that the Protestants, either through pressure or through incentive, would soften their position. Melanchthon and the papal legate, Cardinal Campeggio, met, and while the Lutheran thanked the cardinal for not speaking of war, nothing came of their deliberations. Well into the summer, Charles held on to his hope for a third way, a council where the Protestant cause would get a full and fair hearing, while the Church would commit to correcting its abuses. In desperation, he wrote to Clement VII with a final appeal:

"If the heretics refuse so generous an offer, they will have everyone against them. But if there is no council, Germany, the strongest, most war-like nation in Christendom, would fall into the gravest peril. At present the world is at peace, so a council can easily be called to prevent further breeding of schism. If it should again come to war, then at the very worst, we could dissolve the council. We then, Your Holiness and I, would have done what we could, and others would bear the blame. God, I hope, would then punish those who were answerable for the evils that would fall on Christendom. Therefore, I entreat and beseech you to consent to the council so that we may avoid the burden of blame and win the praise of all good men."

The emperor seemed to know that he was whistling in the wind. The pope had consistently expressed only horror at the idea of a council. This was about heresy against Church doctrine, not about the Church itself. Still, the emperor appended to his appeal a coda for the Church: "It would be best if Your Holiness would do your own part and get rid of such abuses as can readily be stopped. That would be a great help."

On August 3, the Catholic side formally answered with its own point-by-point rebuttal called a Confutation. With that, Philip of Hesse packed up and left in disgust. Melanchthon, in turn, would eventually answer the Catholic rebuttal with his Protestant surrebuttal, which he called his Apologia.

In Coburg, Luther worried that his colleague might surrender into compromise and concession. He fretted at Melanchthon's dignified tone and his deferential references to the "apostolic see," while Luther, as if to stiffen his representative, referred to the pope as "a low Italian" and "the son of a harlot." While Melanchthon spoke of priestly celibacy as ungrounded in Scripture, Luther wrote openly about the secret love lives and homosexuality of priests and popes: "Roman sodomy, Italian marriage, Venetian and Turkish brides [i.e., male sex partners], Florentine bridegrooms." While Melanchthon labored to keep the door open to an accord, Luther wanted the door slammed shut. In August he wrote to Melanchthon, "All talk of harmonizing our doctrines displeases me, for I know it is impossible unless the Pope will simply abolish the papacy." In September, he wrote, "If we yield a single one of our conditions, we deny our whole doctrine and confirm theirs. I would not yield an inch to those proud men. I am almost bursting with anger and indignation. Pray break off all transactions at once and return hither."

Almost lost in the noise was the Turkish question. At the start of the diet, Charles had hoped to impose taxation on the German estates to support a crusade against the Turks . . . if not an offensive crusade, at least taxation for the defense of Vienna. Archduke Ferdinand went further. He proposed that the lands of rebellious German princes be confiscated and sold to raise money for a defensive army in the Balkans. By late summer, taxation of any sort seemed out of the question. Increasingly, Charles's options were reduced to two: use force or do nothing. With authority from the Vatican, Cardinal Campeggio advocated for force.

The Diet of Augsburg broke up in failure and alienation. Charles V formally accepted the Confutation, renewed the Edict of Worms, and issued an ultimatum to the "heretics." By the spring of 1531 they must reconvert to Roman Catholicism or else. On September 8, he dismissed the representatives of the German states.

The Lutheran princes departed in disgust and trepidation. War seemed in the offing. Once again, Philip of Hesse took the lead in organizing the opposition. He called for a conference of the dissidents, to be convened in Schmalkalden in central Germany in December. There, two months later, in February 1531, eight Lutheran principalities and eleven independent German cities formed a defensive alliance against their emperor. Their creed was the Augsburg Confession. If one of their numbers was attacked, all would come to its defense. An army of ten thousand soldiers and two thousand cavalry was authorized for the coalition.

Ironically, Martin Luther himself opposed the league in principle. He favored theological opposition, but not military action. And he professed an enduring admiration for the emperor personally as a man "who stood his ground as firmly as a rock." Resistance was now the issue. Reluctantly, he wrote a tepid endorsement:

"If war breaks out, which God forbid, I will not reprove those who defend themselves against the murderers and bloodthirsty papists, nor let anyone else rebuke them as being seditious. I will accept their action and let it pass as self-defense."

As the Lutheran princes affixed their signatures to the Schmalkalden League, Philip Melanchthon now answered the Confutation with his Apologia. Between its theological grounding now committed to writing and its military alliance, the Lutheran movement was firmly established as a Protestant theocracy within a Catholic empire. The idea of a universal Christian dominion, guided by a pope and a Christian Caesar, was finished. It appeared that sectarian war could be the only result.

But Suleyman the Magnificent was soon to change all that.

35.

CEREMONY OF AMNESIA

On June 27, 1530, two days after the reading of the Augsburg Confession was staged for Charles V in Germany, a very different kind of theater commenced in Constantinople. For the next eighteen days, the eastern imperial capital uproariously celebrated the circumcision of Suleyman's three oldest princes: Mustafa, Mehmet, and Selim. The elaborate spectacle had been in the planning for months, partly to make the populace forget the sour memory of Vienna, partly to show once again that Suleyman stood above all others in the world in his magnificence and munificence, power and wealth. At all costs, the ceremony had to surpass in its grandeur the coronation of the Holy Roman emperor in Bologna.

On the first day, Suleyman's cavalcade emerged from the Seraglio on a wide boulevard that only a few months before had been a narrow street leading from the Topkapi to the old Byzantine Hippodrome. Houses had been leveled on either side of the street to create a fitting processional route. Accompanied by imperial gatekeepers, masters of the throne room, aghas, members of the divan, Islamic scholars, pages of the Inner Service, and his viziers, the sultan was carried to the parade ground on a golden palanquin. The Hippodrome was decked out in festive garb. Two tall obelisks had been erected, along with a bronze column shaped like a mythical, three-headed serpent. As the sultan entered the parade ground, fanfares from trumpets melded with the roars of lions in nearby cages. Ibrahim Pasha came forward on foot to greet his master and escort him to his golden throne at the far end, from which tapestries had been hung and from which fine silk blew in the breeze.

The days that followed featured brilliant processions and amazing displays of skill and bravery. On the second and third days various dignitaries such as emirs and former viziers and ambassadors approached the throne to offer homage to Suleyman and to place magnificent gifts at his feet: Syrian damask, bolts of Egyptian cotton, Tartar furs, and Venetian velvet. Gorgeous Ethiopian and Hungarian slaves were presented to the sultan, along with Arabian stallions. The sultan reciprocated with gifts. It was said that the gifts he presented to Ibrahim were said to be worth fifty thousand ducats.

An elaborate Venetian delegation led the diplomatic contingent, for ever since the naval victory of the Turks over Venice in the Battle of Sapienza in 1499, the watery city-state had pursued a policy of accommodation. Venetian diplomats actually lived within the royal compound. They had learned, the Turks said wryly, "to kiss the hand that they could not cut off." But the rest of the European presence was meager. Russia and France had representatives. Indeed, Francis I and Suleyman were engaged in an active correspondence about the Holy Land. Francis was expressing an interest in traveling to Jerusalem and en route visiting "his patron and friend, Suleyman."

And he had a request. He wanted an ancient Christian church in the Holy City that had been converted into a mosque to be returned to its original faith. To this, Ibrahim had replied that if "the king of France demanded a province, Turks would not have refused. But in matters of religion, they could not gratify the king's desire." This was followed by Suleyman's own letter, in which he invoked the Koranic injunction that there be no compulsion in religion. "The Christians there shall live peaceably under the wing of our protection," the sultan wrote to Francis. "They shall be allowed to repair their doors and windows. They shall preserve in all safety their oratories and establishments that they actually now occupy without anyone being allowed to oppose or torment them." The operative words were *that they actually now occupy*.

Soon enough, the parades and games began. Artisans of various guilds paraded floats with their wares before the imperial grandstand. There were circus acts and concerts and musical plays. Soldiers engaged in mock battles, assaulting wooden towers with muskets and swords, and whoever prevailed was rewarded with beautiful slave girls or handsome boys. A new game was inaugurated, a contest of throwing long sticks; its inventer, a renowned mathematician, was lavished with gifts for his creativity. Footraces and chariot races were held, and even combat between wild animals. In one such event, the German ambassador offered a sacrificial wild boar to fight a lion. To the dismay of the Turks, the boar, which had one leg tied with a rope anchored to a stake, comported itself ably, dispatching two lions. "With the last lion," wrote an observer, "the hog tumbled him over and over in the dust before the lion shamefully ran away. This happened to the great confusion of the Turks, who compare themselves to lions, and compare Christians, especially Germans, to hogs."

In the evenings the mosques of the city were illuminated, and when this light mixed with that of fireworks and burning wooden towers, Constantinople took on an orange glow. At the Seraglio elaborate banquets were put on, in which lambs were sacrificed (the custom of circumcision ceremonies) and sheep were roasted whole. When the latter came off the spit and were presented to the throng, birds suddenly flew from the charred cavities of their carcasses. Jugglers and acrobats performed for the banqueters. The sultan and his sensual, cunning, and self-assured wife, Roxellana, entered with high ceremony.

Suleyman presided over the festivities seated on a magnificent throne and surrounded by Roxellana and other ladies of the court, while black eunuchs and slave girls, known by names of flowers (Lotus Blossom, Little Rose Leaf, Splendor of the Tulip) and dressed in chemise and transparent, billowing sky-blue silk, served his food. Court gardeners passed through the assemblage, carrying baskets of fragrant flowers, while the scent of amber perfume and oriental spices wafted through the reception hall, next to the fountain in the Court of the Favorites. A high point came when a specialist stepped forward to ply the ancient art of reading the prophecy in the sultan's coffee grounds and whispering the results into his ear.

The fabulous orchestra of the harem provided the music, its melodies anchored by the haunting plucked notes of the *qanun,* the rattle of the tambourine, the strains of the viol that Ibrahim played so well, the thumps of the *derbuka.* Dancers emerged from the wings, their faces smeared with a mixture of almond paste and white jasmine. At a climactic moment, which was greeted with great anticipation, the sultan released one of his favorites from the harem and presented her to a loyal dignitary as a wife. When the gorge drew to an end, buckets of multicolored sorbet, crushed ice mixed with the snow of Mt. Olympus and flavored with violet and lemon, were brought forward.

As the Turks feasted and the city glowed, one wry Western observer whispered that the aureole of the city "announced to the shepherds in the mountains of Asia and to the sailors on the Sea of Marmara the orgies of the new Babylon."

Suleyman was well pleased with his great feast of amnesia. Finally on the eighteenth day, the three princes, aged fifteen, nine, and six, rode through the streets in the midst of a rowdy throng of youths their own age. They were led by heralds carrying candles attached to palm fronds, and a contingent of half-naked former unbelievers who held in their left hands darts pointing toward their hearts as a confession that the weapons would have pierced their hearts if they had not finally embraced Islam. Along the way the princes were presented with baskets of fruit and flowers.

On the balcony of Ibrahim Pasha's mansion, the sultan awaited his sons, for in affection and as an honor to Ibrahim, the circumcision was to be performed at the grand vizier's residence. As Suleyman and Ibrahim watched the remarkable conclusion to the carnival, Suleyman turned to his friend.

"In your opinion, Ibrahim, between the two magnificent ceremonies of your wedding to my sister and the circumcision of my sons, which was the most spectacular?"

"A wedding like mine has never been seen since the world has existed and will never be seen again," Ibrahim replied. The wedding festivities had lasted fifteen days.

"How so?"

"Because, Your Majesty, you have many splendid guests here, but no one can compare with a guest I had at my wedding. The padishah of Mecca and Medina, the Solomon of our time, blessed my wedding with his presence."

"Shall you be blessed a thousand times," Suleyman replied to his friend, at this flattery, "for over the years you have set me straight countless times."

As his sons approached the balcony, if Suleyman had any thoughts about their future, they are not recorded. Only one of them could succeed him, and the history of losers in the Ottoman court was not rosy. They came toward him in order of their age. The eldest, Mustafa, was the crown prince. The sultan looked down upon his firstborn with great pride. The boy, fair-haired like his mother, was developing as the perfect prince and successor. In the palace school, he had excelled in mathematics. He had learned Persian, Italian, and Arabic with ease. He had mastered the Koran and proved himself an excellent swordsman and equestrian. Popular with his mates, he showed courage and exuded the easy charm of a natural leader.

Only one liability burdened him. He was the son not of Roxellana but of the sultan's first favorite, the Circassian beauty Gülbahar, known as Rose of the Spring. The rivalry between these two fiery slaves had roiled the harem from the earliest years of Suleyman's reign. Technically, Gülbahar remained the first lady of the harem, who stood in line to assume the exalted role someday of the *valide* or mother of the sultan. But Roxellana had been scheming for years to undermine her rival and had even, so the rumor had it, been behind an attempt to assassinate Mustafa with poisoned oranges. In the year after this ceremony, Suleyman bowed to the imprecations of Roxellana and dispatched Mustafa, with his mother, to Manisa as governor, partly to get them out of the Sublime Porte. It would take Roxellana another twenty-three years to accomplish her ambition. In 1553, despite heroics in eastern campaigns, Mustafa was accused of high treason on a trumped-up charge. In the traditional Ottoman way, he was strangled with a bowstring by deaf-mutes, as his father listened behind curtains close by.

Next came Roxellana's two sons. Mehmet, at age nine, was Suleyman's favorite and would remain so, until at age twenty-two, while serving as governor in Manisa, he died. The third son, Selim, was to compete with a fourth son, Bayezid (who was not included in this circumcision ceremony). Nearly thirty years later, the two would fight for the crown, and Selim would prevail. Bayezid was executed with four of his sons. The youngest son of Suleyman and Roxellana was named Cihangir. Born a hunchback, he would die in the same year as Mustafa . . . of heartbreak, so the story was told, over his brother's execution.

ACT NINE

LAST GASP
IN EUROPE

✠

36.

TWO WIVES

From the fall of 1529 through the spring of 1531, the timid, irresolute, overwrought pope, Clement VII, wept often over the state of Roman Catholicism. His dominion was threatened with invasion from without and insurgency from within, and there seemed no end to the growing peril. The victory at Vienna had been a wonderful, almost miraculous respite, but it was probably temporary. The reconciliation with Charles V and the coronation spectacle at Bologna had marked a happy moment, but probably it was an empty ceremony along the lines of the Field of the Cloth of Gold. Then the Diet of Augsburg and the Schmalkaldian agreement had hardened the Lutheran heresy into a formal alliance of rebellious states. A war in Germany seemed inevitable if papal authority was ever to be reestablished. The Turkish menace hovered like the sword of Damocles. Now the pope had to turn his mind to the dysfunctional House of Tudor.

In July 1529 the dispute between the king and queen of England had been removed to Rome. But there it languished for many months. The pope's natural inclination was to vacillate and delay, for making a definitive decision often made him physically sick. Delay and vacillation had actually worked in England, and the pope hoped the same thing might happen in Rome. Wanly, he prayed that Henry would tire of his manipulative courtesan, Anne Boleyn. With the distractions of Vienna, Bologna, and Augsburg, the pope had good excuses for avoiding Henry's demand for divorce and Catherine's demand for vindication.

When the case was first shifted to Rome, Catherine expected a quick decision in her favor. At her Blackfriars trial she had argued successfully that the commissioners lacked competence and impartiality, though she had benefited mightily by the impartiality of the papal legate, Cardinal Campeggio, by forcing him to declare in her favor. In Rome his voice would be all the more influential. And she had forced the king's chancellor, Cardinal Wolsey, into disgrace, ironically with the help of Anne Boleyn. He was now headed for the Tower of London and the grave. But Henry initially sent no advocates to Rome to press for a decision that he knew would go against him. Instead, through the winter of 1530 he mobilized support for his case by gathering favorable opinions from compliant academics in English and French universities. Though these experts could argue all manner of legalisms, only Catherine could testify to the key point of the case: whether she had actually had carnal relations with Henry's brother, Arthur, before she had had them dutifully as Henry's obedient and loving wife.

With his ear to the ground for gossip, Clement VII felt compelled on March 7, 1530, to issue a stern warning to Henry, Anne, and their chief advisers. If Henry and any woman should contract to be married while his legal wife's case was still under consideration in Rome, they would be subject to the most severe ecclesiastical punishments. Impetuous as ever, Henry considered this a provocation. By July he had his case ready and changed tactics. In Rome the English ambassador presented the pope with a statement of Henry's experts:

"In the opinion of learned men at universities in England, France, and Italy, the King's cause is now found just, which ought to persuade the Pope, and he ought to confirm their judgment." Civil wars and grave mischief could only be prevented by the king marrying another woman, from whom he might obtain a male heir. "This can not be done till his present marriage is annulled. And if the Pope would still refuse to do this, they must conclude that he has abandoned them, and so they must seek other remedies. Most earnestly do they pray him to prevent this, since they do not desire to go to extremities till there is no more to be hoped for at his hands."

The pope replied promptly and pointedly. Uncharacteristically, his back-bone stiffened. He forgave them for their letter's "vehemence"; he put their combative tone down to their great affection for their king. But learned men were by no means of one mind about this matter. Writing in the third person about himself, the pope wrote, "He wished their king might have male issue, but he was not in God's stead to give it." As for their threats to seek other remedies, he cautioned them to beware and reminded them, "It is not the physician's fault if the patient will do himself harm." He had never denied their king anything that he could grant with his honor. "He wished to put this matter to a speedy issue and would do everything he could with-out offending God."

No doubt the speed and definitiveness of his response caused the pope acute physical distress, for he now felt himself to be between a "hammer and an anvil." If he ruled in Catherine's favor, legitimate as her case was, Henry might act on his threat to break with Rome. If he ruled in Henry's favor, he would surely alienate his temporal brother, Charles V. If Henry did break with Rome, millions of devout Roman Catholics in England would be separated from their spiritual roots.

At this latest rebuff, Henry's advisers came up with a new and bizarre idea. Why not bigamy? Instead of subtracting the first wife, why not add a second? Two wives, Catherine and Anne Boleyn, a double marriage. Their reference point for this outlandish notion was as bizarre as the idea itself. They invoked the wisdom of Martin Luther! They referenced the heretic's permissiveness toward the champion of the Reformation, Philip of Hesse!

In 1523 Philip had had the misfortune to marry one Christine of Saxony, a sickly, ugly, and alcoholic maid. Three years after this misguided union he began to explore the notion of adding a second wife and appealed to Mar-tin Luther for a theological opinion on the matter. At first Luther discour-aged the idea. Unless the wife suffered from something like leprosy, bigamy was not a good idea. But Philip's question seemed to intrigue Luther, and

the next year he sermonized on it. Bigamy, he concluded, was not specifically contrary to Scripture. Indeed, in the patriarchal era, described in the
book of Genesis, Abraham had had three wives, Luther pointed out, and he
was "a true nay perfect Christian." Moreover Jacob had had four wives.
Luther might have added that King David had eighteen wives and Moses
had two. The law of Moses still applied. On the basis of this biblical evidence, Luther said in his sermon, "It is not forbidden that a man should
have more than one wife. I could not forbid it today." To this he added a
coda: "But I would not advise it." Should such a necessity arise, Luther said,
it was advisable to keep the second marriage secret to avoid scandal. Philip
took this counsel to heart and, later, married a second wife.

Using Luther's arguments, Henry's advisers now formally requested a
papal dispensation for the king to take a second wife. Ironically, Luther's
arguments about the patriarchal era of the Bible persuaded some important
figures in Rome, including, of all people, Luther's chief antagonist in the
early days of his rebellion. Cardinal Gaetanus Cajetan advised the pope that
bigamy was neither contrary to the law of nature nor forbidden in Holy
Scripture. Indeed, for sound political motives, the pope would be wise to
grant a dispensation "to avoid a greater evil." Wiser counsel prevailed. After
consulting with a consistory of his cardinals, the pope informed the English
envoys that such a dispensation was not possible. Henry reacted in anger.
The pope, he said coarsely, was in the pocket of Emperor Charles V and the
Spaniards.

Catherine of Aragon apparently knew nothing of these back-channel
communications. She knew only that after fifteen months her case had not
even been opened in Rome. Through this period her frustration rose in
torrents. She wrote often to the pope, each letter more pointed than the
last. Importantly, her exasperation was with the pope and not with Henry.
She deluded herself that evil advisers were misleading her husband. If only
the pope would act, her husband's affection for her would return. "I trust
so much in my Lord, the King's, natural virtues and goodness," she wrote to
the pontiff on January 6, 1531. "If I could only have him with me two
months, as he used to be, I alone would be powerful enough to make him

forget the past." Henry's advisers were jeopardizing the king's honor and his soul. "From these people spring the threats against Your Holiness. Therefore, put the bit in their mouths! Proceed to sentence! Then their tongues will be silenced and their hopes of mischief vanish. Then they will set my lord at liberty, and he will become once more the dutiful son of Your Holiness, as he always was."

The day before Catherine wrote this letter, Clement VII in Rome wrote a papal brief reaffirming his edict of the previous year, warning Henry not to marry another woman while his case was still active in Rome.

Henry now took his first formal step toward a breach. In mid-January 1531 he called a general convocation of the English clergy. Invoking an arcane and largely forgotten law called *praemunire* that dated back to the time of Richard II, in which the pope was forbidden to interfere in the internal affairs of England, Henry had himself proclaimed the "Protector and Supreme Head of the Church and Clergy of England." The effect of this action was to bludgeon the English clergy into submission and obviate any chance that they would resist him.

In April 1531, Henry's case had lain untouched in the Vatican offices for nearly two years. Francis I now entered the debate on Henry's side, ever eager to stir up mischief for the emperor. He suggested that the case be removed to a "neutral" site in France, a prospect that would occasion even further delay. Desperately, Catherine appealed to her nephew Charles V for pressure on the Vatican. "If the pope grants further delay, as the King of France is said to have requested him to do, you can expect that before long their people will obtain all they are aiming at. I beg you not to consent to the delay but insist on the pope's giving sentence before next October when Parliament reconvenes. I am sure that the delay is solicited only to work my ruin."

The remainder of the year saw no advance in the legal case, but Catherine's situation changed. In late summer Henry banished her from the court. She departed obediently with the parting remark that no matter where she was, "nothing could remove her from being his wife." As the queen vacated her royal apartments, Anne Boleyn moved into them.

Eventually, word of this banishment reached Rome. The pope waited until the new year to react. Finally, on January 25, 1532, he wrote to the king. Again the pope referred to himself in the third person: "He has heard reports—which he unwillingly believed—that the King had put away his Queen and kept one Anne about him as his wife. Which as it gave much scandal, so it was a high contempt of the Apostolic See to do such a thing while his suit was still pending, notwithstanding a prohibition to the contrary. Therefore the pope, remembering his [Henry's] former merits, which were now likely to be clouded with his present carriage, did exhort him to take home his queen, and to put Anne away; and not to continue to provoke the Emperor and his brother by so high an indignity, nor to break the general peace of Christendom, which is its only security against the power of the Turk."

This papal brief did not reach the king for another five months. Seven months after that, on January 25, 1533, Henry VIII, once the Defender of the Faith, soon to be an excommunicant, married his second wife in a secret ceremony.

37.

FUTILE DIPLOMACY

After Europe's close call at Vienna in late 1529, European leaders began to alter their view of Suleyman and his Ottoman Empire. Gradually, it had dawned on the West, and Charles V in particular, that this was no wild-eyed barbarian from the steppes of Central Asia, no pagan worshipping false idols, no voluptuary in the fleshpots of his harem, and that his empire was a worthy adversary equal to any collective of principalities of which Europe could boast. Reports, mainly from the Venetian envoys who lived within the Sublime Porte, painted a picture of Suleyman himself as cultured, well-read, and elegant in a distinctive oriental fashion, as well as determined, visionary, and dangerous. Far from the ferocious, backward image of his father, Selim the Grim, Suleyman's reputation began to take on a romantic cast. His features were described and his values defined by diplomats who were both fascinated and awed by him. His visage was "deadly pale," one wrote, given to a melancholy cast, stern but majestic. His neck was long, his nose aquiline, his grip strong rather than delicate. He was "addicted" to women, two in particular, even as he had at hand in his harem three hundred of the most beautiful women in Asia Minor. He was "liberal, proud, and hasty," with wide swings in mood, one day harsh and overbearing, the next quite gentle and humble.

His public events such as the circumcision festival had been avidly described, but there were also glimpses into the sultan's private life: how he slept on crimson mattresses, covered in the winter with a comforter of soft sable or black fox, in summer between delicate satin sheets, his head on green tasseled pillows, beneath a tapered canopy of gold silk. His apartments deserved the word *magnificent*. Among his favorite amusements was watching dwarfs dance. As noteworthy was his fixation with the life of Alexander the Great, whose empire had stretched from India to the heart of Europe. Reportedly, an account of the Great Conqueror's life, by a Persian writer, lay at the sultan's bedside, and this seemed to lend more credence to Suleyman's stated ambition that he would one day extend the dominion of Islam to the Rhine and the Indus rivers. His reach already extended deep into Mesopotamia.

Moreover, the envoys of European aristocracy were struck by the emphasis on merit rather than pedigree in Ottoman society. "No one is distinguished from the rest by his birth," wrote one diplomat, "and honor is paid to each man according to the nature of the duty and offices which he discharges. There is no struggle for precedence, every man having his place assigned to him by virtue of the function that he performs. The Sultan pays no attention to wealth or the empty claims of rank. He only considers merit and scrutinizes the character, natural ability and disposition of each. Each man is rewarded according to his deserts."

In the summer of 1530 at the Diet of Augsburg, Charles V had rattled his saber at the Lutherans and issued his ultimatum to them. He would give them until the following spring to recant their errors. If they did not, they would face military action. In the spring of 1531, however, he had done nothing, and he would do nothing for an obvious reason: he had come to realize the gravity of the Turkish threat. His mandate at Bologna, to protect the Christian patrimony against all threats, must now take precedence over his desire to purify the faith. All of European Christian civilization, Catholic and Protestant, faced extinction if the factions did not come to an accommodation. In April 1531 Charles wrote to his brother, Ferdinand, that the archduke should seek a truce with the Ottomans, while Charles would attempt a compromise with the Lutherans.

In the fall of 1531 both these diplomatic fronts opened tentatively and unsatisfactorily. The news from Constantinople that Suleyman was preparing for a second invasion of Europe heightened the urgency. In October, Ferdinand dispatched a delegation of twenty-four ambassadors to the Ottoman capital, led by Nicolas Jurischitz, a Croatian nobleman and the commander of a small fortress at Güns on the Austrian-Hungarian border. For nine days the envoys were sequestered in confinement before they were granted an audience. They came with an offer to pay Suleyman an annual "pension" if the sultan would recognize Ferdinand as king of Hungary, abandon his vassal János Zápolya, and withdraw his soldiers from Buda. Under the circumstances, these outlandish demands did not make for a strong negotiating position, since Ferdinand's soldiers had been attacking the Turkish defenses at Buda during this period. Ibrahim Pasha scoffed at the terms. He lectured the diplomats on the cowardice of their archduke for not meeting Suleyman at Vienna. He heaped contempt on a religion that would imprison its religious leader and allow its spiritual capital to be sacked. When it was suggested that Ferdinand be acknowledged as king of Hungary, Ibrahim Pasha flew into a rage.

"The Empire is at war!" he shouted. "Peace remains impossible so long as Ferdinand lays claim to Hungary and until he returns every piece of land he has seized." At the suggestion of a "pension" from the archduke, Ibrahim pointed out to the towers of the Topkapi. "Look hither, do you see those seven towers? They are filled with the finest jewels and treasures." The great Ottoman civilization had no need of a paltry Christian bribe. The Turkish quarrel now was not with Ferdinand, the mere emir of Vienna, Ibrahim continued, but with Charles. In private conversations Ibrahim was now referring to Ferdinand as "only a little fellow of Vienna, and worth small attention." Charles V, meanwhile, was never referred to as an emperor, but merely as the king of Spain.

After a delay of another eight days, the Austrian ambassadors were finally granted a personal audience with Suleyman. The arrangements for the meeting were such to convey awe and fear, as the diplomats were conducted through an impressive array of janissaries, valets in golden hats, and personal guards. Two elephants, ten lions, and two leopards guarded the entrance. When they approached the throne, the sultan left them in no doubt about the situation.

"For a long time the king of Spain has declared his wish to go against the Turks. I, by the grace of God, am proceeding with my army against him. If he is great in heart, let him await me in the field, and then whatever God wills shall be. If, however, he does not wish to wait for me, let him send tribute to my Imperial Majesty."

Suleyman was now casting the conflict as a contest for the mastery of the world. There could be only one emperor of the world, only one superior civilization, only one true faith. Who would be the true lord of the age, this so-called Holy Roman emperor with his baby brother in Vienna, or the Rampart of Islam, the Possessor of Mecca and Medina, the Lord of Damascus and Egypt, the Caliph of the Lofty Threshold, the Lord of the Residence of the Pleiades?

Meanwhile, toward the end of 1531 peace negotiations between the Lutherans and the Catholics became more productive. Luther himself was more open to concessions in certain church ceremonies, while the Catholics backed off on their demand for a final solution to the doctrinal differences. An unexpected development in October changed the dynamic. Luther's rival in the Reformation, Huldrych Zwingli, had embraced violence by taking his evangelicals to war against the five Catholic cantons in Switzerland. On October 11, in a battle at Kappel, the Zwinglians were roundly defeated, and Zwingli himself was killed. A public hangman quartered his body and had the parts burned with horse dung. When he heard the news, Luther was only contemptuous. That Zwingli had borne arms in battle was blasphemy, and Luther ridiculed the notion of Zwingli as a martyr, regarding his death as divine punishment for distorting the meaning of the Lord's Supper. The political effect of Zwingli's death was to weaken the influence of his adherents in southern Germany while it strengthened the Lutheran hold there.

By February 1532 the Catholic side was offering to formally recognize the current status of the Lutherans in return for military support against the Turks. Thus, in effect, Suleyman became a tacit ally of the Reformation. With the Vatican's concurrence, a solution to religious disagreements was put off indefinitely; in fact, the Vatican had taken itself out of play. Clement VII cowered in the wings of the Vatican, so terrified about the possibility of another Turkish invasion that he was considering gathering up all the money in the treasury and fleeing to Avignon, leaving Italy to fend for itself. In March a diet convened in Regensburg. Luther was pleased to be negotiating at last not with the pope but with the emperor, and he well appreciated the emperor's desperate need for Protestant soldiers. There, the Lutheran side agreed to make no more "innovations" to its doctrine. By the time negotiations moved to Nuremberg in June, the major points in dispute had been resolved, though the sides were still quibbling over what to do about any German province that might yet swing over to the Lutheran side. But this too was finally resolved, and a formal peace accord was reached on July 23, 1532. This "general stable peace" prohibited armed conflict between the two Christian sides.

38.

STUCK AT GÜNS

By this time, Suleyman was already in Belgrade.

His arrival in this "gold key to Europe," as Belgrade was called, had been an occasion to put the sultan's magnificence on full display. The city's streets were adorned with triumphal Roman arches, every bit as grand as those that had adorned Bologna for the coronation of Charles V. Indeed, the Belgrade spectacle seemed intended specifically to surpass the opulence of the Bologna event. Standard-bearers carried banners with Mohammed's name embossed in jewels and other flags displaying elegant Ottoman symbols. Pages carried fantastic gold-and-jeweled helmets, more amazing than the crown Charles had worn in Bologna. Other pages carried a box containing the actual mantle of the Prophet and two of his swords. The sultan, wearing an immense turban and a fur-lined purple caftan, sat astride a jeweled saddle on an enormous horse that was caparisoned with brocade and whose bridle contained an egg-sized turquoise gem.

The sultan tarried in Belgrade for several weeks, combining military strategy and diplomacy with dazzling ceremonies. Ambassadors from Vienna turned up again, first at Nis and then at Belgrade, offering a much larger annual tribute and withdrawing previous demands about Buda and the recognition of Ferdinand. They were treated roughly at first by Ibrahim, before they were ushered into the presence of the sultan. The audience was choreographed by Ibrahim to induce the utmost awe and amazement.

Suleyman sat upon a golden throne whose supports were fashioned to look like quivers containing golden arrows and that were covered with jewels. Upon his head was a stunning golden helmet that had been made by the finest goldsmiths of Venice and that was designed as four golden crowns, one superimposed upon the next, and sprouted jewels as if they were starbursts. The helmet bore a vague resemblance to the tiara of the pope, but was far more magnificent. One observer called the helmet-crown "the trophy of Alexander the Great."

In this audience little was said, for, according to a Venetian report, the ambassadors were rendered "speechless corpses." To them Suleyman again delivered his stark challenge to Charles V. Was he great of heart? If so, let him await me in the field. With that the ambassadors were dismissed unceremoniously to return home empty-handed.

Treated with greater dignity and even more elaborate pomp was a delegation that came from Francis I. Despite the French king's promise in the Peace of the Ladies three years before to give up consorting with Turks and to join in the defense of Christian Europe, Francis had actually made a secret alliance with Suleyman's vassal János Zápolya to support the Transylvanian's claim as king of Hungary. In return, Zápolya agreed that Francis's second son would succeed Zápolya on the Hungarian throne. The French envoys were taken for audiences with commanders and viziers, and treated to parades by the Anatolian and Rumelian armies. In their audience with the sultan, the French ambassadors tried to dissuade the sultan from going forward with his European invasion, lest it do what in fact it was doing: uniting the Catholics and Protestants and making the Holy Roman emperor even more powerful. Ibrahim Pasha turned the request aside gently. Matters had proceeded too far. There was no turning back from this epic duel for the mastery of the world. The matter had become personal.

If he turned back now, Suleyman said, "They would say that I am afraid of the king of Spain."

From his golden throne the sultan could survey his vast Balkan dominion with satisfaction. The Turks held virtually all of Croatia to the west with the exception of a few coastal cities like Dubrovnik. They held the territory between the Sava and Drava rivers known as Slavonia. They had occupied Bosnia and Herzegovina for nearly seventy years, and Serbia south to Kosovo for almost one hundred and fifty years. In all of these territories, conversion to Islam had been spirited. When Suleyman's army moved into Hungary, it would encounter a more mixed situation, but the campaign ahead offered the opportunity to reward those who supported his vassal János Zápolya and to punish those who had defected to Archduke Ferdinand.

In the second week of July 1532, the Ottoman army decamped and moved north, while a formidable Turkish fleet on the Danube shadowed the ground forces. At Osijek, the armies crossed the Drava River over twelve pontoon bridges and soon entered southern Hungary. Heavy rain and interminable swamps hindered the progress, but not as dramatically as during the previous invasion. Eight thousand janissaries led the way, their heavy drums and reedy horns announcing the advance. They were followed by more than a hundred cannons, by a contingent of tribute boys with their long hair and scarlet caps festooned with white feathers, and a group of harriers with their hawks and hounds. The Eagle of the Prophet, encrusted with pearls and precious stones, preceded the suite of the sultan himself. Behind him came tens of thousands of soldiers and an immense baggage train pulled by camels and elephants.

The juggernaut moved north through western Transdanubia, taking the more direct overland route to Vienna through Székesfehérvár and Györ, slogging through the swamps south of Lake Balaton (and leaving many of their heavy siege cannons in the mire), skirting the lake itself and avoiding Buda altogether. At town after town, fortress after fortress, local commanders under the sway of Zápolya came out to greet the Turks and offer the keys to their garrisons. Rewards were handed out accordingly.

At Györ the Sultan tarried for discussions with his advisers. There, the Turkish high command made an important strategic decision. The Ottoman navy would continue upriver to Pressburg, and an advance division of sixteen thousand light-armed raiders would proceed to the environs of Vienna, while the main body of the army would proceed west overland to the southern edge of Lake Neusiedler. From there it would turn south to the town of Güns, the first of the small fortresses under the sway of Ferdinand I. After the army made quick work of that tiny fortress, it would move west into the grasslands and meadows of southeast Austria. They hoped Charles V would be lured from his refuge across the Alps to the open and lovely landscape of Styria into the final apocalyptic battle between emperors and religions and continents to determine whether Islam or Christianity was the dominant and superior force in the world.

By now it was early August, prime fighting season, and the Christian force was indeed massing in southern Bavaria at Regensburg. Charles had been elated at how quickly and enthusiastically his army of defense had mobilized itself. On August 9 he had written to his wife that all the states of Germany, including the Protestant ones, had acted with dispatch and zeal. Within a matter of a few weeks, a combined force of Germans, Austrians, Italians, Spanish, and Dutch had been joined by some twenty thousand Lutheran landsknechts. The total strength of the force was about eighty thousand. Charles was well pleased. The moment for which he had been born and risen to power had arrived. This clash would mark his fulfillment as the secular defender of the faith. This was the highest calling of chivalry. In the words of the Order of the Golden Fleece, the society of European Christian nobles of which he was head, he had been brought to this place and this time to lead the fight "for the reverence of God and the maintenance of our Christian Faith, and to honor and exalt the noble order of knighthood."

On August 9, the first elements of the Turkish army under Ibrahim Pasha arrived in the environs of Güns. To their dismay, instead of a meek and subservient official bowing and offering the keys to the town, the Turkish advance guard was confronted with Hungarian knights in full battle armor. Upon further inspection, it was determined that all the surrounding villages around Güns had been set aflame, the fields of fodder torched, and the wells poisoned. By the time Suleyman himself arrived three days later with the main army, it was clear that not only would the fortress not surrender, but it planned a stiff defense.

The stubborn leader of this affront was a familiar figure, the Croatian nobleman Nicolas Jurischitz, who just months before had presented the tribute offer for Archduke Ferdinand to the Sublime Porte in Constantinople. Against the mighty Turkish army of over seventy thousand soldiers, Jurischitz had arrived in Güns several weeks before in the company of ten fully armed knights and twenty-eight light cavalrymen. The town itself boasted about a thousand able-bodied men and several thousand women, children, and old people. Güns was a classic "castle town," with low walls, a fortress, and a barbican or gate tower; its walls were surrounded by a moat that was fed by a millrace that coursed down the hill from the north.

Jurischitz saw his mission clearly. To Ferdinand I he wrote, "I have volunteered to fight against the Turkish emperor and his army. I fight not because I presume to equal his force, but only so as to delay him a little while to give time for Your Royal Majesty to unite with the Christian Holy Roman Emperor." Slowing down the Islamic cyclone, therefore, was his sole purpose.

That the Christians dared to challenge so overwhelming a force was, at first, a source of bemusement to the Turkish high command. Wrote the sultan's chancellor, "As soon as the mind of His Highness, Ibrahim Pasha, became enlightened as to the situation of the castle, he, like so many lions in courage, intended to break the pride of those locked within and to open the gate of triumph and attach this castle to the string of other fortifications he had conquered." It would not be so easy.

In classic fashion, the light cannons known as falcons and falconets opened a barrage against the walls, to little effect. The Turks quickly realized they needed the heavy cannons that they had discarded in the swamps of Lake Balaton. Moreover, the defenders had the brio to sally out of their fortress and inflict considerable loss on the besiegers. Six days into the siege a number of all-out assaults had been repelled, and the Turkish forces grew restless. Grumbling about Ibrahim Pasha's command began; he had promised quick victory and plentiful booty. Men began to drop from starvation. Heavy rain and hail complicated the situation, and supplies started to run short. "We are short of bread," a Turkish dispatch read. "We have enough grain, but there are no mills to grind it, so we are short of flour." Twelve days into the siege, Turkish mines brought down a forty-foot section of the wall. But the charge of the janissaries into the breach was turned back.

If the siege was faltering, the will of the defenders was also waning. Scrolls were lobbed over the walls to the Turkish side, describing a desperate situation and encouraging negotiations. But Jurischitz rallied his motley force. Finally, on August 27, after another furious assault was turned back, Ibrahim Pasha offered to talk. The first exchanges stalled, and the siege resumed. At one point eight Ottoman flags were planted on the walls, but they soon disappeared. With no further progress, Ibrahim offered to talk a second time. His sudden interest in peace negotiations had behind it a considerable incentive: his janissaries were on the verge of revolt.

After two full weeks, the garrison still held out. Their exasperation tinged with grudging admiration, the Turks turned to diplomacy in earnest. Messages began to be exchanged between the sides. Did the fortress commander propose to continue his "futile display of arrogance and pride?" If he would surrender, a free passage to freedom was promised. Jurischitz replied that he was merely the servant of the Holy Roman emperor, who had entrusted the town and fortress to his care. As such he would surrender to no one as long as he lived. Next came an offer of money to the defenders, one gold ducat for every house in the town, though their superiors would have to pay considerable tribute for the trouble they had caused the great Suleyman. To this Jurischitz replied that the town did not belong to him but to his master. He was in no position to take money for it. As for the ducats for the sultan's troubles, he barely had enough money to pay his own soldiers. As each of these retorts were reported to Suleyman, he grew more livid. He ordered one more furious assault. Word was passed through the Turkish ranks. "I will have the head of my enemy, or he will have mine," Suleyman was quoted as saying.

When huge wooden, pyramid-shaped assault towers were rolled close to the high walls, the defenders filled barrels with sulfur, tar, and tallow, set them on fire, and burned the towers. As their defense went into folklore, it was said that during this last assault "a rider of vast and imposing stature appeared in the sky, brandishing a flaming sword. This engendered such fear in the Turks that they retreated from the walls." St. Martin himself had become, in folklore, the savior of Güns.

When the dust of this final assault settled, a Turkish herald approached the walls and shouted a question. Was the commander still alive? Jurischitz was, in fact, wounded. Half his garrison was dead, and his remaining soldiers were ready to give up. The store of gunpowder was virtually depleted. But the Croatian shouted back that he lived still. Then, shouted the herald, the grand vizier demanded a conference with him. Safe conduct was promised, and two Turkish hostages came forward to remain in Christian hands while their leader talked to the enemy.

Jurischitz instructed his comrades that if something happened to him, they were not to surrender the castle. "Thus, alone and timid," he wrote later, "I left the fortress with my escort that consisted of a thousand janissaries with their captain riding by my side."

At Ibrahim Pasha's sumptuous tent the Croatian commander was greeted with ceremony and respect. The grand vizier rose to welcome him warmly and conveyed him to a seat of honor. Ibrahim inquired about the commander's injuries with evident sincerity. Were the wounds dangerous? he asked. Soon enough, he came to the point. Why had Jurischitz not surrendered? Ibrahim went down the long list of other commanders who had done so in the face of so mighty a force. So much pain and suffering could so easily have been avoided. Ibrahim then turned to the status of Jurischitz's Christian masters, displaying a precise awareness of where Charles's Christian army was now encamped. Did the Croatian expect the king of Spain to come to his relief? There was almost a note of hope in Ibrahim's voice.

If Jurischitz had at Güns proved himself a great warrior, he was no less a diplomat. To each of the grand vizier's questions, he had an elegant response. He thanked Ibrahim for his concern about his wounds. Only his honor had prevented him from giving up, for he could not endure the humiliation of surrendering without being forced to do so. Gradually, it dawned on Jurischitz that Ibrahim was attempting to lure him over to the Turkish side. How could the Croatian bear to live under so tyrannical a rule as this? Ibrahim asked. The great Suleyman was offering a gift of his grace for the castle, the city, its citizens, and the commander himself. As long as the sultan had ruled, never had his people fallen to such a low state as the people of Güns. Rising decorously, Ibrahim Pasha offered his hand and proposed to take Jurischitz for an audience with the Grand Turk, only a short distance away. The commander needed only to bow before the sultan and he would be saved.

Jurischitz declined.

"I know the power of your grace over the Grand Turk," he said. "My respect for him will not allow me to present myself to him in such a weakened state. I am too weak to bow."

It had been a delicate dance. "I noticed how pleased Ibrahim seemed to be by showing my reverence and great esteem for him," the Croatian wrote to the archduke a day later. Flattery had gotten him everywhere. He knew full well that had he given offense, another assault would have followed and that would have been the end of it. At the parting, Ibrahim presented Jurischitz with a magnificent robe of honor.

As the Christian commander was escorted back to the castle, the janissary captain asked if he might come inside the walls to congratulate the brave defenders. Jurischitz did not think it was a good idea. Unruly Germans and Spanish soldiers were inside over whom he had little control, he said. The captain's safety could not be guaranteed. Not long after, Ibrahim Pasha appeared in person outside the walls. Please do not harm further any injured Turks who might be inside the walls, he shouted to Jurischitz. There were none, the commander shouted back.

"If you are well and wish to ride to the gates of Vienna with His Majesty's ambassadors, it can be arranged," Ibrahim shouted. There would be no last assault, only a last effort at recruitment. Again the Croatian thanked the grand vizier for his generous offer, but he must decline. He had fought them for twenty-five days, he shouted back. His defense was more important to him than any major battle or any other honor could be.

Ibrahim nodded his understanding. "You speak the truth," he said and rode away.

The strangest of conclusions was arranged for this historic David-and-Goliath affair. To save face, a contingent of janissaries was permitted to occupy a breach in the walls for several hours. There they planted their huge flag in the rubble, green in its background, with thick white Arabic lettering: "There is but one God, and Mohammed is his prophet." As the janissaries sang and chanted boisterously, accompanied by loud drums and horns, Ibrahim sent his congratulations to Suleyman. Heavy rain began to fall, but it did not dampen the farce. Suleyman himself wrote the good news in his diary, as if he were writing for the historical record:

"The Grand Vizier held a Divan with the ceremonial hand kiss. With the joyful news of the surrender of the fortress the Grand Vizier was given five hundred gold coins and a caftan. The Pashas kissed the Sultan's hand to congratulate him for conquering the castle."

In his heart Suleyman must have had a very different emotion. His mighty army had been detained and rebuffed by a puny force for more than three critical weeks. In these campaigns against Christian infidels he seemed cursed to encounter brilliant commanders: Philippe de Villiers de L'Isle-Adam at Rhodes, Graf Nicolas von Salm at Vienna, and now Jurischitz here.

At an agreed-upon time, 11 a.m. the next day, the Turks withdrew from the breach, and to this day the bells of Güns (now the Hungarian border town of Köszeg) chime at that hour every morning.

The Turks had wasted three precious weeks on this pointless assault. The chill of fall was not far away. Notwithstanding the lame efforts of Turkish propaganda to turn defeat into victory, the siege of Güns would later be compared to the humiliation of Xerxes at Thermopylae.

IT WAS TIME to take stock. If seven hundred determined, well-commanded enemy soldiers in a well-conceived fortress could tie down the mighty Ottoman army for three weeks, what were the prospects for Vienna itself? From the irregulars who had been harrying through the Vienna woods, the Ottomans learned that Italian, Spanish, and Lutheran troops had been pouring into Vienna. The city would surely be far better defended this time.

Moreover, the Ottomans realized that their supply of heavy cannons was insufficient, and they had not brought enough siege equipment. Their supply of wooden siege towers had been depleted at the walls of Güns. What then was the purpose of this fifth imperial campaign? Suleyman and Ibrahim Pasha had to remind themselves why they had come this far north and this deep into the Christian dominion. They had not necessarily come to capture Vienna, they convinced themselves, but rather to engage this so-called Holy Roman emperor in an epic battle of empires, civilizations, and religions.

Within a few days of the Güns humiliation, more bad news came from the north. The Turkish irregulars around Vienna had been outmaneuvered by a group of Saxon Lutherans and had run foursquare into an Austrian battery of heavy guns. The Turkish commander attempted an escape by splitting his army to avoid the vise, but both elements had been overwhelmed and slaughtered mercilessly. Only a handful of the sixteen thousand advance troops limped back into Suleyman's camp. Among the dead was the Turkish commander. Missing was his magnificent helmet, studded with precious jewels and festooned with vulture feathers. A few days later it was presented to Charles V as a trophy, and much was made about the triumph of the German eagle over the Turkish vulture.

How might the Ottomans lure the king of Spain into a pitched battle under the most favorable conditions? Eschewing any more attacks on fortified bastions, a strategy of scorching the earth was adopted. If indeed the king of Spain had a great heart, if indeed he was the defender of his faith, surely he would not allow his dominions to be ravaged without a fight. Instead of turning north to Vienna the juggernaut moved slowly southwest toward Graz, traveling through the low hills and green pastures of Styria, leaving utter ruination in its wake, and avoiding the mountaintop bastion of Riegersburg. ("It is said that the Germans do not own a better castle," Suleyman wrote wistfully in his diary.) Orchards were burned, grasslands set afire, towns plundered, especially their churches. Ironically, some of those churches were Lutheran, for the Reformation had come to Styria two years before.

At this unspeakable devastation Charles reacted by doing . . . nothing. Instead of coming to the rescue of his lands, he tarried in his safe remove behind a range of Alps in southern Bavaria. He was content to let the Turkish fury spend itself. Lower Austria was expendable for the greater good. The line of defense for Europe ran along the mountain range through middle Austria. From past experience the Christian side could count on the Ottomans to start home with the first frost.

By the time the Turkish army reached Graz eleven days after leaving Güns, the absence of any challenge from Charles seemed to intensify the fury of the invaders even further, and they took out their frustrations on the local populace and landscape. One of the Turkish chroniclers waxed eloquent about the pleasant city: "In the majestic and grand city, the gardens and vineyards resemble paradise." That was before the Turks reduced paradise to hell, plundering its villas and torching its churches. In the middle of the city, however, stood its imposing castle, the Schlossberg. This the Turks left untouched. They had learned their lesson at Güns: no more sieges against strong fortresses. After a day of rage, the Turks turned south toward home. Suleyman and Ibrahim had given up on the pusillanimous king of Spain.

"The lands of the king are just like his women," Ibrahim wrote contemptuously of Charles, implying not only personal cowardice but collective infidelity to his people and his dominions.

So again, even as the Ottoman army beat its retreat south into Slovenia, then southeast along the Drava River to Belgrade, the chroniclers from Suleyman and Ibrahim Pasha downward were spinning their narrative of triumph. Along the way, Ibrahim picked up another gift of a bejeweled horse for his management of a river crossing.

On September 23, with laurels rather than a battle helmet on his head and with the great bells of St. Stephen's Cathedral tolling joyously, Charles V entered Vienna in triumph. There, he was reunited with his brother, Ferdinand, and together they went to receive the acclamations from their troops. When the Holy Roman emperor rose before his soldiers, he shouted out in Spanish, "I will kill this Turkish dog! And nothing will prevent me from being on the battlefield myself!" Despite these histrionics, an ulcer infected his leg, and he was incapacitated for several weeks thereafter, tied to his bed. When the news came that Suleyman had reached Belgrade, Charles V departed for Italy.

To be sure, the Turks had spread terror through Europe. The second invasion had thrust deeper into Christian lands than ever before. The plunder had been huge. Many castles had surrendered. The land was ravished. But the invasion had not captured Vienna or any other important place. It had stumbled at Güns and failed to subdue the fortresses at Graz and Riegersburg. The mark it had left was psychological, not physical, but the importance of that was not to be underestimated. The "Turkish terror" would reverberate for centuries. Though Suleyman had boasted that he would extend the Islamic world into the heart of Europe, the Rhine River lay another three hundred miles west of Graz. His dream of becoming another Alexander the Great would have to be realized in the east, in Persia and beyond. And when he was back in Constantinople in November 1532, as he presided over a five-day celebration of his imaginary victories in Austria, he was contemplating that very thing.

39.

THE POMPOSITY
OF IBRAHIM PASHA

Fifteen thirty-three was to become a year of complicated diplomacy. In mid-January, Jerome of Zara, an envoy from Ferdinand I, arrived in Constantinople with a new offer of peace. Jerome was the elder brother of Nicolas Jurischitz, the hero of Güns. Breaking all precedent, Jerome was speedily ushered into the presence of the sultan himself, a sure sign that after his reverses in the Balkans Suleyman was now inclined toward peace. The Sultan of Sultans and the Caliph of Islam could find scriptural sanction in the Koran for his instinct:

"If [your enemies] incline toward peace, you also incline to it and put your trust in Allah" (sura 8:61).

Within a few days Jerome wrote ecstatically to Ferdinand in Vienna, "I, through the grace of God, have achieved all the desired points and have concluded an honorable, glorious, useful, and long-lasting peace between the most serene and invincible emperor of the Turks and your sacred kingdom." Suleyman, according to Jerome, was ready to treat Ferdinand as his son, and his wife and her sister as his daughters. Instructions had been sent to all Ottoman commanders and governors to cease hostilities toward the Christians. In early February, Suleyman and Ibrahim Pasha went off to the woods outside Adrianople for a hunting excursion. They would give Ferdinand and Charles two and a half months to reply to their offer of peace.

Inevitably, there were sticking points.

On the borderlands of the Ottoman and Holy Roman empires, three irritants and one major dynastic question needed to be addressed if peace was to be possible. On the southwestern tip of the Peloponnesian peninsula, the Christians still held a strategic outpost called Koroni. Commanding the sea routes between Rumelia and Crete, it monitored and harassed Turkish naval activity in the Ionian Sea and the Sea of Crete. If Suleyman decided to attack Italy next, Koroni would be a problem. Its existence was more than an annoyance to the Ottomans, for apart from its military function, its unruly Christian soldiers were regularly attacking the Turks and Albanians who lived in the neighboring villages.

Then in the north of Hungary, on the Danube River between Buda and Pressburg, Ferdinand's soldiers still held the great Moravian fortress of Esztergom. So long as this river bastion remained in Christian hands, it deterred the Turks from another invasion of Austria. And lastly, far away on the coastline of northern Africa, a rowdy Ottoman admiral named Kheir ed-Din Barbarossa held Algiers as an important foothold for the Turks on the Barbary Coast. For more than a decade, Barbarossa had ventured out of his redoubt to attack Spanish interests and threaten Sicily.

More important than any of these flashpoints was the conundrum of the Hungarian throne. Suleyman had made a solemn commitment to his vassal János Zápolya. Ferdinand's main goal in these negotiations was to get the Ottomans to abandon their vassal and recognize his dynastic right to the throne.

So, as the Austrian envoys went north to confer with their masters, Ferdinand and Charles, they took with them the Turkish demands that the keys to Esztergom be handed over, and that the rogues of Koroni be brought under control, as prerequisites for peace. Ibrahim had told them, "Peace is always to be desired, and it is the duty of any prince to seek it." If the Turks were really ready to call Ferdinand their brother, perhaps they were now ready to forsake their puppet.

Three months later, in late May, the Austrian envoys returned to Constantinople with their instructions. Deferentially, as a sign of submission and to satisfy Suleyman's first requirement for peace, Jerome of Zara handed over the keys to the hilltop fortress of Esztergom. At this gesture, Ibrahim chortled and told the diplomat to keep his keys. The demand had been merely symbolic. (He did, however, accept the gift of a golden medallion and a handful of diamonds and rubies that came with the keys.) The envoys also brought with them letters of response to the peace initiative from both Ferdinand and Charles V. When Jerome handed Charles's letter to Ibrahim, the grand vizier treated the missive reverently, even admiring the imperial seal. The sultan too had an imperial seal, he observed. "And I have a seal similar to his, which I carry with me, for my lord does not want there to be any difference between himself and me. Whatever clothes he orders for himself he orders also to be made for me. He does not want me to spend anything in building. He does the building for me." Then Ibrahim laid Charles's letter aside without opening it. "This is a great lord," he said of the Christian emperor. "We must honor him."

Over the next seven weeks, the envoys had a series of intense and revealing negotiations with Ibrahim Pasha. In the talks, Ibrahim was alternately expansive, arrogant, accommodating, boastful, and menacing. At one moment he boasted that the Ottomans had an army of Tartar troops who could destroy the whole world and intimated that the Sublime Porte was planning an invasion of Italy with an army of three hundred thousand. At another moment he spoke of peace and commended the Austrians for their soft-spoken diplomacy. "The tongue is a small part of the body," he reflected, "but it is of the highest importance."

The talks ranged widely and were at many points discursive and dilatory. Once the grand vizier launched into a discourse on the qualities of the lion as the most terrible animal in the jungle: "He can not be tamed by force but only through ruse . . . by the food he receives from his guardian and by the influence of habit. The guardian must carry a stick to intimidate him. No other person but the guardian should feed the lion. The lion is the prince.

The guardian is his minister and his adviser. The stick represents truth and justice."

What was the point?

"I guide my master, the Great Emperor, with the stick of truth and justice," Ibrahim blurted out. "King Charles is also a lion. His ambassadors must tame him in the same manner. What I do is done. I can appoint a groom to be a pasha. I can subjugate countries and kingdoms if I please to do so, and my master will not question it. If he makes an order that I disapprove of, his will has no effect. If, on the other hand, I make an order and he disapproves, my will is executed and not his. Peace and war are in my hands. The imperial treasures are at my disposal. I am dressed as glamorously as my master and my fortunes remain constant at all times as he takes charge of all my expenses. His kingdoms, his lands, his coffers, he confides in me, and I do with them whatever I please."

In short, the diplomats should take note: Ibrahim Pasha was the real power in the land, not Suleyman. If his sultan had attributes of Jupiter, he, Ibrahim Pasha, was the true Caesar of the world.

"All power rests in me," he said. "I delegate tasks, I distribute provinces. What I give is given; what I refuse remains refused. Even in instances where the Grand Padishah would like to delegate or when he has delegated certain tasks, if I do not give my approval, it will be forgotten."

To this grandiosity and braggadocio, the diplomats could only listen in silence and awe.

If he were pope or Charles, Ibrahim continued, he would have no problem in arranging a council between the Catholics and the Protestants. None would dare excuse themselves from his order. "If I wanted to, I could put Luther on one side of a room and the pope on the other and force them both to hold a council." His attitude toward the pope and the Christian kings reeked of contempt. Look at this ring, Ibrahim told the envoys. Its ruby once belonged to the king of France when he was captive in Madrid. "I have bought a diamond from the pope's tiara for sixty thousand ducats!" His implication was that Charles V was trafficking in stolen jewels. Did they really think after the sack of Rome and after the pope's cruel captivity in Orvieto that a friendship between Charles and the pope was genuine?

The grand vizier also ranged over the events of the past ten years. On Hungary, he said, "If King Louis had died in bed, Ferdinand might have claim to Hungary. But now, since we have twice taken that kingdom by force of arms, the kingdom is ours!" On the previous year's campaign he spoke of the two envoys who had come from Vienna to Belgrade to ask for peace. "We gave them peace because we give peace to all who ask it of us, and we inquired whether they were also requesting peace for the Emperor Charles. They replied that they knew nothing of Charles because he had not been with their lord Ferdinand. Thus we continued with our army. When they asked us where we were going, we said that we were on our way to seek out the elusive Emperor Charles, wherever he might be." On the defeat of Güns, turning to Jerome of Zara, Ibrahim repeated the standard line: "We gave your brother, Nicolas, back his castle, and the rest rendered an oath of fealty to us. We remained for as long as we wanted in our kingdom of Hungary, and we saw no one to offer us resistance. Nor did we hear anything from Emperor Charles. When it seemed best to us, we came back here, and now here we are!"

Eventually, the grand vizier stated his opening position. On Koroni, the Ottomans owned a thousand fortresses like it, and thus the Peloponnesian outpost was of little importance. They would rather conquer it by force than secure it through negotiation. On the throne of Hungary, the sultan had committed himself to King Zápolya and could not break his word. As for Algiers, the sultan could control his governor and could ensure the safety of Christians in the area if he chose, but he would resist any effort of Charles V to take the outpost.

At the end of one of these insufferable sessions, sweetened water was brought. While the diplomats, their brows no doubt beaded with sweat, drank from silver cups, Ibrahim drank from a turquoise vessel. "My lord receives these stones every year, as much as two horses can carry," Ibrahim said.

Charles V had written his response to the peace offer two months before on March 26 from Lombardy in Italy. It began by reciting his seventy-odd titles. After this bit of posturing, the contents were characteristically careful and courteous. The Holy Roman emperor welcomed the initiative, but emphasized the hereditary rights of his brother to the throne of Hungary. "Whatever friendship Your Serenity has shown to our own most serene brother, we deem it have been shown to ourselves," Charles wrote. He insisted that an agreement should be negotiated not only with him but universally with "all Christian princes." In a separate letter from Ferdinand, the archduke indicated that he could persuade Charles to give up the provocative fortress of Koroni. Before now, the contents of Charles's letter had not been discussed.

On June 2, Ibrahim summoned the Austrian envoys to his grand palace on the Hippodrome with urgency. As they were ushered into the reception room with a sense of foreboding, they found the grand vizier seated, dressed in an exquisite golden caftan and inner robes of deep blue. Seated with him was the private secretary of the sultan. This was to be a command performance, every word to be reported to the sultan.

After the usual courtesies and obsequies, the conversation began benignly enough. Ibrahim inquired idly about the various estates of the king of Spain in Iberia, then pondered the relative merits of France and Spain. Was it not true that France had more than forty navigable rivers and Spain only a few? he wondered. Then with more edge, he said, "Why is France so much more cultured than Spain?"

Jerome of Zara must have sensed that something ominous lay behind this dilatory conversation, and he answered with startling candor. The deficiencies of Spain, he said, came about because Catholic kings of Spain, Ferdinand and Isabella, forty years earlier, had expelled the talented and skilled Jews from the country, then expelled the diligent and cultured Moors who were such good farmers and great architects. Moreover, the machismo in the Spanish character made the Spaniard more suited for the front line of a battle rather than the backside of a horse and plow.

"Such manliness is mere hotheadedness," Ibrahim replied. "Such false pride is in the blood."

Then, the grand vizier reached for Charles's letter. "This letter does not come from a prudent or wise sovereign," he began menacingly. "The king of Spain has enumerated a number of titles in utter arrogance. Many of them do not belong to him at all! How dare he say he is the king of Jerusalem! Does he not know that the sultan rules Jerusalem? Answer me!" Ibrahim shouted.

Jerome of Zara mumbled something about this title being merely a diplomatic convention, signifying nothing.

Ibrahim Pasha cut him off. "I hear great Christian lords go to Jerusalem in the garb of mendicants. If the king of Spain should think that he could become king there by making a pilgrimage in the guise of a beggar, he is mistaken. I shall forbid any Christians from ever going there, either him or anyone else!"

The stunned diplomats could merely listen and hope that Ibrahim's rage would cool.

"Duke of Athens? There is a small ruin called the Acropolis there, and it is mine. By what right does he try to usurp my possessions?"

Perhaps the diplomats were not aware of the contents of this offensive letter, Ibrahim suggested, softening momentarily, offering an out. The Austrians took the opening, saying the letter was sealed, and they had not presumed to open it.

"Look at this!" Ibrahim continued, waving the parchment in the air. "Your lord presumes to put Ferdinand and my master on the same level! Reducing my master to the level of yours? The sultan has many governors more powerful and far richer in land and men than Ferdinand!"

How different was this arrogance from the "much greater, truly regal modesty" of Francis I, he hissed. He had signed a recent letter to the sultan merely as Francis, King of France. "Once Charles has made peace with us, only then will we refer to him as an emperor." As the envoys were dismissed, they must have wondered when that peace might take place. They were told that Ibrahim would not show this insulting letter to the sultan, lest it anger him and destroy any chance for peace.

In the next three weeks, frantic diplomatic consultations took place around Constantinople to try to diffuse the tense situation. Alvise Gritti, the Venetian mediator representing Zápolya, had arrived and became involved in the discussions. Harsh words were exchanged. When Jerome of Zara, arguing the case for Ferdinand, said of Charles V that no Christian leader since Charlemagne had been so powerful in Europe, Gritti said, yes, but not all Charles's subjects obeyed him. Look at the Lutherans. European Christianity was in disarray. Look at Henry VIII's divorce proceedings and Francis I's new designs on Genoa. By contrast, in Suleyman's realm, every subject obeyed the sultan. In fact, "if right now he should send a cook to kill Ibrahim Pasha, nothing could prevent his death."

It soon became apparent that Suleyman had seen Charles's insulting letter and was putting the worst possible construction on it. If the sultan was merely on the level with Ferdinand, then Charles must consider himself superior. It would take considerable effort to calm the sultan's wrath. This was no small question of bruised feelings. Suleyman tartly issued instructions that there should be no more talk about Koroni, and he renewed his support for Zápolya.

Passions cooled, however, as the larger issue of peace asserted itself. Ibrahim and the Austrian envoys, along with Ludovico Gritti, worked diligently to repair the damage. Ibrahim reassured the diplomats that at the least the sultan was prepared to extend a three-month truce to Ferdinand, "his son." If Charles wanted peace, however, he would have to send his own envoy to Constantinople to sue for it and not hide behind the representatives of his brother. With good faith on both sides, the outlines of an agreement were hammered out.

On June 23, as evidence of progress, the Austrian envoys were finally accorded the honor of meeting the sultan himself. The day before, Ibrahim had sent them instructions in writing about how they were to act and what they were to say to the Sultan. This time, there could be no mistakes, no loose language. A battalion of 150 cavalry in gold and silk uniforms escorted the diplomats to the Sublime Porte. When they were ushered into the sultan's presence, they found him on a dais seated on jeweled cushions. As they had been instructed, they knelt to kiss the hem of his garment and delivered a formal greeting, calling the sultan "magnus Caesar." They deigned to hope, Jerome of Zara said, for a "benign response" to their request for a "long and lasting peace." It fell to Jerome to explain and apologize for the misunderstanding caused by Charles's letter.

Suleyman listened silently and stoically to these comfortable words. Finally he answered them in Turkish, and his secretary translated his words. Although six previous envoys had failed to make peace, these diplomats would be honored with a favorable response to their request. "The great Caesar grants you a firm, propitious peace, not for seven years or twenty-five or a hundred, but for two hundred, three hundred years, indeed for an eternity, so long as you shall want this peace and so long as you do not break it." As the sultan's son, if Ferdinand needed something in the future, he need only ask for it, and it would be given.

The following day the Austrian diplomats sat down with Ibrahim Pasha at his palace for a lavish meal and to discuss the final details of the agreement. The grand vizier was warm and well pleased with their work. "Not all Turks are barbaric, cruel, and inhumane as our Christian enemies say that we are," he observed. When they were ready to break up, Ibrahim Pasha said, "Today you took bread and salt with us. Now we are friends, for I cannot be your enemy after we have eaten together."

Nearly another year went by before the fate of the first ever agreement between the Christians of the Holy Roman Empire and the Muslims of the Ottoman Empire was decided. In the summer of 1533, as the diplomats were making their way slowly to Charles and Ferdinand, Constantinople lapsed into a terrible plague. The plague raged into the fall, with fifteen hundred dying in a day. Before it was over, some fifty thousand Turks had perished. When the Austrian envoy finally returned from Spain the following spring (April 1534), he found the atmosphere in the imperial city much changed. The Sublime Porte had turned its gaze eastward to Baghdad, the "Belgrade of the East," and beyond to Persia, in the grip of the Shi'ite heresy. Ibrahim Pasha was somewhere on the Silk Road, and Suleyman was preparing to join him.

The Austrian envoy came with instructions from Charles to make peace "in our name and on behalf of Christendom." The Holy Roman emperor was prepared to give up Koroni to secure peace, although Christian leaders, especially the tremulous Pope Clement VII, were pressuring him to retain it. When the diplomat was brought into the presence of the sultan, the envoy regretted the absence of Ibrahim Pasha as a mediating force. Suleyman was in a surly, volatile mood, swinging unpredictably between friendliness and hostility. The plague and the Persian campaign seemed to unsettle him. European problems had shifted to the background. When the diplomat expressed Charles's wish that all Christian princes in Europe be included in the peace, the sultan scoffed at the notion that all Christian princes were Charles's subjects and slaves. No, replied the diplomat cautiously, some were his subordinates, the others his friends. What about Francis I? Suleyman retorted, then wryly suggested that perhaps he, as the friend of Francis, could act as the mediator in the dispute between the Christian kings. When the diplomat suggested that the pope needed to bless the agreement, Suleyman flew into a rage.

The audience broke up unsatisfactorily, and the Christian diplomat instantly regretted having arranged it. As he left the Topkapi, janissaries jostled and jeered him. There would be no formal peace, lasting seven or two hundred years or an eternity, only a fragile truce. Only the decision of the Sublime Porte to concentrate its resources in Asia Minor gave Europe a chance to take a deep breath.

In early June Suleyman crossed the Bosporus into Asia and would be gone for another year and a half. But before he left, he took the extraordinary step of marrying Roxellana, the love of his life. Making Roxellana the first concubine in Ottoman history to be freed and then married constituted an enormous breach of tradition, in which it was customary for sultans to have single children by multiple slaves. But Roxellana had now borne him four sons, and his affection for her was unstinting. To underscore that love Suleyman married off nearly all the eligible concubines in the harem to worthy men in his retinue.

The wedding occasioned a great ceremony. "This week there occurred a most extraordinary event, one absolutely unprecedented in the history of

Sultans," wrote an Italian observer. "The Grand Signor has taken to himself as his Empress a slave-woman from Russia. Both Christian and Muslim knights have celebrated the event, along with tumblers and jugglers and a procession of wild beasts, and giraffes with necks so long it was as if they touched the sky. There is great talk about the marriage, and none can say what it means."

In fact, the public was troubled by the unnatural act, and it was whispered, especially among the janissaries, that she had bewitched the sultan, using love charms and magic arts. "They call her *Ziadi,* which means witch," wrote another Venetian. "For this reason the Janissaries and the entire court hate her and her children as well, but because the sultan loves her, no one dares to speak."

ACT TEN

The Natural
Enemy

✠

40.

TWO IRAQS

In Suleyman's lifetime Persia rather than central Europe had been the natural and traditional enemy of the Ottoman Empire. His father, Selim I, had devoted his short reign to the east, campaigning as far as the Persian capital of Tabriz in an effort to purify Islam under the traditional doctrine of Sunnism. Selim's great adversary was the founder of the Safavid dynasty, Shah Ismail I, who had come to power in 1501, who had done much to consolidate the tribes of that ancient land under a powerful head, and who had established Shi'ism as the official creed of his domain. In his early campaigns Ismail had secured Azerbaijan and, in 1508, had captured Baghdad. His ambition was to establish a great Shi'ite empire that would encompass eastern Anatolia, Azerbaijan, Persia, and Iraq.

Importantly, Shah Ismail's embrace of Shi'ism was as much political as religious. If the majority Sunnis were known as the traditionalists, Shi'ites were "separatists," and so his Shi'ite empire would be separate from the influences of the dominant sect. The dispute between the sects was genealogical; the question was who was the rightful leader of Islam and what was the correct relationship of the believer to Allah. The doctrine of the Shi'ites proclaimed a God-given caliphate by which a line of twelve imams, beginning with the fourth caliph, Ali, were considered to be sinless and infallible and to be the leaders of Islam by divine right. Fanatics had assassinated the first imam, Ali, and the twelfth, Muhammad al-Mahdi, had disappeared around A.D 874. But the last imam is believed to be still living. The return of Mahdi, like the second coming of Christ, is to this day eagerly awaited by Shi'ite believers, a time when he and his army will reestablish the Shia faith in the world during the last days. In this tradition Shah Ismail claimed to be the representative of the twelve imams on earth and thus put himself forward as a demigod.

To the Sunnis of Ottoman Turkey, this arrogation represented a profound heresy. Suleyman had devoted the first fourteen years of his reign in battle with the Christian infidel. Now he would turn his attention to the Islamic heretic.

Selim I had won a great battle over Shah Ismail in 1514 at Chalderon just west of Tabriz, a conflict that was ultimately determined by a greater Ottoman force and its use of cannons and firearms against the Persian bows and spears. This was the Ottoman victory that earned Selim his reputation for savagery and conferred upon him his sobriquet "the Grim" when, after the battle, the sultan had massacred all his Persian prisoners, and, for good measure, another forty thousand Shi'ites within his own dominion. But Selim had been forced to abandon Tabriz after his victory for logistical reasons—his supply line to Turkey was simply too long—though his campaign against Persia had added Kurdistan and Georgia to the expansive Ottoman Empire and had consolidated Ottoman rule over eastern Turkey. Nevertheless, the Persian Empire, the Safavid dynasty, and its Shi'ite faith had survived. Tabriz became the Persian capital once again without a struggle.

Ismail had died in 1524, and his eldest son, Tahmasp I, who was only ten years old, succeeded him. To this stripling, Suleyman had sent an insulting and threatening letter of anticongratulation (see Act Five). Only the focus on the Balkan campaigns and Rhodes had prevented Suleyman from turning his attention to the east. An eastern campaign was, at some point, inevitable, both as an act of faith and a filial duty. Apart from the religious and political motivations, Suleyman felt a personal obligation to complete the unfinished work of his father.

Suleyman's concentration on Christian Europe during the first decade of his reign had provided the Persian rival an opportunity for consolidation. Persian agents had done their best to encourage the Ghazali revolt against the Ottomans in Syria. In the years after 1524 Persian forces had seized a number of important fortresses along the border between the two empires, even encroaching well into eastern Anatolia. As the Persians moved into Turkey, various governors switched sides. There were other provocations. The most significant happened in Baghdad, the Rome of Islam. When Suleyman labored in frustration before the walls of Güns in Austria, he was informed that the governor of Baghdad, who had sworn his allegiance to the sultan and had promised the keys to his great city, had been assassinated and replaced by a Persian satrap. During the 1532 campaign toward Vienna, Suleyman was informed that the Persians had seized Bitlis, an important bastion in eastern Turkey. For these provocations as well as religious reasons, Ibrahim Pasha had long been urging an eastern campaign on the sultan.

The grand vizier had left Constantinople in the fall of 1533 with a formidable army. His first objective was the recapture of Bitlis near Lake Van. Once this was accomplished, Ibrahim quartered his army in Aleppo for the winter. When spring came, the plan was to proceed directly to Mosul in Iraq on the way to the great prize of Baghdad itself. But tensions in the high command altered this plan. Within Ibrahim's army he had a fierce rival, his vice general, Iskender Chelebi, the finance minister of the Empire. Chelebi was a powerful and immensely wealthy exhibitionist, who owned six thousand slaves, a favored three hundred of whom wore turbans adorned with gold. When he went into battle, he had with him a personal guard of twelve hundred horsemen, and he was quite popular with the army at large. By virtue of his tremendous wealth and popularity the minister had the ear of the sultan. He envied and coveted the high perch of Suleyman's "favorite."

As the Turkish army marched east through the dominions of Armenian and Turkmen princes from whom the Ottomans were descended, a dispute over strategy developed between the two men. Personal ambition and animosity lay beneath these disagreements. At this serious challenge to his authority, Ibrahim was forced into compromises to maintain the loyalty of the army. While Ibrahim wanted to move on Baghdad, Chelebi urged an assault on Tabriz, the Persian capital and the seat of the heresy. Playing to Ibrahim's vanity, Chelebi convinced Ibrahim that to defeat the shah at his own capital in a glorious holy battle would secure Ibrahim's place in history forever as the Conqueror of Tabriz. In reality Chelebi expected that an insufficient Ottoman force would surely face stiff resistance and would probably be defeated as the shah defended his capital. Suleyman would then blame Ibrahim for the failure, and Chelebi would supplant Ibrahim in the sultan's affections. The march on Tabriz was Chelebi's trap, and Ibrahim fell into it.

Meanwhile, leaving his son Mustafa in charge of the capital, Suleyman left Constantinople on June 13, 1534, with a considerable force of his own and with the expectation of joining up with the grand vizier somewhere in the Persian borderlands. Initially, the sultan was in no hurry. Instead of taking the direct route east, he proceeded languidly southwest to the city of Konya. There he paid homage to the memory of Jalal ad-Din ar-Rumi, the transcendent thirteenth-century poet and mystic who rivaled Omar Khayyám as the greatest literary figure of Sufism.* Born in Afghanistan, Rumi represented the ideal of the perfected human being, and he believed that the path to God was to be found by way of poetry, music, and dancing. The sacred dances of the whirling dervishes sprang from his teachings, and dervishes performed their mystical dance for the sultan. This pilgrimage for Suleyman seemed to be a spiritual preparation for the travails that lay ahead. On Rumi's magnificent green tomb was his epitaph: "When we are dead, seek not our tomb in the earth, but find it in the hearts of men." The pilgrimage may also have been a contemplation of Suleyman's possible death, for on his deathbed Rumi had written:

How do you know what sort of king I have within me as a companion?
Do not cast your glance on my golden face, for I have iron legs.

---

* Sufism is the literary and philosophical movement within Islam that focuses on the relation between the soul and the Almighty.

Ironically, Sufism had its origins in the Shi'ism of the eleventh century, and Rumi himself was a Persian who wrote in the ancient Persian language. Before he left Konya, Suleyman left instructions that the mausoleum of Rumi be elaborately restored.

While Ibrahim's army moved on Tabriz, Suleyman resumed his march east. The sultan was receiving dispatches from his grand vizier, mainly good news about fortresses along the way that had surrendered without a fight. But the tone of these dispatches changed in the early summer. Come quickly, Ibrahim wrote as he got closer to Tabriz. A confrontation with the shah's army was imminent. But Suleyman could not come more quickly. His army proceeded through the mountains of eastern Anatolia with difficulty, encountering snow in August. The sultan did not receive Ibrahim's urgent appeal until September 20, two months after the issue had actually been resolved.

As Ibrahim's inadequate force approached Tabriz and hovered perilously over Chelebi's trap, Shah Tahmasp abruptly ordered his army to retreat east to the shores of the Caspian Sea, and thus the great holy battle between Sunnis and Shi'ites was, at least temporarily, avoided. To Chelebi's dismay Ibrahim entered the Persian capital unopposed on July 13, 1534. Graciously, in contravention of a fatwa against the heretics, Ibrahim spared the residents the traditional three days of plunder. Swept away by his own glory, he proclaimed himself not only the Conqueror of Tabriz, but also the sultan of northern Persia.

Thus, flushed with triumph, Ibrahim decided to spring his own trap. Mysteriously, some thirty soldiers were arrested near the sultan's military coffers and charged with an attempt to steal from the royal treasury. When they were put to the rack, they blurted out that Iskender Chelebi had put them up to the dirty deed. Why the finance minister would want to steal from his own treasury was a puzzle. As word of the charge swept through the army, the soldiers scoffed at the charge, assuming, correctly, that Ibrahim cooked up the hoax to dispose of his rival. Ibrahim's standing among the troops plummeted as Chelebi's rose.

Unaware of this sideshow, Suleyman arrived in Tabriz with his army on

September 30 and was joyously greeted by his supreme commander, his vice general, and the local population. As he took up residence in the shah's palace, the animosity between Ibrahim and Chelebi was papered over as Suleyman congratulated his commanders and distributed the customary gifts. Ibrahim bided his time.

Baghdad was next.

41.

Charles and
the Barbary Sea Dogs

When the agents of Charles V reported that the mighty Ottoman Empire had shifted its attention to Persia and away from Europe, the emperor must have considered it both divine providence and the realization of an old stratagem. As far back as 1518 the powers of Western Christendom had been trying to encourage the Persians to open up a second front in the east. Various envoys had been dispatched to the Safavid dynasty, and in 1525 Charles had written to the shah offering an alliance. But nothing came of it. Then in 1529, with a full appreciation of the danger that the Ottoman Empire posed to Europe and highly alarmed by the first assault on Vienna, Charles sent yet another envoy to Shah Tahmasp I pleading for a military diversion. While nothing came of this either, the shah in an exchange of letters expressed his "friendship" for the Holy Roman Empire, just as the Ottomans had expressed their friendship for France. Therefore, the fortuitous campaign against Persia represented not only Charles's deliverance from a third invasion of Europe but a counterbalance to the initiatives of Francis I with Suleyman. The French-Turkish alliance was still a worry. Intelligence to this effect had come to Charles in 1533, after the pope met with Francis I in Marseille.

"Not only will the King of France not prevent the coming of the Sultan against Christendom," the pope told Charles. "He will advance it." Francis I was the bad penny who kept turning up unwanted.

With the pressure relaxed in eastern Europe and accommodation reached with the Lutherans in Germany, the action shifted to the Mediterranean Sea. For nearly three centuries, the coastline of North Africa had been the lair of the notorious Barbary pirates, who had bedeviled shipping throughout the inland sea, making slaves and oarsmen of their Christian captives, blackmailing and looting at will, and reaping immense rewards along the way. These privateers had been tolerated largely because they were so slippery and such skillful seamen. They were masters of deception and knew all the hiding places of the African coast: its inlets and islands, its currents and shallows. Their lightning raids terrorized coastal towns and villages. They tormented native Berber princes as they sallied out of Algiers to threaten isolated Spanish outposts that dotted the North African coastline from Melilla to Tripoli. Among their favorite targets were the galleys of the papacy, but they did their best to avoid open battle with the great galleons of established navies.

With its proximity to Africa, Spain and Spanish interests were the most affected by this scourge. Ferdinand and Isabella had attempted to control the menace by exacting tribute and by building a formidable fortress called the Peñon in the harbor of Algiers. At the turn of the century, the Spanish dilemma grew more severe after the Catholic kings of Spain expelled the Islamic Moors from Andalusia in southern Spain. Many of these Muslim refugees fled to Algiers, full of hatred and obsessed with a passion for righteous revenge. The pirates took full advantage of this new group of fresh, well-motivated recruits. After the death of King Ferdinand in 1516 the Barbary pirates were emboldened further to cease their payment of tribute to the Christian infidels.

In their struggle against the Spanish the Muslims of North Africa turned to two swashbuckling Turkish corsairs, known as the brothers Barbarossa. The elder Barbarossa, Arouj, was the more daring of the two, and he cut a vivid figure. His beard was red, hence the name Barbarossa, and his arm had been shot off in a battle with the Spanish in 1513. Once a prisoner of the Knights of Rhodes for two years, he had a reputation for ruthlessness that spread far and wide, as he killed and supplanted one Berber prince after another and spread his dominion from his headquarters in Jerba to Jijelli and Tlemcen. But in 1518 Arouj was killed by the Spanish, fighting in a civil war in Tlemcen, and his more prudent younger brother, Kheir-ed-din, succeeded him. Though the beard of the younger pirate was auburn rather than red, he too was known abroad as Barbarossa.

In this struggle with the Spanish, Kheir-ed-din turned to Constantinople for help, first to Selim the Grim, and eventually to Suleyman the Magnificent. The sultans supplied him with arms and financial support, dispatched a contingent of two thousand janissaries to him, and made him governor-general of Algiers, honoring him with the accoutrements of high command, horsetails, and a scimitar. His pirate navy grew to thirty-six swift galliots. But still the Spanish clung to their fortress at Peñon, and Barbarossa was unable to supplant them until 1529.

During the 1520s a drama unfolded between Kheir-ed-din Barbarossa and the great Italian admiral Andrea Doria. For years they had shadowed one another, always avoiding direct confrontation. Now they had become old warhorses, both in their sixties, and their rivalry had become personal. A final epic duel between them seemed inevitable. In 1532, events moved in that direction when Barbarossa sailed north to Sardinia in search of oarsmen to propel his growing fleet of swift, narrow galliots. The mission was a disaster, as a storm drove many of his vessels onto the rocks. Instead of bolstering his teams of rowers, he lost over twelve hundred men in the storm. But when news of this raid reached Charles V, the emperor realized the need for more vigorous naval action in the Mediterranean, partly to exterminate the wily old pirate of Algiers, partly to protect Spanish interests in North Africa, partly to safeguard the boot of Italy. Andrea Doria was pressed into duty, and his fleet bolstered. His capture of Koroni in southern Greece was a direct result of this renewed interest in naval power. A year later, ships from Doria's fleet disrupted a Turkish attempt to recapture the Christian outpost in Greece. (As part of the peace negotiations after the second Turkish invasion of Austria, Spanish soldiers abandoned Koroni in April 1534.)

Tensions in the Mediterranean escalated. The weak showing of Ottoman warships at Koroni, coupled with the prowess of Andrea Doria, convinced Suleyman that something major had to be done about the antiquated Ottoman navy. So he turned to Barbarossa. The old sea dog had been the sultan's vassal since 1518, but he had been kept at arm's length, sometimes causing more trouble than he was worth. Now his services were needed in a wider role, for clearly the Ottoman navy, made up of outdated and poorly led ships, was unsatisfactory for a great empire. Andrea Doria might, at any time, choose to threaten the Bosporus itself. The sultan insisted, however, that the pirate meet with Ibrahim Pasha first. So in the late fall of 1533 Barbarossa was forced to travel overland to Aleppo, where Ibrahim was wintering with his army. Once Barbarossa passed this preliminary round satisfactorily, he was summoned to the Sublime Porte for an imperial audience.

He arrived in grand style, eighteen of his sea captains accompanying him, including his most famous captain, known as "Caccia Diabolo," the Devil's Hunter. Bearing silver and gold artifacts and bags of money, with throngs lining the streets to watch the extravagant show, the old corsair paraded to the Topkapi with a bevy of beautiful African slave girls, bejeweled and clothed in silk, followed by a collection of exotic African animals, led by their trainers. When Barbarossa came into the presence of the sultan, he was honored with ceremonial robes and promptly put in charge of rebuilding the navy. With dispatch some sixty new ships with modern fittings were added to the navy. As Suleyman went east to Persia, Barbarossa set sail west as the admiral of the Turkish fleet, with one hundred ships, a regiment of janissaries, and ten thousand soldiers.

For weeks he terrorized the west coast of Italy from the tip of its boot all the way to Naples. Castles were plundered; towns were burned; and panic swept to the inner sanctum of the Vatican. Clement VII, no doubt, imagined this to be the long-expected invasion of Italy by the infidel. A number of times, Ibrahim had boasted to Christian envoys that one day the flag of the Prophet would fly over St. Peter's Basilica. The Ottoman raiders were now less than one hundred miles southwest of Rome. Hastily, the pope mobilized a force of six thousand soldiers, under Ippolito de' Medici, but by the time they came on the scene, the pirate had wreaked his havoc.

Amid this general mayhem Barbarossa savored a special mission given to him by Ibrahim Pasha. The pirate was to attempt to kidnap the most famous belle in all of Italy, Giulia Gonzaga, painted by many artists, including Sebastiano del Piombo, and coveted by many. This ravishing beauty was the widow of a Colonna prince, and therefore the mission would bring the Turks into conflict with the powerful family that had sacked Rome a few years earlier. Ibrahim's scheme was for the Italian prize to be delivered to Suleyman's harem, and to supplant Roxellana, the sultan's wife, who was giving the grand vizier fits. But when the Turks stormed her castle at Fondi, Giulia Gonzaga fled into the night nearly naked in the company of a single knight and escaped the clutches of the Turkish pirate. In reprisal, Barbarossa burned her village and torched a nearby convent, massacring the Benedictine nuns within. When the Turks were safely gone, Giulia Gonzaga had the knight who aided her escape killed, for he had seen too much.

Two weeks later, the Turkish fleet, said to comprise 250 galliots, appeared off Bizerta in Tunisia. This was the domain of a dissipated pasha named Muley Hassan, ruler of the Hafsid dynasty, who was notorious for having poisoned his father to secure his throne, then for having exterminated forty-four brothers, and who had recently enlarged his harem with four hundred young boys. At the news that the famous pirate was hovering nearby, Hassan gathered up his immediate family and fled into the desert. Barbarossa sailed into Tunis without a fight and took charge of the strategic city.

Barbarossa's raid on the Italian coast and, more important, his capture of Tunis sent shock waves through Europe, ending the complacency that Suleyman's eastern tilt had induced. The Mediterranean suddenly presented a new and dangerous peril. It was one thing to have a pirate's nest in Algiers in the western basin of the Mediterranean, but quite another to have a menacing Ottoman fleet in Tunis, little more than a hundred miles from Sicily.

The alarm spread, and Charles, in Spain, pondered his options.

42.

TUNIS: THE LAST CRUSADE

The crisis in Tunis evoked in the Holy Roman emperor once again his providential duty to his Christian dominions. A new kind of crusade was now called for because "God's honor" and the well-being of Christendom, not to mention his own honor and reputation, were at stake. Instead of the ancient tradition of an aggressive campaign to occupy the Holy Land and recapture the Holy Sepulcher of Jesus, this was to be a defensive crusade to safeguard Western Europe and its Christian religion. The naval crusade in the Mediterranean was linked to the land crusade of protecting Vienna and the eastern flank. After Vienna and Güns, Charles now fully appreciated the peril to Western civilization. Among his titles was king of Spain, and Spain's history for five hundred years was defined by a Christian struggle against Islam. The Mediterranean and Austria were now extensions of that historical struggle, and Charles rose to his role. While Portugal, the Netherlands, Italy, and the Empire offered money, ships, and soldiers, the flower of Spanish nobility rose enthusiastically to the cause; Spanish soldiers and Spanish galleys would form the backbone of the grand enterprise. If he was successful at Tunis, Charles fantasized that he might move on to the ultimate crusade, an assault on Constantinople itself. That, he said, was "the great ideal of my life."

The preparations for the African campaign needed to go forward with the utmost secrecy and discretion. If Francis I caught wind of the mobilization, he would surely tip off Barbarossa. And other hot spots within the Empire had to stay quiet while the mobilization went forward, for the French king could cause trouble elsewhere. While Charles wished to advocate passionately for the cause of his aunt Queen Catherine in the divorce proceedings with Henry VIII, to do so might drive England even closer to France. And Charles needed, at least for the time being, to defer his desire to crush the heresy of Martin Luther, since pressure on the Protestant German states might drive them as well into an alliance with Francis I. For the moment, Luther was behaving himself, preoccupied as he was with his scholarship. In 1534 his complete German Bible was issued, and a year later he began his famous lectures on Genesis. On the Austrian front Charles encouraged his brother to forbearance.

"We must take things as they are," Charles wrote Ferdinand.

Another event during the period marked the end of one era and the start of another. The Ottoman seizure of Tunis made the military order of the Knights of St. John of Jerusalem relevant once again. Ever since their poignant departure from Rhodes in 1522, the Knights Hospitaller, under the command of their elegant leader, Philippe de Villiers de L'Isle-Adam, had wandered aimlessly as refugees without portfolio, first to the islands of Crete and Sicily, then to Viterbo, and finally to Nice. With the scourge of Barbarossa and his Barbary pirates, and with the still active ambition of Francis I to reclaim Milan, Genoa, and Florence, the emperor finally donated the island of Malta to the order as its permanent home, with an outpost in Tripoli, Libya. As the Knights of Malta the order found new life, just as life itself drained out of the grand master himself. Villiers de'LIsle-Adam died in September 1534, as Barbarossa took charge of Tunis. Soon enough Suleyman would come to regret his generosity toward the ferocious Hospitallers twelve years before.

As Charles planned his novel crusade, he also pursued a covert strategy in the high tradition of medieval skulduggery. Perhaps there was an easier way to solve his North African problem. A Genoese merchant named Luis de Presenda was recruited for a desperate mission. His instructions were to travel to Tunis under the cover of a commercial venture and make contact with the refugee pasha in an effort to stir up a rebellion against Barbarossa. At the same time he was to present himself as Charles's accredited ambassador to the pirate and to offer more money, more ships, and a grander title than Suleyman had given him. He was to become the "Lord of North Africa." To cover all bases, if these efforts failed, this agent of high-minded Christianity was to attempt termination with extreme prejudice. He was to hire an assassin who could either poison the old pirate or slit his throat, preferably when the pirate was drunk, which he frequently was. Unfortunately for Christianity, the purpose of de Presenda's mission was soon found out, and he was executed.

In the late spring of 1535 Charles V gathered his naval expedition in Sardinia under the supreme command of Andrea Doria. With the Spanish in the majority of the force of thirty thousand, it also included Germans and Italians and seven hundred Knights of Malta. The fleet numbered more than four hundred ships, of which about a hundred were men-of-war. Leaving Sardinia on June 12, the fleet arrived on the Barbary Coast in twenty-four hours and moved eastward on their objective.

Tunis was an ancient city, having existed in the time of Carthage, whose ruins were only a few miles to the northeast. Its natural circumstance made it a daunting challenge to any invader. With its eighty thousand inhabitants, the city was protected by a shallow circular saltwater lake, some six miles in diameter. Entrance to the lake was only through a narrow canal that was defended by a major fortress called La Goletta, "the collar." To defeat the forces of the pirate and, hopefully, to capture the villain himself, Charles V would have to subdue La Goletta, then surmount a second obstacle, the walls of the city itself. Knowing from his spies that a Christian attack was coming, Barbarossa had reinforced the bastion of La Goletta and put in command one of his best captains, Sinan the Jew.

On June 20 the Christian armada arrived in the vicinity of La Goletta and found it to be defended by five thousand wily Turks and determined Moors. In the days that followed, the invaders found it difficult to gain a foothold. From a distance, Barbarossa skillfully deployed Moorish commandos in small skiffs to harry the Christians in shallow water, while other defenders harassed the invaders as they attempted to advance through nearby olive groves. Bombardment from La Goletta was intense and continuous, and the invaders noticed that the Moorish cannonballs bore French markings such as the fleur-de-lis and the motto *Nutrisco et extingo* ("I nourish and I extinguish"). The weather was also a complication. When fierce winds were not causing sandstorms, heavy rains bogged down the siege. As the days bled into two weeks, Charles found it difficult to keep peace within his multinational force. The Spaniards hated the Italians, and the Protestant Germans had little respect for the authority of their Catholic commander. One drunken German actually pointed a pistol at Charles and was promptly hanged. Moreover, in the withering heat, good drinking water was in short supply. To satisfy their thirst, the invaders relied on wine and bitter fruit, and for their hunger, they ate sea biscuits, only to have dysentery break out in their camp.

As the frustration continued, a Moorish defector approached Charles with a familiar suggestion: he knew how Barbarossa could be assassinated. Since others were present when this nefarious proposal was presented, Charles puffed himself up in a pose of indignant self-righteousness and proclaimed that no Christian prince could possibly countenance such a wicked act.

At the siege of Tunis Charles V was for the first time a battlefield commander. The challenges were considerable, and he comported himself with skill and courage, rallying his men to greater exertion and often exposing himself to enemy fire. More than three weeks into the siege, he set July 14 as the day for the pivotal assault. A bombardment from seventy ships began at dawn. By midday, one of the main towers of La Goletta came down. As a contingent of Spaniards advanced on land, the Knights of Malta waded ashore with assault ladders, and after a furious battle they poured over the walls and through the breaches. At last, the defenders fled. Charles strode into Goletta with Muley Hassan at his side.

"Here is the gate open to you," Charles said to the king of Tunis, "by which you shall return to take possession of your dominions." Once in charge of the Lake of Tunis, the Christians captured eighty-four pirate ships, which for some reason Barbarossa had not brought into play. With this haul Charles might well have imagined that he had eliminated the entire navy of the Barbary pirate. An objective of the expedition had been accomplished, but not the main objective. That was the killing or capture of Barbarossa himself.

The defenses of Tunis itself seemed to present a somewhat lesser challenge, for its walls were weak and the loyalty of its Moorish and Arab defenders to Barbarossa was uncertain. Perhaps more worrisome for the pirate was the presence of thousands of Christian prisoners within the city's alcazar. If they revolted and seized arms, Barbarossa knew that his defense would quickly collapse. As the pirate pondered what to do, the Christians dragged their cannons across the sandy shoreline of the lagoon under a blistering sun and finally came within sight of the city.

Instead of defending his suspect defenses, the pirate ordered a general attack on a broad plain three miles outside the walls, supposing that the Christian force would be exhausted from the heat and difficulty of dragging their heavy cannons across the sand. Though the Muslim force was depleted from desertions, its numbers were still superior. But it met a disciplined, well-commanded Christian army, spearheaded by heavy cavalry. Still, the battle for Tunis was fierce. As he deployed his soldiers on the battlefield, Charles had his horse shot from beneath him, and a personal page was killed by his side. The Christians fought bravely, motivated by the need to reach the wells near the city walls. With his assault repulsed, Barbarossa retreated into the city.

For him the situation had become desperate. The Christians in his midst were his worst nightmare. He came near the decision to burn the alcazar, incinerating the Christian prisoners, but Sinan the Jew talked him out of it. The rumor of the impending massacre reached inside the prison, and as Barbarossa feared, the captives revolted and seized control of the fortress. With that, Barbarossa fled the city. On July 21, Tunis fell without a fight.

Indeed, the keys to the city were presented to the emperor by the mayor, who pleaded with the conqueror not to sack his city. But Charles V had promised his soldiers the traditional three days of plunder. Tunis was but a nest of pirates, the Christian commanders told their soldiers, and the soldiers went about their work gleefully, massacring thousands of inhabitants and enslaving thousands more, an atrocity that would stain Charles's reputation and would stand in marked contrast to the mercy that Suleyman would soon show to his captives in Baghdad. While the Christians wreaked their havoc, Barbarossa made his way west to Bône, and Andrea Doria was unable to retrieve his sailors to give chase. In Bône, Barbarossa had kept a handful of his best galleys in reserve, and he sailed away to Algiers unmolested, while Charles V struggled to bring his greedy soldiers under control. The dissolute pasha Muley Hassan, reviled by his own people, took possession of his throne amid the carnage, and a contingent of Spanish soldiers was left to garrison La Goletta.

Across Europe the Christian victory at Tunis was hailed as a glorious achievement. Charles at last basked in full magnificence as the unrivaled champion of Christendom, the supreme defender of his faith. The contemporary historian Paolo Giovio led the exultation: "Your glorious and incomparable victory at Tunis seems to me, by my faith as a Christian, to have a dignity that far surpasses all others of everlasting memory." Victory parades were planned for the conquering hero in Italy and Spain. The glory and prestige of Tunis became the stuff of poetry and song. A new order of chivalry was created called the Cross of Tunis. Its motto was *Barbaria*.

Months later, the conqueror of the Muslims knelt before the pope in front of St. Peter's Door and followed him to the altar for a ceremony of thanksgiving. By the time Charles was in Rome, he had been the object of so many celebrations and flatteries that he had lost his natural reserve and wallowed in vainglory. Once again, with grand gestures and raised voice, he turned his ire on his old rival Francis I. In a long speech before the pope and his court, he recited his grievances against Francis over the years and reiterated his challenge for single combat. "Let us not continue wantonly to shed the blood of our innocent subjects. Let us decide the quarrel man-to-man, with what arms he pleases to choose, in our shirts, on an island, a bridge, or aboard a galley moored in a river. Let the Duchy of Burgundy be put in deposit on his part, and that of Milan on mine. These shall be the prize of the conqueror. And after that, let the united forces of Germany, Spain, and France be employed to humble the power of the Turk, and to extirpate heresy out of Christendom." This harangue mystified the assemblage of cardinals and ambassadors who had come to celebrate peace and goodwill among Christian princes. The next day, Charles had come to his senses, withdrawing it all.

Lest this fawning adulation of Charles register too sharply in his opponents' minds, Barbarossa popped up mischievously within a few months in the Balearic Islands, off the eastern coast of Spain, disguised as a Christian commander, and flying the flag of Spain. There, he subdued a Portuguese galley and carried off the residents of Port Mahón in Minorca as slaves. Finally, he had enough rowers for his revitalized fleet.

But for all the hullabaloo over this "famous battle" in Europe, the struggle for Tunis would, in time, become only a footnote in history. This temporary victory was followed by a more permanent defeat. Muley Hassan remained on his throne for another five years, detested by his people as a traitor to Islam, reviled for the slaughter of his own people with the infidel's weapons. In 1540 he was dethroned by his son, imprisoned, and blinded. At about the same time the Spanish abandoned their fort at La Goletta.

In the meantime, Kheir-ed-din Barbarossa rapidly reclaimed his dominance of the high seas. Within five years of his defeat at Tunis, he was once again the master of the Mediterranean and the intimidating bogeyman in the imagination of southern Europe. He persevered into his seventies, never slowing down in terrorizing the Barbary Coast, living on to command an Ottoman fleet in support of Francis I in the 1540s. As Constantinople remained the center of the vast Ottoman Empire, Algiers anchored its western dominion. When he finally retired from the fray, Barbarossa lived out his last years in splendor in a Constantinople palace. (A statue in his honor now graces the naval museum in Istanbul.)

His was a more glorious ending than that of Ibrahim Pasha.

IF THE YEAR 1534 was defined by Suleyman's invasion of Persia, Barbarossa's conquest of Tunis, and Charles's call to crusade, it was also defined by England's final split with the Roman Catholic Church. The year before, after Henry VIII appointed a compliant archbishop of Canterbury, his marriage to Catherine was declared null and void, and the English Parliament supplied the secular sanction. The king's second marriage, to Anne Boleyn, was made public, and in June of 1533, she was crowned queen of England. Pope Clement VII responded with a formal sentence of excommunication against the English king. The papal representative in England was recalled, and diplomatic relations with the Holy See were broken off. Early in 1534 the English Parliament severed all connection with Rome. Only in March of that year, after so long a delay and so much procrastination by the pope himself, did a papal council finally pronounce Henry's marriage to Charles's aunt Catherine to be valid. Thus, as Charles looked to the rest of Europe to support his naval crusade to Tunis, England had become a pariah state. Just as Protestantism was now secure in central Europe, so it was in England as well.

With that, a turbulent era of European history was ending. In September of 1534 Pope Clement VII, who had presided over Rome's losses in Europe and the British Isles, passed away. Among the last things he heard from Charles before he died was this:

"I am beginning to fear that God intends us all to become Muslims. But I shall certainly put my conversion off to the last!"

43.

BAGHDAD,
ABODE OF PEACE

Baghdad. Noble city of peace. Home of the great caliphs. Bulwark of saints, so called because so many holy men and martyrs are buried here. Refuge of poets and scholars. Built in the eighth century A.D. by Mansur, the second caliph of the House of Abbas. The center of the enlightened Abbasid dynasty and its greatest caliph, Harun ar-Rashid, a dynasty of which Suleyman considered himself to be a natural descendant. The scene of romantic Arabian nights. Famous for its rice plantations and gardens and date orchards, for its silks and tiled buildings. The crucible of sacred Islamic cosmology. The source of the first tables regulating the times for Islamic prayer, and of the first tables determining the direction of Mecca for all longitudes and latitudes. The final resting place of Abu Hanifa an-Nu'man, called the "greatest imam," as the founder of the Hanafi sect of Islam, to which the Ottomans belonged. The current home of Fuzuli, the most prominent poet of the day and destined to be a giant of Turkish literature.

For Suleyman, going to Baghdad was a spiritual quest, a pilgrimage to the place that was once the highest civilization of the world. It pleased him to think of the extremities of his empire as poles of peace and war. While Belgrade was called Darul-jihad, the House of Holy War, Baghdad was known as Darus-selam, the Abode of Peace. With the capture of Baghdad and an extension to Basra on the Indian Ocean, Suleyman would fulfill the promise of his great-grandfather Mehmet II as the Lord of Two Parts of the Earth and Sovereign of Two Seas.

But Baghdad was no longer a great city. In A.D. 1258 the Mongols of Genghis Khan's grandson had sacked it, shattering the irrigation system that had made the Tigris valley a fertile paradise, leveling its monuments, including the great center of learning, the House of Wisdom, and throwing thousands of invaluable books and manuscripts into the Tigris River. And worse, in A.D. 1400 the Tartars of Tamerlane had swept down from the steppes of Samarkand to destroy its walls and buildings, including the palace of the caliphs, leaving only the mosques standing and putting on display 120 columns of severed heads. The enfeebled Abbasids had fled to Egypt after the Mongol invasion, removing the spiritual heart of the holy city, until Selim the Grim, Suleyman's father, had transferred the caliphate, empty and pointless, from Cairo to Constantinople. The once proud city of peace was now a dusty byway, prey to a succession of forgotten occupiers like the Black and White Sheep of Iraq. Shah Ismail had taken the city from the White Sheep.

Suleyman tarried in Tabriz for merely five days before he set his united army on the road again. It was the fall of 1534 now. The weather was closing in, and the way ahead was difficult. A divan had decided to pursue the shah, who had retreated east to the shores of the Caspian Sea. With the Rumelian army, Ibrahim led the way; Suleyman followed with his janissaries and the Anatolian army; the light cavalry took up the rear. But when the Ottoman columns reached a town called Sultaniye, the intelligence came that the Persians had escaped and were beyond reach. And so the Turks regrouped, returning to their original objective and turning south toward Hamadan and Baghdad. Because they had marched so far east and south, however, the Ottoman army would now have to cross the rugged, mountainous terrain of Azerbaijan and Kurdistan. The going was slow and arduous, and the losses to equipment and animals were huge. As the quartermaster of the army, Chelebi bore the blame, for it was his duty to guard against such losses, no matter what the adversity. When the sultan saw how many camels and cannons were being lost in the march, when he saw no letup in the weather, he receded into a foul humor.

"The day brought thick fog, making visibility impossible," Suleyman wrote in his diary. "Numerous animals were lost. The night is unbearably cold."

Ibrahim chose this moment of dark moods to tell the sultan of Chelebi's "crime." "And as for the male thief and the female thief," it is written in the Koran (surah 5:38), "cut off from the wrist joint their right hands as a recompense for that which they committed, a punishment by the example of Allah." Predictably, Suleyman flew into a rage. The finance minister was immediately relieved of command, arrested, and held for trial, his possessions confiscated and his slaves redeployed to the sultan's household.

With Chelebi in chains, the campaign continued through the ancient biblical city of Hamadan, where it was said (Ezra 6:3) that Cyrus the Great, in the fourth century B.C., had given the order to rebuild the first Temple of Jerusalem. After Hamadan, the army struggled over still more difficult terrain, over the snow-covered passes of the Zagros Mountains, shedding more cannons and dead animals by the roadside. After they passed a castle that marked the border between the two Iraqs, Persian Iraq and Arab Iraq, the Ottoman columns finally spilled into the valley of the Tigris River. They found their city of peace to be undefended.

On November 28, Ibrahim Pasha entered the city by the Gate of the Great Imam and followed the avenue to his tomb, only to find that Shi'ites had destroyed the mausoleum of the famous expounder of Sunni Islamic law and burned the hero's bones. After Ibrahim received the keys to the city from its caretaker, he ordered the gates locked, including the bridge gate across the Tigris, and took the keys to Suleyman. The sultan entered the city two days later. Despite the fatwa that sanctioned pillage, and despite his anger over the profaning of Sunni holy sites, Suleyman ordered that the inhabitants of the city and their possessions were not to be touched.

In appreciation, the poet laureate of Baghdad, Fuzuli, a Shi'ite and custodian at the holy Shi'ite city of Karbala, sat down to compose an ode to the new conqueror.

Protector of the Faith, the refuge sure
For all of Islam, Mecca sings your praise.
Medina knows you, lightning of revenge.
Protector of the right, dread foe to wrong;
O great Sultan, thine alone is the gift
Of Justice, and to every man of art,
Turk and Arab and Persian too,
Sure hope of refuge and shelter sure
Who, like the ocean, in each stroke of time
Bestows the hope of favors yet to come.
Who gives the pearl to all those near at hand
And sends the cloud refreshing those afar,
Who makes his pearl the light of all the world
And moistens thirsty lips with water pure;
Like Fortune's wheel, your kindness manifests
And prodigally spreads your treasure round
Like all the sun when in munificence
It scatters pile on pile its golden coin.
Great Suleyman, emblem of the line
That first in Osman brightened all the world
The breaker of the petty lords of war,
You remain apart in purity and faith.

The sultan stayed in Baghdad for the next four months. Much of his time was spent in reorganizing Mesopotamia for permanent Turkish administration. He appointed governors, designated a viceroy for Baghdad, set up garrisons, surveyed property, and repaired the walls of the ancient capital. He had come as a pilgrim as well as a conqueror. The triumph of the Ottomans and of Sunnism was total, and yet the sultan set out not only to restore the legendary Abode of Peace to its former splendor, but to reach out to the very heretics he had come to exterminate. His first act was to rebuild the mausoleum of Abu Hanifa an-Nuʿman, the founder of Sunni Islamic rites and lawgiver of Sunni jurisprudence. The sepulchre was in the northeast quarter of the city, in a neighborhood called al-Azamiyyah. Simultaneously, a search for the saint's bones was instigated. Miraculously, the former custodian of the grave site came forward to tell the story that before the imam's grave had been violated by the Shi'ites, he had had a dream in which the imam himself had appeared and asked that his bones be moved to a safe place. The caretaker had done so, substituting the holy bones with the corpse of an unbeliever. Ibrahim Pasha was led to a secret refuge, and when the diggers began to dig, they hit a stone. Suddenly, as the legend is told, the scent of fragrant musk filled the air, proof that the relic they sought was nearby. Beneath the stone lay the saint's grave. When the news of the discovery spread, it was interpreted as evidence that Allah indeed favored the greatest of all sultans and the Conqueror of Baghdad. Suleyman ordered a mosque to be built around the sepulcher and madrassas for the study of law established nearby. Suleyman the Magnificent was becoming Suleyman the Lawgiver.

The tomb of Abu Hanifa was not his only preoccupation. He seemed to revel in the physical manifestations of the Islamic legends, sacred equally to Sunnis and Shi'ites, of which there were so many in the valley of the Tigris and the Euphrates. This cradle of civilization contained the supposed burial sites of the earliest prophets—Adam, Noah, Ezekiel, and Esdras—and the tombs of six of Mohammed's imams, starting with Ali. The Sunni sultan made a point of making a pilgrimage to Ali's sepulcher at Najaf and to the site of the Battle of Karbala, a place that stood only behind Mecca, Medina, and Jerusalem in holiness to the Shi'ites. It was as if he wished to demonstrate his respect and his desire to unite the sects of Islam into one universal faith. Babylon was not far away, where in Islamic scripture (sura 2:102) God sent Harut and Marut down from heaven in possession of ten carnal temptations, to see if angels could resist these temptations any better than mere mortals on earth. And he would be told of the hole in this sacred valley that by Shi'ite belief had swallowed up the last imam, Mahdi, and from which he would emerge before the Day of Judgment.

Through the winter Ibrahim's anger and resentment toward Chelebi remained intense, and he worried that if the trial of his rival were delayed until the army returned to Constantinople, Chelebi might marshal his considerable influence to challenge the flimsy accusation. Thus in March 1535, during the last days in Baghdad and at a propitious moment, Ibrahim pressed Suleyman to issue the execution order. Hours later, Chelebi was dragged to the horse market and hanged.

In the hours before his execution, Chelebi would exact his own vengeance. Calling for paper, he wrote a letter to his lord and master. In Islamic tradition this was a most revered document, for a last testament carries the weight of forty witnesses. Whatever he had done, Chelebi wrote, Ibrahim himself was even more guilty, for Ibrahim with his Persian gold was planning to assassinate Suleyman and claim the title of sultan for himself.

On the night after the execution, and now in possession of Chelebi's last testament, Suleyman, according to Turkish sources, had a terrible dream. In it Chelebi, bathed in celestial light, appeared to Suleyman, berating him for murdering an innocent man and trusting his treasonous vizier. Then the phantom threw himself on Suleyman and tried to strangle him, before the sultan woke up screaming.

The next day, acting as if nothing had happened, Suleyman accompanied Ibrahim on a visit to the tomb of Ali, the first imam of the Shi'ites in the revered place of Najaf. The last testament and the dream left a lasting impression, but another year would pass before the poison pills took effect. Two weeks later, in an effort to prevent further disclosure of his hoax, Ibrahim had Chelebi's father-in-law decapitated.

On April 1, with the city secure and on the rebound, the Ottoman army left Baghdad and moved north. The distressing news had arrived that Shah Tahmasp I had reoccupied his capital of Tabriz. So it would be necessary to recapture the heretic's lair before the army headed home. Ninety-one days were needed to accomplish the distance of four hundred miles. But to Suleyman the route was pleasant because the weather was good, and good weather always brightened the sultan's mood.

"There are many snakes in this land," Suleyman noted in his diary.

44.

THE ABRUPT END
OF A GREAT FRIENDSHIP

Once Tabriz was secured, it took the great Ottoman army four more months to march home. On January 8, 1536, the citizens of Constantinople welcomed their sultan home with customary adulation.

Almost immediately, the murmurings against Ibrahim spread through the capital. Old complaints, once consigned to whispers, now were spoken openly. The colossal statues of Hercules, Apollo, and Diana that Ibrahim had shipped from Hungary and installed in front of his palace had horrified many believers when they first appeared. Their ostentatious display flouted the Muslim rule that forbade graven images as idolatry and profaned the story of the prophet Abraham, who had destroyed idols (sura 21:58). Now the statues were openly cursed. A popular poet penned a few lines that stuck:

Two Ibrahims came into the world.
One destroyed idols. The other set them up.

As Ibrahim still clung to power, he had the poet paraded around Constantinople on a donkey for his impertinence before he was strangled. This only intensified the grumbling.

It was whispered that in Iraq Ibrahim had lost his belief in Islam and had recaptured his humble roots as a Christian. Whereas once he revered the Koran and pressed it piously to his forehead, it was said that in Iraq he had turned holy men away with distaste when they appeared before him to present a decorative holy book as a gift. Rumors flew that because he now called Ferdinand of Austria his brother and Charles V his cousin, he had gone over to the other side. Secret correspondence was said to prove his treason. Absurd though this charge of collusion was, it now found many willing believers. His commercial acquisitions with Venice, which resulted in expensive personal purchases, raised the question of his greed, his vanity, and his ambition, as if he wished to surpass Suleyman in magnificence and supplant him as sultan. As the news of Chelebi's execution swept through the capital, the popular finance minister took on the aura of a martyr among the Turkish soldiers. A famous Turkish poet composed an elegy, "On the Execution of Iskender Chelebi":

> Dust lit on the face of his fair fame
> Borne by the blast of traitorous calumny
> Word went forth for his elevation
> Full sudden from the court of equity
> Straightway they reared him up toward the skies,
> They raised him from the dust of obloquy
> And dervish-dancing went he, circling round
> From exile to the Land of Amity.
> A slave neck-bounden stood he at the court;
> They loosed him from the bonds of villainy.
> For joyfulness he set no foot on earth
> What time his head was freed from misery.
> Right gladly soared he on his ascent
> Delivered from the world of Infamy.
> So never was the life or death of him
> Found to be empty of sublimity.
> And this our hope, that in the world to come

Likewise, he win to lofty dignity.
The host of Heaven spoke his inscription
"Upward he journeyed through his courtesy."

Even more damaging was Ibrahim's appropriation of the title of *sultan* in Iran. His rebellious predecessor Ahmed Pasha had done the same thing in Egypt twelve years before, and for his transgression the previous grand vizier had been drawn and quartered by Ibrahim Pasha's own order. Now Ibrahim himself had stepped over an important line of demarcation between a slave and a sovereign. Such an offense threatened the authority of Suleyman himself. Members of the court came forward to tell of Ibrahim's boasts of being the real power in the Ottoman Empire, while Suleyman always did his bidding. "He loved himself better than he did his lord," wrote a Venetian diplomat, "and he wished to be alone in the dominion of the world in which he was much respected." The long-seething resentment over all the gifts and privileges that he had received from Suleyman over the years boiled to the surface.

No one was more delighted to take advantage of these rumors and resentments and complaints than Suleyman's wife, Roxellana. She had always resented the influence that Ibrahim exercised over her lover and had long advocated his ouster. The year before, Suleyman's mother had died, and this had removed a figure who protected Ibrahim. Now Roxellana did her best to embellish the rumors and poison the sultan's mind.

In this twilight period during the first two months back in the imperial capital, Suleyman gave no outward sign that he was aware of this court intrigue. Business went forward as usual. Indeed, Ibrahim's first act was to negotiate an important commercial agreement between the Empire and France that would form the basis of the relations between the countries for years to come. The grand vizier continued to live in the royal palace and sleep in the bedroom next to the sultan's.

Into this mix came the searing memory of Iskender Chelebi's last testament and his terrible visitation to Suleyman on the night after Chelebi's execution.

Whatever Suleyman was thinking about the machinations swirling around him he kept to himself. What was rumor and what was truth? What were the ambitions of the detractors compared to the ambition of Ibrahim himself? A lifetime of trust bound the two men. What value did Suleyman place on Ibrahim's lifelong friendship and upon the distinguished thirteen-year service to his reign as a great battlefield general, a master diplomat, a consummate administrator? If Suleyman was to believe the worst and bow to the wishes of Roxellana and Ibrahim's other enemies, had he not made an honorable vow to Ibrahim never to disgrace his friend so long as he lived?

On this latter point, the story is told that Suleyman consulted with his learned men. How he could honorably dispose of Ibrahim and still keep his vow? "You have promised never to kill him so long as you lived," one wise man is supposed to have said. "Life consists in conscious action, and he that sleeps does not truly live. So there is a way to punish his disloyalty and not violate your oath. . . .

"Have him strangled while you are asleep."

Ibrahim had caused the death of an innocent man, and thus his own death would be according to Scripture:

"Verily all glorious Allah is master of revenge."

On March 15, the ides of March well appreciated by the Ottoman Caesar, the sultan invited his grand vizier to dinner as usual in the private quarters. They dined and conversed amiably as usual and parted amicably for bed. The next morning the body of Ibrahim Pasha was discovered outside the main gate of the Topkapi Palace. He had been strangled, with signs of a great struggle. The corpse was loaded on a wagon and buried unceremoniously in an unmarked grave in a dervish cemetery near the Galata Bridge.

EPILOGUE

The reigns of Suleyman the Magnificent and Charles V did not end with this ten-act drama after these pivotal, dramatic sixteen years, for history rarely conforms to the neat package of the stage. Their intrigues and battles and animosities continued unabated for the next several decades. The causes of the conflict were essentially the same. Both epic leaders continued to be almost constantly at war until their old age, but the balance of power for their respective empires remained basically the same.

An old world had passed into oblivion, and a new, modern world had taken shape. A reformation of the Catholic Church had been accompanied by a new way for Christians to worship their God. Protestantism was now firmly and permanently established. The Ottomans had pushed their farthest into central Europe, establishing in the Balkan Peninsula a patchwork of Christian and Islamic communities that would disintegrate into conflict at subsequent eras of history right into the late twentieth and early twenty-first centuries with the terrible religious wars in Bosnia and Kosovo. The European memory of Turkish terror and religious jihad would find resonance in the twenty-first century with the issues of Turkish immigration into Europe, a kind of de facto invasion, and the question of Turkish accession to the European Union as the union's only Islamic partner. Not only tactical lines but psychological lines had been established in these sixteen years that exist even today as barriers between East and West, Asia and

Europe, Islam and Christianity. And finally, Suleyman's failure to subdue the Shi'ism of Persia and thus to consolidate Islam under one theology would leave a deep division between the two sects of Islam that is still being played out in modern Mesopotamia.

Suleyman would launch another six imperial campaigns, returning four times to the Danube but never again threatening Vienna. He returned twice again to Persia, but never subdued the Shi'ite reign of the Safavids, though the Ottoman dominion was extended to the Arabian Sea at Basra and in Aden. In 1555 the Ottomans and the Safavids signed a peace treaty that ended their hostilities for the rest of Suleyman's reign. Whereas the sultan had succeeded against the Knights of St. John at Rhodes in 1522, he failed to supplant the same pirate-monks in their new home in Malta in 1565. Although the Ottomans continued their domination of the Barbary Coast and although Barbarossa defeated Andrea Doria in a great naval battle at Préveza off the coast of Greece in 1538, the victory was not followed up by an invasion of Italy, as the Christians and especially the Vatican feared.

Charles, in turn, would fight battles against the Ottomans in Hungary and in the Mediterranean, but they were essentially battles to prevent Islamic conquest and contain the Ottoman expansion, rather than to extend the boundaries of the Hapsburg Empire. Those boundaries, he knew, were best extended through marriage rather than combat. Though Charles had succeeded in Tunis in 1535, the city reverted to Islamic rule in the next generation, and Charles failed disastrously at Algiers in 1541 when a hurricane destroyed his fleet. The rivalry between Charles and Francis I continued unabated, but Francis profited little from his alliance with the Ottomans. (In 1543 Francis permitted Barbarossa to winter his fleet in Toulon, but this was the Turks' only tangible benefit from the Franco-Ottoman alliance.) Charles invaded Provence in 1536, while Francis made gains in the kingdom of Naples in southern Italy. They would fight their last war between 1542 and 1544. That would end with the Peace of Crépy. Francis I died three years later. After he came into his own as a battlefield general at Tunis, the emperor became a formidable military commander, taking the field against the French in Provence and Germany, leading the naval expedition at Algiers, crushing a rebellion in Ghent in 1540. With these exploits he was widely perceived, in his own lifetime, to be a kind of classical hero.

Meanwhile, during the last two decades of his reign, Charles presided over a handful of additional diets, pursuing his abiding hope of reuniting the Protestants with the Roman Catholic Church. After the stalemate in the Balkans and the Peace of Crépy, he finally resorted to military force against the Lutheran states of Germany. After imperial forces captured the elector of Saxony, and Philip of Hesse surrendered, Charles defeated the Lutheran states in 1547. This led to the so-called Armed Diet of 1548, which marked the high-water mark of Charles's power in Germany. But military conquest could not shake the hold of Lutheranism, for Protestantism was now firmly established both in Germany and in England. (In the company of his sixth wife, Henry VIII died in 1547.) Instead of imposing an inquisition, Charles instead pursued a policy of conciliation, suspending penalties against the heretics and steadfastly pushing a reluctant Vatican toward reform.

In his declining years Luther preoccupied himself with his writings, penning more controversial commentaries on the Bible and refining his translation of the New Testament. He died in 1546 and thus did not witness the military surrender of his great supporters to the Holy Roman emperor. At his funeral he was likened to the second angel of the Apocalypse, who cries, "Fallen, fallen is Babylon the Great!" His prophecy was remembered: "In life I was thy pestilence; dying, I will be thy death, O Pope." Philip Melanchthon delivered his funeral oration and placed the Reformer in the company of the original patriarchs and the great prophets of the Church. "His heart was true and without falseness," Melanchthon said, "and he strove ever to observe the Apostles' command [Philippians 4:8] 'Whatsoever things are true, whatsoever things are honest, whatsoever things are just . . . and pure . . . and lovely . . . and of good report, if there be any virtue, if there be any praise, think on these things.'"

In 1556, worn-out, world-weary, and suffering from gout, Charles abdicated his throne as Holy Roman emperor and turned it over to his brother, Ferdinand. A year later, he resigned his Spanish, Dutch, and Sicilian crowns, as well as his rule over the county of Burgundy, and gave them to his son, Philip II. Then Charles retired to a remote monastery in the Extremadura in the Gredos Mountains of western Spain at a place called Yuste.

For the next year and a half, Charles lived a quiet, pious, and indulgent life, feeding the ducks, fishing, happy in the company of his wolfhounds, his confessor, his majordomo, and his clockmaker, Torriano. As Torriano labored away at a clock that not only told time but also displayed the day, the month, and the year, the emperor watched in fascination as if he were counting the minutes and the hours. The ingenious engineer also made mechanical toys for the emperor's amusement. In his dotage, the Defender of Christianity in Europe was afraid of mice and spiders. Meanwhile, to the despair of his physician, European potentates sent him barrels of oysters, anchovies, and Dutch sausages. "Kings," wrote the majordomo, "must surely imagine that their stomachs are made differently from those of other men." As his Portuguese cook prepared mountains of spiced food, Charles V gradually ate his way toward death.

As his health disintegrated, Charles gave himself over to the pathos of his imminent demise. Among the many priceless objects that he had brought with him to Yuste was Titian's painting of the Last Judgment known as *La Gloria,* in which the famous painter had included images of Charles, his beloved Queen Isabella, and their children, on their way to their just rewards. This epic painting hung over the altar in the monastery's chapel. On the anniversary of Isabella's death, the emperor insisted on a three-day celebration of burial rites. After they were over, he turned to his confessor and wondered if it would not be well for him to witness his own obsequy. "Would it not be good for the soul?" Charles asked. The confessor replied that indeed burial rites would be more effective in life than in death. So the chapel was again draped in black, the household dressed again in mourning, and a huge catafalque was placed before the altar. A service for the burial of the emperor was then held, as the emperor himself watched, holding a tapered candle and surrendering his soul to the Almighty. As this story was later told over the centuries, it was embellished, with the added detail that the emperor actually crawled into his casket to meditate upon his forth-coming celestial journey.

A month before his death, Chalres called for his will, desiring to add a codicil to it. Long in preparation, the document was of immense length and specified how his fortune was to be distributed to his children and his attendants down to the lowest servant. The codicil required thirty thousand masses for the benefit of his soul to be said across the Hapsburg dominion. Moorish captives in prisons were to be released. But the most noteworthy additions concerned religion, as his latent anger and regret and bigotry were given full vent. He enjoined his son, Philip II, to reinstate the Inquisition in Spain with its full force, so that every heretic in Spain would be brought to justice. (This was a charge that Philip was only too glad to satisfy. In the classic Hapsburg manner of concluding marriages to expand its dynastic reach, Philip had married Queen Mary of England in 1554. But Catholic "Bloody Mary," the daughter of Henry VIII and Catherine of Aragon, died in 1558 and was succeeded by Queen Elizabeth I, the daughter of Henry VIII and Anne Boleyn. It would be Philip II who would several decades later launch the Spanish armada against Protestant England.)

In perhaps the most startling addition to the will, Charles expressed his regret that he had honored his promise of a safe passage to the Reformer, so that Martin Luther could attend the Diet of Worms unmolested.

Charles died in late September 1558.

As CHARLES V dwindled in Yuste, Suleyman the Magnificent, a world away, was moving into the last years of his spectacular reign. For ten years, from 1555 onward, the Sultan had avoided the imperial campaigning that had characterized his role as Conqueror in the previous thirty-five years. His attention, instead, was on his capital and his culture and the Ottoman system of governance. In these last years of Suleyman's reign Constantinople became the most vibrant, creative city in the world. With a leader who was himself an admired poet and an accomplished goldsmith, the arts flourished: calligraphy, wood carving, carpet weaving, architecture, painting, bookbinding, theater, scholarship, spectacle, science, geography, and literature. Within his employ was perhaps the greatest architect in Turkish history, Sinan, who in 1557 completed the spectacular Suleymaniye Complex, a collection of buildings around a monumental mosque, dedicated to Suleyman himself and including a mausoleum for Roxellana (who died in 1558).

In their own times, if Charles was perceived as a classical hero to the Christian world, Suleyman was no less a hero to the Islamic world. He had lived up to his name and his promise as the second Solomon, the perfect embodiment of power, justice, and creativity. In 1555 a literary diplomat, Baron Busbecq, who was the Austrian ambassador to the Sublime Porte, described him vividly: "His expression has a sternness that, though sad, is full of majesty. He is beginning to feel the weight of years, but his dignity of demeanor and his general physical appearance are worthy of the ruler of so vast an empire."

In this twilight period he was being praised as much for his domestic accomplishments as for his foreign campaigns. He had reformed both military and civil administration, codifying specific rules and laws for governance, especially those laws that affected the taxation and treatment of the common man. He had laid down standards of behavior for the Islamic scholars, the *ulema,* and he set out to protect the rights of Christians within his Islamic dominion. Beyond the religious laws of the *sharia,* which were derived from the Koran, Suleyman's "sultanic laws" formed a lasting basis for Turkish constitutional law and earned him the additional sobriquet of Suleyman the Lawgiver.

His last years, a period of consolidation and acclamation, also saw great tragedy. He watched his heirs expire one by one: Mehmet, his first son with Roxellana, in 1543; Cihangir, the hunchback and his favorite, ten years later; Bayezid, his fourth son with Roxellana, in 1561 when that son lost the dynastic competition to Suleyman's least accomplished son, Selim, and was executed. But Suleyman's greatest tragedy came of his own doing, with the murder of Mustafa, his first son with Roxellana's predecessor and rival

Gülbahar. For the great sultan had allowed himself to be maneuvered into believing Roxellana's jealous and conspiratorial whispers that Mustafa was plotting to overthrow his father. To his immense grief later and to his discredit, Suleyman acquiesced one dark day near Konya in the execution of the most natural leader of his brood. That left Selim—Selim the Sot, as he was known—as the sole survivor for the Osmanli line. In Suleyman's last years, he was tormented by his son's debauches, badgering his heir to give up "that mad red thing" and actually executing one of his son's drinking companions. But Selim would not give up his wine and his other indiscretions. After Suleyman died, the few years of Selim's rule marked the beginning of the decline of the Ottoman Empire.

In 1562 Suleyman had concluded a peace with the Austrians, and this seemed to close the books on the quest to invade Europe that had so dominated his ambitions of a lifetime. Two years later, Charles's brother, Ferdinand, died. But Ferdinand's successor was making trouble again in Hungary, and so in May of 1566, at the age of seventy-two, Suleyman left Constantinople on his twelfth and last imperial campaign. He was too weak to ride a horse now and was transported in a carriage, surrounded as always by the relics of the Prophet and the accoutrements of glory.

Like the conflicts at Güns and Vienna and Malta before it, the Battle of Szigetvár would find its way into classical folklore. A famous Hungarian epic poem called the Peril of Sziget would be written about the siege in the next century by an ancestor of the heroic defender of the fortress. Its epic form was said to have influenced John Milton in his writing of *Paradise Lost*. In the Hungarian epic Suleyman is portrayed as the instrument of the Christian God, angry that the Hungarians have abandoned their faith. Inevitably, after fifteen parts, written in quatrain, Suleyman is killed by the heroic commander of Szigetvár, and the Magyar knight is in turn dispatched by janissaries and thus achieves Christian martyrdom.

And so too would the death of Suleyman inspire lasting poetry. An elegy was written to him by the greatest of the Turkish lyric poets during this classical period, named Mahmud Abdul Baki:

Will not the king awake from sleep, when comes the light of day?
Will not he move forth from his tent, bright as high heaven's display?
Long have our eyes dwelt on the road, and yet no word is come
From that far land. . . .
Across the face of the earth thou hast hurled the right
From east to west thine armored champions have borne it
As sweeps a sword. . . .

If this last campaign had the dull feel of repetition, so would the last battle of Szigetvár. The immense Turkish army found itself once again in front of a modest fortress, commanded by an ingenious Christian general, with a stubborn set of defenders. Again one hundred thousand Turkish soldiers faced several thousand determined warriors behind unprepossessing walls, and again it would take several critical weeks to bring the place to heel at tremendous cost. The difference this time was that the aged sultan stayed within the gossamer confines of his tent and received the bleak reports of his aghas and viziers. Burdened by anxiety, he died of natural causes on his own battlefield.

ACKNOWLEDGMENTS

Defenders of the Faith completes a cycle, begun in the early 1990s, in which I have focused on turning points in history from A.D. 1000 to the trial of Galileo in 1632. In this book, as with *The Last Apocalypse, Warriors of God,* and *Dogs of God,* I've paid close attention to the clash of Christianity and Islam, first with the beginning of the Christian reconquest of Islamic Spain, then with the third crusade of Richard the Lionheart and Saladin, further with the completion of the Spanish "reconquest" during the time of Christopher Columbus, and here with the press of the Ottoman Muslims at the portals of Western Europe. In each of these four instances, had the fortunes of the battlefield altered just slightly, the landscape of Western civilization into the modern age might have been very different indeed. *Galileo: A Life* ends the quintet with the eternal struggle between religious doctrine and modern science.

The residue of these historical struggles is very much with us today: in the clash of Western crusade versus Eastern jihad in Iraq and the Islamic world generally, in the controversy over Arab and Turkish immigration into Europe, in the scandals over torture and other abuses in the American occupation of Iraq, in the growing fundamentalism of both Christianity and Islam, in the violent clashes between Sunnism and Shi'ism, in the romanticizing of Ottoman and Arab culture in current Eastern Mediterranean politics, in the resistance of Europe, especially Austria, to Turkey's application to join the European Union.

In general, these five books have each taken three years to write, and *Defenders of the Faith* fits the pattern. As in previous work, for the research I shuttled between my small office at the Library of Congress and the Woodrow Wilson International Center for Scholars. At the library, the Turkish and Ottoman specialist, Christopher Murphy, was unfailingly helpful and responsive to my numerous requests. In addition, I was ably assisted, as in the past, by stellar reference librarians, Thomas Mann, David Kelly, and Mary Jane Deeb. Phoebe Peacock helped with my occasional requests for Latin and Greek translation. At the Wilson Center, I was again blessed with whip-smart, diligent young interns: Corinne Ilgun, Duden Yegenoglu, and especially Anthony Bodin, who stayed with me far beyond his normal tour and who was invaluable as a translator of French and German texts. (Many important Ottoman sources are in French and German, but not yet in English.) And the center's lead librarian, Janet Spikes, was always ready with a prompt and cheerful response to my many queries.

For the Italian portions of this story, I was twice in Italy. For two weeks in the fall of 2006, when I was working on the sack of Rome, the American Academy in Rome took me in once again, and for that productive foray at the academy and the Vatican Library, I thank the academy's president, Adele Chatfield-Taylor, and its director, Carmela Vircillo Franklin. The following summer, when I was working on the Battle of Pavia, my old friends Cosimo Mazzoni and Antonella Berardi gave me elegant shelter and sustenance for a month at their lovely villa above Florence.

In the spring of 2008, toward the end of my process, I made a valuable trip abroad to retrace Suleyman's steps from Istanbul to Vienna. I arrived in Turkey just as Turkish soldiers had invaded northern Iraq in search of Kurdish rebels, as the debate over the wearing of head scarves by Turkish women in the new Islamic republic was at its height, as trials against Turkish writers for writing supposedly "anti-Turkish" things about dark episodes in Turkish history were in full swing, and as the approval rating of America had fallen from over 50 percent in the late 1990s to 12 percent in the Bush presidency. Many of my discussions with scholars dealt with the relevance of this story to the modern age. With political scientists Suhnaz Yilmaz and Ilter Turan in Istanbul, with former Turkish ambassador to the United States Faruk Logoglu in Ankara, and with a longtime student of modern Turkish politics, the Swedish cultural attaché in Istanbul, Ingmar Karlsson, the role of Ottoman history, especially Suleyman's story, in contemporary affairs was the central topic. On the specifics of this story, I benefited from the wisdom of Ottoman scholar Asli Niyazioglu at Koc University and the dean of Ottoman scholars, ninety-two-year-old Halil Inalcik, at Bilkent University in Ankara. My visits to the fabulous Topkapi were made especially memorable by my long conversation with the palace's bombastic director, Ilber Ortayli.

In early March 2008 I arrived, a bit nervously, in Belgrade only a few days after Serbia's "medieval heartland" of Kosovo declared independence from its motherland. The week before, the Bush administration, along with other European countries, had recognized the new country, causing much consternation in Serbia. At the Bulgarian-Serbian border, the border policeman looked at my American passport skeptically and proclaimed ominously, "Americans are not welcome in Serbia right now." In Belgrade, my Serbian driver went out of his way to show me the buildings in Belgrade that American bombs had obliterated in the 1990s and the bridges over the Danube that our planes had destroyed. After my introduction to him by my colleague at the Wilson Center Martin Sletzinger, I spent many pleasant hours with the important political commentator Aleksa Djilas, walking the ramparts of Belgrade's medieval fortress and trying to understand why the memory of the Battle of Kosovo, in which the Ottoman Turks defeated the ancient Serbs in A.D. 1389, was felt so intensely in Serbia in the twenty-first century.

Moving into southern Hungary, I toured the battlefield of Mohács, before I had profitable discussions in Budapest with Ottoman scholars Geza David and Korpas Zoltan. Then in western Hungary, in the charming border town of Köszeg, as Güns is known, I walked the castle walls in the rain with Pocza Zoltan, the director of that stout holdout against the Ottoman juggernaut.

And finally I arrived in Vienna. There the task was to visualize the vulnerable medieval walls along what is today the famous Ringstrasse and to imagine what that venerable city might have looked like if Suleyman had prevailed in 1529 or 1532 and had turned the spires of St. Stephen's Cathedral into minarets. Twice in the sixteenth century, the Austrians had turned away an Ottoman army of over one hundred thousand soldiers. Today Austria is the most vociferous country in its opposition to Turkish entry into the European Union.

"We have defeated you twice before," an Austrian newspaper had editorialized. "We can do it again."

SELECTED BIBLIOGRAPHY

Alberi, Eugenio. *Relazioni degli ambasciatori veneti al Senato.* Ser. 3, vol. 1. Florence: Societa editrice fiorentina, 1839–63.

Andrews, Arthur Irving. "The Campaign of the Emperor Charles V against Tunis and Kheir-ed-Din Barbarossa." Doctoral diss., Harvard University, 1905.

Armstrong, Edward. *The Emperor Charles V.* London: Macmillan, 1929.

Arnaldez, Roger. *Les grands siècles de Bagdad.* Alger: Entreprise nationale du livre, 1985.

Atil, Esin. *Süleymanname: The Illustrated History of Suleyman the Magnificent.* New York: H. N. Abrams, 1986.

Atkinson, James. *The Trial of Luther.* New York: Stein and Day, 1971.

Bagley, J. J. *Henry VIII and His Times.* New York: Arco Publishing, 1962.

Bainton, Roland H. *Here I Stand: A Life of Martin Luther.* Nashville, TN: Abingdon Press, 1990.

Bariska, Istvan. *A Contribution to the History of the Turkish Campaign of 1532.* Köszeg, Hungary: Institute for Social and European Studies, 2007.

Bauer, Josef. *Die Turken in Österreich: Geschichte, Sagen, Legenden.* St. Pölten: Niederösterreichisches Pressehaus, 1982.

Bedford, W. K. *The Order of the Hospital of St. John of Jerusalem.* New York: AMS, 1978.

Blockmans, Wim. *Emperor Charles V.* London: Arnold, 2002.

Bourbon, Jacques de. *A briefe relation of the siege and taking of the city of Rhodes.* London, 1809.

Bowle, John. *Henry VIII.* Boston: Little Brown, 1965.

Bradford, William, ed. *Correspondence of the Emperor Charles V.* London: Richard Bentley, 1850.

Brandi, Karl. *The Emperor Charles V: The Growth and Destiny of a Man and of a World-Empire.* Trans. C. V. Wedgwood. Atlantic Highlands, NJ: Humanities Press, 1980.

Braudel, Fernand. *The Mediterranean and the Mediterranean World in the Age of Philip II.* 2 vols. Trans. Sian Reynolds. London, 1973.

Brecht, Martin. *Martin Luther: Shaping and Defining the Reformation, 1521–1532.* Minneapolis: Fortress Press, 1985.

Bridge, Anthony. *Suleiman the Magnificent, Scourge of Heaven.* London: Granada, 1983.

Brockman, Eric. *The Two Sieges of Rhodes, 1480–1522.* London: John Murray, 1969.

Bucholtz, Franz B. *Geschichte der Regierung Ferdiandn des Ersten.* Graz: Akademische Durck- und Verlagsanstalt, 1971.

Busbecq, Ogier. *Life and Letters.* 2 vols. Trans. C. T. Forster and F. H. B. Daniell. London, 1896.

Cellini, Benvenuto. *The Autobiography of Benvenuto Cellini.* Ed. Charles Hope and Alessandro Nova. Oxford: Phaidon Press, 1983.

Champillon-Figeac, Aimé L. *Captivité du roi Francois I.* Paris: Imprimerie royale, 1847.

———. *Poésies du roi François I.* Geneva: Slatkine Reprints, 1970.

Charriere, Ernest. *Négociations de la Fance dans le Levant.* Paris: Imprimerie nationale, 1848.

Chastel, Andre. *The Sack of Rome, 1527.* Princeton, NJ: Princeton University Press, 1982.

Clot, André. *Soliman le Magnifique.* Paris: Fayard, 1983.

Coeke van Aelst, Pieter. *The Turks in MDXXXIII; a series of drawing.* London and Edinburgh: privately printed for W.S.M., 1873.

Coignet, Clarisse. *Francis the First and His Times.* New York: Scribner and Welford, 1889.

Concina, Ennio. *Il Doge e il Sultano: Mercatura, Arte e Relazioni nel primo '500.* Roma: Logart Press, 1994.

Crabites, Pierre. *Clement VII and Henry VIII.* London: Routledge, 1936.

Creasy, Edward Shepherd. *History of Ottoman Turks.* Beirut: Khayats, 1961.

Creighton, M. A *History of the Papacy from the Great Schism to the Sack of Rome*. Vol. 6. New York: Longman's, Green, 1897.

Dennistoun, James. *Memoirs of the Dukes of Urbino*. London: J. Lane, 1909.

Djevad, Ahmed. *État militaire ottoman depuis la fondation de l'empire jusqu'à nos jours*. Constantinople: Imprimerie du Journal la Turquie, 1882.

Doernberg, Edwin. *Henry VIII and Luther; an account of their personal relations*. London: Barrie and Rockliff, 1961.

Downey, Fairfax D. *The Grand Turke, Suleyman the Magnificent, Sultan of the Ottomans*. New York: Minton, Balch, 1929.

Eliot, Charles. *Turkey in Europe*. New York: Barnes & Noble, 1965.

Engel, Joahnn C. *Geschichte des Ungarischen Reichs*. Wien: Camesina, 1813.

Evilya, Efendi. *In the Days of the Janissaries*. New York: Hutchinson, 1951.

Ferdinand I. *Die Korrespondenz Ferdinands I*. Wien: A. Holzhausen, 1912.

Feridun, Bey. *Tagebuch der ägyptischen Expedition des Sultans Selim I*. Weimar: G. Keipenheuer, 1916.

Fischer-Galati, Stephen A. *Ottoman Imperialism and German Protestantism, 1521–1555*. Cambridge, MA: Harvard University Press, 1959.

Friedensburg, Walter. *Der Reichstag zu Speier 1526 im Zusammenhang der politischen und kirchlichen Entwicklung Deutschlands in Reformationszeitalter*. Berlin: R. Gaertner, 1887.

Füessli, Peter. *Peter Füesslis Jerusalemfahrt 1523, und ein Brief über den Fall von Rhodos 1522*. Zurich: Schulthess, 1982.

Galea, Michael. *Grandmaster Philippe Villiers de L'Isle Adam, 1521–1534*. SanGwann, Malta: Publishers Enterprises Group, 1997.

Gatteschi, Riccardo. *Vita di Raffaello da Montelupo*. Florence: Edizioni Polistampa, 1998.

Gibb, E. J. W. *A History of Ottoman Poetry*. London: Luzac, 1965.

Gibb, H. A. R., and Bowen Harold. *Islamic Society and the West*. London: Oxford University Press, 1957.

Gibbons, Herbert Adams. *The Foundation of the Ottoman Empire: A History of the Osmanlis up to the Death of Bayezid I, 1300–1403*. London: Frank Cass, 1916.

Giono, Jean. *The Battle of Pavia*. London: P. Owen, 1965.

Goffman, Daniel, and Virginia H. Aksan, eds. *The Early Modern Ottomans: Remapping the Empire*. New York: Cambridge University Press, 2007.

Goodwin, Godfrey. *The Janissaries*. London: Saqi, 1997.

Granvelle, Antoine P. *Papiers d'état du cardinal Granvelle*. Paris: Imprimerie royale, 1841.

Gregorovius, Ferdinand. *History of the City of Rome in the Middle Ages*. Vol. 8. London: G. Bell & Sons, 1912.

Grisar, Hartman. *Luther*. London: Kegan, Paul, Trench, Trabrer & Co., 1913.

Guicciardini, Francesco. *The History of Italy*. New York: Macmillan, 1969.

Guicciardini, Luigi. *The Sack of Rome*. New York: Italica Press, 1993.

Hackett, Francis. *Francis the First*. Garden City, NY: Doubleday, Doran, 1935.

Hadfield, Andrew, ed. *Amazons, savages, and machiavels: Travel and colonial writing in English, 1550–1630*. Oxford: Oxford University Press, 2001.

Hakluyt, Richard. *Principal Navigations, Voyages, Traffiques & Discoveries of the English Nation*. Glasgow: J. MacLehose, 1903.

Halman, Talat S., ed. *Suleyman the Magnificent, Poet: The Sultan's Selected Poems*. Istanbul: Dost, 1987.

Hammer-Purgstall, Joseph. *Campaigns of Osman Sultans*. London: W. Straker, 1835.

——. *Geschichte des Osmanischen Reiches*. Pest, C.A: Hartleben, 1827.

Hazlitt, Wm C. *The Venetian Republic: Its Rise, Its Growth, and Its Fall*. 2 vols. London: Adam and Charles Black, 1915.

Helm, Claudie, and Jost Hausmann. *1495: Kaiser, Reich, Reformen: Der Reichstag zu Worms*. Koblenz: Landesarchivverwaltung Rheinland-Pfalz, 1995.

Hendrix, Scott H. *Luther and the Papacy: Stages in a reformation conflict*. Philadelphia: Fortress Press, 1981.

Hibbert, Christopher. *The House of Medici*. New York: William Morrow, 1975.

Historisches Museum der Stadt Wien. *Wien 1529: Die erste Turkenbelagerung.* Wien: Bohlau, 1979.

Hogenberg, Nikolas. *The Procession of Pope Clement VII and the Emperor Charles V after the Coronation at Bologna.* Edinburgh: Edmonston & Douglas, 1875.

Holy Roman Empire. *Deutsche Reichstagsakten: Jungere Reihe.* Gotha: F.A. Perthes, 1893.

Hook, Judith. *Sack of Rome.* London: Macmillan, 1972.

Howorth, Henry H. *History of the Mongols from 9th to the 19th Century.* 4 vols. London: Longmans, Green, 1878.

Huber, Alfons. *Geschichte Osterreichs.* Wien: Bohlau in Kommission, 1967.

Hummelberger, Walter. *Die Befestigung Wiens.* Wien: P. Zsolnay, 1974.

Inalcik, Halil. *The Ottoman Empire: The Classical Age, 1300–1600.* New York: Praeger Publishers, 1973.

———. *Turkey and Europe in History.* Istanbul: Eren, 2006.

Jenkins, Hester Donaldson. *Ibrahim Pasha: Grand Vizier of Suleiman the Magnificent.* New York: Columbia University Press, 1911.

Kane, J. E., ed. *François I: Oeuvres poétiques.* Geneva: Slatkine, 1984.

Kemal pacha Zadeh. *Histoire de la Campagne de Mohacz.* Paris: Impr. Imperiale, 1859.

Khalifeh, Hajji. *The History of the Maritime Wars of the Turks.* Trans. James Mitchell. London, 1831.

Knecht, R. J. *Francis I.* Cambridge: Cambridge University Press, 1982.

———. *Renaissance Warrior and Patron: The Reign of Francis I.* Cambridge: Cambridge University Press, 1994.

Kohler, Alfred. *Ferdinand I, Fürst, König und Kaiser.* Munchen: C. H. Beck, 2003.

———. *Karl V: 1500–1558, eine Biographie.* Munchen: C. H. Beck, 1999.

Konstam, Angus. *Pavia 1525: The Climax of the Italian Wars.* Westport, CT: Praeger, 2005.

Kretschmayr, Heinrich. *1529 allgemeine Betrachtung.* Wien, 1929.

———. *Geschichte von Venedig.* Gotha: F. A. Pethes, 1934.

Kunt, Metin, and Christine Woodhead, eds. *Suleyman the Magnificent and His Age.* London: Longman, 1995.

La Jonquiere, A. *Histoire de l'empire Ottoman.* Paris: Hachette, 1914.

Lamb, Harold. *Suleyman the Magnificent.* Garden City, NY: International Collectors Library, 1951.

———. *Tamerlane, the Earth Shaker.* Garden City, NY: Garden City Publishing Co., 1932.

Lane-Poole, Stanley. *Story of the Barbary Corsairs.* New York: G. P. Putnam's Sons, 1890.

Lewis, Bernard. *Istanbul and the Civilization of the Ottoman Empire.* Norman: University of Oklahoma Press, 1963.

Lewis, Raphaela. *Everyday Life in Ottoman Turkey.* London: Batsford, 1971.

Lopez de Gomara, Francisco. *Annals of Charles V.* Ed. R. B Merriman. Oxford: Clarendon Press, 1912.

Luther, Martin. *Martin Luthers Werke.* Weimar: H. Böhlau, 1883.

Lybyer, Albert. *The Government of the Ottoman Empire in the Time of Suleiman the Magnificent.* New York: AMS Press, 1978.

Mackinnon, James. *Luther and the Reformation.* London: Longmans, Green, 1929.

MacLean, Gerald, ed. *Re-orienting the Renaissance: Cultural Exchanges with the East.* New York: Palgrave Macmillan, 2005.

Mattingly, Garrett. *Catherine of Aragon.* London: Jonathan Cape, 1942

McConica, James Kelsey. *English Humanists and Reformation Politics under Henry VIII and Edward VI.* Oxford: Clarendon Press, 1965.

Merriman, Roger B. *Suleiman the Magnificent, 1520–1566.* Cambridge, MA: Harvard University Press, 1944.

———. *The Rise of the Spanish Empire.* Vol. 3. New York: Macmillan, 1925.

Michelet, Jules. *Histoire de France jusqu'au XVIe siècle.* Paris: L. Hachette, 1852–67.

Mignet, M. *Rivalité de François I et Charles-Quint.* Paris: Perrin et Cie, 1886.

Mignot, Vincent. *Histoire de l'empire Ottoman.* Paris: Le Clerc, 1771.

Mijatovitch, Elodie Lawton. *Kossova: An attempt to bring Servian national songs at the battle of Kossova into one poem.* London, 1881.

Miller, Barnette. *Beyond the Sublime Porte.* New Haven, CT: Yale University Press, 1931.

Mitchell, Bonner. *Italian civic pageantry in the High Renaissance.* Florence: L. S. Olscheki, 1979.

Möhirng, Rubina. *Turkisches Wien*. Wien: Herold, 1983.

Morgan, David. *Medieval Persia, 1040–1797*. London: Longman, 1988.

Mouradgea d'Ohsson, Ignatius. *Tableau général de l'empire othoman*. Paris: Imprimerie de M. Didot, 1787.

Mullett, Michael A. *Martin Luther*. London: Routledge, 2004.

Murphey, Rhoads. *Ottoman Warfare*. New Brunswick, NJ: Rutgers University Press, 1999.

Mustafa Celebi Celalzade. *Geschichte Sultan Suleyman Kanunis von 1520 bis 1557*. Trans. by Petra Kappert. Wiesbaden: Steiner, 1981.

Nasuh, Matrackci. *Beyan-I Menazil-I sefer-I irakeyn-I sultan Suleyman Han*. Ankara: Turk Tarih Kurumu Basimevi, 1976.

Ney, Julius. *Die Appellation und Protestation der evangelischen Stande auf dem Reichstage zu Speyer 1529*. Darmstadt: Wissenschafftliche Buchgesellschaft, 1967.

Öhlinger, Walter. *Wien zwischen den Turkenkriegen*. Wien: Piechler, 1998.

Olin, John C. *Christian Humanism and the Reformation: Selected writings of Erasmus*. New York: Fordham University Press, 1987.

Penzer, N. M. *The Harem*. London: Spring Books, 1936.

Perjes, Geza. *The Fall of the Medieval Kingdom of Hungary: Mohács, 1526–Buda 1541*. Boulder, CO: Social Science Monographs, 1989.

Petiet, Claude. *Au temps des chevaliers de Rhodes*. Paris: Editions Ferdinand Lanore, 2000.

Pitts, Vincent J. *The Man Who Sacked Rome: Charles de Bourbon, Constable of France*. New York: Peter Lang, 1993.

Porter, Whitworth. *A History of the Knights of Malta*. London: Longman, Brown, Green, Longmans & Roberts, 1858.

Raby, Julian. *Venice, Dürer, and the Oriental Mode*. Totowa, NJ: Sotheby Publications, 1982.

Reissner, Adam. *Historia der Herren Georg und Kaspar von Frundsberg*. Leipzig: R. Voigtlaender Verlag, 1863.

Robertson, William. *The History of the Reign of the Emperor Charles V*. London: Lippincott, 1904.

Rogge, Joachim. *1521–1971: Luther in Worms*. Berlin: Evangelische Verl.-Anst., 1971.

Rouillard, Clarence D. *The Turk in French History, Thought, and Literature, 1520–1660*. New York: AMS Press, 1973.

Russell, Joycelyne. *The Field of Cloth of Gold: Men and Manners in 1520*. London: Routledge & Kegan Paul, 1969.

Sanuto, Marino. *Diarii di Marino Sanuto*. Bologna: Forni Editore, 1898.

Schaff, Philip. *History of the Christian Church*. Peabody, MA: Hendrickson Publishers, 1996.

Schimmer, Karl-August. *The Sieges of Vienna by the Turks*. London: J. Murray, 1847.

Setton, Kenneth. *The Papacy and the Levant, 1204–1571*. Philadelphia: American Philosophical Society, 1976–84.

Simanyi, Tibor. *Er schuf das Reich: Ferdinand von Habsburg*. Wien: Amalthea, 1987.

Stadtwaldt, Kurt. *Roman Popes and German Patriots: Antipapalism in the Politics of the German Humanist Movement from Gregor Heimburg to Martin Luther*. Geneva: Librairie Droz, 1996.

Stirling-Maxwell, William. *The Cloister Life of the Emperor Charles V*. London: John C. Nimmo, 1891.

Stripling, George. *The Ottoman Turks and the Arabs*. Urbana: University of Illinois Press, 1942.

Summer-Boyd, Hilary, and John Freely. *Strolling Through Istanbul*. London: KPI, 1972.

Szakály, Ferenc. *Lodovico Gritti in Hungary: 1529–1534*. Budapest: Akadémiai Kiadó, 1995.

Taylor, Henry O. *Thought and Expression in the Sixteenth Century*. New York: Ungar, 1959.

Terrasse, Charles. *François I, le roi et le règne*. Paris: B. Grasset, 1943.

Turetschek, Christine. *Die Turkenpolitik Ferdinands I von 1529 bis 1532*. Vienna: Verlag Notring, 1968.

Tyler, Royall. *The Emperor Charles the Fifth*. Fair Lawn, NJ: Essential Books, 1956.

Vatin, Nicolas. *L'Ordre de Saint-Jean de Jerusalem, l'empire ottoman et la Méditerranée orientale entre les deux sièges de Rhodes*. Paris: Peeters, 1994.

Verres, J. *Luther, an Historical Portrait*. London: Burns & Oates, 1884.

Vertot, Abbé de. *Histoire des Chevaliers hospitaliers de St.-Jean de Jerusalem*. London: printed for G. Strahan, 1728.

Wylie, James A. *The History of Protestantism*. London: Cassell, 1874.

SIGNIFICANT JOURNAL ARTICLES

"Charles V in Bologna: The self-fashioning of a man and a city." By Konrad Eisenbichler. *Renaissance Studies*, 1999.

"Luther and the War against the Turks." By George W. Forell. *Church History* 14 (December 1945).

"The Ottoman Empire." *Metropolitan Museum of Art Bulletin*, 26, no. 5 (1968): 204–24.

"Ottoman Imperialism and the Lutheran Struggle for Recognition in Germany, 1520–1529." By Stephen A. Fisher-Galati. *Church History* 23, no. 1 (1954).

"Suleyman the Magnificent and the Representation of Power in the Context of Ottoman-Habsburg-Papal Rivalry." By G. Gulru Necipoglu. *Art Bulletin* 71, no. 3 (1974): 401–27.

INDEX